THE GRAVE OF BISHOP MACKENZIE.

THE STORY

OF

THE UNIVERSITIES' MISSION

TO

CENTRAL AFRICA,

FROM ITS COMMENCEMENT UNDER BISHOP MACKENZIE, TO ITS
WITHDRAWAL FROM THE ZAMBESI.

BY THE

REV. HENRY ROWLEY,

ONE OF THE TWO SURVIVORS OF BISHOP MACKENZIE'S CLERICAL STAFF.

With Portraits, Maps, and Illustrations.

SECOND EDITION.

NEGRO UNIVERSITIES PRESS
NEW YORK

Originally published in 1867
by Saunders, Otley, and Co.

Reprinted 1969 by
Negro Universities Press
A DIVISION OF GREENWOOD PUBLISHING CORP.
NEW YORK

SBN 8371-1299-0

PRINTED IN UNITED STATES OF AMERICA

TO

THE RIGHT REVEREND

SAMUEL LORD BISHOP OF OXFORD,

CHANCELLOR OF THE MOST NOBLE ORDER OF THE GARTER,

LORD HIGH ALMONER TO HER MAJESTY THE QUEEN—

TO WHOSE UNTIRING

ZEAL AND MATCHLESS ADVOCACY IT IS

UNDER GOD MAINLY OWING THAT THE CHURCH OF ENGLAND IS MORE

FAITHFULLY FULFILLING HER OFFICE AS A

MISSIONARY CHURCH—

THIS SIMPLE NARRATIVE OF AN EFFORT MADE FOR CHRIST AMONG

THE HEATHEN OF EAST CENTRAL AFRICA

IS

BY PERMISSION

AFFECTIONATELY AND GRATEFULLY DEDICATED.

PREFACE.

THIS STORY of the Universities' Mission to East Central Africa is simply my African Journal adapted to the narrative form. I have been led to publish it partly by the urgent request of many who thought that a full and unreserved account of the Mission was needed, and partly because friends in whose judgment I have great confidence have thought that it would find readers, not only among the professed supporters of Missions, but also among the many who, from whatever cause, are interested in the African race.

The portrait of Bishop Mackenzie is from a photograph taken at Cape Town after his consecration; the portraits of the Rev. H. De W. Burrup, the Rev. H. C. Scudamore, and John Dickinson, Esq., are from photographs taken before they left England; while those of the Ajawa are from photographs which my friend Horace Waller, Esq., had taken at Cape Town. Several of the other illustrations, as will be seen, are from sketches by Dr. Meller; the rest from sketches by myself.

OXFORD: *September*, 1866.

PREFACE TO THE NEW AND CHEAPER EDITION.

THIS Edition of the Story of the Universities' Mission to Central Africa, is not an Abridgment. Some verbal alterations, and a few modifications and additions, have been made; but, with these exceptions, the present Edition, save in outward appearance and price, is like unto the first.

H. R.

OXFORD, *May*, 1867.

CONTENTS.

CONTENTS.

LIST OF ILLUSTRATIONS.

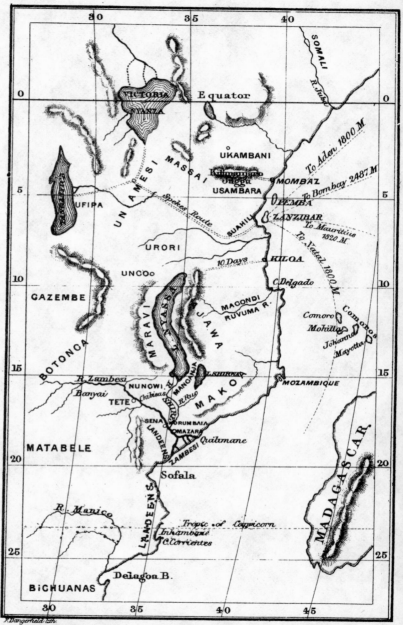

SECTION OF EAST CENTRAL AFRICA.

Scale

THE UNIVERSITIES' MISSION

TO

CENTRAL AFRICA.

CHAPTER I.

INTRODUCTORY.

In 1857 Dr. Livingstone, at Cambridge and Oxford, appealed to the Church of England to enter upon the field of missionary labour which his discoveries had opened out in Africa. And he did not appeal in vain. It was resolved that a mission, to be called 'The Oxford and Cambridge Mission to Central Africa,' should be founded. The universities of Dublin and Durham subsequently joined in the mission.

The object intended was to establish stations in Central Africa, which should serve as centres of Christianity and civilisation, for the promotion of true religion, the encouragement of agriculture and lawful commerce, and the ultimate extinction of the slave trade.

And to accomplish these designs, it was proposed to send into Central Africa at least six clergymen, to be headed by a bishop ; also a physician or surgeon, and a number of artificers, European or African, capable of conducting the work of building, of husbandry, and especially of the cultivation of the cotton plant.

Charles Frederick Mackenzie, then archdeacon of Natal, was chosen for the bishop ; the support of the general public

1

was solicited and gained; and no similar enterprise in modern times excited such great hope, or was honoured with more distinguished advocacy.

For some time, however, considerable difficulty was felt with regard to the best locality for the mission. But, in 1858, Dr. Livingstone had returned to Africa, and, in the course of his explorations, had ascended the river Shire, which takes its rise in Lake Nyassa, flows southward for 400 miles, and enters the Zambesi at about 150 miles from the coast. Here Livingstone discovered a highland lake region, and the descriptions given of this particular country by himself and companions, at once influenced the promoters of the mission in its favour.

It was resolved that, on the highlands of the Shire, the mission should make its first effort.

There were few who did not look upon this fresh discovery of Dr. Livingstone's as a direct interposition of Divine providence in favour of the exertions then making for the evangelisation of Africa. Hitherto, so easy an access to the healthy regions of Africa had not been imagined, and a mission field so promising as that described had scarcely been hoped for.

Of the Zambesi, as the future highway for religion and commerce, great expectations had been raised, but the Shire was said to promise even better things. As a river, it was described as far superior to the Zambesi for steam navigation, deep, and free from sand-banks, and navigable at all seasons of the year. The valley of the Shire was declared to be of boundless fertility, where anything would grow but Iceland moss, capable of an immense development—the future rice and cotton field for the world. The Shire highlands were spoken of as a magnificent healthy country, some three or four thousand feet above the level of the sea, well watered and wooded, well adapted for cattle and sheep, with a rich soil, and growing cotton largely. The natives were said to be brave, industrious, ingenious, and friendly. It would have been strange indeed if great hopes had not been raised by such intelligence as this, especially as the access to this highland country was declared so easy that, with the exception of thirty miles over which a road could be readily made, there was water communication all the way from England. Added to all this, the deadly effects of the climate of the lowlands seemed at last fairly met and overcome; for, owing to a supposed happy combination of medicines, fever, immediately beyond the coast itself, was a thing no longer to be dreaded, being seldom or never fatal, more like common cold than fever, so harmless, indeed, that no loss of strength resulted from its attacks; and, thus armed, Europeans might at most seasons of the year go up to the highlands in perfect safety. From all that was said on this subject, it was imagined by many that, through the good providence of God, so successful a treatment of African fever had been discovered, that it was now no more dangerous than many of the diseases which we at home suffer slightly from, but which in times past were ordinarily fatal.

A great impetus, therefore, was given to the mission by these communications. Men of all habits of mind ceased to think the thing impracticable; even the 'Times' honoured it with its approbation, and the necessary funds were quickly raised.

The object of the mission was to civilise as well as Christianize; to instruct the natives in the arts of civilised life, as well as to preach the Gospel; to encourage and direct their labour; and to substitute a lawful Christian commerce for the slave trade. The mission staff, therefore, consisted of laity as well as clergy.

On October 22, 1860, a farewell service was held in Canterbury Cathedral, and four days afterwards, the Bishop elect, the Rev. L. J. Procter, the Rev. H. C. Scudamore, Mr. Horace Waller (Lay Superintendent), S. A. Gamble, carpenter, and Alfred Adams, agriculturist, sailed from Plymouth for Cape Town, where the consecration of the Bishop was to take place. It was arranged that other members of the mission should follow in the course of a few months; and, so lightly were the difficulties of the country to which we were going estimated— and from the information we had received, I cannot see that this favourable estimation was unwarranted—it was further determined that the Bishop's sisters, and other ladies, should come out to us as soon as our arrival and settlement in the country was known.

Not having joined the mission until within a few days of the Canterbury gathering, it was agreed that I should leave England by the November mail—the necessary delay at the Cape giving me this opportunity for a longer sojourn at home. Through some misunderstanding with the ship agents I did not leave England until December.

In the meantime the Bishop had been consecrated : stores, for a year at least, barter-goods, tools, and agricultural implements were purchased, and every preparation made that a wise forethought and experience could suggest.

When I arrived at Cape Town, I found that the whole mission party, which had been increased by the addition of four Christianised Africans, freed slaves, had departed. H.M.S. 'Sidon,' taking in tow the 'Pioneer,'—the little steamship sent out by the Government to Dr. Livingstone—and having on board most of our party and stores, had gone on to the Zambesi a fortnight before; but H.M.S. 'Lyra,' with the Bishop, Mr. Procter, and two of the Africans, had left Simon's Bay only the night before I arrived, and purposed staying some days at Natal. There I was enabled to join the Bishop.

There is no mercantile communication between Cape Town and any port on the east coast of Africa, north of Natal, and without the assistance of H.M. ships, we could not have reached our destination.

Upon leaving Natal we at once proceeded to the Zambesi, and on February 7, 1861, soon after mid-day, we sighted the 'Sidon' at anchor, and were soon alongside of her, off the mouth of the river.

Captain Oldfield, the commander of the 'Lyra,' and the Bishop, immediately went off to the 'Sidon.' On their return, we learnt that those of our party who had come up in her had gone into the river several days before with the 'Pioneer,' and that since then there had been no communication with the shore.

A brisk wind was blowing, and a heavy sea running, but by the aid of a glass, we could see the 'Pioneer' safely moored in the smooth water beyond the tremendous surf on the bar of the river.

My first impressions of the Zambesi were not favourable. After the glorious coast-line from the Cape to Natal, the low, mangrove-covered shore before us presented a very discouraging prospect. The ideas I had entertained received a rude shock, for nothing could look more impracticable for ordinary commercial purposes than the entrance to the Zambesi. The anchorage outside is not good; we were seven miles from land, and had but seven and a half fathoms of water, and a more exposed position for ships cannot be well imagined. The officers of the Royal Navy are not apt to magnify difficulties, but those about me in no measured terms condemned the Zambesi. According to them, no sailing vessel could enter the river; no boat, save under very favourable circumstances, could cross the bar without imminent danger to life; and they laughed at the notion of the Zambesi ever furnishing a commercial port. A short time before, one of the 'Lyra's' boats, while taking in letters for Dr. Livingstone, was upset on the bar, and Mr. Paymaster Seveke, a most estimable officer, drowned; and, previous to this, an entire boat's crew, with the exception of one man, had been lost in attempting the same passage for the same purpose. With the aid of a small steam tug, sailing vessels of light tonnage might be towed into and out of the river, but from all I could see and learn, I felt sure that only the prospect of a very large profit indeed would tempt commercial men to encounter the difficulties of the Zambesi.

We passed an uneasy night at our anchorage, the wind did not abate, the ship rolled miserably. Circumstances next day were not more favourable for the passage of the 'bar.' The 'Sidon' signalled the 'Pioneer' to come out, but she did not move from her moorings.

On the 9th the weather was more propitious, and as the morning advanced we fully expected the 'Pioneer' out to us, but she showed no disposition to move; so Captain Oldfield, knowing the Bishop was anxious for news of Dr. Livingstone, offered to take him into the river in his gig. We watched their departure with anxiety, for though the 'bar' looked peaceful, it has a treacherous habit of upsetting boats, even when most placid. And the little boat seemed but a cockle-shell to encounter so formidable an adversary. We saw her approach the bar; saw the breakers at that very moment break out into activity; saw her furl her tiny sail, the men take to their oars, and then we lost sight of her. But a few minutes afterwards a white flag fluttered from the flag-staff on shore, and we knew that the danger was safely passed.

During the next day we were visited by a swarm of mosquitoes and mangrove flies, which bit vehemently, and were a great nuisance.

Soon after five o'clock on the morning of the 11th, we saw the ' Lyra's ' boat coming over the bar, and shortly afterwards we welcomed back the Bishop and Captain Oldfield.

Dr. Livingstone, his brother, Mr. Charles Livingstone, Dr. Kirk, and sixteen Makololo, were reported on shore, and our brethren who had come up in the ' Sidon ' were with them in good health and spirits.

Dr. Livingstone had been waiting at the Kongone since January 1; he had expected the ' Pioneer ' sooner, but we missionaries had taken him by surprise, for he put into the Bishop's hands a letter which he was on the point of sending to England to him.

To my astonishment I learnt from the Bishop, that Dr. Livingstone, thinking a better communication with the interior might be found by way of the Rovuma, a river 450 miles north of the Zambesi, had proposed that, instead of going up the Zambesi, we should go with him and explore the Rovuma, which was thought to proceed either from the Lake Nyassa or its neighbourhood, the very region to which we were bound.

Without stating his own opinions, the Bishop asked what I thought of this plan. I did not like it. It would, it seemed to me, alter our position materially. As Christian missionaries, we must be prepared for all that might fall to our lot in the performance of our duties; but, unless it were unmistakably the necessity of our position we were out of place as explorers.

I was glad to find that the Bishop had taken this view of the case, and had not consented to Dr. Livingstone's proposal.

On the morning of the 12th the 'Pioneer' left the river; Dr. Livingstone and Dr. Kirk came on board the 'Lyra,' and Dr. Livingstone's proposition respecting the Rovuma was again discussed.

It then appeared that the Bishop had not comprehended the full force of the objections to our going up to the highland country by way of the Zambesi and Shire, and the reasons which made, to Dr. Livingstone's mind, the expedition to the Rovuma necessary. Briefly, they are thus stated:—

1. The influence of the Portuguese would be against the success of the mission; they claimed the whole coast-line from Delagoa Bay to Cape Delgado; the Rovuma lay beyond their possessions; if we could, therefore, find a way to the healthy highland country by this river, the delay of a few months, before we commenced our actual mission work, would be amply compensated for.

2. The difficulties in the way of transport of stores from the Shire were very great. We should need a large amount of native labour, and we were not likely to get it, for Chibisa, the only friendly chief, had removed from the Shire, and the rest of the natives were churlish, and would do nothing for us.

3. We had no medical man; were utterly ignorant of the treatment of fever; it was then the most unhealthy season of the year; Dr. Livingstone could not remain long with us, as his duties would call him off in another direction, and fatal consequences would probably ensue.

Dr. Kirk assented to all this, and enforced his chief's plan respecting the Rovuma as the best we could adopt.

Still it seemed to the Bishop, to others, and myself, that, as we expected a medical brother to come out to us almost immediately, the consequences of uncertainty and delay might really prove more injurious to the mission than the difficulties pointed out by Dr. Livingstone. We had commendatory letters from the Portuguese Government, and the African officials were not likely to interfere with us. We might expect trouble for a time with the natives, wherever we went, and so little was known of the Rovuma, that its suitability for purposes of navigation seemed very doubtful. And the Bishop,

very forcibly, put before Dr. Livingstone the fact of our having
left active employment in England, and the desirability of not
longer leading the comparatively idle life forced upon us during
the past four months, and expressed his fear that the uncertainty and delay in commencing the real work of the mission
might expose us to much that it were well to avoid, injuriously
influence those who were to follow us, and cause much painful
anxiety to friends at home.

Dr. Livingstone would not anticipate any ill consequences
from the delay, as we should be but three months in settling
the question of the Rovuma. The Bishop and one other
might come with him, the rest of our party and our stores
might go to the island of Johanna, where they could await the
result ; there they would be preparing themselves for their
future work; and might learn something of the Makoa language, the very dialect, it was said, we should need. There
also they might make themselves acquainted with African
natives, for though the island is under a Mahomedan ruler,
many Africans are there as slaves, and there they might also
learn many things that would be very useful for us to know.
He was very sanguine about the Rovuma, but promised, if it
failed, to return to Johanna, and take all up to the Shire highlands, by way of the Zambesi, as originally planned.

We were not convinced of the necessity of going to the
Rovuma, but it appeared necessary to agree to Dr. Livingstone's proposal. Had we acted contrary to his advice, if
misfortune followed, people at home would have said,

' There, by the good providence of God, these men met
with the only man who was in a position to say what was the
best thing to be done, they rejected his advice, and the result
is entirely due to their own presumption and folly.'

It was agreed, therefore, that it should be as Dr. Livingstone wished, and the Bishop asked me to be his companion.

Details relative to the departure of the ships were soon arranged. The ' Pioneer' was to proceed to the Rovuma at once
and alone ; the ' Lyra' to Johanna, where she was to leave
Mr. Procter and others, and what stores of ours she had on
board, then to the Rovuma with the Bishop and myself; and

from her superior steam-power, she was expected to anticipate the arrival of the 'Pioneer:' the 'Sidon' agreed to land the rest of our party and the remainder of our stores at Johanna. We sighted Johanna early on the morning of the 21st. Like all the Comoros, it is of volcanic formation, a mountain heaved up from the depths of the ocean. It is covered with verdure from its base to its summit—6,000 feet above the sea. I had never before seen so beautiful a specimen of this grand world which God has made for the habitation of man.

Pomoney, the residence and plantation of Mr. Sunley, then British Consul for the Comoros, is on the west side of the island, and is a rendezvous for the east coast squadron. It has a small, but, when entered, safe harbour, formed by the coral reef. The entrance to the harbour is very intricate, and not easy to any but steam vessels; it is a mere chasm, which the caprice of the coral insect seems to have left in the reef.

The area of Johanna is about 250 square miles. The dominant race are Arabs, who conquered the Aborigines many years ago, since which time the conquered have been the slaves of the conquerors. But they are not the only slaves, for out of a population of 10,000, three-fourths are in bondage, the slaves being continually recruited by importations from the African coast. The Arabs are without doubt, the great slave-traders in Eastern Africa. It is said, and I am inclined to believe it, that no less than 19,000 slaves were carried away from Zanzibar and Ibo alone, in the year 1860, and that as many as 600 vessels were then employed in this atrocious traffic on the East African coast. The majority of these vessels were but Arab dhows, but some, and I have seen several, were ships of large tonnage, fitted up for their special purpose, with every appliance. And to keep this fleet of the devil in check were some five or six very slow men-of-war, so hampered by ambiguously framed instructions, that the commanders were frequently afraid to act when their own judgment told them there was sufficient ground for doing so.

The evils of slavery are said to be somewhat mitigated at Johanna—the Arab, as a rule, acting more like the patriarch of old than the modern master of slaves. But the degraded

appearance and downcast bearing of the slaves, contrasted
with the frank demeanour of the Makololo, were sad proof of
the evil of slavery in any form. Until then I had never seen
men as slaves, and until then I had never fully realized the
intense wickedness of slavery.

Johanna has an independent sovereign. Muzumudu, the
capital, is on the north side of the island, and it is there the
mass of the population is found. Pomoney is simply what
Mr. Sunley has made it—a pleasant abode, and a profitable
plantation.

It was the intention of Captain Oldfield to stay at Pomoney
for three or four days, during which time, he thought, with
the aid·of Mr. Sunley, to whose kindness and hospitality we
were greatly indebted, that accommodation could be found on
the island for our friends who were to be left behind.   But
the day after our arrival H.M.S. ' Persian,' a brig of war, and
the last of its race, made her appearance, and reported the
' Wasp,' another cruiser, a wreck on shore, just below Cape
Delgado.   It was at once arranged that both ships should go
to her assistance, the ' Lyra' first taking our friends round to
Muzumudu, where Mr. Sunley had put the disused consulate
at their disposal.   But while dining with the Consul in the
evening, it was announced that an officer, in an open boat, had
just arrived from Mayotte, another of the Comoros, forty
miles distant, with the information that the ' Enchantress,' a
store ship expected at Johanna, had run on the coral reef surrounding that island.   The necessities of Her Majesty's service
put all other considerations aside.   The ' Persian' set sail immediately for Mayotte ; the ' Lyra' could not get away till
daybreak.   That night was a busy night with all : the crew
took in coal, and we missionaries shifted our baggage and
stores on to the 'Vega,' an old slave ship, now used as a permanent store ship at Johanna, on board of which, for want of
better accommodation, our friends were for a time to take up
their quarters.

At daybreak we were away under full steam for the ' Enchantress.'   We soon overtook the ' Persian ;' for the wind
failing, she had been knocking about all night, and only kept

from going ashore herself by aid of her boats. Evidently she could give no aid to the 'Enchantress,' so she turned her prow towards the 'Wasp,' and the 'Lyra' went on alone to Mayotte, which island we were not long in sighting. When we first saw the 'Enchantress' she looked more like a ship at anchor than a wreck, but when we drew near to her we saw she had sustained irretrievable damage: in nautical phraseology, she had 'broken her back,' and was past all hope of being saved. On boarding her it was found she was deserted, but her stores were safe.

We stood off the reef during the night, and in the morning made for Zaoudzi, the residence of the Governor. Zaoudzi was well fortified, sixty-eight pounders were peeping out everywhere, and the French inhabitants (for the French have acquired Mayotte) had evidently done all they could to make residence there as agreeable to themselves as might be. We here found the crew of the 'Enchantress,' for after the officer had left for Johanna, the position of the ship appeared to them so dangerous, that it was resolved to abandon her.

The crew of the 'Lyra' were three days at work on the 'Enchantress,' during which time many thousand pounds' worth of goods were safely removed. She was a beautiful vessel, originally a slaver, but had been captured but a few months before by Admiral Keppel, and bought in by Government to be used as a tender; this was her first voyage in an honest capacity. When we left her she was no longer beautiful, but foul and battered, her deck torn up, her rigging hacked, and her sails ragged, her hull filled with water, grinding and crushing against the rock beneath, and only waiting for a strong wind to go to pieces.

On the 28th we left Mayotte for Johanna, where we unshipped the stores from the wreck, and then started for the 'Wasp.' We found her in a better position than we expected, damaged, but afloat, her crew having got her into deep water again.

On Wednesday, March 6, we left her, and set our faces towards the Rovuma, which river we reached on the afternoon of the 9th.

The 'Pioneer' had been awaiting our arrival twelve days, and was preparing to ascend the river without us, as the favourable time was passing away.

CHAPTER II.

THE ROVUMA.

On Sunday, March 10, Dr. Livingstone and the officers of the expedition attended Divine service on board the 'Lyra,' and some of the Makololo came on board also. They were much surprised at the size of the ship, and called it a town. They soon became friends with the sailors, and told them they liked the English, because they were the only people besides themselves who were not afraid, and liked fun.

On Monday, about mid-day, the Bishop and I left the 'Lyra' for the 'Pioneer'—Captain Oldfield, Lieut. De-Wahl, and Mr. Paymaster Jones accompanying us. As we pushed off, the crew manned the rigging and gave us three cheers. The good Bishop's unaffected piety, cheerful disposition, and manly bearing, had quite won the hearts of the officers and crew, and they had won our hearts too, for they had given us a thousand causes to remember them with gratitude and affection.

As soon as we were on board the 'Pioneer,' she weighed anchor, and began the ascent of the river.

The mouth of the Rovuma forms a noble bay. The entrance to the river is unobstructed by a bar, though at certain phases of the tide there was a 'bore' for a short time, which would make boating just then dangerous. The river at first was quite a mile broad, and very deep, but after a few miles it rapidly shallowed, and sand-banks seemed everywhere. We had to sound constantly for the channel, and every now and then we were forced to anchor and send a boat ahead to find the deeper water. We halted for the night at about ten miles from the sea.

Our experience was not considered unsatisfactory. The

country about us was said to have healthier characteristics
than that of the Zambesi. We had left the mangroves behind
us, and where on the Zambesi mud was said to be, here was
sand; and on either side of us were hills something like our
Sussex downs, but more thickly wooded, and bold mountain
land was seen in the distance ahead.

We passed, on our way, a hippopotamus, a strange sight
when seen for the first time; and a crocodile, a loathsome
sight at any time. Flamingo and pelicans, herons and cranes,
the black and white ibis, and many other curious birds were
numerous. The voyage had been full of interest to me; indeed it was full of interest to all, though all were not interested in the same things.

A native village lay immediately off our anchorage, and just
before sunset a large canoe, having fifteen men in her, left the
village and went up the river. A kind of signal drumming
was kept during the night by the natives on land, who were
evidently alarmed at our appearance.

At daybreak next morning we went on shore. We had
scarcely pulled a dozen strokes from the ship, before the beating of a drum told us that our movements were observed. As
we landed we saw a man running from us towards the bush.
We shouted to him, and told him we were friends, but he
heeded us not. There were a few huts not far from the river,
but the village itself seemed to be on the slope of the hills.
As we went towards these huts we were met by an old man,
decidedly African in feature, but dressed in Arab costume.
Upon being told that we were English and friends, he was gracious enough to say that the English and he were one, good
men and brothers. We followed him to his house, a square-
built hut with an outlying shed or two. This old man was by
no means unsophisticated; he knew all about the slave trade,
and the English cruisers, and had in all probability taken voy-
ages in slaving 'dhows.' He was acquainted with many
things, evidently, and was a Mahometan. Information respecting the source of the Rovuma was asked for, and he said that
the river came from 'a big water,' that people were plentiful
along the river, and would no doubt be glad to see us. But

on Dr. Livingstone saying we were not traders, but had come to teach him and others about our Heavenly Father, and that we had the good Book, he said the people would certainly be glad to see us, but he did not think they would believe us or the good Book either. When we left him he made us a present of a fowl, and in return, Dr. Livingstone gave him a string or two of red beads, which he received in both hands, with bent body, and with every indication that he thought the gift overwhelmingly profuse.

Our progress up the river during the day was considered satisfactory. When we halted for the night, we were about ten miles from the coast. Obstructions had been numerous, but they arose from ignorance of the channel. Every one seemed surprised at the healthy character of the vegetation; it was such as was not found for 100 miles up the Zambesi. There was but little swamp, for the hills on either side were within a few hundred yards of the river. These hills were covered with trees; and ebony, lignum vitæ, and other valuable woods, were seen in the valley. All so far seemed hopeful.

Next day, however, we had scarcely raised the anchor before we were in a difficulty. Sand-banks were so thick ahead of us, that for a long time we could make no progress. We had to send out boats to find a passage, and our stoppages were so frequent, that we did not make more than five miles during the day. When we halted for the night, the hills on either side sloped down to the very bank of the river. Close to the river the soil was a rich sandy loam, but higher up the hills you could see that the earth, where the vegetation was less dense, was of a reddish hue. We passed by several villages during our short journey, and everywhere there seemed indications that the population thereabouts had once been considerable; for, by the different growth of the trees on the hills, you could see that much land had been not long since under cultivation.

We visited a village before we started next morning. We saw no women, but the men came towards us distrustful, and half defiant. They were evidently the natives of the land, genuine Africans, in feature and apparel. Some were armed with guns, others had spears and bows and arrows. These people were certainly not prepossessing either in appearance or manner. We were strangers, and they were suspicious of us, and men under such circumstances do not show to advantage. Now and then, however, one could see indications of something better than was at first apparent, for when Mr. Paymaster Jones, a hearty, florid, loud-voiced, happy-looking man, brimful of fun, tried to rally them from their stolidity, now and then an irrepressible burst of laughter broke forth from them, and the real character of these people manifested itself; and convinced one that first impressions would be very unfair to them. I learnt a lesson from the Paymaster's jollity, which was of use to me in my subsequent experience.

From these people we learnt that the water in the river was decreasing, and that it would get less and less, now that the rainy season was nearly over, until it became so low that people could walk across from one side to the other. This was not cheering information.

On the morning of the 14th, Captain Oldfield, Lieutenant De-Wahl, and Mr. Paymaster Jones left us to return to their ship. I felt sorry to part from these gentlemen, for the unvarying kindness we had received from them made this final parting a trial.

Before leaving, Captain Oldfield expressed to me his conviction that we should not get twenty miles farther up the river, and hoped we should not find it impossible to get down again before the next flood season. This made us feel more than ever the anomalous position we missionaries were in on board the 'Pioneer.' To Dr. Livingstone, as an explorer, a halt of a few months in the river would not be of much importance; he could take land journeys from his ship, and so be doing his proper work, but to us such a position would be most injurious, and the possibility of it made me very anxious.

As soon as they were gone we dropped down the river a few hundred yards in order to get firewood. The Makololo went ashore with their hatchets and commenced work. They had not been thus engaged long, before a number of men came down the hill, carrying on their heads pumpkins, melons, and

other vegetables for sale. Their leader was a half-caste Arab,
who wore a turban and a robe that at one time had been magnificent, but was now soiled and worn. He was a villainous-
looking fellow, and if report speaks truly of these half-caste
coast Arabs, they are not belied by their physiognomies.
These men were evidently the masters of the country about
us ; the natives seemed to live in fear of them, and where they
were not subjected to actual bondage, were evidently greatly
oppressed by them.

Some of these people came off to the ship, and Dr. Livingstone was very courteous to them; but they had no sooner
returned to the shore than the head man began to talk very
big, said the country was his, the trees his, and that we should
not cut wood unless we paid for it—a thing unheard of, for
property in trees, unless banana trees, seems to be unknown
among the natives generally. So he was told that the trees
were as much ours as his, that we would pay his people for
anything to eat, and for cutting down wood if they liked to
work, but that we would give them nothing for the wood we
cut down ourselves. Upon this he became more presuming,
used threats, and laid hands upon the wood the Makololo had
cut. This man, and most of his companions, had guns ; they
had not seen guns with us, and no doubt imagined themselves
stronger than we ; but when Mr. C. Livingstone, who was on
shore with the Makololo, saw the temper of these fellows, he
sent off the boat to the ship to bring his revolver, and the
muskets of the Makololo. This to the Makololo was capital
fun; they jumped about with greatest alacrity, and evidently
longed for a skirmish with these Arab fellows, who had dared
to interfere with their *white* men ; and so, when the boat
returned to the shore, they seized their guns, and without
further parley rushed upon the malcontents. A loud shout of
laughter followed, for the Arab leader and his followers scampered off as fast as their legs would carry them. In their
fright they left behind them all they had brought down for sale.

The Doctor said it was ever so when the natives imagined
themselves the stronger ; that it was always wisest to show
your teeth at once, and then there would be no occasion to bite.

The Makololo had been warned not to fire, and unless the others had fired, though it is not in their nature to be forbearing, there was no fear of their disobeying orders, for Dr. Livingstone had them well in hand. He said they murmured against his moderation now and then, for they are a war-loving set of fellows, and delight in showing their prowess.

The runaways did not remain long in hiding, for finding they need not fear, they came forth again, this time slinking along like hounds, called to the hand that had just beaten them. No more was said about the right of cutting wood : the things they had for sale were bought, and they were told if any harm came to them it would be their own fault entirely, as we were disposed to be friends.

Before leaving, the chief began to assume something of his old bearing before his followers, and, taking off the covering of buck hide that protected the lock of his gun, assured them that had he chosen to fight, he could have done great things, for his gun would go off. The Makololo heard this piece of boasting, and they so laughed at him, that he was glad to get away.

We weighed anchor soon after this, but we did not go very far, for we had to find our way through a very labyrinth of sandbanks, and the higher we went the more difficult seemed the navigation. Captain Oldfield's prediction was in a fair way of being realized.

From midday to sunset the weather was stormy. We had heavy rains, and much thunder. The sunset was past description beautiful. I had never before seen such gorgeous manifestations of colour. And after the rain ceased, the temperature was delightful. We sat upon the deck, and the soothing, satisfying influence of the hour seemed to leave scarcely anything to be desired. The Bishop, while watching the refulgence about the setting sun, began to hum "Jerusalem the Golden." I joined him. Then the Makololo came round about us, and sat at our feet, and asked us to sing again, so we sang Keble's evening hymn, and "Father, by thy love and power." Then Dr. Livingstone asked Moloko, the principal man among the Makololo, to sing, and he sung a solemn melody composed by his great chief Sebituane. It was like a grand old Latin tune, and, set to sacred words, it would have passed as such. Dr. Livingstone told us that he first heard this song when Sebituane was dying. Hundreds of his chosen warriors sang it, while seated around his hut, at his request. It must have been grand, but sad in the extreme. The dying chief was a hero; the people had, under him, become heroic also; and his spirit left this world while the voices of those he had made eminent were singing in his ears the melody his own soul had conceived.

I grew to be very fond of the Makololo, of Moloko especially, for there seemed in him capacities for good which none of the others had; he was much more reflective than they. Ramakukan had immense physical powers, and when angered he would be a formidable adversary, but he was somewhat besotted by the excessive use of " bhang," Indian hemp. This pernicious plant is smoked by most of the tribes almost as much as tobacco. Indeed, among many it is preferred to tobacco, and it is more exciting. But its effects are so injurious, that Dr. Livingstone forbade the use of it among the men with him, and so they consoled themselves with excessive snuff-taking. Most of the Africans I have met with are snuff-takers, but these Makololo consumed enormous quantities. This prodigious snuff-taking is not pleasant to look upon. The men's eyes became inflamed, and streamed with water; they panted for breath, and seemed ready to choke; but they enjoyed it nevertheless, for, to use their own expressions, " It lights a fire in the head, which is very good." This habit, and their method of feeding, were their most unpleasant characteristics. You soon got used to their scant apparel, for it is natural to them, and not at all indecent. As a rule they were a modest set of men, but in their eating they were downright savages, and must have had the digestion of wolves.

I recollect a dinner of bullock's hide. It was cooked by being exposed to the fire until it looked like burnt leather. They then pulled it to pieces with their hands, or, when too tough, chopped at it with their knives, putting monstrous pieces into their mouths, and evidently begrudging the time necessary for mastication. The hide of any animal seemed at that time much esteemed by them, that of the hippopotamus having the preference. If properly boiled, this hide softens and swells until it is four inches thick, and of the consistence of very firm jelly.

On the 16th we were under steam early, and after five or six hours' tedious work, had accomplished five or six miles. Then we halted for wood, started again, and dropped anchor for the night about three miles further up the river.

There was still time for a stroll, and some of our friends went after game. I went with Dr. Livingstone for a ramble, with no other object than to get on the top of a hill ahead of us. The vegetation was very beautiful here. Wild flowers and fruit abounded. The wild grape was there, also the date and the fig, and a large and plum-like fruit of a very peculiar flavour, and a tree, belonging to the Strychnos variety, which bore a noble fruit, like in appearance to an orange, but larger. The pulp of this fruit was good for food, but the pips were pronounced poisonous.

We met with the footprints of hippopotamuses, buffalo, and deer, but saw no animal larger than a pigeon. Insect life was very abundant, and very beautiful. But on returning the Doctor discovered the tsetse, and the presence of this terrible fly quite dispelled the visions I had indulged, of future herds of cattle quietly feeding on the profuse herbage everywhere about us. As night advanced the fire-fly came out in great force, the grass-hopper chirped as it only chirps in these regions, and the frogs did their best to fill the air with their melodious utterances.

During the next day the ship remained at anchor, and it being reported that there was a village near at hand, the Doctor and others, immediately after breakfast, went in search of it. We had not gone far before we came up with a native armed with a bow and arrows, who had evidently been watching us. Dr. Livingstone did not understand his dialect, but a man he had with him did, and upon being told that we wished to go to his home, he, without hesitation, led the way.

The word " near" has a relative meaning in Africa; the size of the continent, not the actual distance, is certainly the thing considered. In England, if told a place is near, in the same way that a man would tell you that a certain house was just round the corner, you would not expect to have to walk five miles before you come to your destination. In Africa it is otherwise: a man pokes out his chin to intimate that the distance you have to go is small, really nothing; but it will frequently be at least two hours, walk as hard as you will, before you reach your destination.

It was a delightful walk, however—my first march beneath a tropical sun; and I enjoyed it.

There were but seventeen huts in the village to which we were taken, and they were in a miserable condition, tumbling down and filthy. We seated ourselves under the shade of a large tree, and our guide stood before us looking uncomfortable and irresolute, evidently not knowing what to do with himself, and suspicious of our motives. No other people were to be seen. We asked him for water. He professed to have none; but a hearty slap on the back, an assurance that we meant no harm, and the gift of a bright-coloured cotton handkerchief, sent him off laughing. When he returned several other men made their appearance, and sat down in front of us, and finally, some women and children came out of their hiding places. These people were genuine Africans; the men looked unhappy and downtrodden; the children were well fed and cared for, and were of prepossessing appearance; but the women were simply hideous. Their heads were shaved as bald as the palm of the hand, and they wore in an aperture in their upper lip a circular block of wood fully two inches in diameter. A similar custom prevails among all the women in the Nyassa lake regions, though in many places they wear rings something like a table-napkin ring, made of the wood of the castor-oil plant, instead of the block. In all cases the effect is frightful. Anything more repulsive cannot be conceived, and it is a fashion as inconvenient as it is ugly. The women cannot pronounce many of the words of their own language: eating and drinking are by no means easy, for if a woman would drink, she has to throw back her head, open her mouth, and pour the liquid down, for suction is out of the question; and though the mothers have as much affection for their little ones as our own mothers have, they cannot manifest that affection in the same way as our mothers do, for, with that monstrosity standing out at right angles to the teeth, kissing is impossible.

A chief, upon being asked why the women wore this hideous thing, replied, 'I am sure I can't say why they wear it, unless it is because they are women; what they would be if they did not wear it, I don't know: they would not be men—and it is very certain they would not be women—so they wear it, I suppose, because they *are* women.'

A cogent reason truly.

AKWIKALONGA, AN AJAWA WOMAN.

I once asked a woman why she so disfigured herself, and she told me it was not proper to show the mouth, though by its use the mouth becomes more than ever the most prominent feature; while another woman answered my inquiry thus:— 'Do you think any woman among my people would ever get a husband if she had not a good large "pilali" (lip ring)? not she!' It was a long time before I could get used to the faces of women thus outraged, by this the most hideous fashion the perverted fancy of woman has ever devised.

There was no sign of food about the village we were in, no bleating goat or cackling fowl. The people were certainly an

oppressed race, and in great poverty, and were no doubt compelled, by the exactions of the dominant Arab, to simulate even
a greater poverty. And yet the land was a fertile land, capable
of sustaining twenty times the number of people living upon
it. But here, as elsewhere in Africa, there is no security for
property, for if a village becomes comparatively rich by its
industry, sooner or later it will certainly be attacked, and its
inhabitants enslaved by a less industrious but more warlike
neighbour. And in lands entailing little labour, and producing
abundantly, the population is probably less than it was centuries since, and the people are ever on the verge of starvation.

Nipa was the name of the head man of the village, but
Nipa, with true African policy, was not visible. We wished
to see him, and our friend the guide ran off to fetch him, but
returned saying he was not to be found, and brought us a
large melon instead. As we practised it, melon-eating was
not a refined proceeding. We each had a lump, so large that
both hands were necessary to hold it; at this lump we bit,
filling our mouths with the refreshing pulp, by no means a
pretty process, but the only way, I think, of finding out
what a lemon really is; for, as we manage it at home, a melon
is an insipid unsatisfactory thing. While resting, an Arab,
accompanied by his slave, a tall emaciated African, came into
the village. When he saw us he hesitated, for he was one of
those who had been unamiable about the wood; but upon Dr.
Livingstone bidding him come forward and fear nothing, he
came and sat in front of us, pushing the natives on one side,
and taking the mat they were sitting upon. The way in which
this was done, and the effect his presence had upon the villagers, showed that these half-castes were the scourge and
terror of the aborigines. Dr. Livingstone did not allude to a
previous acquaintance, and seeing he had some young Indian
corn with him, offered to buy it; he was ready to sell, and
the transaction was satisfactorily accomplished. He did not
stay long after this, and when he went away he wished Allah
might be with us—a wish which, from the wicked expression
of his face, and the ugly voice he had, sounded more like a
curse than a blessing.

When he was gone the villagers came forward again, the women found their tongues and the children their confidence. Seeing this I went towards them, meaning to have played with the little ones, and to have made myself generally agreeable; but, to my consternation, the women ran off with a shriek, taking the children with them, and the result of my amiable intentions greatly amused my companions.

Dr. Livingstone's object in visiting this village was to get information, and we were informed that the country was called Chiungura, that the supreme chief was Doni, who lived some distance up the river; that the river—Oovooma, they called it—came from a ' big water,' and that the water in the river was certainly falling, and would soon be so shallow as to be no deeper than a man's middle.

Nothing more was to be learnt, so Dr. Livingstone gave presents, and after inviting the people to the ship, we departed.

Towards evening, Nipa, attended by our guide of the morning, and others, made his appearance. He was a grim-looking old man, grey-headed, dirty, and disagreeably odorous. He and his attendants came on board, and were awe-struck with all they saw. One man nearly went into fits with astonishment on seeing the reflection of himself in a looking-glass; while another, upon being shown a china tobacco-jar, fashioned and coloured like a Sir John Falstaff, and which opened just where the corpulence was greatest, was so alarmed that he leaped clean overboard in his fright.

It was very stormy just before and after sunset, but cleared up in time to allow us to sleep on deck as usual. The mosquitoes were numerous, but our curtains were an effectual barrier between us and them, and protected by a blanket coat, and trousers of the same material, which had been provided for us by the kindness and forethought of Captain Oldfield, sleeping on deck was far more comfortable than in the close atmosphere of the saloon.

On the 19th it became evident to all that we had gone up the river as far as we could safely go without the risk of being stranded for months. The water was so rapidly falling that there was a decrease of seven inches in one day; the difficulties ahead seemed increasing, and the question was, what should we do—go on, or at once return?

It was clear that the mission could find no settlement where we were; for, however attractive the land about us, it was too near the coast, and too much under the influence of the half-caste Arabs, to answer our purpose. Dr. Livingstone had a day or two before stated that it might be necessary to resolve upon one of two plans.

The first was, that we should force our way as far as we could up the river; and then that the Bishop and I should stay and do what we could among the people as missionaries, while Dr. Livingstone and party proceeded overland to Lake Nyassa. Their return, it was thought, would be simultaneous with the next rise of the river—in six months. If the overland route was found practicable, and the country and people favourable, we were then all to return to Johanna, come back again with our whole force, and go up to the lake region by way of the Rovuma.

This plan, to our minds, was open to gravest objections.

The second suggestion was more in accordance with the original idea; viz., to return at once to Johanna, take up our friends, &c., and go up to the highland country by way of the Zambesi and Shire. But, instead of all returning, the Doctor proposed that Mr. May, the commander of the 'Pioneer,' and Mr. Charles Livingstone, should accompany us; while he, Dr. Kirk, the Makololo, and several others, should at once go up to Lake Nyassa by the Rovuma, and so meet us in the highlands. This was an important modification of the original proposal, but, considering the nature of Dr. Livingstone's position, we could not object to it, though it did not satisfy our judgment. The Bishop was very anxious, and we had many conversations together on this subject. That our presence was an embarrassment to Dr. Livingstone, was manifest: he had long been waiting for increased means to carry out his work, and he was naturally anxious to make at once the best use he could of the means Government had now placed at his disposal; he had also to consult the feelings of those associated with him, men who, having purely scientific ob-

jects in view, could not be supposed to have more than a
secondary interest in our mission, and who were naturally
anxious to shield themselves from all suspicion of not having
made the utmost of every opportunity, when opportunities are
so rare as they are in African explorations. Nevertheless, I
could not help feeling that Dr. Livingstone was in a great
measure responsible for our speedy settlement, since it was
owing to his representations and promises that we came out,
and that it was his duty, therefore, to consult the welfare of
the mission, even though he had to defer his own plans. Dr.
Kirk and others were naturally anxious for the land journey,
for to have ascertained the source of the Rovuma, and to have
opened out another route to the interior, would have added
greatly to the reputation of the expedition; but Dr. Livingstone, with a disinterestedness for which we missionaries felt
very grateful to him, said, when the subject was finally discussed, 'I am anxious to do the best that can be done for
Africa, irrespective of my own personal feelings, and taking
all things into consideration, I think the best thing that can
now be done will be to get the mission established as quickly
as possible, and in order to do that well, we had better not
divide our forces. We will go down the river to-morrow,
and return to the Zambesi all together.' And thus it was
arranged.

We were in trouble as soon as we pushed from the shore,
for in turning the ship the stream caught her and swung
her on to a sand-bank, and we had to work hard till sunset before we could get her afloat again. The Bishop worked in the
boats, taking out anchor and cable as though bred to such service; he was the admiration and wonder of the sailors. Next
morning we had not been steaming more than an hour and a
half, before we were once more aground; and it required three
days of incessant labour from all on board to get the ship
afloat. The Makololo worked zealously. I encouraged and
superintended their efforts at the capstan, and their hearty
laughter, and droll attempts at vocalisation, for as we worked
I made them sing, were very cheering. It was impossible not
to like these men. The efforts they made to please, their inva-

riable good humour, and exceeding modesty, would mark the
man a churl who did not like them.   With us, doubtless, the
best part of their character was uppermost, and they were
really pleasant companions; under less favourable circumstances, they would probably appear less amiable, for a certain
latent ferocity glittered in their eyes at times, which showed
them to be men who were capable of doing terrible things.

A number of the natives of the country came down to the
river and watched our efforts to get afloat.   Most of them
had brought provisions for sale, but for a time their timidity
made barter impossible.   Two or three for the moment bolder
than the rest came off to the ship in a canoe, but a sudden
panic seized them, and before we could purchase what they
had for sale, they paddled off as though their lives depended
upon the speed with which they could get to shore.   On the
third day of our halt, however, a canoe came down the river,
managed by a man and a boy.   Without hesitation, they
made fast the canoe to the ship, and jumped on to the deck.
The man was our old acquaintance, the guide.   We had won
his confidence, and through him we were not long in winning
the confidence of those on shore, for as soon as he heard of
their fear he laughed heartily, and after selling us all he had
for sale, he went off to them, leaving his boy with us, and
brought the entire party to the ship.   Poor fellows! as soon
as they found we had no desire to eat or enslave them, they
opened out in a marvellous way.   They laughed and talked,
jumped about the ship, and became quite jolly—acted indeed
like children who boast that they are 'not afraid.'   They
looked like an oppressed people, and their very ornaments testified to their poverty, for their bracelets and necklaces, instead
of being of brass or beads, were of plaited grass, or the hair
from the elephant's tail.

After halting a day to give the crew a rest, we again commenced the downward journey.   The current was in our favour, the water had risen several inches, and we hoped to do
in a few hours the distance that had taken days in the ascent.
For a time all went well with us; our hope seemed in a fair
way of being realised; we were in full sight of the sea, within

three miles of our purposed anchorage, when the ship went at full speed on to a sand spit, and there stuck hard and fast. It was vexing, for the channel, several fathoms deep, was within a few yards of us. Anchors were taken out at once, but the men were tired and dispirited, and the attempt to get afloat that night entirely failed. The tide when it rose did not do much for us, for in the morning the sand was piled up on our port side several feet above the water. It was Sunday; but, after morning prayer, we all turned to work with a will, and by vigorous effort, as the tide again flowed, we moved the ship once more into the deep water, and then without further accident proceeded to the mouth of the river.

And so ended this attempt upon the Rovuma. But notwithstanding our disappointment, the novelty of our position, the glorious climate, the beauty of the scenery, the strange forms of animal life we had seen, and the thorough heartiness of those with whom we were associated, made life very enjoyable. There was not a sign of sickness among us, the unhealthiness of African rivers seemed a fable; I never had better health, or larger appetite, and, save when hungry, was never less conscious of having a stomach. But this happy state of things did not continue. We had not been more than a few hours at the river's mouth before a sailor sickened with the fever. Then the Bishop was attacked, and then one after another fell ill, until of the Europeans on board, I alone escaped the fever. It did not affect all alike. Some had it severely, others but slightly; some lingered in it for many days, while others recovered after a day or two of pain and inconvenience.

Our position was not well chosen. Where we were anchored the sea-breeze came to us across a mangrove swamp, and was therefore laden with malaria, and a creek that ran through the swamp emptied itself into the river just opposite the ship, and poisoned the water which we drank.

So many were down with the fever at one time, that our departure was delayed until the 29th—Good Friday. We had not then sufficient men recovered to work the ship in case of severe weather; but it was more perilous to wait than to put to sea, and our engineer being convalescent, we got up steam and stood towards Johanna.

CHAPTER III.

RETURN TO THE ZAMBESI.

It was not long before I succumbed to my old foe, sea-sickness, and for three days I was useless. The Bishop, Dr. Livingstone, Dr. Kirk, and others took the helm by turns, and kept watch. Having but one engineer fit for work, we could not steam at night, and our sails were not of much use to us. By Saturday afternoon we had exhausted our stock of wood; we had but little coal, and as it was thought advisable to keep that in store in case of need, we hoisted sail. The 'Pioneer' sailed badly; we drifted with the current, and instead of making for Johanna, the ship bid fair to carry us to Ibo.

On Easter Eve, Dr. Kirk slung a hammock for me from stanchion to stanchion, athwart the ship's stern, in order that I might not feel the motion of the vessel. It was a glorious night; never had I seen the stars so lustrous. My mind, however, was running upon the loving preparations made by many at home for the great to-morrow. We had hoped to have been at Johanna on Easter-day, but the delay in the river had made that impossible, and the necessities of our position made us unable to have a celebration of the Holy Eucharist on board ship. This gave the good Bishop and myself much concern; and so I kept awake during the night, noting the many cruciform constellations in the southern hemisphere, and thinking of Him who, as at that time lay in the grave, ready to burst the bonds of death, and thus consummate His victory, and make certain our salvation. About three o'clock the moon shone out brilliantly, and with the exception of a dense dark ridge of clouds, skirting the eastern horizon, all was serenely beautiful. As morning advanced, a gleam of light appeared in the east, and broke up the bank of cloud into strangely fantastic forms. As light increased, these sinister looking masses of vapour assumed appearances truly diabolical. There they were like the foul spirits of hell, such as painters of old delighted to pourtray as embodiments of sin: long-necked, big-headed, puffy-bodied, weird, and horrible looking creatures, huddled together as if in fear, gazing as if fascinated, or re-treating in headlong terror; while above all rose the glorious sun, and then those hideous forms melted away, and nothing remained but a brightly illumined cloud, that might have been, and perhaps was, a causeway for the angels of heaven. And so I sang to myself, 'Jesus lives,' and despite my sickness, was very happy.

On the evening of the 31st I was able to report myself fit for duty. I kept the first watch that night. Heavy showers of rain fell at intervals. The wind was fitful, and occasionally violent. The old quartermaster and I were on deck alone for some time—he at the helm, I on the look-out. Our orders were to keep the ship before the wind, but the wind played pranks with us, and 'Davy Jones,' instead of Johanna, was, according to the quartermaster, our certain destination. We were right out of course, and could not get the ship up to it again. Mr. May, the commander, was below, shaking with fever; I took the helm, and sent the quartermaster to call him up. When he appeared he took the helm, and ordered us to 'brail the sails.' What that meant, and what it would accomplish, of course the old sailor knew, but I was in profoundest ignorance. I followed him, however, and did what he told me, and for a few minutes it was, 'Pull away here, sir,' 'Let go there, sir,' 'Make all fast here, sir.' And so the sails were brailed, and the ship brought up to her right course. But now the old tar growled and grumbled so that it was past bearing with gravity, and I laughed heartily.

'It's all very well for you to laugh, sir,' said he, 'but it's no laughing matter. Though I s'pose the longer we lives the more we sees. I've seen many things in my day, but what I've seen lately beats everything else hollow; for, I never did expect to see a bishop a taking out o' anchors, and a hauling in o' cables, and a ship managed by the likes o' you and him, sir.'

As days went on the fever did not lessen, for though some recovered, others were smitten. We were so short-handed that we could scarcely keep the ship going. Our stoker fell ill.

there was no one to supply his place; and to his other labours, the Bishop added that of stoker; for I saw him emerge from the engine-room as black as a sweep : he had been stoking for several hours.

We sighted Comoro very early on the morning of April 2, and we anchored close to Mohilla, about midday. We had then consumed our last shovel of coals, and had scarcely a gallon of fresh water left, for by an oversight the tanks had not been filled in the Rovuma. It was close work, and it was only by the good providence of God that we escaped a great disaster.

Mohilla is the smallest of the Comoros, but certainly the most beautiful; it is pre-eminently an isle of beauty. We anchored opposite to a pleasant looking village, and a canoe containing a grand looking individual, in turban and flowing robes, at once came off to us. This man spoke a little English, and he wanted to know who we were, where we had come from, and where we were going to. We satisfied him on those points, and made known our wants—water and wood, fresh meat and vegetables. But nothing but water could be immediately had. The island was governed by a queen, and her consent was necessary to all trading transactions with strangers. The queen lived at Fomboni, five or six miles further along the coast, so messengers were at once sent to her, and we went on shore. The village was well kept, clean, and orderly. The natives, a mixed population of Arab, Malagash, and African, were not so very dirty; the children were prepossessing, and intelligent. Men were sitting about under the trees chanting the Koran, for they were in the full fervour of the Ramadan, when all good Mussulmans fast and pray from sunrise to sunset, but feast and sin from sunset to sunrise. Bananas and other fruit were tempting the palate in all directions, but until the queen's permission to sell was received, not a single thing could we purchase.

In the morning a messenger arrived from her majesty, graciously inviting us to her palace. Abdallah Ben Ali, the messenger, a quiet-looking, soft speaking man, announced himself first, as the queen's treasurer; secondly, as a general dealer ready to sell you anything and everything you needed, eggs or firewood, bullocks or negroes. He sent away his canoe, and returned with Dr. Livingstone and Dr. Kirk, the Bishop and myself, to Fomboni. Four of the Makololo manned our boat. As we went along we wanted to know all about Mohilla, and Abdallah was quite ready to tell us. It was an abode of bliss, a paradise of happiness, nothing discordant ever entered there, and he, Abdallah Ben Ali, was the happiest of men, for did he not live at Mohilla. "Was the queen married?" Yes, she was married; her husband, however, was not at Mohilla; he had gone to Zanzibar, and was not expected to return: but there was nothing unamiable in this little arrangement, all were content; it was just as it should be.

Fomboni consisted of a fort mounting forty small guns, the queen's palace, a mosque, and 300 or 400 houses. Its position was charming. Several large dhows were moored close to the shore, one of which was pointed out to us by Abdallah as the queen's, but which we learnt she never used. Why should she? Once at Mohilla, who would wish to leave it. The whole masculine population were awaiting our arrival, and, shouting and screaming, accompanied us to the palace. The Makololo excited much curiosity, for though Africans were numerous enough on the island, such stalwart, swaggering fellows as these four Makololo were rare. We passed the fort, and saw there a number of men armed with muskets. Entering the court of the palace, we found a body-guard, drawn up, armed with spears only. We were conducted to the council chamber of this little state. It was a long, narrow, whitewashed room, with benches on either side. The walls were ornamented with ancient looking guns, pistols, and spears. At the end of this chamber sat various grey-bearded men with rosaries in their hands; for, like certain Christians, the Mussulman regulates his prayers by his beads. As we entered these men arose, and beckoned us to the seats of honour. The Makololo followed, and squatting down on their haunches right in front of these venerable greybeards, surveyed them with fearless curiosity.

Then the principal personage opened his mouth, and gravely said—

' How you get along ?   What's the best news ?'

Dr. Livingstone detailed our wants and our woes, told him who he was, where he had been, and where he was going.

They elevated their eyebrows, were excited, and expectorated vehemently.   For a few minutes there was a considèrable mastication of betel-nut.   Those who filled the lower part of the room pressed forward ; dingy heads were thrust in at the windows ; all were eager not to lose a word.   Curiosity made the people rude; those outside crushed those inside ; a disturbance was the result.   The mighty men ejaculated angrily, and the spearmen thrust at the disturbers savagely, as though they would terminate their curiosity by sanguinary measures.

Then it was announced by a man in scantiest apparel that the queen was ready to receive us, and we ascended by steps, and through a trap door, into a large ill furnished room, and found ourselves in the royal presence.   At the end of the room furthest from the entrance, the queen sat on a handsome Turkey carpet.   She was habited in a flowing robe of red and gold, and wore a mask glittering with spangles, which prevented us from seeing the whole of her face, yet left sufficient revealed to show that she was young and good-looking.   At her side, dressed in Arab costume, stood her son, a pretty child about three years old.   Ladies in waiting, old and ugly, and by no means cleanly, who were chewing betel-nut, and copiously expelling saliva, sat on the floor around their royal mistress.   The queen did not chew ; but she did royalty gracefully and well, and motioned us to chairs with much dignity. She did not speak English, though she spoke French fluently, which none of our party did, for one after the other, to her great amusement, broke down in attempting to reply to her in that language.   So a grand Johanna man present, who was proud of his English, acted as interpreter.   The queen was curious, and showed much intelligence by her questions and remarks.   Hearing that the Makololo were below, she expressed a wish to see them, and they, nothing abashed, stalked into the royal chamber, and squatted before the queen.   Sherbet, of true oriental flavour, was then brought to us ; permission was given to purchase what we needed, and we then bowed and retired. The Makololo saluted upon leaving. Moloko, indeed, strode forward a step or two, and with a force of expression which first startled the queen and then made her laugh, said in his native tongue—

'Remain well, and live long, Queen of the Nations!'

As we were leaving the Palace, the Johanna man, with bated breath and mysterious air, informed us that the queen's prime minister, who was not present on account of sickness, wished to speak to us on affairs of moment. We went towards the ministerial abode. On our way, to our surprise, we were met by two Frenchmen—one, Le Père Finaz, the other Monsieur Arnoud, both Jesuits. They demonstrated much joy on seeing us; invited us to their house; and we accepted their invitation, promising on our return to visit them.

The prime minister was a stout old man, with a black skin, and a white beard; a disagreeable, restless, wicked-looking old man, whose illness was evidently assumed. Dr. Livingstone expressed his willingness to hear what he had to say; but he spoke no English, and deputed to the Johanna man the task of making known to us the cause of his anxiety, who, with the air and action of an actor, proceeded to say,

'Twenty years ago, the brother of the King of Malagash came to Mohilla. He brought with him very many dhows, filled with very many people, and he made war upon the people of Mohilla, and won very many battles. He was very strong, and the people of Mohilla could not defeat him. But they were very good Mussulmans, and loved their religion, while the Malagash are dogs, and have no religion; so they said to him: "If you wish to be our king, let you and your people become of our religion, and we will fight no more; but if you will not do this, we will fight every day until there is not one of us left alive." He said, very good, and he and all his people became good Mussulmans, and so we were all happy again. Then the king sent for his wife, and she brought with her a babe not yet born, and that babe is our queen. In a little time the old queen died, and then the king died also. They had but this one child. But before the king died, he called to him this gentleman (pointing to the prime minister), and this (pointing to another old man), and he took his little daughter in his arms, the present queen you know, and he said to them, " Be kind to her, take care of her, and rule for her until she become a woman." This they did, and all were very happy. The queen becomes a woman, and must have a husband, and so she marries an Arab man who came here from Zanzibar. After this all were very happy, but only for a short time; for this Arab man, because he married the queen, thought himself a king, and would not let any one but himself rule : would not let any one but himself see the queen ; and treated all the people of Mohilla as though they were dogs, dirt, swine. He took from them their goods; he would not let any ships come to the island to buy what we had for sale; he made the people very poor; and then he went away to Zanzibar, and took with him 300 men, to show the Zanzibar people what a great man he was. But when he returned to Mohilla he only brought 100 men back, and said all the rest were dead. He said that, but we did not believe him. We say he sold them for slaves. So the people of Mohilla became very angry, and drove him away from the island, and swore by Allah that he should never come back again. Was that right ?   Say,?'

'Right! quite right !' said I, in a glow of most undiplomatic fervour, and to the amusement of my companions.

'There! there! you hear this !' said the Johanna man, patting the prime minister on the back. And then he proceeded—

'But listen again. This Arab man goes to Zanzibar, and the queen is very sorry that her husband is away from her; she has a very good heart, but a very bad head. No sense, none, women never have; and so she is not happy without her husband, she wishes him to come back, and she sorrows very much. Well, this Arab man is afraid to come back alone, so he tries first of all to get the king of Zanzibar to bring him back; then he goes to the French, and they listen to what he says, and send two men here. One of them says he comes to teach, the other says he comes to farm ; but they do not teach, they do not farm. They go to the queen day after day, and they talk a great deal to her; what they say no one knows; but the Zanzibar people tell us that the French are going to bring back the Arab man, and if we will not have him, then they will take Mohilla themselves, give the queen money, give the Arab man money, and make Mohilla like Mayotte—a place where they can grow sugar. Now we do not wish the French to come, for they make the people work very hard, and do not pay them. We would like to have a consul, like Mr. Sunley, at Johanna, and then the French will keep away. We do not like the French—we hate the French. If they do come, the people of Mohilla swear by Allah that they will all go away. But they will come, we fear, and they will make this Arab man come too. What do you advise? Say?'

And this, Abdallah Ben Ali, was the paradise of content you pictured to us!

What was advised is not of much consequence. That the French wish for Mohilla there can be no doubt, and I dare say they will get it. A better sugar plantation could not be found in that part of the world.

We left the prime minister looking more sinister than ever, and though there was without doubt much truth in the narrative we had just heard, yet my sympathies went with the little queen. She was in a bad position between her Arab husband, those plotting, selfish, old rascals, those ministers of hers, and Messieurs the Frenchmen. All had their own ends to serve at her expense.

As we went toward the French residence we were followed by a curious crowd of men and boys; but when we drew near to the house, one after the other dropt off, until we approached the door alone. Le Père and Monsieur were very hospitable. Absinthe and cigars were offered with an irresistible politeness. The priest had a head nobly proportioned, but the expression of his countenance was not pleasing. Monsieur was in look, word, and gesture essentially French; a very clever man, evidently, and as unlike an agriculturist as could well be conceived. He understood English a little he said, and I gave him credit for more than he cared to own to. They had both lived for some time at Madagascar, and were very cautious of what they said about Mohilla; though they called the people demons, wild beasts, and detestable. Monsieur declared they had tried to poison him.

Before returning to the ship we negotiated with Abdallah for the supplies we needed. But next day, as Dr. Livingstone found we could get better supplied at Fomboni, we steamed to that place.

We stayed here several days in order to recruit the crew; and the fever-smitten profited by the halt, though several were much shaken, and few fit for work. Those of the crew who went ashore were grievously disappointed, for they could find no intoxicating liquor on the island. One old sailor declared that, though he had been sailing about the world ever since he was a boy, Mohilla was the first place he had been to where it was impossible to get drunk.

I made a good many friends among the children of the island. The little creatures—they were all boys, the girls being rarely visible—came around me whenever I went ashore, and begged me to teach them to speak English. So I walked with them, talked with them, and told them the English for any-thing they pointed out to me; or sat down, and described on the sand the letters of the alphabet. Most of these boys had pleasing features, and they were quick in thought as well as in feeling. They hated the French intensely, and whenever Le Père and Monsieur were spoken of their countenances fell, and they all spat vehemently on the ground, with disgust and vexation. I had never seen such an Anti-Gallican feeling. The last evening we spent at Mohilla I went on shore to take trifling presents to some of my young friends. I stayed with them, talking and singing, until the mueddin, on the top of the mosque, called the faithful to evening prayer. The sun was gone down, and the little ones held up their hands in silence, and went quietly off towards their homes. As I turned, however, towards the boat, one of these children came back to me. He put his hand in mine, and entreated me to take him away. He said he wanted to be all the same as the English, and tried to make me say, 'finish,' the word with which they concluded all arrangements satisfactory to them-selves.

A few hours' steaming brought us to Pomoney (Johanna) and we then learnt that the whole of our brethren had gone to the other side of the island. The Bishop and Dr. Kirk resolved to walk across to Muzumudu. I kept to the 'Pioneer.' News of our arrival had preceded us, and when we anchored off Muzumudu, Captain Stirling of the 'Wasp,' who was at Johanna, awaiting orders, came off to us, bringing Mr. Waller with him. We then obtained more particular information about our brethren. It appeared that after we left Johanna for the Rovuma, they stayed a few days on the Vega, then went round in a dhow to Muzumudu, and occupied the disused consulate, which Mr. Sunley had kindly prepared for them. Here they were attacked by fever. Mr. Scudamore and Adams suffered severely. But all were now convalescent, for they had left the consulate, which was close to the filthy town, and were living on the top of a hill nearly a thousand feet above the sea. This place was a perfect paradise. The cottages they there occupied also belonged to Mr. Sunley, and to this gentleman we were largely indebted, for his kindness and hospitality were exceeding and invariable.

When I went on shore I found myself once more in the presence of royalty, for close to the principal mosque there was a crowd of gaily-dressed men, one of whom came forward and offered me his hand. Waller at the same time introduced me to him as the king of Johanna. He was a mild-looking, intelligent young man. There were various other little mightinesses, and ' Mr. Rowley, Prince Mahomet;' ' Mr. Rowley, Prince Abdallah,' &c., &c., occupied the next five minutes. Our brethren seemed in favour with these people, and the king had left his country residence in order that he might have the benefit of their society. He was reading English with Waller, and one and all seemed anxious to improve themselves in our tongue, if not to profit by our religious instruction. The people of Johanna, generally, had acted with much good feeling; and the English missionaries were evidently greatly esteemed by them.

When we arrived at Lindaani—the name given to that part of the island where our friends were living—we found that the Bishop and Dr. Kirk had arrived. The Bishop had fever again; it came on while walking from Pomoney, and he had the utmost difficulty in reaching his destination.

At evening prayer, the whole mission staff met together for the first time.

Poor Adams had lost the bonny look he had on leaving England; he was much pulled down. Gamble was greatly weakened, but Procter and Scudamore looked well. A good report was given of the coloured men we brought from the Cape, for though as open to sickness as Europeans, their conduct hitherto had been admirable.

When we returned to the 'Pioneer,' next day, we found Dr. Livingstone preparing to pay the king a visit. I went with him. The approach to the king's house was not pleasant. The streets were so narrow, that extending your hands you touched the houses on either side. The road was so out of repair that we were in constant danger of tripping up, and the foulness under our feet was so abundant and disgusting, that had we fallen, we would have felt defiled for a month to come.

The Johanna monarch had an extraordinary residence for so exalted a personage. The entrance hall was a mere barn; foul water in filthy vessels, cocoa-nut rubbish, and a variety of other abominations, made it repulsive to sight and smell. The reception-chamber was free from such actual defilements, but it was far from clean, though much care and some money had been expended in fitting it up after the oriental fashion.

We were before our time, I suppose, for some of the ladies of the harem were there when we entered. We just saw the skirts of their raiment as they rushed out, uttering frightened exclamations. And one of our conductors ran forward and held a curtain before an opening that had to be passed by other ladies before they could get clear away from us infidels. But the curtain was too small. We saw several lightly-clad females pass by, and as they could not resist the temptation to look in our direction, we were able to judge of their beauty; their faces were flat and fat, dingy and dirty.

The king came in shortly after this, and made no attempt to act the king. He was much interested in Dr. Livingstone; had read his travels; and asked many questions relative to Africa, and pleased all by his intelligence, and gentlemanly behaviour.

That day was a great day; the last of the Ramadam; the king and all his courtiers went in gayest apparel to the mosque as soon as we left them. At night the people were excited, drummed, and fired off guns incessantly, and sleep was impossible. I always have a disposition to 'rejoice with those that do rejoice;' but this night, I could scarcely keep from execrating the rejoicing that deprived me of the rest I needed so greatly—for I had been for days without sleep.

We passed the next day at Lindaani. The Bishop was very unwell, and caused us much uneasiness. About midday we were surprised by a messenger, who ran breathless into our house, and exclaimed, 'The king!' And in a few seconds afterwards, followed by a numerous and motley-attired suite on foot, his majesty alighted at our door—from his donkey! King and courtiers made themselves at home, for this was no visit of ceremony. He expressed himself sorry to hear we were going to leave Johanna, and said if a missionary would come to live at Johanna he should be glad, and would give him land, for he wanted to perfect himself in the English language, and the explanations of a person were better than that of a dictionary —though 'Walker was very good.' He and his people had come up the mountain to pray, at a certain sacred spot by the side of the stream flowing close to us, and they left behind their cloaks and swords, while they went to their devotions. When they returned, the king again expressed his regret at losing us so soon, and bade us farewell. His departure was a strange sight. The donkey, a fine animal, was brought to the door, and when he mounted, his attendants arranged themselves in order about him. For a few seconds this order was observed, and the whole assemblage, some in bright-coloured and plentiful drapery, others without drapery of any kind, moved gravely away. The altogether of the thing was novel. Mountain and valley, cascade and river, a vegetation equal to anything under heaven, the blue sea in the distance, and this petty monarch in his poor pomp and splendour, constituted a picture which was striking. But when the king had passed by the grove of palms growing about our house, he forced his steed suddenly into a gallop, and the effect was perfectly ridiculous. The dignitaries strove to keep their places, but most of them were fat and short-winded, and burdened with their holiday attire, notwithstanding all their efforts were soon left behind, to curse and to pant, as they saw their places assumed by the sturdy half-naked slaves, who, less pampered, were fleeter of foot.

At night there was another great rejoicing; the people were not drunk with wine, but they were madly drunk with excitement.

Our stay at Johanna was longer than we anticipated. Several members of the expedition were far from well, and the condition of the 'Wasp' was so bad, the ship's doctor, and the majority of the crew being down with fever and other illnesses brought on by exposure and hard work on the coast, that Dr. Kirk attended to the sick for a few days.

Several of the crew of the 'Pioneer,' who had suffered most from the fever, were sent on board the 'Wasp,' invalided, and six Johanna men were taken in their places. Those invalided were in a miserable condition, for the fever, owing probably to previous disease, had punished them wofully.

The 'Wasp' supplied the 'Pioneer' with sufficient coal not only to steam across to the Zambesi, but to carry her past the woodless districts of the river. But when this coal was on board, it became apparent that little else could be taken. The 'Pioneer' was then as heavily laden as she should be, and Dr. Livingstone informed the Bishop that instead of being able to take back to the Zambesi all our stores and material, as he had promised to do, he would only be able to take about one-third of them. This was a grave matter; for there was now no possibility of getting any other conveyance to the Zambesi. What we had provided for ourselves we should doubtless want, for those best informed on the subject of our probable necessities for the first year or so, had selected our stores at the

Cape, and I could not look at the future without gloomy fore-boding, when I found that nearly two-thirds of the stores pronounced absolutely necessary were to be left behind. Truly the Rovuma arrangement was proving to us most unfortunate in its issues. It was the beginning of troubles ; the first of an unhappy series of events which have made the Universities' Mission sadly famous.

Had we gone up the Zambesi in February we should have secured all our stores, for then there would have been no need for the coal which crowded the decks of the 'Pioneer' at Johanna. But we were not men to waste time in useless reflections, or to meet troubles half way, and having received an assurance from Dr. Livingstone that he would have no difficulty in helping us to get our second year's stores, as he would not take a sea-voyage, and would not need coal, we were somewhat consoled. It was a grievous thing truly to leave so much that was valuable behind, to be wasted, spoiled, or pillaged ; yet, following our good Bishop's example, we made the best we could of our position. Comforts we did not want, and we trusted that our bread would be sure, and that our water would not fail. It was in such emergencies as these that the grand features of Bishop Mackenzie's character shone out ; his faith, hope, and charity were inexhaustible. His certainly was the 'charity that never faileth,' and it was good to be with him, for he had the rare faculty of developing in others that which was their best.

We left Muzumudu on the morning of the 18th, and steamed round to Pomoney. As soon as we arrived, the Bishop (who was now better), Waller and myself went to the storeship, and getting up our stores from the hold, made a selection of those things we could take with us. We were unable to finish our work that day, and it was not until sunset on the following day that we had made all arrangements.

When all was on board, the 'Pioneer' was laden to within an inch or so of what she could safely carry in smooth water, and our voyage across to the Zambesi was considered a des-perate venture, especially as Mr. May, the commander, had resigned, the monsoon was changing, the weather threatened

storm, and Dr. Livingstone was to act as captain. It was a
bold thing for a man whose knowledge of navigation was so
limited as his, to take the entire command of a ship; and so
the professional commanders thought, and shrugged their
shoulders, and wished us a safe voyage, evidently not expecting what they wished.

It could not have been otherwise, in so far as we missionaries were concerned; we had no notion of holding back, so
we committed ourselves to God's mercy, and as no better
guardianship could be desired for us, we were content.

We left Johanna on Monday, April 22. Fever still prevailed among us, and from the foul and crowded state of the
little ship, this was not to be wondered at. At most there was
but healthy accommodation for twenty people on board the
'Pioneer,' and there were forty-eight, with an amount of baggage, &c., disproportionately large. The deck was blocked up
with boxes, bales, and sacks of coal. The saloon and after-
cabin were offensive with the odour proceeding from the mass
of stuff stored in them. For three days, when unwell and
unable to remain on deck, I lay up in a corner of the saloon
with my head close to a number of sugar-cane tops which were
fermenting and developing vinegar, while piled about me were
reams of paper, containing between their leaves botanical specimens, many of them imperfectly dried and rotting. Indeed,
every available space in the ship, fore and aft, was blocked up
with stores, baggage, and natural history specimens, not
only preventing a free current of air, but poisoning what
we had.

During the first three days of our voyage the ship went
heavily through the sea, and had we experienced anything like
the rough weather predicted, we must have thrown overboard
all that was stored on the deck. After the third day our
course was easier, the coal we had consumed lightened the
ship, the wind and waves abated, and we no longer felt anxious
about our safety. On the fifth day we shut off the steam and
hoisted sail.

Fever did not leave us during these days. On Sunday, the
28th, the Bishop and several others were suffering severely.

Mr. Scudamore preached in the morning, and while preaching was suddenly taken ill with fever, and was unable to finish his sermon. These attacks were generally of brief duration, though their return was to be expected at any moment.

On the 29th we sighted land, which proved to be the Quilimane coast. We were not more than six miles from the shore, too close to be safe under sail, so we steamed the rest of the distance to the Zambesi, about eighty miles.

We arrived off the Kongone mouth of the Zambesi about one o'clock P.M. on the 30th. For three hours we waited for the rise of the tide, and then we attempted the passage of the 'bar.' The huge unbroken rollers were setting in fast and furious from the south. The crash and confusion when they burst was deafening. Such a tumult of water you rarely see; look where you would there was an angry, hungry-looking foam. The sense of danger in one's position gives to existence an intensity not by any means disagreeable, for though fully conscious of the peril, it is far from unpleasant to discover so much vitality in yourself. In a small boat it might be otherwise; though I have heard say that the feeling of being shot along before a huge roller, which every moment threatens to break and overwhelm you, is delightful. It may be so, but I have no wish to experience such a delight. As it was with us, in a stout little ship, with a man for captain who knew the channel, and whose nerves were iron, our spirits were raised by the state of things about us, from the conviction that we were able—humanly speaking—to set the danger at defiance.

For a few minutes all went well with us. I was beginning to look forward to a night of comfort, undisturbed by the rolling and pitching of the ship, when the soundings attracted attention. The leadsman called out first—'A quarter two,' then immediately afterwards, 'A quarter less two,' while another throw proclaimed, 'A half one,' and the next 'A quarter one.' It was a breathless moment; we were evidently out of the channel, and close to danger. Huge rollers were rushing at us broadside on. The vehemence of the surf was tremendous, but the little ship behaved admirably. A hundred yards more and we might be away from the danger. Could we do it? The risk was great; failure would have been destruction. A battered ship, and a dead body washed on to the shore from time to time, would have told the tale of our disaster. The risk was too great. Dr. Livingstone gave the signal to put the ship right about; she answered to her helm beautifully, and skimmed like a duck over the angry waves that but a moment before were all but overwhelming her. We anchored for the night about five miles from the shore.

Next morning—SS. Philip and James' Day, a happy day I thought for a missionary Bishop and staff to enter the heathen land where they were to work—our attempt to get into the river was successful. There was less southing in the wind, and the swell was not so heavy. The passage was turbulent, but by no means terrible; and we anchored without mishap in the smooth water of the Zambesi.

There can be no doubt that this bar is a formidable obstacle in the way of making the Zambesi the highway to the interior of Africa. I think it an insurmountable obstacle, for, though a steam-tug might be able, four days out of every seven throughout the year, to go over the bar, with a sailing vessel in tow, yet the hope of making this mouth of the river a commercial port must be very small, as the anchorage for ships, both outside and inside of the river, is as bad and as insufficient as can be; and a passage for boats is practically impossible.

The East Luabo is said to offer greater facilities for navigation, and according to the Portuguese, was at one time used by their sailors. Should the Kongone in course of time become blocked up, and it seems not improbable, the increased rush of water may sweep away many of the obstructions at the Luabo; but until that takes place, the best port on this coast is that of Quilimane. At most seasons of the year, sailing vessels of a certain draught have no difficulty in getting to and from Quilimane. The bar is not so formidable, the channel is wider and less tortuous, and at Quilimane there is much more convenience for shipping than can be found either at the Kongone or East Luabo. The great objection to the

THE KONGONE MOUTH OF THE RIVER ZAMBESI.

Quilimane river is this—*it is not a branch of the Zambesi*. At Quilimane you must unlade your vessel, put the cargo into canoes, carry it up the river a four days' journey, unship again, and then carry it *overland* some distance to the Zambesi; for the Naquaqua, the feeder of the Quilimane river, takes its rise among hills somewhere behind Mount Morumbula, and practically does not communicate with the Zambesi.

CHAPTER IV.

THE ZAMBESI RIVER.

THE Portuguese Government, since Dr. Livingstone has made the Zambesi famous, have asserted their exclusive right to the river by erecting a custom-house at the Kongone, and keeping a few soldiers there. We found the military to consist of a corporal and three or four privates, coloured men, dressed in blue cotton uniforms. A European officer was their com- mandant, but he was not at his post when we entered the river.

As soon as we were anchored Dr. Livingstone went on shore and found letters from the Governor of Quilimane, in one of which he stated that the Bishop and his party had been strongly recommended to his good offices by his Government, and he therefore offered all the assistance in his power. This was satisfactory, though we did not at that time think we should avail ourselves of his assistance, as it seemed determined by Dr. Livingstone that we missionaries were to have nothing whatever to do with the Portuguese.

Inhamissengo, the island formed by the Kongone mouth of the Zambesi and the West Luabo, is not an unhealthy looking place. It consists more of sand than mud, though a little inland, among the mangroves, mud, and nothing but mud, meets one's eye as the tide recedes. Nothing in the way of food, save a few beans, grows on Inhamissengo, though it is a famous liquor plantation. The dwarf palm abounds, and the natives, mostly slaves of the landowners higher up the river, where the Delta is very fertile, extract a juice from this tree, which, unfermented, is a delicious drink, and, distilled, yields a pleasant and a wholesome spirit, which they call nipa.

NATIVE DISTILLING NIPA FROM THE JUICE OF THE DWARF FAN PALM.

The natives on and about the Delta are, physically, a fine race, broad-shouldered, and deep-chested ; in outward appearance, as good specimens of humanity as you meet with south of the Zambesi. And were it not for the degradation forced upon them by the Portuguese, I should think them capable of a higher elevation than the southern tribes ; they are more genial, and have quicker sympathies.

The Portuguese, wherever they acquire territory in these parts of Africa, divide the natives into two classes ; the colono and the slaves. The colono are the original owners of the soil. They are nominally freemen, but are ground down by such rigid rules and exactions, that their condition is little better than that of the slave. The whole of the Portuguese possessions are divided into districts called pracos, which, with the exception of a few crown lands, are assigned to individuals who hold them at a nominal rent for a certain number of lives. The colono have to pay tribute, equal to a bushel of corn per head, per annum, to the owner of the praco on which they live ; and this tribute is enforced by fines, imprisonment, and slavery. Added to this they are compelled to give personal service without remuneration, whenever called upon, not only to the possessor of the soil, but to the crown officials, and to supply with food, free of charge, soldiers, and others employed by the government, when travelling. There are laws professedly regulating the relation of these colono to the owners of the pracos and others, but like all laws in these Portuguese colonies, they are but a dead letter ; the colono are not only subject to the caprice and extortion of the landowner, but to that of every soldier or official in their neighbourhood, and their condition is truly wretched.

The slaves are acquired by purchase, or by violence from the tribes inland. As a rule the Portuguese do not go into the interior, attack the villages, and bring away the inhabitants as captives ; now and then, however, an enterprising man among them may make a raid, and plunder and enslave, but generally they send their agents, natives whom they have degraded and trained to the purposes to which they put them, in order to purchase slaves. They are able to do this, because throughout the land slavery is an institution among the natives themselves. Not the same kind of slavery that exists among the Portuguese in America and elsewhere, for there is little in common between the two systems. With the natives there is no such great distinction as master and slave. Among the tribes we dwelt with, the word slave had no equivalent in their own language ; the term used had been introduced by foreigners; but a certain number of the people hold a similar relation to their chiefs and great men that Abraham's servants held to him. Their system is therefore patriarchal, for the chief is recognised as and called the father, and those who are subject to him, are spoken of and regarded as his children. But this system is without doubt the source, and in some respects the cause of the other system of slavery. For, tempted by those articles of European manufacture which the slavers take with

them, the chiefs will frequently, as by their laws they have the
right to do, sell their children—those people who are subject
to them. Beads, thick brass wire, and unbleached calico are
the usual barter-goods, the last being most generally in request;
indeed it is the main currency of the country, with which the
traveller may buy whatever the natives sell, and so greatly is
it desired, and so lightly are men, women, and children
esteemed, that two yards only, worth one shilling, was, when
we entered the land, the price frequently paid for a man or a
woman. In this way, doubtless, many slaves are acquired.
But when the demand is great, or the chiefs and others refuse
to sell those over whom they have power—and though sorely
tempted by their necessities, they do frequently refuse to sell
their people, for they are a kind-hearted race, and have often
much affection the one for the other—the slavers then take up
bribes, such as guns and gunpowder; they stir up strife
between village and village, between tribe and tribe; they
kindle and keep up wars with diabolical ingenuity, in order
that they may purchase the prisoners which each side makes
in the war. The chiefs object usually to sell their own people,
but they have no scruple in selling those they make prisoners
in war. It is thus the vast majority of slaves are acquired.
Do away with the traffic in human beings, and you do away
with the greater part of those wars which keep the African
tribes in a state of constant terror and demoralisation. I have
no hesitation in saying that for every slave so acquired, twenty
lives have been sacrificed in getting him; and for every plantation of so-called 'happy slaves,' a district of twenty square
miles has been devastated in order to secure them.

In common with ourselves the Portuguese have made the
slave trade illegal, but because they still permit slavery to
exist in all their colonies, the slave trade exists also; for
wherever you make it lawful for a man to regard his fellow-
man as something less than man, as property in common with
his cattle and swine, which he may sell as he would his horse
or his pig to his next-door neighbour, you cannot prevent
him finding the best market for his property. And, then, as
the price paid by the foreign purchaser is ten times greater

than he can get from his neighbour, he will use the utmost exertion to get the foreigner for his customer. So we find that slaves are still being exported from these Portuguese colonies, notwithstanding the presence of officials who are placed there to prevent this abominable traffic. The fact is the Portuguese Government pay their African officials such miserable stipends, that the comforts of life, so longed for in that climate, are beyond their means, and it is to be feared that some are not able to resist the slave-trader's bribe when it is offered. Honourable, kind-hearted men, I know, are there, who regret as much as we can do the demoralization which they are unable to prevent.

To illustrate the impunity with which law is sometimes set at defiance, 'I will tell a tale as it was told to me,' by one who was so intimately acquainted with the transaction that I suspected him to have borne some part in it.

Senhor ——, a well-known merchant entered into a negotiation with a house at Bourbon to supply it with 2000 slaves —a period of nine months to elapse between the delivery of the first and second thousand. In due time, either by barter or by violence, the first thousand of men and women were got together. Until the ships were ready to receive them, these poor creatures were kept outside the town, and fed from its stores; everyone therefore must have known what was being done. When the ships were ready, the slaves were marched through the town (at night it is said), embarked at its port, and having escaped our cruisers, were carried safely to those for whom they were intended.

In full reliance upon the good faith of the Bourbon house, the Senhor had no sooner got rid of the first consignment than he sent out his agents, far and near, and collected the second thousand. The ships returned, but instead of the payment he expected, they brought a notification from the house at Bourbon which drove the Senhor nearly wild. The money was not forthcoming, and in his anger he hoisted sail and proceeded at once to Bourbon, giving orders that the second thousand of slaves should be supported at his expense while he was away. The voyage was long, provisions meanwhile became scarce and dear, a large sum was soon owing for food supplied to his slaves, and when the Senhor returned without his money, (for the house at Bourbon had completely failed him), he was nearly a ruined man, and having no market for his slaves at that moment, he gave orders to release them. That was done. But they were not so readily disposed of. They could not return to their own country, they were destitute of food, they began to pillage, and to commit violence when resisted ; no one cared to make slaves of them again ; for the scarcity of provisions continued, and slaves were worth less than dogs. So they became a nuisance and a scandal ; it was necessary for the public good that they should be got rid of, and the soldiers had a grand battue—they shot down these poor creatures like vermin.

It is not all slave-trading speculations however which turn out so unprofitably as this, nor are they frequently of this character. In this instance, the Senhor united in his own person, procurer, agent, and shipowner, and had his speculation succeeded he would have realized at least £50,000, and have returned to Europe, and passed the rest of his days full of honour and senatorial dignity, the uncompromising advocate of constitutional liberty ; as it was, he was impoverished and laughed at.

Generally, the profits of slave-trading are shared among several. For instance, some well-known Spanish or American trader advises the agent on the coast that he needs a thousand slaves, and will be at such and such a place at a certain time to receive them. The agent communicates with his brother merchants further up the river; they and their servants acquire the human property, and send them down to the coast agent, gaining by so doing at least 200 per cent. upon their outlay ; the agent gets as much, for slaves at the ship are worth from £8 to £12. But insomuch as the greatest risk is incurred by the owner of the ship, his profit is enormous, for at Havannah, able-bodied slaves are frequently sold for £150 up to £200. So if 100 slaves be deducted from the 1000 for expenses, and another 100 for deaths on the voyage, you have as much as £100,000 as the profit on a cargo of 1000 slaves.

The Government of Portugal seems anxious to ameliorate the condition of the slave in its colonies. The laws respecting slavery are admirably framed, and express in high-flown language most benevolent sentiments. Not possessing the means to compensate the owners of slaves, they have given the masters the benefit of a term of twenty years ; this term expires in 1878, and then by law so will slavery also terminate. Meanwhile various enactments exist for bettering the condition of the slave, until the time when he is to be a slave no longer. All slaves are to be registered, and in the estimation of the law, none are slaves unless registered. None can be slaves, legally, longer than ten years ; children of slaves are born free ; masters may not punish at pleasure, the authorities alone being empowered to inflict punishment. It is murder to kill a slave ; and, lastly, no baptized native can be a slave. I fear the slave is not much benefited by this philanthropic legislation. Not a tithe of the slaves are registered ; the children of slaves are as much in bondage as their parents, and are sold as openly ; the masters punish at will, are often guilty of great barbarity, and have in reality the power of life and death in their hands. The regulation about baptism is a farce : as a rule, they make no attempt to Christianize the natives, bond or free.

The colonists consist of Europeans, half-castes, Goa men, and Banyans ; the latter, however, are confined exclusively to the coast settlements. The Europeans are few in number, the half-castes the most numerous. The European is not so hard a master as the Goa man ; but the half-caste is merciless. He is said to hate both black and white—the former because he has so much in common with him ; the latter because he is not regarded as his equal, and the most pitiless inhumanity towards their slaves is frequently practised by them. In this country there seems really nothing to protect the slave from the cruelty of the master, if the master be cruelly disposed. Law exists but in name. His value is but nominal, and so the self-interest of his owner affords him no protection, as it does where slaves are valuable. The usual instruments of punishment are a three-thonged whip made of buckhide, each thong consisting of a plait of three, and a rod of hippopotamus's hide, hard as

iron. These scourges inflict severest injuries, and I have seen
men mutilated for life by the severity of their punishment. It
is a mistake to suppose that the slaves receive a kinder treatment from their masters because of the native tribes around.
In America the masters could afford to be merciful if so disposed, for masters predominate; but in these Portuguese colonies a reign of terror seems the necessity of the position which
the Portuguese have assumed. By cunning and violence, the
slave is here reduced to a greater degradation than he ever was
in the vast slave states of America; and, where the master
cannot ensure obedience, he kills—not always openly, though
some care not to resort to secrecy. Bound hand and foot, in
the dead of the night, recaptured runaways, or rebellious slaves
have been taken by well-trained agents in a canoe, and when
in the middle of the stream the canoe has been upset and the
victims drowned. The agents then swim to shore and report
the disaster as an accident, so appearances are saved. While
in some localities, wretches, who have become what they are
through the diabolical training they have received, will not
scruple, if a refractory slave, man or woman, be sent to them
with a present, to provide that they be no more seen. It is by
these and similar means that the master in this country, aided
by his knowledge of the superstitions of his slaves—which
knowledge he uses against them—is able to keep up his authority.

I once rebuked a man severely for the inhuman way in
which he punished a boy for neglect of some trifling order.
His whip was the most ferocious looking thing I ever saw; a
few lashes were sufficient to reduce the child to insensibility.
He did not attempt to deny I was right, in the abstract, but
he argued thus:

' You see, in order to live out here I must have slaves, and
in order to keep slaves I must have a whip. My whip is no
worse than any other whip that I know of, but I do not justify
it as a right, I simply defend it as a necessity. Wherever
slavery exists discipline must of necessity be brutal. You
English, because you do not keep slaves, take the philanthropic,
the religious view of the question; we, who do keep slaves

take the material view, which regards the man as property, in the same way as you regard a horse, to be broken in and flogged to your will. I admit the philanthropic view is the best, for in the eyes of God all men are equal; and, though the African be a degraded man, I know enough of him to be sure that he can be raised by kindness and religion into a position not very inferior to our own. But, if you keep slaves, and mean that they shall give you the labour of their bodies, and of their minds also, in so far as you permit them to have minds, you must degrade them by the whip, and by all other means at your disposal, until, like dogs, they are the unhesitating servants of your will, no matter what that will may be, and live for your pleasure only. I know the philanthropic, the religious view of the question, is the best. I feel it is the best; but it will never pay me to adopt it. I am here. I must be here. What am I to do? Starve? Not if I can help it. I do as others do. I keep slaves, and while I have slaves I must act as the master of slaves. I must use the whip. When I first came into this country I was tender-hearted, for I had been well nurtured at Lisbon; but that soon passed away—it could not last. I was the laughing-stock of my companions. Just to explain my position, I will tell you of a circumstance which happened soon after I came here. The Governor invited me to a party of pleasure. The party consisted of himself, his daughters, some officers, and others. We were to go in boats to a favourite island resort several miles off. I took one of my slaves with me, a lad that I kept about my person. As we were going along this lad fell into the river. He could not swim, and the tide was carrying him fast away to death. Dressed as I was, in full uniform, I plunged in after him, and saved him. The wish alone to save the boy's life prompted me to risk my own. And for this I became the jest of the party; even the ladies tittered at my folly. Next night the Governor gave a grand dinner, when others besides those at the boat party were present. I had taken cold, and coughed slightly; remarks were made, and the Governor in scoffing terms alluded to the yesterday's exploit. A shout of laughter followed. "Were you drunk?" said one.

"Had you lost your senses, to risk your life after a brute of a negro?" said another. "Rather than spoil my uniform, I would have knocked him on the head with a pole," said a third, and it was a long time before my "folly" was forgotten or forgiven. You think I am worse than others. I am not; but I do not condescend to their hypocrisy. And what I am now, this country and its associations have made me.'

And nothing, not even that of the slave, can be worse than the condition, the moral and physical condition, of the masters. The degradation and debasement they force upon the natives have certainly reacted upon themselves. The consequences of their godless lives and flagrant immoralities are visible in their wretched looking persons.

But to return to the ship. As soon as we were anchored in the river the crew commenced clearing the deck and re-arranging the stores. And next morning the Bishop and others of our party commenced upon the after-cabin. The work fell to our lot, because our property was stored there. By opening the port-holes, a thing impossible at sea, we got rid of the offensive odours that had pervaded the saloon, and by a vigorous application of broom and brush, and a more judicious stowage of stores, we made a like griev-ance again impossible. In short, the ship had a thorough cleansing, and great was the comfort therefrom.

There is no good wood for steaming purposes at the Kon-gone, so we went round to Luabo. Our course was along a narrow canal-like channel of the Zambesi; of the river itself you get no fair idea until you get beyond the Delta. The mangrove-trees hem you in on either side. Green as churchyard grass are the leaves of the mangrove, and equally suggestive of death. Monkeys were numerous among the trees, and scampered, and chattered, and barked at us as we passed them. A few pelicans and hawks were the only birds we saw.

We halted for the night opposite the residence of a Por-tuguese named Augustinian, about fifteen miles from the sea. Augustinian was on the bank, his slaves, a sturdy set of men and women, around him. He saluted us courteously, and invited us to his house. He was not a thorough-bred Portuguese, though he showed very little of the darker-blood in his veins ; but he was one of the most miserable looking objects I had seen. His debilitated frame, so debilitated it pained you to look at him, showed how terribly the sins of the father were affecting the son, for the general depravity is so great, and its consequences so hideous, that it is few you meet with out here who have not in some way been branded with this fearful inheritance of sin. Among the slaves were two or three men that could have overthrown fifty such men as their master ; and I could not help wondering at the deep mystery which keeps them in bondage.

Augustinian's first inquiry related to the Landeens, who are an offshoot of the Zulus. He was dreading an invasion of these people. The Landeens exercise authority from the Zambesi to Delagoa Bay, and they make the Portuguese pay tribute to them for some of their best estates on the south bank of the river. They are invaders and conquerors, and their history is this :—Some years since, the father of Panda, the present chief of the Zulus, sent out Manikoos, one of his great men, and a number of his warriors to drive the Portuguese from the coast positions they held south of the Zambesi. They failed to do this ; they could only shut them up in their forts from the land side. It is or was a law among the Zulus that an unsuccessful general on his return should lose his head. Manikoos was unsuccessful, but wished to keep his head. He saw that though he could not drive the Portuguese out of their forts, he could easily subdue the natives of the country about them, and he proposed to the people with him, that instead of returning home, they should form a kingdom where they were, and make him king. His proposal was accepted, and Manikoos in course of time subdued all the tribes about him, who had more affinity with the Manganja than the Zulu, and made his name terrible. If it were not for the Zambesi, which they dislike to cross, these Landeens would have no difficulty, supposing they had guns, in driving the Portuguese out of the land ; as it is, wherever they have estates in the neighbourhood of these people, the

tenure by which they hold them is of the most uncertain
kind.

The Luabo mouth of the Zambesi is more pleasing than the
Kongone. It is at least a mile broad, and its characteristics
are more cheerful and attractive. There is plenty of game of
all kinds on shore; the spoor of buck, buffalo, and hog was
everywhere seen. We had not been at anchor long before two
of our party, well used to the gun in England, went after
fresh meat. But the experiences of an English sportsman
aid him but little in Africa, and Dr. Livingstone, anticipating the issue, called to him one of the Makololo, and
said :—

'Mobeta, take your gun; go ashore, and bring us back a
buck; we have not had fresh meat for some days.'

Mobeta was delighted, and running down below brought up
his gun, a genuine 'Brown Bess,' and started. He returned
before the others, and was the only one who brought back
game. He shot a bush-buck; the others, nothing. But African venison, after all, is a mistake; it is not so good as inferior
mutton—that is, as far as my experience of it goes.

Hippopotamuses seemed numerous; we passed them repeatedly on our way round, and they walked about on a
sand-bank just ahead of where we were anchored, papa,
mamma, and little one, quite unconcerned at our presence.

While waiting at the Luabo, I had my first attack of fever.
I was not very well for two days; I felt indeed, as though I
might be seriously ill. Then my ankles, my knees, my hips,
my back, my eyes, and my head began to ache, and the pain
increased until it was almost beyond quiet endurance. I could
scarcely move, was unable to stand, and found little relief
from lying down. The Zambesi 'Rousers' were administered;
but, for a time, the fever symptoms increased. Now I was
burnt with heat, then I shivered with cold, then I became a
little delirious, and I had hard work to keep from talking
nonsense. The excitement of the brain was most distressing.
But it was not of long duration, for, on the third day, the
remedies administered gave me so much relief that I fell into
a sound sleep of some hours' duration, and when I awoke, I

felt not much the worse for this my first attack—a very slight attack—of African fever.

On May 7, all being ready, we began the real ascent of the river, and it was thought by Dr. Livingstone, that in less than three weeks we should be at Chibisa's village, where we were to disembark. We made a long run, and when we halted for the night, were fully sixty miles from the sea.

The growth of mangrove-trees did not extend twenty miles up the river, and we felt glad to be rid of them, despite the uninteresting character of the country succeeding.

The Zambesi is a magnificent stream to look at. When I first caught sight of its broad water, I was not surprised at the exaggerated feeling which had called it an inland sea, for it is a mighty looking stream, more than a mile broad. But though so broad it is very shallow, and for several months in the year you cannot navigate it with any vessels drawing more water than the ordinary canoes of the country. It is a wilderness of sand islands, the water flowing in small streams between. On either side is a vast plain of grass, giant grass, six or eight feet high. You don't see a tree, scarcely a tree. Here and there a clump shelters the house of some Portuguese settler. Here and there a tall palm tree rears its head, but these trees only make the painful nakedness of the country more conspicuous. The sameness of the scenery wearies you. Nothing can be more disappointing than the characteristics of the country about the Zambesi for the first hundred miles.

During our day's progress we passed several villages and Portuguese residences. The gentlemen did not appear, but the natives did, and a wretched looking race they seemed. They were slaves, probably, and their abject bearing was very painful to witness. It was very humiliating to me, as a Christian, to think that these poor creatures were what they were through the selfishness of Christians.

We passed numerous hippopotamuses, saw several crocodiles, and many kinds of birds rarely seen in England, save as stuffed curiosities. Flamingoes gorgeous in apparel and magnificent in height; herons of more graceful build, but of more sober hue; and a legion of others of more delicate structure, with

whose names, habits, and characteristics I am not familiar, and
about whom, therefore, I shall be silent.

Dr. Livingstone was anxious to get to Mazaro before halting,
but the sun went down, and we were still three or four miles
below it.   The last gleam of light gladdened our eyes with a
peep of the wood-covered hills about Shupanga, and with a
glimpse of the summit of Morumbala, which looked beautiful
in the purple reflection shed by it.

We were in motion early in the morning, the whole population turning out to see us.   The size and speed of the
'Pioneer' astonished them, for hitherto they had not seen so
formidable a vessel.

We did not stop at Mazaro, but dipped our bunting in
compliment to the Portuguese flag flying there, and were
saluted in turn.   Not a European was discernible among the
crowds on the shore, until we came to the estate of Senhor
——, where we halted.   The Senhor was waiting to receive
us.   He was a miserable looking man, prematurely old, nearly
blind, and very deaf.   As he came tottering down to the bank
to greet us, shading his eyes with his hand, and making vain
efforts to distinguish those on board, his appearance was so
repulsive you could not sympathise with his infirmities, which
were manifestly the result of vice long continued and still perpetrated.   This man was the great man of the district, the
medium through which all communications would pass from
us to the higher Portuguese authorities in this part of the
world.   He was a notorious old slave-trader, and from his
extensive transactions in slaves ought to have been wealthy,
but he was not; a curse is, as a rule, upon the ill-gotten gain;
a rich slave-dealer in this part of the world is scarcely known.
Yet they keep the traffic up; the excitement it produces—and
it is to them as great as gambling—and the diabolical power
it puts in their hands, prove irresistibly attractive.   Blind,
deaf, and incurably diseased, retribution was laying its heavy
hand upon the Senhor; his boatmen had plundered him; all
seemed at war with him; even she who held the position of
wife to him, had risen against him.

Above this place the country rapidly improved.   The vegetation was superior, large trees were numerous, and hills were opening up to view on all sides.

Shupanga is on the south bank of the river. The house was large, and so situated as to command a view of Mount Morum-bala and adjacent hills, and the extensive country intervening. Surrounded by plantations of mango, orange, and cocoa-nut trees, with a soil, properly cultivated, capable of producing in profusion all things necessary to strengthen and make glad the heart of man, there are few places in this part of Africa more desirable. But the house was uninhabited and falling into decay, for the Landeens drove away the residents by their threats and exactions.

Dr. Livingstone kindly suggested to us to take from Shu-panga cuttings of orange, mango, and lemon trees, and the roots of pine apples, these things being little known on the Shire highlands; and as the best plantation lay below the house, in order to get near to it, the ship was taken up a part of the river where sand-banks and shallow water prevailed. We gathered our cuttings and roots, but a heavy price was paid for them, for in trying to get away again, the ship swung on to a sand-bank, and there remained for three days.

Dr. Livingstone sent to a friendly Portuguese for assistance, and he sent to our help a large canoe, capable of holding three or four tons of cargo, and a dozen men. We found the canoe better adapted for taking out anchor and cable than our light boats, and so it and the men, who of course were slaves, were of much use.

After we were out of this difficulty, the engines refused to work, and we had to halt while the engineer repaired them.

Whilst waiting here, some of our friends took their guns and went in search of game, which they did not get, but they brought with them several of these much-dreaded Landeens. They were magnificent fellows, but had the look of unmitigated savages. They wore a kind of kilt made of monkey-skins, and their loins were covered with strips of monkey-skin and buck-skin alternately arranged. It is a far more picturesque attire than the bit of dirty calico I had hitherto seen worn by the natives. Their necklaces were made mostly of the horns of a

diminutive antelope, strung through the roots, though one
fellow, the medicine-man, had a forest of chips about his neck.
He also had at least twenty bracelets of steel wire on each
arm, and on the fingers of each hand were many rings of the
same material. Their snuff-boxes, which were made of a section
of bamboo or reed, were about a foot long, an inch in diameter,
and ornamented with elaborate carving, very skilfully executed.
One man carried his snuff-box in a hole made in the lower lobe
of his ear.

They were well pleased with their visit to us, for Dr. Livingstone conversed with them freely, and gave them trifling presents. There was nothing servile in their bearing; indeed
they regarded all the natives around as their servants and
slaves. They do no work, but quarter themselves upon the
tribes they have subjugated. Those who visited us were, with
many others, living upon the villagers near to Shupanga, and
they assumed the air and manners of lords and masters. They
carry off the stalwart lads as recruits, and the young women as
wives. The Portuguese are really unable to do anything with
them. Once, when repelling an invasion of these people, they
captured two of them, and carrying them to Quilimane, did
their best by flogging, &c. to subdue their spirit. But they
only evoked threats of vengeance and defiance. Until death
they breathed out threatening and slaughter against their cap-
tors. They were as little moved to supplication as the North
American Indian.

As yet nothing has ever been attempted in the way of Chris-
tianizing this fine race. It is very sorrowful that such noble
specimens of humanity, who would be as powerful for good as
for ill, should be left in the darkness and debasement of heathenism.

Our progress into the Shire was pleasant and unobstructed.
The character of the country on the Zambesi improved the
higher we went. Well-wooded and picturesque hills, and lofty
mountain-land gratified the eye. It was with feelings of sadness that you looked from the country to its inhabitants, the
sinister, degraded men and women, gazing at you from the
bank of the river. Beholding the fair landscape only, listening

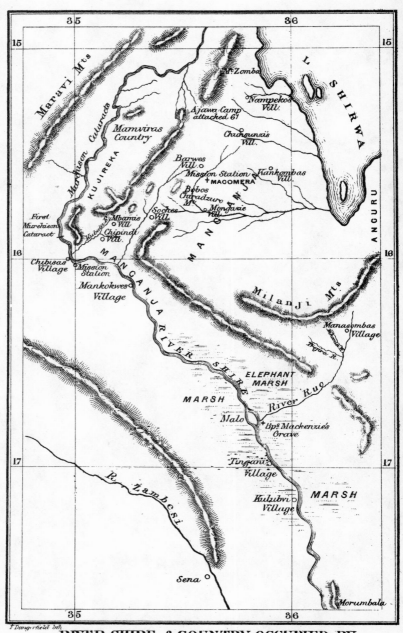

35   36

15   15

Maravi Mts

L. SHIRWA

Mt Zomba

Nampekoo Vill.

Ajawa Camp
attacked 61

Mamviras
Country

Chadsunzais
Vill.

Madason Cataracts

Barwes
Vill.

Mission Station
MAOOMERA

Kankombas
Vill.

Bobos
Curadzuro
Mt

KUJIREKA

Sochos
Vill.

Monguaie
Vill.

First
Murchison
Cataract

Mbamis
Vill.

Hubvas

Chipindi
Vill.

MANGANY

ANGURU

16   16

Chibisas
Village

Mission
Station

Mankokwes
Village

MANGANJA RIVER SHIRE

Milanji Mts

Manasombas
Village

Tigora R.

ELEPHANT
MARSH

River Ruo

MARSH

Malo

Bps Mackenzie's
Grave

17   17

R. Zambesi

Tinganu's
Village

MARSH

Kulubvi
Village

Sena

Morumbala

35   36

F. Daug. field lith.

RIVER SHIRE, & COUNTRY OCCUPIED BY
THE MISSION.

to the voices of unceasing praise put forth by the meaner of
God's creatures, the birds and insects, for the chirp of the
grasshopper is truly a cry of praise, you feel inclined to ex-
claim, 'All things are very good;' but, casting your eyes on
the dark crouching forms before you, men in whose veins runs
the blood of which all the families of the earth are made, the
descendants with you of one common parent, and the noblest
effect of God's creative power, you shudder at the visible
presence of evil—of evil so long inherited and intensified,
that it has all but shut out knowledge of the existence of
good, and has blinded its victims to the presence of itself.
Great is the mystery of evil: and great is the faith that is
required to behold it hoping, without doubt, without fear, but
with humility and awe, that in the effort to lessen it you may
find your duty, and in the right performance of that duty your
own soul's progress towards that blessed land where evil
entereth not.

CHAPTER V.

THE SHIRE RIVER.

WE ascended the Shire a few miles and then halted. Our halt
extended to several days, for Dr. Kirk went on business to
Sena, and we awaited his return.

The Shire is a much narrower river than the Zambesi, in no
part being more than 500 yards broad, in many parts not 100.
For the first seventy miles the channel is deep, and navigation
is easy ; after that, as the river widens, it becomes shallower,
and, except for canoes or vessels drawing no more water than
canoes, it is practically useless. Our experience in the 'Pioneer' will show that we did not find it the splendid stream for
navigation it was described to be. About two hundred miles
from its confluence with the Zambesi, navigation is stopped for
at least sixty miles, by a series of cataracts. Beyond these
obstructions the river, I am told, for more than eighty miles
is favourable to navigation, its source being the Lake Nyassa,
into which you may sail without let or hindrance.

The Shire Valley varies in width from ten miles to fifty. It is shut in by two ranges of hills which run in the general direction of the river. For the first hundred miles the valley of the Shire is mainly swamp land. Stand on Morumbala, the first hill of any importance you meet with up the Shire, and the view you have is extensive, but cheerless past description. Swamp, swamp—reeking, festering, rotting, malaria-pregnant swamp—where poisonous vapours for several months in the year are ever bulging up and out into the air, lies before you, as far as the eye can reach, and farther. If you enter the river at the worst seasons of the year, as I think we did (for in the month of May the swamps are drying up) and if you are detained any great length of time in the neighbourhood of these pestiferous localities as we were (for instead of being eighteen or twenty days in getting to our destination, we were nearly eighty) then the chances are you will take the worst type of fever, which will be again and again repeated, and though you do at last get on to the healthy highland plateau, it will probably go very hard with you. If, on the other hand, you go into the river during the best season, when the swamps are fairly dried up—say from July to the end of October—you have everything in your favour; you will probably take so mild a form of the fever, that it will not inconvenience you more than an ordinary attack of influenza at home; and, if you pass rapidly up to the highland region in boats or canoes, you will soon eliminate what fever you may have in your system, and will be able to exist as free from physical inconveniences as in most other tropical countries in the world. My experience will not let me say much more for the Lower Shire Valley than this; for though its characteristics after the first hundred miles are healthier, and it is really beautiful in many of its features, it never can be a suitable residence for Europeans, and I think its fertility has been much overrated. In some parts, doubtless, you could not exaggerate its productiveness, but generally I think it much less fertile than it was at first imagined and described to be.

The population of the valley for the first hundred miles was scant. That it could ever have been thickly peopled seems to me impossible. Under the hills that shut out the Zambesi

from the Shire Valley, and also under those trending towards
the Milanji, amid clumps of trees here and there, villages may
have existed, but the inhabitants were without doubt few, and
from the specimens we saw of them, most miserable. The
principal occupant of these marsh-lands is the elephant, and
you may at times see several hundreds of these monster animals in one herd, feeding like cattle in meadows, together
with buffaloes and other creatures, who are at home in such
regions. Along the course of the river are birds innumerable.
The river itself abounds with animal existence; fish, unknown
to European rivers, ferocious-looking things some of them are,
with teeth outside the mouth; crocodiles, so numerous that
you meet with them perpetually, and once I counted seventy-
nine of these disgusting reptiles at one time on one small
island; while hippopotamuses are more numerous than street
dogs in London. Above these marsh-lands the population,
though never dense, greatly increased.

Not far from where we halted was a native village, the inhabitants of which looked poverty-stricken and oppressed. For
a day or two they supplied us with fowls, but we soon exhausted their stock; there would seem nothing to prevent
them rearing hundreds, but two or three dozen were all they
could produce. They were, however, very eager for our unbleached calico, for they had but a very poor supply with
which to cover nakedness.

No great way from where we halted lived a half-caste Portuguese, who in that wicked land was notorious for his wickedness. Instead of the whip he used the gun, which, in his
ferocious facetiousness, he called his 'Minister of Justice.'
And in mere wantonness he was known to have taken life
again and again, yet no steps were taken by the authorities to
restrain, much less punish him. Men heard of his murders,
but they shrugged their shoulders, and did nothing. It was
only a 'wild beast of a negro' that was killed, and what was
that! They thought less of it perchance than if he had shot
a hippopotamus. One of his murders was painfully notorious,
even to its minutest particulars. Over the female slaves employed in the house and adjacent lands is placed a head woman,

a slave also, usually chosen for such an office for her blind fidelity to her master. This man had one such woman, one who had ever been faithful to him and his interests, who had never provoked him by disobedience or ill conduct, and against whom, therefore, he could have no cause of complaint. One day, when half drunk—I give this wretched man what excuse can be made from this fact—he was lying on a couch in his house; his forewoman entered, and made herself busy with some domestic work. As her master lay watching her, his savage disposition found vent in a characteristic joke: 'Woman,' said he, 'I think I will shoot you.' The woman turned round to her master, and said, 'Master, I am your slave; you can do what you will with me; you can kill me if you like; I can do nothing. But don't kill me, master, for if you do, who is there to look after your other women; they will all run away from you.'

She did not intend to anger her master by this reply—to exalt herself at his expense; but instantly the man's brutal egotism was aroused; he had no will or power to restrain his deadly passion; the savage joke became a murderous reality, and he shouted with rage:—

'Say you that! say you that! fetch me my gun. I will see if my women will run away after I have killed you.'

Trained to implicit submission, the woman did as she was commanded. She fetched the gun, she handed him the powder and the ball; at his command she knelt down before him, and the wretch levelled the gun and fired at her breast. In his rage he missed his mark, the ball passed through her shoulder. She besought him to spare her: he was deaf to her entreaties, and called for fresh powder and ball, and, though wounded and in agony, she again handed them to him. Again the gun was loaded; again it was levelled at the woman's breast, and this time with fatal accuracy, for when he discharged it, the woman fell dead at his feet. I exaggerate nothing; the facts, as I state them, were known far and wide; the Governor was made acquainted with them; the ministers of justice—save the mark! knew of them, but no one put forth a hand to punish this bad man for what he had done, or to protect his slaves from further cruelty from his hands. But a righteous retribution overtook him nevertheless. He was, some time after the event I have narrated, going down to the town of Quilimane, with the full odour of his bad deeds upon him, and vaunting in his wickedness. He was on the Zambesi in his canoe. The canoe-men were his slaves. Something they did offended him. He uttered his usual threat, that he would shoot. The cadamo—captain of the crew—wrought up to desperation, and knowing that the deed invariably followed the threat, turned round and said—

'Master, you say you will shoot, do you? Well, shoot! and if you do, you will kill one man; but you will kill no more!'

'Ah! what! you threaten to kill me, do you? Well, we will see!' replied the master, rousing himself up and taking his gun.

'I can't say, master, what will happen if you fire; but if you fire, I say you will kill no more;' was the dogged rejoinder.

The answer to this was the discharge of the gun. One man had his arm broken, but the rest sprang upon the tyrant; a pair of muscular hands were quickly round his throat; there was for a short time a desperate struggle, and then the guilty soul fled this earth, to await the righteous judgment of Him in whose ear the cry of the afflicted is ever present, and who 'executeth righteousness and judgment for all them that are oppressed with wrong.' A bag of salt was tied to the dead man's body, and then the Zambesi received it.

But mark this. Though the government, and magistrates, men sworn to administer justice between man and man, irrespective of race or colour, allowed this man to murder at will, unmolested, yet no sooner did they hear that the slaves, under this strong provocation, had avenged themselves, than they showed ceaseless energy and resolution in punishing those who slew him. The country was in commotion. A master slain by his slaves!—no matter the provocation—aroused almost to madness the cowardly fears and fierce resolves of all. Once admit the possibility of retribution, and what master is safe?

So soldiers were sent out in all directions; some of the canoe-
men were shot down like wild beasts, and the others re-cap-
tured, and publicly whipped to death.

Dr. Kirk returned from Sena on the 17th. We waited two
days longer for a canoe that was to follow, bringing various
things belonging to Dr. Livingstone, and also thirteen slaves
belonging to Senhor Feróa, of Sena, Dr. Livingstone having
borrowed them to help him up the river, and on his journeys.

Senhor Feróa is the magnate of Sena, and the best specimen
of a man the Portuguese have there. His position towards
his slaves is said to be more that of a chief than a master.
Village after village is occupied exclusively by his people, from
whom he exacts little labour, in whose quarrels he adjudicates,
and whose wants he supplies when, as is sometimes the case
they are in need through bad harvests. It pleases him to act
the patriarch. He is without doubt a benevolent man, and
would be a richer man had he fewer slaves; and while he lives,
many of his slaves may in some sense, be better off than if
free. But varnish it as you may, there is nothing so exten-
sively and lastingly degrading as slavery, as instituted and
carried on by Christians. The Landeens, and other savage
tribes, carry away people into captivity. The Makololo, for instance, enslaved the Batoka and Bashubia; and the Matabele
have done, and are still doing, the same thing with regard to
other tribes: but the subjugation of these people is productive
of far less evil than the servitude imposed by the Christian's
system of slavery. They are degraded, it is true, are looked
upon and treated as inferiors, but sooner or later they become
incorporated with the tribe that conquers them, and partake
of equal privileges. But take the position of the slave, even
when the master is as good a man as Feróa, a man who aspires
to be the father of a family rather than the master of slaves,
and still few states can be more miserable than that of his
slaves; for, in reality, he is not what he aims to be; he is a
master, and they are slaves; and like all other slaves, liable at
any moment to be visited with the full consequences of their
position. At the present moment they may be more than
content, for they have doubtless been brought so low as to be

unconscious of the degradation of slavery; but the time may come when they will be roughly awakened to a sense of their true position. Feróa may die at any moment, and, like dogs, they may be sold by his heir; and if not sold as dogs, treated much worse, for man's flesh is cheaper than dog's flesh, and as I have shown, it costs a brutal master next to nothing if he chooses to exercise his brutality. The men lent to Dr. Livingstone, were, I dare say, a fair specimen of Feróa's household slaves, and the appearance of the elder among them, those that had been longest in servitude, was most suggestive of everything degrading to man. Few things are so painful to behold as the debasement of your own kind, from whatever cause arising; but when one knows, as in the case of the slave, that this debasement is systematically forced upon the debased, that it is the certain result of a system which the few strong exercise against the weak many, a system which not only robs man of his freedom, but of his manhood, and reduces him to the condition of the brutes, one feels more than pain, shame, rage, and a host of sensations antagonistic to equanimity. I felt all this when these men came on board. The elder looked as if their lives had been encircled with evil, that evil of the worst conceivable form had been so constantly kept before them, that its very essence had moulded itself into their natures, they seemed to me the incarnation of vice. The younger presented a far more hopeful appearance, and under our influence they developed in a very amiable way; the expression of the slave in a great measure left their countenance, they bore themselves almost as free men. They were quickwitted, and readily attached themselves to you, and were anxious, when once you had their confidence, to be of service to you. But with the others, the deadening influence of slavery had dulled their faculties, stultified their instinctive sense of right, and made havoc with their affections. They were like most are who have been long inured to bondage, something less than men, slaves indeed, with the very instinct of servitude ineradicably fixed in their natures; and their degradation of soul was stamped on every feature, and was apparent in every movement.

Feróa may be all that he is said to be; but the system
which had brutalized these men, his property, who were becoming old in his service, and in his service alone, is devilish
and nothing else.   The presence of these men was a perpetual
cause of pain to me.

We left Shamo on May 20.   There was nothing to obstruct
our progress on that day, for though the river was narrow,
and ever winding about, it was deep as an artificial canal.   We
had but to keep in the middle of the stream, and all went
well.   We anchored for the night at the foot of Morumbala.

The hills about Morumbala appear as if they had been thrust
from it in the convulsion that projected it above the surface of
the earth; while others, a little way off, looked as though
they had been squeezed through the earth's crust in a semi-
liquid state.

As the sun set the clearness of the atmosphere brought out
the outlines of Morumbala with great distinctness, while the
shades of colour on it, about it, and above it, were delicate
and varied: the rising glory of the moon cast a broad belt of
silver light along the rippling river, and brought clearly into
view the more prominent features of the mountain.   It was
some time before we felt inclined to turn into bed that night.
We sat and talked of the work we had before us, and sang
hymns of praise to the Giver of all good.

When morning came a cloud was on the mountain top, and
during most periods of the year the condensation of vapour
about the summit of this hill is great; this adds to its beauty,
but it detracts from its suitableness as a residence.   Being an
isolated mountain, and the first high land from the coast,
storms congregate in the neighbourhood of Morumbala, and
though on the night before peace seemed to reign perpetually,
yet in that land nowhere are storms so frequent.

We steamed more than thirteen hours that day, and accomplished more than sixty miles; we were too low down to see
the swamps, and the vegetation along the banks of the river
was in many places very pleasing.

The valley widened when we had passed Morumbala, and
the country beyond was mountainous.   Mount Clarendon

loomed up high in the air, while others less lofty arrested the attention by their peculiar and oftentimes grotesque formation. Towards evening we caught a glimpse of the Milanji range; it was but a glimpse, yet it enabled us to form some idea of the mountain features of the country to which we were going. A bank of cloud was resting on their summit, yet as viewed from where we were they looked awful in their grandeur.

Here and there we passed a few huts, and now and then a column of smoke farther inland told of additional habitations, but the population was scant. The people living near the river ran out to see us as we passed by, and we could see others standing on the ant-hills, which are very numerous, and often fifteen to twenty feet high. We also passed several fishing stations, things of rudest contrivance, where a few men and boys were drying fish in the sun. Towards the close of our day's journey the population seemed increasing, and we halted just opposite to a considerable village called Kulubvi, which seemed to be from all accounts the only place along the river where corn and rice could be bought in any quantity, and we trusted to it to supply our deficiencies.

When Dr. Livingstone first came up this river the people were everywhere suspicious of him, and lined the banks in warlike attitude. This was very natural, for I doubt if they ever before had reason to regard with favour any with a skin lighter than their own; but now the spirit of the people was changed, we no sooner halted than men, women, and children flocked to the river side to welcome us, and several canoes filled with noisy loud-mouthed fellows came off to the ship. It was past sunset, and we did not wish to have anything to say to them then, but it was difficult to get rid of them. Long before daylight next morning we were awakened by the boisterous laugh and the loud clamour of the people on shore, and when the fog cleared away we saw that they had brought out rice and other things for sale.

I was curious to see these people, for they belonged to the tribe we purposed to live with, and so I went on shore with the Bishop to purchase what things we needed. For two fathoms of cloth (unbleached calico) we bought a bag of

cleaned rice weighing about thirty-five pounds; the un-
cleaned rice was half this price. A small kind of bean was
still cheaper, and fowls went at the rate of ten for a fathom.

It was merry work, this bartering with the natives, for notwithstanding there was a fixed price for a certain quantity, the
quantity brought was often uncertain, less than that commanding the stated payment; so you had to regulate your pay-
ments accordingly. This led to a great deal of talk, mirth,
and assumed indignation; they would stipulate with great
vehemence for two or three inches more than you felt inclined
to give, and the lookers-on roared with laughter, or shouted
encouragement to their friends, as these transactions were in
progress. They did not seem downcast when your firmness
overcame their friends' request, but shouted as though they
had succeeded. When the women were associated with the
men in the bargaining, their shrill sharp voices were heard
above the deeper utterances of the men, and if the affair did
not take the exact form they wished, if they found they stood
but little chance of getting what they wanted, they elevated
their arms as well as their voices, and strutted about in
apparent ire, giving vent to their feelings in language that
must have been the reverse of complimentary. Fortunately I
was in blissful ignorance of its meaning, for beyond the names
of the things we needed I knew nothing of what they said.
The end of all this was utmost good humour, and indeed while
they scolded and expostulated, they seemed barely able to
keep under their cachinnating inclinations; and at last the
women accepted with evident pleasure the very things they
had but a few moments before refused with so great a show
of scorn and indignation.

I was much struck with the regard which the men appeared
to have for their women. They did not by any means seem
to be in the degraded position they are said to be in among
some of the African tribes. Their position was unrestrained,
and they seemed to be regarded by the men as in no way
inferior to themselves. Instead of the women bringing down
the heavy burdens and the men stalking along with a stick,
you saw the men carrying the rice they had for sale, and the

women walked unburdened behind. This hopeful state of things was no doubt owing in a great measure to the fact of these people being quite agricultural. Where the tribes are pastoral the men are fond of war, and when not fighting are hunting, or are out with their herds, and so the drudgery of field labour falls to the woman, and she comes in course of time to be regarded as the drudge of the man, a creature never admitted into his confidence, existing only for his convenience and gratification. But here the men seemed evidently a domesticated race; some were nursing their children, and fondling them with much apparent affection. It was amusing at times to see the deference they paid the woman, going to her and asking her opinion before they concluded a bargain. There seemed but little of the savage in these people. The low, sensual, cruel disposition was not as a rule indicated in their physiognomies and cranial formation. Heathen and barbarous they were, but savage I could not think them; I doubted if it would be right to regard them as " the vilest and most degraded of men, whose sins have blackened and defiled the earth," for I felt in a purer atmosphere when among them, than when standing by the side of Senhor —— on the Zambesi. That some among them would answer to the worst description given of them as a whole, I saw clearly; for now and then a face came across your view, so repulsive in its for- mation and expression, that you felt that the man who owned it belonged to a class not confined to any one part of the world, but common to all communities; a class which, if your life stood between them and the attainment of their desires, would, if they could, unhesitatingly sacrifice it. But as a set off there were others that not even the long ages of hereditary ignorance and heathenism had been able to degrade, men who you felt sure would under more favourable circumstances have had few superiors in character and intelligence. The majority were those whose faces expressed nothing beyond what you might suppose to be the common-place qualities of the com- munity in which they lived. Indeed, take them altogether, they were naturally very much like men anywhere else.

The women wore the hideous lip-ring of which I have spoken

when in the Rovuma, and most had shaved off their hair. The men were not disfigured, save by a triangular notch in their front teeth, and they wore their hair dressed in fashions often becoming. It seemed *their* glory, but the woman's shame. Fancy the loveliest of God's creatures in this part of the world with her upper lip thrust two inches beyond her nose, and a bald head! I am no artist, but I have an artist's admiration for grace of form and beauty of feature, and treasure the remembrance of a beautiful face, whether of man or woman, as I do that of a beautiful passage in music or poetry. In England it is, perhaps, difficult to find a female face, unless expressive of wickedness, which it is not pleasant to look upon; but in Africa, wherever I took my walks abroad, I met with a feminine ugliness almost overpowering, and for which the possessor was alone responsible, for many of the women would have been really good looking had they not disfigured themselves so vilely.

The people in the Shire Valley were nominally under the rule of two great chiefs, Tingani and Mankokwe. These chiefs were called Rundos. Mankokwe's government extended to the highlands up as far as Lake Shirwa, and Tingani was, I believe, paramount lord over that portion of the highlands below the Ruo.

Up to May 25 we met with no obstructions to our voyage up the river. On the night of the 25th we halted near to Tingani's village; the chief himself we did not see, but his brother, an insignificant looking fellow, and apparently of no reputation in the eyes of his countrymen, came down to the ship. With the Portuguese Tingani bore the reputation of a fire-eater; he had attacked and plundered some of their trading parties, and he, in all probability, was the organizer of the opposition that met Dr. Livingstone when he first ascended the Shire.

It was at this village that we first met with indications of the growth of cotton. Some—a small quantity, not more than a pound—was, on being asked for, brought to the ship for sale, and a yard of calico was given for it. Dr. Kirk also purchased a large piece of native cloth for an equal length of un-

bleached calico. It seemed surprising that having the power
to provide themselves with raiment so suited to their need as
this cloth of their own make, they should desire our own
manufacture so greatly. Their own is coarser than ours; it is
something like jack-toweling, but it is much more durable than
our calico, and does not so soon look shabby. But with them,
as with ourselves, fashion is everything.

This village was famous as the resort of guinea-fowl, and
those skilled in the gun or who had sporting proclivities went
off to see what they could secure for the table; we heard them
banging away, and in a few minutes they returned, having met
with a covey close to the village, of which they gave a good
account. But they complained dismally of the mosquitoes
which beset them on shore, and with reason; for ever since we
had entered the Shire these provoking insects had been an increasing quantity, giving us their company both day and night,
but about here they appeared to culminate.

It is great fun, however, when safely curtained for the night
to hear the angry utterances of the swarms of these little pests
around you, as time after time they make ineffectual attempts
to get at you. These creatures are without doubt a trial to a
man's temper if he be easily excited, but I cannot understand
people 'foaming with vexation and rage' through the night,
when a few yards of muslin properly made up and a little tact
would save them from such an unseemly manifestation.

Immediately above Tingani's, the valley of the Shire becomes
more and more marshy, and the difficulties of the river navigation commence. The marsh draws off much water; a multitude of islets intercept and turn aside the stream; the passage
in many places becomes so narrow, the windings so frequent
and acute, sandbanks so numerous, and the current in most
places so rapid and perverse, that progress in a vessel like the
'Pioneer' was all but impossible, and not attainable without
much patience, labour, and loss of time. Our experience in
the Rovuma was severe, but it was nothing compared with that
which followed us from the entrance of the Elephant marsh
almost up to the village of Chibisa. As day by day went on,
it seemed more and more unlikely that we should be able to

force the 'Pioneer' up to our proposed destination. It would
be wearisome to give at length our day by day experiences, but
it is needful to say something about them, in order to give a
fair idea of the difficulties that had to be encountered, and the
time we consumed.

On the 25th we did not come to any lengthened stoppage,
but our progress was continually checked, and the distance
done during the day was trifling.

The 26th was Sunday, we halted therefore. The Elephant
marsh is not a desirable place to halt in. The sickly odour of
the mangrove is not present, but the exhalations of the marsh
are more offensive, and, as predisposing causes, equally ac-
celerate and aggravate fever.

On the 27th we got up steam early, but had to halt almost
immediately, and were some hours before we could go ahead
again, and as soon as we were over the obstruction, a snag
smashed one of the port paddle-floats. Then the channel became so narrow that we were obliged to track the ship along
the bank, and keep her off with poles whenever the curves of
the river sent her nose into the muddy bank. But perseverance
and cheerfulness overcame, and we succeeded in getting the
ship out of this channel into broader and more promising
water; but a run of a few hundred yards brought us to a bend
of the river round which the water came with the force of a
mill-stream, and catching the bow of the ship made her helm
useless. Again and again we backed, and tried to round this
corner; but it was all in vain, failure succeeded failure, and we
had to anchor for the night.

It took us a long time to get away from this place on the
28th, but at last it was accomplished by the aid of hawsers fore
and aft, though we had not proceeded more than a mile before
we were fast on a sandbank, from which the ship was not removed until the morning of the 30th.

There was no avoiding these delays; every care was taken to
prevent the repetition of such accidents, but without avail.
We were now in a place where firewood was not to be obtained;
a few miles onward it was in abundance; nothing hindering,
the coal would last till then, but a broad belt of sand stretched

itself across our path before we had gone a mile, and it was not until the afternoon of the next day that we forced the passage. At this place the ship was driven so violently against the bank that the starboard paddle-wheel was damaged. The iron boss was smashed, and several of the girders bent about in a strange fashion.

After resting a day or two in order to cut fuel, we started again on June 3, with mingled hope and apprehension. The apprehension alone was realized, for after dropping down the river a few hundred yards in search of a better channel, and endeavouring to get back, we found ourselves aground before we had reached the place we had just left. Expedient after expedient was tried day by day, but it was six days before success rewarded our efforts. We then steamed a little distance, and dropped anchor until Monday, the morrow being Sunday.

The next entry in my journal runs thus :—

' *June* 17.—Afloat once more! But if the experience of the last fifteen days may be looked upon as a criterion for the future, it will not be many hours before we shall be aground again. It is above three weeks since we entered the Elephant marsh, and we have been twenty-four days in getting over half as many miles!'

On the 10th we made a fresh attempt, but in less than half an hour were again arrested. On the 12th we were once more in deep water, and on the 13th had a run of three or four miles, but on the 14th we were again in grief. The ship was aground midships, and we could not move her an inch forward; she revolved as on a pivot. Saturday night came, and no apparent progress had been made. The next day, Sunday, was very unlike our previous Sundays on board the ' Pioneer.' The ship's position was too critical to permit us to defer our labour, and so all the fore part of the day was spent in efforts, fruitless efforts, to get her where she ought to be. When we left off work, at three P.M., she seemed worse placed than ever. Hour by hour she had been setting more and more on to the bank and having her broadside to the stream she dragged her three anchors after her. We had Evening Prayer and the Litany at

five o'clock; but the usual harmony of the day had been spoiled
by the necessary noise and confusion attendant on the efforts
made to get the ship afloat.   There are times, such as these,
when you must work hard, though it be Sunday.   You love the
first day of the week more abroad than at home; it is to most
men the one link binding them to home observances; the day
when home associations have most power; for the associations
connected with the Lord's day at home have, I feel, a truly
salutary influence on the hearts of most in a foreign land.   I
have seen men of roughest nature subdued by the recollections
of this day.   The Bible that the father gave is looked upon with
filial reverence; the gentle voice of the mother, unheard amid
the clamour of the six days' wear and tear of life, is heard once
again, inculcating in loving language those sacred truths which,
believed and acted upon, would take the soul to paradise; the
church where the sacrifice of prayer and praise was offered rises
up in the imagination before the traveller in a strange land;
and sacred melodies, at other times forgotten, come so forcibly
to the mind, that he cannot do otherwise than give them
utterance.   I am no Sabbatarian, but I have seen so much of
the good effect of the English veneration of the Sunday on the
hearts and minds of men abroad, that I should lament any
change which would tend to lessen the reverence with which,
despite the ungodliness of many, it is now regarded.

We were all somewhat downcast by the difficulties of the
river.   The hope of getting to Chibisas appeared to be dying
out of us, and the long sojourn in the pestiferous neighbourhood of the marshes was acting unfavourably on the health of
all.   Among the clergy of our party Procter was affected most,
he did not have fever severely, but he was almost continually
depressed by its influence.   Among the laity Waller suffered
least; in fact he nearly escaped it altogether.   Adams was
cruelly punished; and Gamble presented symptoms that seriously alarmed us; for he seemed in so bad a way that we
doubted if he would ever be strong again.   Indeed, the physical
condition of our whole party was bad.

Dr. Livingstone did not anticipate so much trouble in getting
up the Shire; he had overrated its capacities, in thinking that

a fathom-channel would easily be found all the way up to the Murchison cataracts.

His patient perseverance, dogged energy, and never-faltering purpose, were strongly manifested in our repeated difficulties on the Shire. On the night of the 16th, he sat beside me on the bulwarks, and explained all that had been tried, and how each effort had failed. To me it seemed quite likely that the ship would remain where she was, for she was at the sport of the current, and her position seemed worse every hour : but he spoke of renewed efforts on the morrow, and did not seem to dream of a difficulty which he could not get over. He was spared those efforts, for about nine o'clock the action of the stream did more for her than we had been able to do; she swung round into the very position wanted, and two hours' work next morning quite released her.

By this time both our capstans were smashed by constant hard usage, and the carpenter had to fit up some clumsy substitutes.

The weather at this time was pleasant, though the temperature for some days had been steadily increasing. The difference, however, between the temperature by day and by night was considerable. At eight o'clock A.M. the atmosphere was generally from 25° to 30° colder than at an hour after midday. Once I noticed the mercury at 54° at eight, when at two it stood at 86°. One morning it was as low as 49°, but on that day it did not rise higher than 77°. A sojourner in Africa would complain of cold when the same marking in the thermometer at home would declare an oppressive heat. A temperature varying from 85° to 90° was not unpleasant. The heavy morning dews were the worst features of our experience. I do not think they are exactly unhealthy, but they necessitate great care. We were by this time fairly out of the rainy season, though now and then we caught a shower, but generally day succeeded day with undiminished brightness. The sun is a glory in these lands. I once heard of a Persian, who, on an Englishman expressing surprise that his countrymen worshipped the sun, replied, 'Not at all surprising! you English would worship it too, if you ever saw it.' There was some truth in this sarcasm on the density of our atmosphere; for see the sun in undiminished brightness, the English at home rarely do.

For several days we had before us an immense grove of palm trees, they stood right between us and the west; some of these trees were of great height, and their graceful stems and beautiful foliage stood out in bold relief against the glowing sky of evening. The effect of the sunset was always very soothing, for though day by day we had to labour hard, and suffer much anxiety on account of the ship, and endure much physical inconvenience from fever and lassitude, yet it was with feelings of thankfulness and peace that we watched for the evening star, shining like an atom of burnished silver through the fiery atmosphere in which it made its appearance.

The few people living about this marsh were very different from those we saw lower down the river. It may have been owing to the deleterious effects of the marsh atmosphere, but more sinister, more wretched-looking creatures were surely never seen. They were churlish and greedy, for though they showed considerable anxiety for cloth, they brought down to the ship but a scanty supply of corn, and did not seem to like parting with what they did bring, and yet corn abounded in their villages. For a week or more we were without fresh meat. We had been able to buy but one goat since we entered the river, and so while halting we made an effort to get another goat. I went with Dr. Livingstone to a village about two miles from the river; cocks were crowing, hens were cackling, goats were skipping about, and around the village were heaviest crops of grain. Food was evidently in abundance. The Doctor offered to purchase a goat. Said the man spoken to—'I must go and consult my friend, he is but a little way off;' and picking up his bow and arrows off he ran. He was some time gone, and when he came back with his friend great was the talk that ensued. The friend negotiated: and first he thought he would not sell; then he eyed the cloth and beads, and thought he would sell; then he sent a boy to drive all the goats before us. The Doctor made a choice; his choice was objected to: he chose again, and that after a little demur was assented to. Then the length of the cloth, and the quantity of beads underwent a severe discussion; but at last all seemed settled; the goat was brought forward, the price was paid, and a little boy of the village began to thread the beads. But the man who sold the goat looked miserable after the transaction was ended. He looked at his cloth, he looked at the beads, he looked at the goat, and at last he exclaimed: 'No, I will not sell. I shall wear out the cloth, but if I keep the goat she will cost me nothing, and will bring forth more.' He seemed, however, reluctant to give back the cloth, and we had to look sharply to see that none of the beads stuck to his fingers. We bought three fowls on the way back to the ship. Dr. Kirk reported that, while out shooting, he had come to another village where was a goat, an old goat, an only goat, which was reported to be the father of all the goats around: this might have been bought, but the creature emitted such an insufferable odour that it would have been impossible to eat him.

The women we saw here seemed more degenerate than the men. I cannot say they were exactly

> Naked, foul, unshorn, unkempt—
> From touch of natural shame exempt;

yet naked they nearly were, wearing no more cloth than the men, and not caring to cover so much of their persons; foul they certainly were, they looked as though water had not touched their bodies for years; unkempt they were not, because they were shorn, and the repulsive fashion and position of their tattoo inclined one to think them from 'touch of natural shame exempt.' It must be a deep depravity which leads women to disfigure themselves so horribly. Here, too, the women seemed the labourers; for while we saw them at hardest work, the men would be sitting round the fire in the centre of the circle of huts, watching the pot boil, smoking, or spinning cotton. These were the most degraded natives I ever met with.

On the 18th we lay at anchor all day, and I and several others were down with fever. On the 19th we got several miles up the river, and seemed fairly beyond the Elephant marsh. The valley was narrowing, and the hills had a cheerful appearance: they were covered with a healthy-looking

vegetation, and varied in height from one to three thousand
feet. At night I could not help congratulating Dr. Livingstone on the progress of the day; it was quite delightful to
think that from sunrise to sunset we had actually steamed six
or seven miles. But this delight was short-lived; we had not
gone half a mile next morning before we came to a regular
barrier of sand, and three and a half feet of water was the
greatest depth we could find. This obstruction was several
ship's lengths in breadth, the current was not strong, and the
bottom therefore was harder than usual. Selecting the best
spot we could find, where the water was in a line with the deep
channel beyond and the current strongest, anchors were taken
out ahead, and the ship was drawn up to them by the use of
the capstan. It was very slow and very hard work. One day
we did not move a foot. Then we emptied the boilers, and
succeeded in getting over a hundred feet. Then we found it
necessary to unlade the ship of everything weighty, and so
after eight days' constant labour the ship slipped into deep
water once more.

These delays were very wearisome; save as an exercise of
patience, there was not a redeeming feature in them. They
were tiresome in themselves; they are tiresome to think about,
and tiresome to write about.

Of course there were compensations even to this wearying
life. No one need be dull in such a river as the Shire, where
animal life is so abundant. The hippopotamus was a constant
source of amusement to us. Once indeed he provoked an
amusement that was very out of place. It was Sunday; all
hands were mustered for Divine service. I had heard one of
these brutes feeding quite close to us during the night, and
early in the morning he dodged about the ship as though he
knew hippopotamuses were safe on that day. When service
commenced, finding no one moving about, he grew bolder,
came quite close to the ship, and gave us the full benefit of
his huge lungs. His utterances were distracting, for a tremendous ha! ha! at the end of a solemn supplication was certainly no aid to devotion, and a running accompaniment of
the same jovial ejaculations was quite sufficient to impair the

effect of the Bishop's sermon. The sailors were ready to explode with suppressed laughter, and so was I.

When the sermon was concluded, all ran to look at this brute; he caught sight of our eager faces and suspected mischief, dived down, and reappeared some distance below. Then he gave another look as though measuring the distance between him and the ship, was not quite satisfied, dived down again, and rose still farther below, looked at us once more, thought himself safe, and shouted defiance all the day long.

The flesh of the hippopotamus, when young, is in tenderness and taste something like veal, but when old it is unmistakably tough, and unlike any animal I have tasted. One day a dead hippopotamus—it had been killed by a trap—floated by the ship. The Makololo threw themselves into a boat, and started in pursuit. They cut and hacked away at the huge carcass, and plunged about it so excitedly that an old sailor said it was difficult to say which was hippopotamus and which was

CUTTING UP THE HIPPOPOTAMUS.

Makololo. They brought to the ship the bowels—the choice part to the native taste—and the hind-quarters. One quarter, a delicate joint which had to be hoisted on to the deck with ropes, was Dr. Livingstone's portion. Then they went on shore, lighted fires, cleaned the intestines, cut the rest into long thin strips, and hung them upon the smoke over the fires, and squatted round it till morning.

I looked well at the joint on deck. It resembled beef in appearance, and I expected considerable satisfaction from the *experimentum gustûs* next morning. But anticipations of a pleasant meal of fresh meat were a little chilled when I heard Dr. Livingstone tell the steward to stew the steaks for breakfast for at least four hours. Had they been stewed for forty, they would still have been tough. We did what we could, but to save our teeth we endangered our digestion. We were glad to see the last of this meat; for, before the Makololo had got rid of theirs, there was an odour about the ship that was barely tolerable.

Like our own country, Africa has its musicians and mountebanks. We were visited by both during our long halt, but I cannot say much for the performances. One man showed considerable wit; his instrument was a one stringed fiddle, and in his songs he showed considerable humour—to judge from the laughter they provoked. His voice was horribly discordant, and he introduced into his vocalisation a series of grunts, sneezings and coughings which seemed to tickle the fancy of his friends amazingly, and he wound up with a song in praise of 'the Beardies, the Beardies, the great white Beardies,' meaning the English. Another fellow, whose head was elaborately decorated with white feathers, danced for our entertainment; and a wretched exhibition he made of himself, accompanying the movements of his feet with a horrid horn-blowing, and leaving off now and then to oscillate the lower parts of his body in a very repulsive fashion. He met with no encouragement on the ship: so he and his friends re-entered the canoe, and, going on to a sand island in the middle of the stream, danced and sounded his abominable horn for hours.

Then a band of drummers came on board, and their leader

was a man whose right arm had been bitten off by a crocodile;
the beast had made a clean bite of it. These drummers stunned
us for a while, but upon the whole their performance was
satisfactory. Their drums were of various sizes, the smallest
about eight inches in diameter, the largest eighteen. They
kept capital time, and the variation of tone produced by variety
of size was pleasing. Had they confined themselves to drumming, all would have been well; but they took to singing, and
then the effect was truly horrifying. They illustrated their
songs by certain histrionic displays, elevating their hands,
clenching their fists, putting their arms round each other's
necks, screeching down each other's throats, and finished off
with a hideous sound, made by forcing the breath through the
closed lips. Altogether, these musical displays of the Manganja did not give us a high opinion of their musical capacity.

In a village not far from the place where we were aground
so long, we found several groups of men crouching round their
respective fires, smoking and being smoked, and apparently
enjoying the latter operation as much as the former, for they
thrust their heads into the pungent fume from the wood fires,
and twisted themselves about as though experiencing the height
of physical gratification.

One group consisted of travellers. They were Ajawa, and
Dr. Livingstone told us that the Ajawa were the slaving tribe,
in league with the Portuguese, who provided them with guns
in order that they might attack and destroy villages, capture
the women and children, and what men they could lay their
hands upon. They were not a pleasant looking set of men certainly. I shall have to say much of this tribe; so I will only
here say that in this, as in all other matters relating to the
country and the relative positions of the tribes to each other,
we implicitly accepted Dr. Livingstone's statements.

About this time we had much conversation with regard to
the course we should adopt, as Christian missionaries, in case
we were ever attacked by the natives. Two questions arose:

1st. Should we take guns with us on the journey to the
highlands?

2nd. If we took them, for what purpose should we take them ?

The Bishop was against taking guns for any purpose whatever, but Dr. Livingstone and others belonging to the expedition had very different ideas upon this matter. Dr. Livingstone said, 'By all means take them, and, if necessary, use them; but if you take them there will be no need to use them, for they are the greatest pacificators in the world if you have peaceful intentions yourself. The Ajawa and all other tribes, knowing you to be well armed, would assist you, for the natives will never dream of attacking you unless you are defenceless.'

I felt, and others of the mission felt, that this was good advice; and though I yielded to no one in desire for peace or in horror of blood-shedding, yet I could very well imagine circumstances when a policy of non-resistance would be simply impossible. I might be able to resist taking life, if my own life alone were in danger; but should the life of any one of my brethren be at stake, and I knew that I had the power to save his life, but could only do so by taking that of his assailant, the impulse to kill, if killing were absolutely necessary, in order to save, would, I felt, be irresistible. This was also felt by the rest of our staff, and ultimately it was agreed that when we went up to the highlands we should take our guns with us. We were greatly concerned about this matter.

We were appalled occasionally at the greatness and difficulty of the work before us, and the strength of the enemy we were going to encounter; but these anxious moments were but brief passages in our life : on the whole we were more inclined to rejoice than complain, to be cheerful than to be sad. Indeed it could not be otherwise, where Bishop Mackenzie was, for he was not only the most hopeful, but the most hope-inspiring man I have known. 'The silver lining' was always visible to his eyes.

We were now close to the village of Mankokwe, the Rundo, or great chief of the Manganja; and Dr. Livingstone, Dr. Kirk, the Bishop, and others, took boat and went to visit this potentate. They arrived at the village at a very sorrowful moment; a sad calamity had just befallen Mankokwe's people. Some women and a child, when crossing in a canoe from the gardens on the opposite bank of the river, had been carried by the force of the stream beyond the point where they wished to land, and were finally upset, and three of the women and the child were drowned. This accident was looked upon as a public calamity, and the wail of woe was general. Mankokwe, however, was inclined to be gracious. Up to this time, his exalted position in the country had not been known; for he had avoided the English during their previous visits, and was not supposed to be the great man he was.

Of course a conference with such a man is a very ceremonious affair. It is not etiquette to address yourself to his mightiness personally; he has a speaker, and you must have a speaker. What you have to say you must deliver to your spokesman, who tells what you have said to the other spokesman, who thereupon makes known to his lord what he knows already, seeing he must have heard it twice before. Charlie, one of the Makololo, acted as Dr. Livingstone's spokesman, and an old man named Chimbeli officiated for the Rundo. The Doctor began by introducing the Bishop, and saying something of his objects in coming into the country; but Charlie added a little of his own to this, for he described the missionaries as the sons of God, and said that our Father had sent us to the Manganja to teach them His word. Mankokwe expressed himself glad to see the Doctor and the Bishop, but upon our purpose in coming to his country he said nothing. On mentioning the chiefs it was intended to visit, he replied,—'You are going to Chinsunzi? he is a child of the Rundo.'

'We are going to Chibisa,' said Dr. Livingstone.

'He also is the Rundo's child.'

'And we also want to see the Rundo.'

'You see him before you—I am he,' was the calm reply. The result of the interview was so favourable that Dr. Livingstone wished to leave the ship where she was while the land journey was undertaken, and Mankokwe did not then seem to object.

Next morning Chimbeli, accompanied by three fine young men, came down to the ship in a canoe, bringing a goat as a present from the Rundo, a return for the presents Dr. Livingstone and the Bishop had made the day before. They all came on board. The young men were fearless and frank in their deportment; but poor old Chimbeli seemed smitten with fear: it was quite distressing to witness his agitation. When the ship was first put into motion he shook with apprehension, but by judicious handling his courage revived, and he was shown the wonders of the ship. The old man was filled with amazement; he lifted up his hands, and exclaimed, 'I have no more breath. My heart is taken away. It is wonderful!'

Just before we arrived off Mankokwe's village, and while close into the bank, we disturbed a monstrous crocodile from its slumbers. We were close upon it, and its huge abdomen was so horribly full, it seemed to have great difficulty in getting out of our way. Most likely the beast had been feasting on one of the poor women drowned the day before.

Mankokwe's village was situated in a spot where the luxuriance of vegetation was such as could only be in tropical climes. Bananas laden with fruit, or throwing out their huge egg-shaped rich purple blossom, were there; the wild vine threw its graceful tendrils from tree to tree, while huge clusters of grapes, unfortunately not edible, bright and yellow, every where met the eye; and strange varieties of the fig tree, higher than all other trees here spread their wide branches over all. Indeed vegetation of all kinds was more prolific at this place than any other part of the Shire.

Nothing of the village could be seen from the river, the huts were hidden by the thick foliage of the banana. Here and there an arcade was made through the trees, down which the people came to the river; and notwithstanding the general mourning which was still going on, a number of the inhabitants came down to the bank to meet us.

We took with us a pair of turkeys, and a ewe merino sheep (the ram died in coming up the river), intending to leave them in Mankokwe's charge, the creatures having suffered much by their long confinement on board ship. Chimbeli preceded, wearing a highly coloured scarf—the gift of Dr. Livingstone—over his shoulder; and the air of importance he assumed as we entered the village was most amusing. The village was larger than any we had before seen. The number of dogs, a mongrel terrier breed, was a nuisance. It was necessary now and then to clear your way with a well-directed kick. The crowing and cackling of the poultry, the vociferations of the goats, and the bleating of sheep—a black short-haired large-tailed variety—made it apparent that where the Rundo lived plenty abounded. Our white sheep was a great curiosity. A sheep with so small a tail, and whose covering was white wool, had not been before heard of by the crowd of well-fed, good-looking natives preceding and following us.

We soon came upon signs of the calamity of the day before. We passed the charred remains of a freshly burnt hut, and seated on the ground were several women, on whose heads was the emblem of woe, who, rocking themselves backwards and forwards, gave vent to their grief in a dismal wail. Their sorrow seemed sincere. They were weeping over the desolated hearth of one of those who had been drowned the day before. Their countenances expressed suffering; tears were falling from their eyes. Strange as must have been the appearance of so many white men, the mourners noticed us not, being absorbed by their own grief. The village rang with their wail of woe. The sorrow of these people was not that

> . . . . unimpassioned grief,
> Which finds no natural outlet, no relief
> In word, or sigh, or tear;

but it was a grief that found expression in one of the most mournful utterances that ever conveyed tidings of sorrow from man to man.

We halted under a large fig tree growing in an open space in the centre of the village, from which locality we were quickly summoned to the presence of the Rundo. Mankokwe was a tall man, with a well-formed head, but with a countenance expressive of no power. Unlike most of his countrymen, he had both beard and moustache; and had it not been for the want of power manifested in his whole bearing, his appearance would have been prepossessing. As it was, though there was an air of superiority about him, yet he looked likely to be the tool of any, through a certain nervelessness, the result no doubt of excess of a certain kind, that was painfully apparent in all he did. He was seated on the projecting roots of a fig tree close to his family residence. He wore cloth of blue; had brass bracelets, brass anklets, and held a brass snuff-box in his hand.

Dr. Livingstone sat down beside him. Dr. Kirk sat down by his chief. Two mats were spread for the Bishop and the rest of us, leaving a space between for Chembeli, who, with profound reverence to the Rundo, sat just in front of us. A little to the right of the Rundo and slightly behind, sat ten shaggy-browed suspicious-looking old fellows. These were the ministers of state, the counsellors of the chief; but they seemed ill at ease, and by no means fit to counsel. The people who followed us, men and boys, arranged themselves in a semi-circle a little way from us, and looked on with eager curiosity.

Before the conference commenced an intelligent-looking woman, with a large tumour, very much like a baby's head, at the nape of her neck, and who was Mankokwe's sister, came up, and falling on her knees and bowing her head, asked in a humble voice permission to be present. The great man inclined his head, and she sat down. The permission granted to her was made use of by other women, all of whom wore the abominable lip-ring, and were elaborately tattooed. One, a young woman, despite the monstrosity in her upper lip, was really handsome. Few European women could boast of such eyes and eyelashes as she had. She was of a lighter colour than the rest, and her head was unshorn.

Dr. Livingstone commenced proceedings by saying he wished to leave the sheep and the turkeys in the village. The animals were brought forward. Mankokwe was interested: he asked no questions, but examined with attention a small piece of the wool which had been plucked from the sheep's side. Then the sister had a pluck, and twisted the wool into thread, and all the other women plucked, and there seemed danger of the poor animal being shorn in a way she had not been used to.

So the sheep and turkeys, consent being given, were let loose, and allowed to wander about at will. But the dogs, true to their nature, began to bark and bite. Of the sheep they seemed afraid, but of the turkeys they had no fear; and a cry from Mankokwe's sister made us understand that the whole pack was in pursuit of the male gobbler. Ramakukan, one of the Makololo, who had been leaning against the tree by which Mankokwe was sitting, chewing sugar-cane, which was found to grow here, and regarding the natives around with an air of supreme contempt—a habit with the Makololo—darted off in pursuit, pushing everybody aside without ceremony, kicking right and left at small boys and dogs, until he rescued the bird. That done, he returned, leaned against the tree once more, and, to the astonishment of the counsellors of state, amongst whom he frequently voided the refuse, recommenced mastication.

Then we were all introduced to the Rundo, and he was told that I was to be left with him, for so it was then arranged, while the Bishop and the rest of the children went up to the hills. To this the great man said nothing disagreeable: he honoured me with a look and a smile, and gaped immediately afterwards. But when Dr. Livingstone again spoke of his ship, it appeared that the wise heads of the state had been talking the matter over, and had come to the conclusion that the ship had better move on. We were in the mazes of African diplomacy. There was plenty of water between us and Chibisas, it was said; we might wait where we liked, truly, but not there: we might have a guide to the hills with much pleasure, and he was quite willing to let any of his men go with us as porters: only considering all things, he thought that it would be better for none of his people to go with us just now. He was not willing to refuse anything asked, but was as evidently unwilling to grant anything needed.

Here the sister again interposed, and apologising for not having anything to place before us in the way of food, excused herself on the ground of the general grief, then going on her knees again begged for permission to retire and mourn; and, consent being gained, she left, all the women following.

The mention of food sent Mankokwe away for a time.
While he was gone, Chimbeli, an inveterate snuff-taker, found
his supply of snuff exhausted, and looked about for a pinch.
Procter carried a snuff-box.   He extended it to our old friend ;
and the look of Chimbeli, when he had fairly mastered a pinch of
the rappee, was suggestive of deepest satisfaction.   One pinch
gone, he took another, and another, and another, and each
time his long-drawn gasps of satisfaction told how fully he
appreciated the foreign mixture ; and then the noses and the
fingers of all around became excited, and all the old fellows had
pinches ; and so great was their satisfaction, and so pleasingly
excited did they become, that when Mankokwe returned, they
were all in a state of hilarity.   He looked enquiringly, forth
came the snuff-box, and a pinch of the wonderful compound
made him almost as forgetful of his dignity as his counsellors
had been of theirs.

Food was brought to us—curried fowl, porridge (nsima),
and pombi ; and a genuine willow-pattern plate was produced,
for Mankokwe ate his food off Great Britain's crockery ! This
was an indication of his dealings with the Portuguese slavers,
and Chimbeli informed us that he had been to Sena.

Before we had finished our repast, information came that
the body of one of the drowned women had been recovered,
and that it was even then being brought into the village.
Upon this news, all, with the exception of the chief and his
counsellors, hurriedly left. We also made haste to depart,
Chimbeli conducting us to the river. The people were everywhere in the full excitement of grief. The women were crying, and wailing, and beating their breasts ; and their lamentations increased to an exceeding bitter cry when the corpse,
rolled up in a sleeping mat, was brought into the village. The
character of their grief was very saddening. It was not only
the expression of a sorrow without hope, but it seemed to
speak of a fear of some greater impending danger.   'An
enemy hath done this,' was the evident thought of all, and
each seemed to think he or she might be the next victim.

Next morning, without any premonitory symptoms, the
fever laid hold of me, and I was obliged to give up ; the

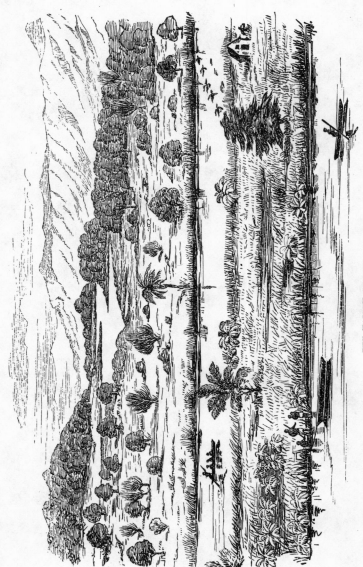

THE VALLEY OF THE SHIRE.

enemy was fairly into the citadel, and the only thing to do was to drive him out as quickly as possible. This was effected in about three days, but the conflict was rather severe, and left me much weakened.

Dr. Livingstone and the Bishop again visited the Rundo, taking with them a variety of presents, shawls, looking-glasses, knives, and beads. The Doctor once more expressed his fear that he should not be able to get the ship up to Chibisa's; Mankokwe had no doubt about it, but added—

'Stay where you like above me. You come as friends; you act as friends; you are not to be driven away like dogs. Stay where you think proper; only I should like you to get up above me as far as you can.'

He afterwards said that, though Rundo, he had very little power over the other chiefs, and if they saw the English with him, they might not like it, they might be angry with him for introducing strangers into the land.

This is the invariable feeling of the African, and he will avoid responsibility if he can. If he introduces you to a place, and evil comes upon that place through you, he, more than you, is regarded as culpable, and he is expected to take the consequences whatever they may be.

The presents excited great interest, and quite put an end to all further conversation on graver subjects, but in the end they produced an effect quite contrary to what it was intended they should; for two days after we had left Mankokwe's, he sent the sheep and the turkeys back to us without any satisfactory reason: we heard he was suspicious of the Bishop, and did not like the idea of his settling in the land, and next day he returned the more valuable of the presents he had received, with an intimation that his land was not to be bought. It was useless to trouble more about this man; so Dr. Livingstone sent him back a proper reply, and resolved to act without his concurrence.

After some more stoppages we arrived at Chibisa's village in the afternoon of July 8.

The village is built on the south bank of the river. This bank is of stratified sand quite sixty feet high, and covered with verdure. The valley here is beautiful, and, the swamp lands being miles below, as healthy as a valley in Africa can be. The view from the cliff surpassed anything I had seen in Africa. The noble river below winding like the ornamental water of a park, the group of islands in the middle of the stream, the valley covered with trees, and then mountain beyond mountain opening out wherever the eye could penetrate. But Dr. Livingstone promised us better things than that when he got us on to the highlands.

From the Chibisians we heard no good report of the highland country to which we were going. There was war there. The Ajawa had invaded the Manganja territory, had occupied villages around Mount Zomba, and were destroying and making captive. The hill Manganja were in a state of greatest excitement and terror, and were quite unable to withstand the invaders, many of whom it was said were armed with guns, while the Manganja had but bows and arrows. These guns had doubtless been supplied to the Ajawa by the Portuguese. It is very certain that the Portuguese traders at Tete were profiting by the strife, for their agents were daily carrying away droves of people who had been captured on either side, and sold to them for slaves. And there is reason to believe that they were not only, in the first instance, responsible for the war, but that they did their best to keep it going.

They were carrying on a peculiar slave trade at this particular time. They did not wish for slaves to send them across the sea, but they were carrying them into the interior, to another tribe, the Banyai, who had lost in war with the Matabele almost all their women and children. These Banyai are great elephant hunters ; the Tete merchants are great ivory traders : their agents went up to the Banyai to buy ivory with the ordinary barter goods, but were told 'We do not want these things; bring us women and children, and you shall have as much ivory as you want.' They then sent their agents to this very hill country to which we were going, a country of which they knew little or nothing until Dr. Livingstone made it known to them, and the cruel war we found raging was the result. I heard afterwards from one of themselves, that at this time they were carrying away at least two hundred people, mostly women and children, out of the hill country every week.

We found at Chibisa's village a party of travellers, men from Mount Zomba. They were Manganja, and on their way to Chibisa, who was living at Doa, on the Zambesi, between Sena and Tete, to beg him to return with them in order that he might bewitch the guns of the Ajawa, and so render them harmless. These poor men looked very woe-begone. They said the Ajawa had burnt their villages, stolen or destroyed their property, killed many of their kinsmen, and carried off their wives and children for slaves. And all their hopes now rested in Chibisa; if he would come all would be well; the Manganja would regain confidence if he would put himself at their head; for he alone possessed the true medicine to make guns harmless. Chibisa was evidently the great man of this part of Africa. Mankokwe might be the Rundo, but Chibisa was the hero; everywhere his reputation was great. Of the origin of this man little was certainly known. He was at first thought to be the descendant of a long line of hereditary chiefs, but there seems good reason to doubt this: more probably he was an adventurer, who by cunning and daring had obtained for himself a position and a notoriety for the time, greater than that of any of the chiefs about him. The Portuguese, who are well informed of the politics of the natives, declared that Chibisa was an impostor, the son of no chief, but originally a slave at Tete; and they account for his rise thus.

The original Chibisa was a woman, a prophetess among the Nungwi, the tribe around Tete, and of great reputation among the natives. In common with other Zambesi tribes, the Nungwi believe in the transmigration of souls, that is, of the souls of their prophets. The lion is generally supposed to be the tabernacle which the prophetic spirits delight to occupy when they leave the human body; and so common is this belief among them, that the lion has the name of Pondora, or prophet, and is held in such estimation in some districts that it is death to the individual who kills a lion, and even the hyæna is

tenderly regarded, for, his whimper being generally heard after
the roar of the lion, he is looked upon as the lion's servant,
and so is spared. In course of time the prophetic spirit gets
tired of its abode in the 'king of beasts,' and leaving his
corpus again enters that of a human being. Chibisa, learned
in the superstitions of his countrymen, ran away from Tete,
and presenting himself at Mikaronko, the capital of the
Nungwi, a large village lying between the Shire and the Zambesi, declared himself possessed of the spirit of Chibisa, the
great prophetess, and so assumed her name. The Nungwi
believed him, for he backed his assertion with the performance
of many, to them, wonderful deeds, learnt probably during his
residence with the Portuguese; and Kapichi, the chief of the
Nungwi, gave him the place of honour at Mikaronko.

Chibisa was not long in making use of his influence, to acquire superior power. He became the head of a number of
people gathered from the various districts around Mikaronko,
who looked up to him not only as a prophet, but as their chief,
and who called themselves by his name. Kapichi was a young
man, and Chibisa was gradually acquiring a complete as-
cendancy not only over him, but over the whole tribe: Kapichi
was chief but in name.

Then war came upon the Nungwi. For some time, Chisaka,
a powerful chief, living to the north of Tete, had been the
terror of the land. The Portuguese at Tete tried to subdue
him, but he defeated them, shut them up in Tete, destroyed
all their outlying establishments, and swept off their flocks
and herds. He pursued his career of successful slaughter
unchecked, laying waste the country along the Zambesi almost
as far down as Sena. Returning to his own country, he
visited Mikaronko, and pretended great friendship for Chibisa
and Kapichi, who entertained him and his people with great
hospitality. But one day, while the chiefs were feasting
together, the report of fire-arms was heard in the village, and
Chibisa, on going to see the cause, found several of his own
people lying dead on the ground, Chisaka's people setting fire
to the village, and making captive the women and children.
Taken by surprise, and having no weapons but bows and ar-

rows, resistance was useless, and Chibisa and Kapichi fled, leaving the village in the hands of Chisaka, who plundered it, and carried off all the women and children he had secured. But Chibisa was not the man to sit down quietly under such circumstances. He sent out spies, who watched the movements of the enemy. He collected his followers, he followed up the foe, and at last in the dead of the night he attacked them so suddenly and vigorously, that he put them to flight, and not only recovered the women and children, and the property of which he had been plundered, but also captured several of Chisaka's guns.

The fame of Chibisa was increased by this exploit, for hitherto it had never been known that men with bows and arrows had overcome those with guns. Chibisa claimed to have a medicine to bewitch the dreaded gun, and the superstition of his followers almost inclined them to pay him divine honours.

Chisaka, however, was not disposed to let his reputation dwindle away. He in turn attacked Chibisa, and in the end, though receiving almost as much damage as he inflicted, the guns, despite the medicine, vindicated their superiority, and Chibisa was obliged to retreat in order to save himself from utter destruction. Chisaka pursued him as far as the Shire, but having no canoes he could not follow him over the river, and so he returned to his own country.

Chibisa and Kapichi then returned to Mikaronko, but the former accused the latter of having caused the war, in order to get rid of him, and a great quarrel arose between them. The tribe divided, part taking the side of Chibisa, part cleaving to Kapichi. Most of the influential men were against Chibisa, for while he ruled they had no power; and the result was, after each had taken muavi—the poisoned ordeal water—the one to prove his innocence of the charge brought against him, and the other to show he had no wicked intention of making a false charge, Chibisa deemed it prudent to retire from Mikaronko, and set up somewhere else for himself. Accordingly with his followers he settled on the right bank of the Shire, close to the island of Dakanamoio.

It was here Dr. Livingstone first made his acquaintance. The natives generally seemed hostile when the Ma Robert first went up the Shire, but Chibisa sought the friendship of the English: he evidently knew the advantage of having such powerful allies.

But he could not rest quietly in his new abode. Circumstances were against him. His people were needy, and became marauders. The river chiefs combined against him; a great mirandu (council) was held, certain crimes were laid to Chibisa's charge, he was accused of plotting against Mankokwe, and to vindicate himself he had to drink mauvi again. Fortunately for him, his stomach was not delicate; he vomited the poisonous stuff, and was once more declared innocent. The combination, however, continued against him; the chiefs feared him, and were jealous of his reputation; and eventually this circumstance made him so uncomfortable that he with the greater part of his people left the banks of the Shire, and went to Doa, a district on the Zambesi, lying between Sena and Tete. He was at this place when we arrived at his village on the Shire.

CHAPTER VI.

SETTLEMENT ON THE HIGHLANDS.

WITH our halt at Chibisa's ended the third phase of our experiences. Each had been very different to the other, each had been more or less trying, but each had its compensating comforts. As the anchor was let go, a feeling of rest came over all of us. The satisfaction of that moment made up for all the unrest and anxiety we had endured in getting up the river. The Doctor congratulated us all, and we all congratulated the Doctor.

On the morning of the 9th (July) we made a formal visit to the head man of the village. It was not so grand a business as that to Mankokwe, but it was more satisfactory. The people were anxious to have us with them; but as we wished to build, the head man thought Chibisa's permission should be gained, and promised that he would himself at once proceed to Doa and get his consent.

This conference being over, the Bishop and I went in search of a site for the house I was to build, and after tumbling about in thicket and brushwood for some time, we found what we were seeking, a spot about a quarter of a mile from the village, and commanding a magnificent view of the valley and mountains beyond.

On the 10th, the ship was drawn up close to the island, in order to facilitate the removal of our goods. A large bell tent was put up on the island; we missionaries at once set to work, and by midday we had the greater part of our stores and baggage out of the ship.

After this the Bishop sent me with a present of cloth to the men from Mount Zomba. I took William, one of our Cape men, with me as an interpreter. I told them that we were very sorry for the great trouble they were in; that God was angry with those who had burnt their villages, and carried away their wives and children as slaves; that we were English, and had left our own country to come and live with the Manganja in order to teach them to be a better and a happier people than they were, to teach them about God, that we were going to live up in the hills near to Mount Zomba, and hoped our presence among them would bring them peace.

The gratitude of these poor fellows seemed great, tears rolled down their cheeks, and on receiving the presents they prostrated themselves on the ground.

During the day a number of the natives came on to the island and seemed much interested in our proceedings. Their bearing was frank and friendly. The women brought their children, a great proof of confidence; and the little ones, after their manner, seemed to be enjoying themselves.

Next day we again went to work, and cleared the ship of all our stores. Much of our biscuit was mildewed: we had lost a great quantity of it through the sea water getting into the tins, and now we had to throw away much more.

An ambassador from Mankokwe made his appearance about noon. His master was indignant, exceedingly angry, because

Dr. Livingstone had returned the goat he had given him as a present, and so he had brought back the remainder of the presents the Doctor and the Bishop had given him. The Doctor laughed at all this, and calling some of the Makololo and Sena men to him, distributed to them the returned presents, to the evident astonishment of the ambassador. Thus the friendship which we had so much counted upon between us and the Rundo was apparently at an end, for these proceedings were almost equivalent to a declaration of war.

Dr. Livingstone decided upon commencing the land journey on the morning of Monday, July 15, and in the mean time we made all preparations.

I made a calculation of all the stores we had, and found that our stock had dwindled to half what it was when we left Johanna. And after we had given the expedition an equivalent for our keep in coming from Johanna, we found that we were quite without certain things, preserved meats for instance, and that we were still greatly in debt to the expedition. But this caused us no alarm ; food seemed plentiful, and we had barter goods in abundance.

The Doctor and Mr. Waller went into the villages in search of men to carry up baggage and stores. They came back disappointed. No one seemed willing to come. They listened and laughed, but would not say yes.

On Sunday the 14th, the good Bishop—who was as usual the life of the whole party—took me aside for a time, and after talking about several things relating to our mutual interests in the good work before us, gave to me Chibisa's village as my parish for the time being. I was not to accompany the land party, and it was expected that I should be some months in the valley.

We all felt dull and sad on this day. We had not been an unhappy party on board the ' Pioneer,' but I have no doubt we most of us felt that when we broke up on the morrow we should never meet altogether again. It is strange how fresh associations grow upon you and lay hold of your feelings. At the commencement of the year we were strangers to each other, and now it seemed as though we had been friends for years.

Indeed the time since we entered the Zambesi seemed thrice the time it really was, and so many events had been crowded into one's existence since we left England, that the months almost appeared years.

Towards evening several natives offered themselves as porters, and this relieved us of a great anxiety, for though Dr. Livingstone kindly placed six of his men at the service of the mission, we wanted six times that number.

By daybreak on the 15th all were ready for the march. It was a dismal-looking morning, and it had been raining during the night; and now threatened more rain: nevertheless all were cheerful and hopeful. I made a last survey of the forty days' supplies I had put up for the mission party, and could not help anxiety when I saw how scanty it looked. Dear Scudamore made us all merry with the quaintness of his arrangements. He was always quaint—always happy—always cheerful—always one of the most loveable, the most gentle and the bravest of Christian men. The health of the whole party was upon the whole good.

The men who had engaged to carry burdens did not make their appearance as early as they promised. We therefore sent William after them, and before we had done breakfast he returned and announced that he had succeeded in getting fifteen. Joyful intelligence! I at once packed up the camp beds; and a little more clothing and certain other comforts were added for each person, and another burden of barter goods was added to the stock. The equipment of the party then seemed quite sufficient; it would have been miserable work travelling all day and lying on the hard floor of a hut all night, with insufficient clothing, and we were warned that the nights on the hills were cold.

The mission had twenty-one porters at its command. Then came the allotment of burdens, and then for the first time we experienced the traveller's difficulty. Some of the burdens were larger than others, some lighter, and the clamour and contention before each man was satisfied with his particular load was amusing. With the expedition party there was no such disputing; the Makololo and the Sena men did just as

they were bidden, and were out of the ship and on to the other
side of the river before we were ready to follow. When all
was settled and we had got our fellows on to the island, they
discovered that they had left their bows and arrows behind.
Miserable discovery! for they would not go without them. I
laughed at them, I coaxed them, I punched them good-
humouredly, I did all that Mr. Paymaster Jones himself could
have done, in order to get them to enter the boat; but they
would have their weapons of war, nobody but slaves went
without, and so off they went to the village again, I and William going with them to ensure their return. When once in
the village they were in no hurry to leave it, they rushed to
their huts and began smoking, and looked as though they
did not intend to leave again for a week to come. It was a
great trial of patience, but it was no use getting angry: so I
kept my temper, and having persuaded one fellow to put down
his pipe, I went down to the boat with him trusting the others
like sheep would follow. And so they did, with the exception
of one man, and his place was well supplied, for nine others
stepped forward and offered their services. I chose one to
supply the place of him who held back, told the others to
await my return, and went off with those to whom burdens
were already apportioned. I found the Bishop had gone on
ahead, but we soon overtook him with the rest of the mission
party. Mr. Waller returned with me in order to equip the
other porters, and the Bishop went onwards with his detach-
ment—pastoral staff in one hand, and a gun in the other.
This pastoral staff was given to him by some of the clergy at
Cape Town. The Bishop thought that as it must go up at
some time to the place where we should halt, it had better go
up at once, and that no person was so fitted by office to carry
it as himself. So he set forward. It was a puzzle to the natives; they were afraid of the staff, and thought it was a new
kind of gun. Said one—

' Mfuti?' (a gun?)

' Aye mfuti ikuri!' (a great gun) said another.

The men who volunteered last were a willing set of fellows.
They made no objections to the burdens we gave them, and

went off with alacrity. I went with them, for it was arranged that I should go some distance on the day's journey and return. The men carried their burdens on their heads, and as they knew the destination of our party they acted as guides, and sped along at the rate of four miles an hour, in order to come up with the main body.

The country we passed through was as wild as the most enthusiastic lover of uncultivated nature could desire—the real thing, an African waste, but certainly not a desert. Villages were there; but unless you stumbled upon them you would not know of their existence, so thickly planted were the trees about them. The grass was often higher than our heads, the bush was all but impenetrable. Large trees abounded; and thick wood, shrubs and creeping plants were everywhere. As we drew near to the hills, we saw mountain behind mountain, rugged rock and wild-looking pass: indeed, everything in nature about us was ' delightfully savage.'

After we had been walking nearly two hours the path led us by a stream, the Kubala. Here we found two women washing. It seemed strange to see so domestic an occupation in so wild a place. Near them, under a tree, we found two of our packages and a note from the Bishop, saying—

' The men carrying these burdens have turned back; bring them on to the next village, and leave them in charge.— C. F. M.'

This looked anything but hopeful, but we did as we were desired, and about half an hour afterwards came up with the Bishop and Dr. Meller. The rest of the party were ahead; Dr. Meller was ready to return—he was left in charge of the ship; and I then took leave of the Bishop and Waller.

As we turned to have a last look, we saw the Bishop marching on with huge strides after the bearers, the gun depressed, the pastoral staff elevated and well in view.

The ship on our return seemed very cheerless, with so many good souls out of it. It was arranged that I should sleep on board until the house was put up. Gamble, who gradually improved in health after he left the ship, and Job, a Cape man—my interpreter—slept in tents on the island.

It was my intention to build two houses, one on the island for stores, the other on the bank for a residence. The spot I chose for a store-house required a great deal of clearing, and it was necessary to raise it above the general level of the island, so I set to work, Gamble aiding me. We had been some time at work when it struck me that I might get some of the natives who were looking on to help us, so Job put me into communication with one Chechoma. This man was a wonderful fellow, a great talkér, a man of reputation among the Chibisians; and he was useful to us in inducing men to act as porters. He was a thin, little man, with a big head. His hair was profuse and long, and thrown back from the fore part of his head, à la Eugénie. Knave and something else—what I need not say—was suggested by this man's personal appearance. It seemed as if his mission was to interfere in everybody's business, and to set everybody right (or wrong), and his countrymen seemingly acquiesced.

So Chechoma came forward, pipe in hand, and made a bow worthy of Beau Nash. I explained to him what I wanted. The thing was novel, had never before been heard of in the Chibisian commonwealth; but Chechoma's mind grasped it, saw the advantage of work followed by pay, and turning to his friends he harangued them on the immense benefits the muzungu (white man) was offering to them.

The result of his eloquence was this : four men, for a certain length of calico, agreed to fetch enough sand from a hillock close at hand to raise the site of the store-house to the required altitude. They worked merrily for an hour, and then they took it into their heads that such an occupation was *infra dig.*, said it was 'woman's work,' and would do no more of it. I laughed at them, and Job, at my bidding, reconciled them a little to the occupation by telling them that in England men always did that kind of work, and that we should think it unmanly to let the women do it. They required constant encouragement, however, before they would finish what they had begun; had I not worked with them, they would have gone off. When I paid them they were highly delighted, and seemed to think that working for the Muzungu Anglesi was not such a bad thing after all. And when, some days afterwards, I again summoned Chechoma and told him I wanted men to work, more than twenty at once came forward and expressed their willingness to do anything I wanted done.

The common idea that the African will not work, that he is a lazy fellow, who sits smoking under a tree all day, caring for nothing under the sun, is by no means correct of all the tribes. Those we were with were not indisposed to work, when they found that labour was profitable to themselves.

On the afternoon of the 17th a large party of men, armed with guns, crossed the river in canoes just ahead of the ship. The captain of this band, a Portuguese, stood on the bank of the river smoking, while his men passed over in Chibisa's canoes. It was evidently a slaving party from Tete, going up to the hills to get slaves. There were nearly a hundred men; most of them had guns, the rest spears and battle-axes. All were Africans but the commander.

It seemed a horrible thing to permit these men to go on their errand of crime unchecked, but we had no authority to interfere with them. We could do nothing but watch them, as they went off on their mission of wickedness.

While watching these people, some of the men who had gone up the hills with the Bishop, to our surprise came on to the island. They were in a state of greatest excitement, and from their statements we learned that they went up as far as Mbame's village, and that when there a party of Chakundas, (slavers) had entered the village; that the English had driven them away, after taking their guns and property from them, and had set the slaves free! Presently more men came, and with them some of the property taken from the slavers—a gun, a number of hoes, earthenware pots, brass armlets, &c. One of these men had a letter from Dr. Livingstone to Mr. Gedy, the officer in charge of the ship, which, after stating that they had the day before released eighty-four slaves and dispersed the slavers, gave instruction to Mr. Gedy to man the boats, and go up and down the river, as another party of slavers had escaped him, and would be down the river with their slaves almost immediately. The slaves were to be retained, the slavers dispersed, and the Chibisians were to be enlisted on our side by a promise of all the booty they could take from the slavers. The freed captives were to be brought to the island, and fed until they could be returned to their own homes.

MANGANJA POTTERY.

I thought this a happy inauguration of our mission work. I felt this one good deed would give us a great reputation among the people of the mountains, that they would feel more confidence in us through this one act, than by a long residence among them without anything done.

The boats were quickly manned, and we went over to Chibisa's village, to enquire into the intentions of those men who had passed over the river during the day. An assembly of notabilities was soon accomplished. Checoma talked for the whole of them, until I stopped his mouth, by saying I wished to hear what the others had to say. From them we learned that the Portuguese and his party came into the village that morning, and had claimed us for brothers, and that they were going to fight the hill Manganja upon some pretence which not one of the Chibisians believed, though they were afraid to say what they did believe. They promised, however, to keep a good look-out along the banks of the river, and to let us know immediately if any slaving party attempted to cross over with slaves.

I saw, through a glass, the last of the Portuguese party going up the hills, and was very wroth, and very sad. We had no authority, had we the power, to interfere with them. Our orders were to release captives, by force if necessary—and that was all. But the old comfort came, in thinking that there was a good God over all, Who knew all; and I was content to leave the issue with Him.

The next day, July 18, was eventless, until about 5 P.M., when Dr. Kirk arrived from the hills. He had left the whole party at Soche's that morning, had brought four of the Makololo with him, and had been unsuccessful in pursuit of a slaving party all day. We told him of the men who passed over the river the day before, and he thought it serious news. He gave me a letter from the Bishop, in which he said:—' Yesterday, six or eight men passed through the village we were in, with eighty-four slaves. They ran away, and all the slaves were freed. I was bathing at the time, and came up only in time to find them all sitting clothed and cooking, as composedly as if nothing had happened. To-day eight more were rescued. Kirk will tell you what he comes for. I am clear that in such cases it is right to use force, and even fire if necessary, to *rescue captives.* I should do so myself if necessary; but I think it more becoming our office to see the guns in the hands of others. Do you as you think best; if you like, volunteer to Kirk to go in a boat with a gun : you have my approval of your doing so. I would say, if you are not required, be glad that you are not called upon. Receive any captives you can get, give them bits of cloth for decency, feed them if you can buy food for them. It is very likely that you may all be called up, that we may concentrate our force, sooner than we expected, and that the shed may not be required; but go on as you are doing till you hear again. There seems to have been great barbarity on the march down. All well; Procter a little upset. Marching *before* breakfast is severe work.

'Scudamore says, " Tell him I'm much obliged to him for packing up my bed. I've got it all right. I've *only* lost my

note-book as yet." "Any more?" "No, no more." *Addendum*
—I hope he won't beat his ploughshare into a spear altogether,
or whatever it ought to be.'

The Bishop, in this, says he found them ' clothed;' the fact
was, Dr. Livingstone had given each of the freed captives, from
the spoils taken from their oppressors, a length of cloth; for
many of the women, as well as children and men, were literally
naked. They were all much emaciated, and when they were set
down to food, they were almost overpowered with astonishment.
One little boy came up to the Doctor, and said—

' Where do you come from? These people (the slavers)
starved us, but you say, "Cook food, and eat:" where *do* you
come from?'

The barbarity alluded to had indeed been great. One poor
woman, the mother of a babe not more than a month old, was
given a heavy bundle of hoes to carry. She was a weakly
woman; she could scarcely stagger along that rough mountain-
path with the babe at her back; her friends said it seemed as
though she would fall down by the way. She could not carry
the hoes and her babe; and the babe—immortal being though
it was—was in the estimation of the slavers of less value than
the hoes, no more than a piece of calico a yard long: so they
took the babe from its mother's arms, and dashed its head
against the rocks, throwing the little body on one side, as
though it had been that of a dog. The men who did this, and
other things like this, were men from Tete, in the service of the
Portuguese living at Tete; and such barbarity is not exceptional, it is the usual conduct pursued by these traders
towards their unhappy captives.

After they had feasted, Dr. Livingstone addressed the people
he had released, telling them that those who had homes and
friends might return to them, that they were as free to do what
they liked as himself. It was found that more than half of
them had no homes to go to; they had seen their homes destroyed in the cruel wars which these slavers had kindled and
were keeping up; women had seen their husbands killed, little
children had seen their parents killed; they were utterly destitute and desolate. So after consulting with the Bishop, the

Doctor said to them, in substance:—' My brothers here have left their own land to come and live with your people, in order to make you a happier, a better people than you are, to teach you about God. If you like, go with them; settle where they settle; they will protect you and feed you until you can support yourselves.' And they all joyfully accepted this offer. Strange to say, they have no word in their language equivalent to our 'Thank you;' but they have the right feeling, for their looks and their actions were eloquent gratitude.

From information gained from Mbame and others, it seemed that the neighbourhood of Mount Zomba was being depopulated by the war. The Ajawa were said to be carrying on a war of extermination. It appeared more than probable that slavers were up there purchasing the captives; and so Dr. Livingstone resolved to go up to Zomba.

Procter and Scudamore were left at Soche's village in charge of the released slaves. The Doctor, the Bishop, and the rest of the party, with the exception of William, were gone on to Zomba.

Dr. Kirk said he hoped that Soche's would be the mission head-quarters, as a more favourable spot could not be found. The country was fertile and well watered, the population abundant, provisions plentiful, and it was nearer to the Shire by fifty miles than Zomba, the place first thought of for us.

It was evident that the armed party, who crossed over the river the day before, knew nothing of these proceedings on the hills; and we felt anxious for the safety of Procter and Scudamore, for the slavers had taken the route to Soche's village.

On the 19th, Dr. Kirk and seven of the Makololo—all who were with us—went along the south bank of the river, towards the Murchison Falls, the fords being between the ship and Matiti, the first cataract, and a boat was sent up the river in the same direction. It was thought that by this plan the slavers would be intercepted; and had the boat done as much as it might have done, we should have cut them off; but to our chagrin we learnt that they had passed over the river just above where the boat halted.

Vexation at this failure gave me fever ; I was ill for several days.   Chechoma was in tribulation on my account.   He came on board ship, poked his head down the skylight, and enquired after my health in a most commiserating voice.   I was impatient to get my house up—fever always makes you impatient—and he seemed to understand this ; for when I spoke to him on this subject, he replied as to a child who wanted an impossibility, and was fretting because he could not have it.

'Wait but a little—only a little—three days—two days—who knows ? one day.   But suppose you wait three days, what is that in the building of a house ?—the men will surely be back from Chibisa in that time.'

They returned on the 28th of July.   They brought good news.   Mankokwe, we learnt, had sent to Chibisa, bidding him not to let us stay at his place ; but Chibisa's answer to us was—

'The white man is a good man.   He is my brother.   If he wants to build, let him build.   If he wants to stay, let him stay.   If he wants to leave his ship and his goods behind him, while he goes about the country, let him leave them, and let my people see that no one touches them.'

The messengers also gave information respecting the armed band which had crossed the river.   The leader had given up his expedition.   He heard, as he went along, of what Dr. Livingstone had done and was doing, and he was afraid.   He went up to within a mile of Soche's village, heard of the English left there, and retreated : when met, he had recrossed the river below us, and was on his way back to Tete.   He sent a message to the officer in charge of the ship, saying he had done no harm, he had committed no violence, he had made no slaves, he was going back to Tete, and there was, therefore, no cause of offence between him and the English.

This is a fact which speaks for itself.   Had this man been unchecked, he would have caused incalculable misery, and would probably have returned with hundreds of captives.

The 28th was Sunday.   On Monday morning early, I went to the village to make arrangements for the house-building ; for, despite the Bishop's hint, I hoped if he settled at Soche's,

that I should remain at Chibisa's. I found the Chibisians
either drunk or getting drunk: the uproar during the night
had been great. The return of the messengers was the cause
of this dissipation. There was a regular pombi-drinking
going on. Chechoma was excited; now boisterous, then sentimental. All were hearty. I was their brother; Chibisa
had said it. They would do anything for the English; and
we might do what we liked in the land; the land was as
much ours as theirs, had not Chibisa said so? Gallons of
pombi were offered me; with a wonderful hand-clapping they
received me, and with a clap! clap! clap! I went away, after
declining from them any assistance for that day.

I cleared the site, and marked out the boundaries of my
house, and then went into the woods and marked the trees I
wanted to cut down.

The general appearance of the Chibisians, next day, was so
unpromising that I resolved to go to work at the house without them; their debauch had thoroughly demoralized them.
My parishioners were not hopeful looking subjects that morning. The state of morality among them did not seem very
high. The Makololo were the admiration of the Chibisian
women. They possessed just those qualities most calculated
to lead women astray, and astray many of them went. There
was quite a rivalry among them for the favour of the Makololo, and the husbands did not seem to be at all disturbed by
this conduct of their wives. They were great 'bhang'
smokers; men, women, and even the children indulged in this
pernicious habit. A child, not more than ten years of age,
seeing his father smoking, would go up to him, and pull down
the pipe from his father's mouth with an expression of countenance indicating quite a yearning for a whiff; and when his
wish was gratified, as it invariably was, the little creature
would inhale vehemently the deleterious fume, and 'sit down
all but stupefied.

The Chibisian children were a pleasing race, when not associated with their elders. When once they had lost fear of
me, they played prettily and merrily, and their laughter—happiest of sounds—was frequent and unrestrained; there was

nothing of that unnatural gravity which I had hitherto noticed among the native children.

No further news came from the hills, and for several days Gamble and I worked very hard at our house. The Chibisians cut down trees for us, and were much interested in our proceedings. I showed them a plan and a sketch of the house, and it was so contrary to their own notions of house-building, that they looked upon it almost as wonderful in its way as the ' Pioneer' was in her way.

Among the Chibisians who volunteered assistance in house-building, was one Tambala (*Anglice* Cock.) He was the Adonis of Dakanamoio, and had a wonderful head of hair, dripping with rancid oil. He was ambitious to earn cloth, so I put him to work to cut me eight poles of a certain length and thickness, promising a certain length of cloth. Off he started, and in about two hours' time he brought me three poles ; then he sat down, looking quite used up, and began talking about the cloth he was to receive, and wanted to make out that I had promised him more than I had done. I showed him my measure : he tossed back his oiled locks in assumed indignation, but after a while he set to work again, and brought another pole, and would do no more work for that day, but wanted payment for the whole number. I refused ; we had high words, and at last I was obliged to drive him away with a manifestation of vigour that astonished him. Next day, towards sunset, he brought the remainder of the poles, but when I offered him payment, refused what I offered. Another dispute was the result, ending again in a manifestation of power on my part, which sent off Adonis flying, while the others round about were convulsed with laughter. After I had finished work for the day, and was sitting reading on the island, Tambala approached, quite subdued, squatted a few yards from me, and watched me with wistful eyes. I took no notice of him for some time ; at last I asked him, through Job, what he wanted.

' Saru anga,' was his reply, in a very penitent voice : that is, ' my cloth.' I threw it to him, and a few minutes afterwards I saw him displaying it to his companions with evident delight.

August 1.—I was at work early this morning, but my labours soon ceased, for about midday a great firing of guns, on the other side of the river, announced the return of Dr. Livingstone. The Chibisians were in great excitement, for as we stood on the high bank we saw, among those getting into the boats, two men with the slave forks on their necks. I made them understand that they were Chakundas—I felt sure of that; and they clapped their sides in amazement, if not with satisfaction.

All belonging to the expedition, with the exception of a sailor named Hutchins, who was left with the Bishop, had returned.

From the Bishop and others I learnt what was done after July 18, when they left Soche's village.

They started for Mongazi's village, about twenty miles off, and there they surprised two slavers, made them prisoners, took from them their guns and baggage, and freed five women and three boys. The slavers managed to escape during the night, and the old chief Mongazi, otherwise Bona, without doubt procured their escape; for he was indignant because his guests, the Chakundas, had been so unceremoniously treated, but was afraid to offer any resistance.

On the 19th, Rowe, a sailor, and one of the Makololo made an excursion into villages where slavers were supposed to be, and succeeded in rescuing eight women and children, the slavers escaping.

The whole party then left Mongazi's and halted at a village belonging to a chief named Nsambo. There they found a man with a gun; under such suspicious circumstances they took the gun from him, and for the time being kept him prisoner. He said he was going on a message from Chinsunzi, the principal chief of those parts, to call up Chibisa. He was told if he were a true man he might return to Chinsunzi, when his gun should be restored.

From Nsambo's village they went on to Magomero, arriving there in the afternoon, without meeting with any other slavers. The whole country was in a state of terror, people fleeing on all sides. Chigunda, the chief of Magomero, declared the

Ajawa were close at hand, and that they were burning, and destroying and making captives on all sides.

The next morning Chigunda offered to show the English the Ajawa camp. Dr. Livingstone was not well that day, and so all remained at Magomero. The object of the Bishop and his party, in coming into the country, was made known to Chigunda, who said that most of the villages about were deserted, but if the Bishop would live with him he would not run away.

The next day, Sunday the 21st, was also spent at Magomero. During this day, continual reports came in of the near approach and destructive operations of the Ajawa.

On Monday, the whole party left Chigunda's for the neighbourhood of Chinsunzi's, where the Ajawa were supposed to be in strength. When at the village of Murongwe, they heard that some Tete slavers were in villages near. They started in pursuit, and during the day released forty-four captives; several others were afterwards found in the bush, to which they had fled from fear; but their fears were soon allayed when they discovered what the intentions of the English were. With the exception of two, the slavers escaped. These two were insolent, and so they were put into the slave forks that had been taken from the necks of the captives, and on their necks they remained until they came down to Dakanamoio. This slave fork is a terrible tamer. As an experiment, I had one put on my neck, and found the helplessness of my condition complete. The strongest spirit would be broken in a few days by it and a course of starvation.

The next day was an eventful one. Dr. Livingstone, the Bishop, and all the rest of the party, with the exception of one or two who were left in charge of the freed people, started from Murongwe, and took the road towards the Ajawa encampment. A number of the Manganja went with them. Everywhere they saw sad signs of the war—villages burnt, gardens uncared for, the beautiful land about them rapidly becoming a desert. About midday they came upon a large party of Ajawa, who were just returning from a successful raid. The smoke of burning villages was seen in the distance. A long train of captives carried the plunder, and their bitter cry was heard, even above the triumphant utterances of the Ajawa women, who came out, as did the Israelitish women of old, to welcome back the victors. The Nsasa, or camp, was built on the slope of a hill, and so securely flanked by other hills, as to be all but unassailable by native enemies. Our friends went on very cautiously, and were quite close to the camp before they were perceived. As soon as the Ajawa perceived them, they came forward defiant, dancing and shouting like savages intoxicated with previous success. Dr. Livingstone called out to them that he came to talk with them, and that it was peace. They disbelieved him, and shouted out that it was not peace but war; and, according to their custom, dispersed themselves in the bush, or hid behind the trees and rocks. Johnson, our black cook, seeing a man aiming apparently at Dr. Livingstone, elevated his gun and fired. Then a fight commenced. The arrows flew fast and furious, and perceiving how few in number the party was to which they were opposed, the Ajawa evidently thought they should make an easy conquest; their shouts of derision rent the air, and they at last came charging down like demons. They were met with a few well directed shots from the rifles; they halted, and returned to cover. But at last they were forced from their stronghold, and their camp destroyed and burnt. The captives escaped during the fight; they threw down their burdens, and fled into the bush. None of the English were hurt; one Manganja was killed, and another had an arrow through his wrist. The Bishop was in the midst of the fight, but did not use his gun; he made it over to Mr. C. Livingstone. It was nearly midnight before our friends reached Morongwe's, having been out without food since early morning, and marched over forty miles.

Next day, the 24th, all returned to Magomero, Dr. Livingstone having arranged to meet Chinsunzi, the principal chief of the neighbourhood, there.

On the 25th Murongwe, and the representatives of Chinsunzi came, and Dr. Livingstone explained to them that though they had seen the English as fighting men, yet it was not as fighting men they wished to be known. They were men of peace and did not come to fight, but to teach them of God,

8

and to promote good-will between man and man and tribe and tribe; but finding the Ajawa murdering, and making captives in order to sell them, and burning villages and spreading destruction wherever they came, he and his friends had gone to stop them. If they would profit by the lesson they had received and would live at peace, he and his friends would rejoice, and be friends with all. He then told them that he was going away himself, but the Bishop and others would stay at Magomero, and make it a strong place to which women and children might flee in case they were attacked. And concluded by saying 'you say selling people is a bad thing— so it is; but you sell them yourselves, you are nearly as bad as the Ajawa.'

Those assembled did not deny the charge, but some asked what they were to do for cloth if they did not sell men and women to the Chakundas. The Doctor told them to grow cotton and he would come and buy it of them, would give them cloth in exchange. They said they had no good seed, only the wild kind; he replied he would give them seed, and having some with him distributed it among them, and promised them more.

Before the day was over Chinsunzi himself came, and a long discussion took place as to whether the English should stay at Magomero or at his village. He was in great fear of the Ajawa, and strongly urged our going to his place.

Dr. Livingstone appeared to think that Magomero offered greater conveniences than Chinsunzi's village, and strongly urged the Bishop to make it his head-quarters. It was quite near enough to the Ajawa to afford protection to those who needed it, and it was just removed from the actual scene of conflict. The Bishop, as he told me afterwards, was strongly in favour of Soche's village; but the Doctor represented to him that if he stayed at Magomero he would save the whole country between him and the river; and so at last it was agreed that our first station should be at Magomero, which was about seventy miles from the Shire.

A letter from the Bishop ordered me up to Magomero as soon as possible. Procter and Scudamore had left Soche's

village, and had gone up with the freed people under their care.
Dr. Livingstone met them on his way down.

Johnson, our cook, came down with Dr. Livingstone, in
order to act as my guide to Magomero.

I was sorry to leave the Chibisians, for I was gaining
ground with them daily.

I left Dakanamoio on the morning of August 5th. Hardisty
the engineer, and Gwillim the quartermaster, went with me
for their health's sake. I had a long train of bearers, more
than seventy ; for by this time most of the Chibisians knew
me, and trusted me. I made them all give me their names,
and made their engagement quite a formal business. Many
of the names were as euphonious as Hiawatha, and others
that have become poetry—for instance, Namalipi, Joanagaru,
Chenanawa, Karakoola, Jasokonisa. In the mouth of a child
the Manganja language sounds prettily enough ; but the men
have a very coarse utterance, and with them it is ugly ; while
the women, with their mutilated lips, can pronounce but few
words perfectly.

I breakfasted on board the ' Pioneer,' and by half past ten
I and all my party were on our way to the hills. There was
no confusion or wishing to return, this time ; every man was
ready with his load, and when I went ahead and called
' Atiendi!' (come on!') every man raised his burden and off
we went. The path did not admit of two abreast : so we
formed a long line, walking in Indian file.

After we had gone over the ground I had previously traversed
we entered a mountain pass. For some time walking was
easy enough, the hills on either side were well wooded and
pleasing, the sun shone brightly, but the heat was not oppressive. But very soon we had indications of a more rugged
path than we had hitherto met with. Huge masses of rock
lay about in all directions. Here, there, and everywhere, we
saw

> ' Crags, knolls, and mounds, confusedly hurled,—
> The fragments of an earlier world.'

We began to ascend rapidly, and for the next three hours the
journey was a severe trial of our endurance. The Kubala

flowed beside us, no longer a peaceful stream but a mountain
torrent; we had to cross it again and again. In the rainy
season the flow of water is at times irresistible; heavy blocks
of stone in the bed of the river indicated by their position
that they had been forced into it by the impetuosity of the
stream The noise of the water as it rushed by us was very
refreshing; sometimes it flowed on a level with our feet, at
other times we were two or three hundred feet above it.
Cascades were numerous, though not remarkable.

After marching about four hours we halted. Of my rear
I could see nothing, for the path was circuitous and the hills
were thickly wooded. It was nearly an hour before the last
man came up. My white companions looked wofully punished;
indeed it had been a toilsome ascent.

Until we halted I had no idea of our altitude. The prospect
was magnificent. Hills, whose summits and slopes were
covered with trees and bamboo, displaying a verdure everywhere beautiful, but everywhere varied, were on either
side; while through the vista we beheld the valley of the
Shire—beheld it in its actual breadth, from the foot of the
hills we were ascending to the mountains that shut in the
Zambesi. It was grand; a sight to dream about.

When we reached the crest of this first range of hills we
were nearly 2,000 feet above the sea. The sun was nearing
the horizon, when to our great relief we beheld our resting
place for the night, a small village at the bottom of a deep
basin-like valley. We were courteously received by Chipindu,
the chief; two of the largest huts were given over to us, and
the head man ordered his people to get us what we needed.
Dr. Livingstone had given me instructions, so when the bearers
came up I made them bring their burdens to me, and I had
them stowed in the hut I intended to occupy. Then I divided
the men into parties of twelve, and gave to each party a fathom
of cloth with which to buy food for supper and breakfast.
By the time this arrangement was made, Johnson, who had
brought the hind quarters of a goat with him, and who had
also bought in the village a yam and some green peas, had a
capital dinner ready. The Chibisians were not idle. Before

we had finished eating there were a dozen fires lighted around us, and as many pots on them.

The sun was lost to us sooner than it would have been in the Shire valley, but for some time its rays illuminated with a ruddy glow the many cloudlets above us, and gave to the mountains around a touch of beauty that was truly delightful. As darkness increased the fires of our black friends multiplied, and lighted up their faces as, eating and drinking, they made the hills reverberate with laughter and mirth. I had no heart to check their merriment, and it lasted far into the night. It pleased me to find them, after their hard day's march, so cheerful.

The inhabitants of the village looked well fed, but they were miserably clad, most of them having nothing around their loins but a strip of the inner bark of a certain fig tree which they soak and otherwise prepare, and beat out with mallets until it is almost as thin as calico. It is the badge of poverty, and makes its wearers look perfect savages.

Next morning we were early on the march to Mbame's, which place we reached in four hours. On the road we had several magnificent views of mountain and valley scenery; but until we came to Mbame's the population was very thin—the first range of hills having but little water. The village of Mbame is situated at the edge of the first plateau, which is a plain about ten or more miles across, well wooded, well watered, and fertile, and with an atmosphere which, after the hot air of the Shire valley, was really delicious.

Mbame was a stout, tall old man, greyheaded and hearty. His village was clean, and the huts were well built; and his people seemed well fed and without care. It was here the first party of slaves were released. I had instructions to bring on a woman and two children who had been among those freed, but were too ill to go on with the rest. The woman had gone away, and the children were still so ill that it was not possible to take them with me; so I gave Mbame cloth for the food he had given them, and promised more if he took good care of them.

We reached Soche's about half-past four o'clock. The country about this place was excellent, capable of great development and already producing abundantly. Before we arrived at our destination several of my porters were quite knocked up, for it had been a most fatiguing march. Gamble and Gwillim brought up the rear, and did good service in urging on those who lagged behind. There was a great deal of kindly spirit shown by those who were less fatigued to their more tired brethren. One man who had a voice like a lion, and a head and face not unlike a buffalo, although his burden had been one of the heaviest, went back again and again to help on those most tired. Indeed, there was so much that was genial and generous among these men that I forgot they were savages, and had no occasion to remember it.

The village was a pleasant village, at the foot of a magnificent hill about 3,000 feet high ; it was surrounded by bananas. When I arrived, the chief was said to be absent; but his presence was announced soon after, and I paid him a visit. He was not a pleasant-looking man by any means. He did not look you fairly in the face, and put you in mind of a man who had committed some great crime, and was living in the constant expectation of being found out. In person he was tall and burly, and as old as Mbame. It was here Procter and Scudamore stayed, so we were welcomed on our arrival by old and young with pleasant faces. When I asked for a hut, I was told I might have which I liked ; and it was my fault, therefore, that I had not a better one—that I had was full of every abomination in the way of vermin and dirt.

Provisions were plentiful, and a better fed, and a more dirty people I had never seen. The higher we got, the better fed the people seemed.

When the goods were stored, I paid the bearers, and gave them cloth for food, and I never paid anything with greater satisfaction ; for they had earned their wage well and truly. They left for home early in the morning.

We stayed at Soche's next day in order to rest and get fresh bearers. The chief behaved admirably, and gave his head man instructions to collect as many men as I needed.

Johnson was something of a musician ; he played the violin in a certain way, and the accordion also. To their delight and wonder, he gave the Socheians a performance on the latter

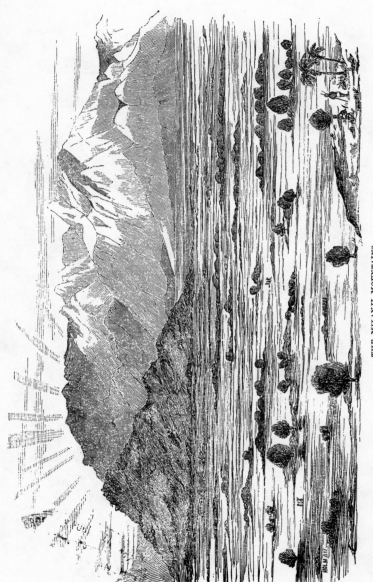

THE MILANJI MOUNTAINS.

instrument. Children left their play, women their work, and
the men were excited. Even old Soche waddled off to listen
to the wondrous music; and 'Jakoma! Jakoma!' (good,
good!) broke from the lips of his admiring audience.

Next morning a crowd of lusty fellows beset my hut, and
all anxiety about the carriage of my luggage disappeared.
Had I a hundred burdens, I could have found a hundred
bearers.

The distance from Soche's to Mongazi's was about twenty
miles. The country we passed through was not hilly, and
the paths were good. For the first two hours our road lay
through a valley of flowers—we were in the Pingwi and
Bangwi pass. The mountain scenery ahead of us was extraordinary. Huge basaltic hills, from 1,000 to 5,000 feet high,
arose in all directions; not in ranges, but, like the mountains
of the moon, apart from one another. Still beyond we saw
the summits of greater mountains; these were the Milanji, a
magnificent range of hills, probably 12,000 feet above the level
of the sea, the grandest mountains in that part of Africa. You
never tired of looking at the mighty mass. Their grayish-white
colour, diversified by the alternation of light and shade when
the sun was full upon them, formed a beautiful contrast with
the verdant plain which lay between them and Magomero.

We halted about half-past ten in a mountain pass. When
we entered it no sign of a storm was apparent; but we had not
been resting more than five minutes before the roll of distant
thunder told us a storm was near. A few minutes more, and
we saw the rain-cloud on the crest of the mountains, filling the
gorge behind, and rolling on towards us in a very ominous
manner. We hoped it would exhaust itself before it reached
us; but it was not so. The rain overtook us, the thunder
leaped from hill to hill, and in a short time the whole
country about us was trembling under the strife of the elements.

About one o'clock we came to a village, and here we rested
for an hour. It did not cease raining until we reached Mongazi's, at four o'clock. An African village is a dirty place on
a rainy day; but Mongazi's was the dirtiest, as well as the
largest, I had seen. Mongazi was an old man, tall, lean, and

ill-looking. His arms were loaded with brass rings, and he
wore a scarlet cloth. He came forth to meet us, and threw
his arms round Johnson's neck with every demonstration of
delight. He was much surprised to see my long train of
porters, and his people came out in crowds, and gazed in
wonder upon the supposed wealth with which they were laden.
But when Hardisty, Gamble and Gwillim made their appearance, they took to their heels and ran. Mongazi stood his
ground, and laughed at his people's fears.

I paid Soche's men for their day's work as they deposited
their burdens : and that done, and the men supplied with food,
I began to think of myself, and found I was shivering and
shaking with approaching fever. I had a fire lighted in my
hut, took a dose of quinine, a dose of wine, and a dose of
something warm, and hoped the morning would find me all
right; but it found me all wrong ; I could not walk without
staggering. I resolved, however, to push on to Magomero, for,
from a note which I had received from Waller about an hour
after my arrival at Mongazi's, I learnt that, though all were well,
they needed many of the things I was bringing up.

Bearers were not so readily procured here as at Soche's :
some misunderstanding prevailed about the number I wanted;
but after much exertion on Johnson's part, we were able to
take all our property with us but six boxes and a bundle of
brass wire. These Mongazi promised to send after us, and he
kept his word.

The march to Magomero from Mongazi's was, in my state of
health, killing work; the road was easy enough, but it was
much longer than I expected.

The country we passed through was magnificent for its mountain scenery ; but the soil did not seem so fertile as lower
down. The trees, save by the side of the streams, were few
in number, stunted, and wizened. We were in a vast plain,
upon which rose hill behind hill, grand and imposing. Zomba
was right before me, like a huge pyramid shorn of its apex.
Chiradzura, an isolated mountain, was really a joy to look at ;
while the Milanaji towered towards the sky, and stretched
along the plain farther than the eye could see.

It was about two o'clock when we reached our destination, the sight of which stimulated my unstrung frame, and for a time I felt free from fatigue of every kind.

Magomero was not a large village; nor was it so pleasantly situated as Soche's or Mongazi's. It was in a hole in the plain; approach it from what quarter you would, you must descend to it. I felt much disappointed when I saw it; for, in a sanitary point of view, it seemed the worse place that could be chosen. It was enforced upon the Bishop by Dr. Livingstone for prudential reasons. Among other things, he thought it a place easily defended; and, in the disturbed state of the country, it did not seem at all impossible but that we might have to defend ourselves.

The country round about Magomero, I have no doubt, was in its best parts as healthy as the mountain districts of India. The air was pure, the heat never great, and existence might be made very comfortable. Magomero, it is true, was 3,000 feet above the sea; but situated as it was, had it been as high as the moon, and crowded as we crowded it, it would have been a pest-hole.

Chigunda lived on a peninsula-shaped bit of land, formed by the course of the stream, about eighty yards broad by three hundred long, and upon this spot also the Bishop had established himself and family. A stockade across the entrance had been erected under Waller's superintendence; so that, by river and stockade, we were quite shut in. It would have been difficult for any Ajawa to get into us, but it would have been equally difficult for us to get out to them. An attack from the Ajawa was indeed expected. No one left the station without a gun, and a watch was kept all night against surprise. We were short of arms, and Dr. Livingstone sent us up four guns, some cartridges, and a couple of rockets. This was the state of things existing when I arrived at Magomero.

When I entered the gate, the little enclosure seemed swarming with life; children were running about, and men and women seemed everywhere occupied.

Close to the entrance, on the right, a large house was in course of erection; it was but the skeleton of a house, and from the ribs of this skeleton emerged the Bishop, who gave me a reception as hearty and as affectionate as the soul of man could desire. Scudamore came forward, axe in hand ; he had been felling trees, and it did me good to see his bronzed and pleasant face. Procter was at work in the house, but looking far from well. Waller I saw lower down, surrounded by a crowd of people, and from him and from all I received so hearty a welcome, that I felt I was among brethren indeed.

The chief, Chigunda, came up and shook hands. He was a mild, intelligent-looking man, but had a very nerveless mouth. He was neither old, tall, nor stout, but about thirty years of age, of middle height, and spare in habit. His appearance altogether was prepossessing.

When I had seen and experienced all this, and paid my men, fever again made itself felt. I was obliged to lie down in the Bishop's hut, which was of such limited capacity that I could not stretch myself out at full length without having my feet outside the door.

CHAPTER VII.

AT MAGOMERO.

I ARRIVED at Magomero at an important moment, for most of the chiefs of the country about us had arrived also. Their object was to solicit our help against the Ajawa. Ever since Dr. Livingstone had left, deputation after deputation had been to the Bishop for the same purpose. The English had declared themselves to be friends of the Manganja; they had driven the Ajawa away at one place, and they did not understand that we could have any difficulty in helping them again, finishing, in fact, the work begun. They could make no distinction between English and English; could not see, especially as there were with us some of those engaged in the conflict with the Ajawa, that what was right for one Englishman was wrong for another. Other bodies of Ajawa were in the neighbourhood, who were doing exactly what those driven away had done, and it was natural for the Manganja to come and ask us to do to them what had been done to the others. Dr. Livingstone, when asked by Bishop Mackenzie whether he thought it possible that circumstances could arise which would necessitate our going to fight, had said, 'No; you will be oppressed with requests, but don't go.' He said this, I have no doubt, under the idea that what had been done would be sufficient. He knew not that other bodies of Ajawa were about us, doing just as those had done whose camp he destroyed. We, however, felt sure that unless we interfered to prevent it, the whole country would be devastated, that we should not be able to occupy the position he had chosen for us, nor save from death or slavery those he had given to our care; and from what he had told us, we could not regard the strife about us as an ordinary tribal war, for he had said that the Ajawa had left their own country in order to enslave the Manganja for the Portuguese. With this impression, and with the additional knowledge we had gained, we thought that good cause did not exist for our interference. And I think few people in our place, however much they might regret the necessity, would have thought that the course we adopted was not necessitated by the position in which we were placed, and by the action that had already been taken. It is true we accepted that position of our own free will, well knowing what it might entail, and no one, therefore, but ourselves can be held responsible for our actions.

The chiefs were assembled close to the Bishop's hut. Chinsunzi and Kankomba were there. They were the two greatest men in the land; in position, only next to Mankokwe; in actual power on the hills, superior to him. On the right sat Chinsunzi alone; on the left sat Kankomba alone; in front of all squatted Chigunda, and he acted as spokesman. Behind these illustrious three, sat about a hundred and fifty others, most of them men having authority—the governing body of the Hill Manganja, in fact. The Bishop, and those with him, sat on a mat facing this imposing assemblage, and William acted as interpreter and spokesman.

There was much deference paid by the subordinates to the

two great chiefs. They themselves said but little, the subordinates much. One after the other got up, and after bowing reverently to their great men, commenced their orations by saying, 'I follow my lord Chinsunzi,' or Kankomba, as the case might be. They were encouraged in their speeches by a regular chorus of ejaculations, now high, now low, now long. When each had done, Chigunda repeated what had been said, commencing with 'Arti' (he says), and his faithfulness in repetition was rewarded by approving remarks. All speeches were uttered in a high-pitched voice, intoned—in fact, for they intone all their speeches and prayers. The purport of all the orations was to enlist the sympathy and the aid of the English against the Ajawa. They pictured the happy state of the country before the Ajawa came, its misery and desolation now they were here. They spoke of villages burnt, of brethren slain, of wives and children carried away; and they concluded by describing the happy state of things that would again exist, if the English would only help them against their cruel enemies.

No other assemblage in the world could have been more decorous or better ordered. Savages these people were not, whatever else they might be, and their oratorical powers were considerable. I could not understand what they said, but I felt it, for action and voice portrayed almost everything they wanted to make known.

After hearing all they had to say, the Bishop told them that in three days he would give them an answer.

From all we could learn, the Manganja appeared to be suffering from want of union among themselves; they seemed to have no real patriotism. This arose principally from the fact of their being a purely agricultural people, and broken up into inconsiderable sections. Small villages were dotted here and there over the country, each village had its head man, and each little community in course of time cared for itself only. They had no great principle to be a bond of union among them, and so when the enemy came, village after village was destroyed in detail, for rarely did they unite in sufficient numbers to repel the invaders. Each cared but little for what befel his neighbour, so long as he himself remained unmolested. But now they expressed themselves willing to unite for the common good, if the English would be their leaders; because, said they, no one could be jealous of them, they were so great and powerful.

Of Chinsunzi we felt little could be hoped; he was an old man, not destitute cf mental vigour, but his physical power was gone. But Kankomba looked like a man that might be made very useful; he was about forty years of age, had a frank, open countenance, and a good head, and was altogether a very manly-looking fellow.

On Sunday, the second day after the gathering of the chiefs, we, after partaking of the Holy Communion, took counsel together upon the answer we should give on the morrow. We all felt the gravity of the occasion; we all felt the extraordinary position in which we should put ourselves with the Church at home, if we consented to go against the Ajawa. But we also felt that the circumstances of our position were so extraordinary, that we were warranted in giving the Manganja aid; and we unanimously resolved, that if they would agree to certain conditions, we would aid them. And in coming to that resolution, we had but one object in view, the promotion of the honour and glory of God in that land.

About two o'clock in the afternoon of the next day, Chinsunzi, Kankomba, and a long train of worthies made their appearance, in order to hear our decision. Before we went out to them, we reconsidered the conditions we were going to propose to them, and then engaged in prayer that God would prevent all that was not in accordance with His will, would guide us aright in this and all our actions, and that He would promote the knowledge of Himself and of His Christ among the people to whom His providence had guided us.

When we appeared, all arose and saluted us with bowed bodies and hand-clapping. This time it was we who had to talk, and so the conference was less lengthy. William, who seemed master of the Manganja tongue, acted as interpreter, as before.

After an exordium, wherein the chiefs were told that all their sorrow of heart and misery came upon them in consequence of the slave trade, in which they had been as guilty as the Ajawa, we said we would help them, if they agreed to the conditions we were about to propose.

Kankomba, on behalf of the rest, said they would listen to the Bishop's words, and if they were good they would agree to them.

The Bishop therefore proposed—

I. That all the chiefs then present should solemnly promise, on behalf of themselves and people, that they would never buy or sell men, women, and children again.

After some silence a deep 'Aye' came from the assembly, and Kankomba said the words were good words—that they all agreed to them.

The Bishop then proposed—

II. That all captives found with the Ajawa should be perfectly free; that no chief or person should claim any one of them; but that all should have liberty to go to whom they liked, and where they liked.

These words also were said to be good, and were agreed to.

Before putting the third condition, the Bishop told them that one of the objects of our being in their land was to put an end to the slave trade, and we could not look upon those who engaged in it as our friends; and then he proposed—

III. That all the chiefs present promise that they will unite to punish any chief who sells his own people or the people of any other chief, and that each chief will punish any of his own people found guilty of buying or selling men, women, and children for slaves.

To this condition they all bound themselves. And then was promulgated condition

IV. That if any Portuguese or other foreign slavers came into the land they would drive them away, or at once let us know of their presence.

And all said 'Aye' to this.

All then stood up, and again solemnly bound themselves by the conditions we proposed. After which the Bishop told them that we would help them against the Ajawa, because after their promises to us we felt we should be doing that which was right, for we should help them against wicked men, who for a long time had been doing things which God our Heavenly Father hated, and we felt sure that God would be with us, and give us the victory. It was then arranged that we should all meet at Chinsunzi's the next day, and that we should go against the Ajawa the day after.

We were deeply sensible that we had bound ourselves to do a very awful thing; but we all felt that the circumstances in which we were placed justified our doing it, whatever might be thought of our conduct at home, where law and order were maintained by a regularly constituted and efficient executive. We all felt that it was more christian to succour the distressed than merely to defend ourselves; more prudent to make an attack upon our station impossible, than to wait quietly until we were attacked, and those we had had taken under our care placed in imminent peril. At no one moment did we forget our character as Christian missionaries, and we did not see, under all the circumstances, that that which we proposed to do was inconsistent with that character.

It was arranged that Procter, Gamble, and William should stay at the station, in order to take care of the freed people and the "stuff."

August 13.—Before we set off on our march to Chinsunzi's, the Bishop gave to Chigunda a present for the huts, six in number, which he had made over to us. Part of this present consisted of a magnificent mantle of red cotton velvet. When we started, Chigunda arrayed himself in this royal apparel, and marched at our head with the gait of a hero; but this heroism was only in his gait, for we had not gone more than five miles out of the fourteen we had to march, when he was missing, and could nowhere be found. Upon enquiry, a lame story was told by Zachuracami, his head man, about his coming on to Chinsunzi's in the morning. We did not believe this, and mentally wrote 'coward' against Chigunda's name ever after. Zachuracami, however, came on, and with him all the men Chigunda could muster. Our path lay over a fertile, well wooded plain, thickly studded with villages, and directly towards Zomba.

We were the first to arrive at Chinsunzi's. The village was larger than Mongazi's, and well built. It was deserted, and looked desolate. A few pigeons flew about the empty huts, and a solitary goat bleated miserably; but not a single human being was to be seen. We had not been in long, however, before Chinsunzi appeared. He explained that all the women and children were in hiding, and had been for some time, and that his men were scattered about, but would all be in before nightfall. He then went away, after showing us to his own hut, the largest and most commodious African habitation I had seen, it was fully twenty-five feet in diameter; but he soon returned with a couple of women to get water, &c., for our use; and the goat was given to us, and slaughtered for our dinner and breakfast.

A party of Kankomba's men was the first of the native force to arrive, but the chief came not. Other bands soon followed, so that by sunset at least five hundred men were encamped in the village. About fifteen of them had guns, but none had ammunition. The guns were serviceable; one or two had the elephant, the East India Company's mark, on them; others had evidently come from the Tower, G.R. and the crown showing their British origin. These guns had been brought into the country by the slave-traders, who buy up our old government stores.

It was a strange sight to see those dusky fellows, looking outwardly very like warriors, with their warlike head-gear, their guns and spears and bows and arrows; and had they felt like warriors, they would have been sufficient for their own protection against any number of men the Ajawa could bring against them; but it was all outside show, they were a timid race, and seemed to take delight in exciting their fears by telling each other unfounded stories of the prowess of the Ajawa; and we were informed that Mutukulu, the great war chief of the Ajawa, had arrived with large reinforcements at the camp only the day before.

As Kankomba did not appear, we sent for Chinsunzi, who

was all activity among his men, to enquire the reason; when, to our astonishment, we learnt that it was not the custom of the Manganja chiefs to go to the battle themselves, and that he, Chinsunzi, would not accompany us on the morrow; but he, as Kankomba had done, would send his son and a deputy. He fetched the deputy, and he pleased us; he looked a brave, resolute man.

Chinsunzi wished us to start at midnight, saying if we waited till morning all the Ajawa men would be away plundering, and none but women and children would be found. We

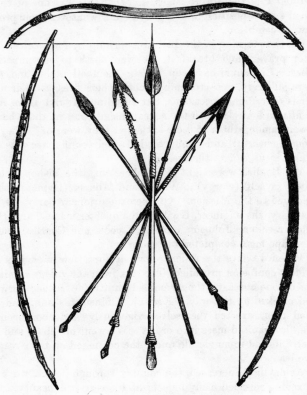

MANGANJA BOWS AND SPEARS

were not at all disposed to listen to this suggestion, and so told him that we should not march until the morning.

Before I lay down for the night I went out into the village; more men had come in, more were coming; every precaution had been taken to keep our expedition secret, and the Ajawa were not thought to know of it; and though so many hundreds were in the village, no noise was made, they sat round their fires in silence, or only spoke in whispers.

I felt, we all felt that night, that it was a terrible thing to be armed as we were against our fellow-creatures, and yet we also felt that there were times, and that this was one of them, when such a position was right for all, whatever their profession or condition.

On the morning of the 14th we were up by four o'clock, and after prayers and breakfast, we went forth to our impatient allies. Chinsunzi had been among them all night, and they were all ready, not crouching round their fires, as their manner is on ordinary occasions, but standing around them forty or fifty in a circle, with their weapons of war in their hands. I went among them to see what spirit they were of. They all seemed cheerful and confident, but their confidence was evidently in us, not in themselves.

We English were eight in number; viz., the Bishop, Scudamore, myself (clergy); Waller and Adams (laymen), these belonged to the Mission. Of the expeditionary party, we had Hardisty, the engineer, Gwillim, the quarter-master, and Hutchins, a sailor; Johnson, our black cook, and Charles, one of the Cape men, completed our party.

When we gave the order to march for a few moments the wildest confusion prevailed. The exit from the village admitted but of one abreast; the assembled multitude rushed forward and blocked up the way. Kapanji, Chinsunzi's son, and the head man, exerted themselves vigorously, and soon brought the disorganised mass into order. We went out first, and the rest followed in single file under the command of their respective leaders.

As daylight increased, the country through which we were marching revealed many objects of interest and beauty. We

were going directly towards Mount Zomba, for the Ajawa
camp was at the foot of its southern face; consequently we
had to ascend for some distance. After we had been marching about an hour, we caught a glimpse of Lake Shirwa, and a
beautiful glimpse it was. The sun was up, and its waters glis-
tened in the early morning glory. For the moment this sight
of the lake made me feel sad, it seemed to speak so forcibly of
the love of the Creator in all His works. I had looked forward to seeing this lake as to one of the pleasures the land
would afford, but I had not dreamt of beholding it under such
circumstances as I was then in. I felt, however, that, painful
as it was, we were doing our duty, that our object was the
glory of God and the good of man, and soon regained equanimity.

As we went along, other parties of Manganja, who were
waiting on the roadside, joined us. Indeed, one old chief,
Kakarara Kabana, brought in this way more than two hundred men, and he marched at their head on to the field. We
were now more than a thousand strong, and our line extended
more than a mile. All marched in perfect silence. If one
ventured to speak, a low whistle passed from man to man until
it reached the offender and silenced him. About eight o'clock
we halted at the foot of some hills from which Kapanji, who
had been as a spy into the camp, said we could see the position and strength of the Ajawa.

I should mention here that the Bishop had resolved to seek
a conference with the Ajawa chiefs in order to induce them to
leave the country peaceably. And so, before ascending this
hill, he called all the Christians around him, and we knelt
down, and he offered up prayer to God that He would be
with us in what we were about to do, that He would incline
the Ajawa to go away peaceably; if not, that He would protect us and give us the victory, and that He would, for Christ's
sake, forgive the sins of those who might fall that day, whether
white or black, friend or foe.

I did not go up this hill, for I thought it would be better
for one of us to remain with the Manganja and keep them in
the order in which they arrived. From the position which I

occupied I could see the ruins of several villages that had
lately been destroyed by the Ajawa; and I could see more
than that, for, stretching before me for miles, was a pleasant
valley, bordered on either side by mountains; and all looked
so beautiful, so peaceful, that for a time I was carried beyond
myself, beyond the impending event, and in imagination I peopled that valley with a happy people, and fancied the hills
echoing to the voice of prayer and thanksgiving from numerous Christian communities.

It was nearly an hour before the Bishop and party returned.
They had had a good view of the Ajawa camp; it was very
large, but in a good position for us to attack, should we find
it needful to do so.

We resumed our march, and in about an hour found ourselves
on a hill just over the encampment, which then proved more
extensive than it had appeared from the hill of observation.
Right in front of us was Mount Zomba. In the valley between us and it were the Ajawa. Their many groups of
roughly-built huts apparently stretched along the entire face
of the mountain. The principal village, where the chiefs resided, lay to the left of us. Their strongest position was a
hill about 200 feet high, which lay opposite to us. How far
their encampment extended to the right, and what their force
was in that direction, we could not tell. It was evident to us
that if we could gain possession of the hill before us, we should
have no difficulty in driving them right off the field.

We were soon seen by them, though our real force could not
have been known, as the main body of the Manganja were some
distance in the rear. As soon as they saw us they uttered their
war cry, and such a horrid ringing of voices I hope never to
hear again. Crowds of people from all quarters ran towards
the left, where the chiefs lived, or took up their position on
the top and sides of the hill before mentioned; while others,
we could see, dispersed themselves in the bush lying between
us and them. It seemed to me that we had come upon a nest
of hornets, and stood a chance of being well stung before we
could get rid of them.

Notwithstanding these warlike manifestations, the Bishop

and Waller, accompanied by Charles, who acted as interpreter, descended to the camp unarmed, and went towards the chiefs' quarter. They promised to keep in sight of two of our party who stationed themselves on a rock to our right, which commanded an extensive view of the valley. It was arranged that if their parley was successful, Waller should hold out a white handkerchief, when we should remain where we were; but if the Ajawa would not listen to us and would have war, he would hold out a red handkerchief, and we were to advance at once.

The hill on which we were was flanked on either side by hills of greater altitude, and their sides, especially that on our left, were rugged with loose masses of rock, behind which a few men might make a great slaughter of an advancing enemy. The path taken by the Bishop and Waller, instead of leading directly down into the valley, ran round the hill on our right, and we quickly lost sight of them. They were, we afterwards learnt, met by four men, two armed with guns, the others with bows and arrows. The Bishop called to them, and said that he had come down because he wished to have a peaceable talk with their chiefs, and desired them to be fetched to him. This they refused to do, and asked what sort of white men the Bishop and Waller were. On being told they were English, they said they would have nothing to do with the English, for the English were their enemies, and had helped the Manganja against them a few days before (alluding to the conflict with Dr. Livingstone), and they came forward as though intending to attack. The Bishop, on seeing this, held up his hands, to show them that he was without weapons, and bade them stay where they were, and, strange to say, they did, and waited to hear what else he had to say. He told them again that he came with a message of peace, but if they would not listen to it, it would be war, and he again desired them to call their chiefs, but the chiefs answered for themselves, for a cry came from their quarters, 'Shoot them, don't listen to them!' So finding further effort for peace useless, the Bishop and Waller and Charles, returned, followed closely for some distance by the four men with whom they had been talking, and expecting every moment to have a bullet or an arrow in their backs, for they were quite within the power of these men.

They had been absent about a quarter of an hour. I cannot express the intense anxiety of that brief period, nor the relief it was to all when we saw them safely back, though the first words, uttered by Waller, were these, 'It is war! they will not have peace! they will have nothing but war with us.' I felt, however, that the great danger of the day was safely passed.

Waller was made our captain, and he saw the great advantage which might arise if a body of men were sent round into the valley behind the hill to our right. So he despatched Gwillim and Hutchins, with old Kakarara Kabana and his men, in that direction, and waited a few minutes before we advanced, in order to give them time to get fairly round.

What a strange thing the human mind is! The Bishop and Waller having returned in safety, I was in no anxiety as to the issue of the day, though I knew that a few seconds would bring me within range of the guns of the Ajawa. A curiously formed and beautifully marked insect alighted on my hand as we were waiting the appointed moment to move on, and I was unfeignedly admiring it, when Waller called upon us to advance. Instantly the Manganja set up their war-cry, a hideous noise truly, but feebleness itself compared with that of the Ajawa.

Going down the hill was exciting work; I fully expected to be shot at from behind the rocks I have mentioned, but the Ajawa had not seized the only good opportunity they had of doing us much harm, and we reached the valley without molestation. We who were in front—and the Manganja adopted the motto of 'After you, sirs'—turned to the right towards a small village, and before we arrived at it were shot at with guns by men secreted in the grass. When we replied, they retreated. The village was deserted, and it was at once fired. The way to the hill, which seemed to be the key of the whole position, was by the left, and the Bishop, myself, Adams, Charles and Johnson struck into a path in that direction, and were fired at from either side, and several bullets whizzed by

rather closer to us than was agreeable. Those who fired, however, did not long maintain their ground; a few shots and they
retreated: we scarcely caught a glimpse of them, for they
slunk through the long grass like snakes. We went some
distance, but finding no Manganja following us, the Bishop
desired me to go back and bring on a large body of men who
were in our rear, shouting in a very warlike way, but only
shouting. I sent on Kapanji with his men to the Bishop, and
they moved readily forward, for they saw the Ajawa were
retreating. I reached the remainder of the shouters and was
going on with them, when to my surprise I saw Gwillim
coming towards me: he was alone. He said that he and
Hutchins with their men went round the hill as directed, and
when descending into the valley met a large body of Ajawa
coming up, who probably intended to attack us in the rear.
A fight ensued, and in the confusion, before the Ajawa retreated, Hutchins disappeared. Gwillim thought him wounded
or killed, and begged me to help in searching for him. I went
back with Gwillim for a short distance, but when up the hill
I heard the crack of a rifle, and repeated shots from a revolver in the direction which Gwillim said the Ajawa he had
encountered retreated, and some of the Manganja with us
pointed in the same direction, and said 'Anglesi, Kakarara
Kabana,' and so we concluded that the fears about Hutchins
were unfounded, and that he was following up the retreating
Ajawa.

I returned at once, in order to rejoin the Bishop. But there
was work for us to do where we were. Some Ajawa were
right in our path; they fired at us, we fired at them, and they
retreated towards the hill I have mentioned as being the
strongest point they had. This hill was about 500 yards from
where we were standing; it was then crowded with men. I
knew the Bishop's intention was to attack it, and the quartermaster suggested to me that it would be as well if we tried to
clear it for him. He had an Enfield rifle, and handed it to me.
I sighted it for 600 yards, and sent a bullet flying over the
heads of those on the hill. Their astonishment was intense,
they ran about and crouched down on the ground; they had

seen me aiming at them, but flinched not, not conceiving our
guns could carry so far; another shot lower down and they
took to their heels. In a few seconds not a man remained on
the hill; they took the road the main body of fugitives had
taken, towards Lake Shirwa.

Immediately after this I saw the Bishop and his followers
ascend the hill, pass over it, and follow on the track of the
runaways. I made signs to the natives with us that I wished
to join the Bishop, and we struck into a path that seemed
likely to take us to him. But the fire from the first village and
from others had spread, and was spreading rapidly in all directions. Again and again we had to alter our course, for the
bush was ablaze. We could not get on to the Bishop's track,
so we struck into another direction which had not been scoured,
and sent some Ajawa flying before us. A wild fear had seized
the Ajawa; they were all in full retreat; and though now and
then some of their principal men, who were armed with guns,
turned and fired, they offered no further resistance. We went
on for some distance until we came upon some low hills, and
then we halted, hoping to see something of our companions.
But nothing could be seen. The air was black with smoke,
for the fire had spread all over the plain, and surrounded us.
Such a sight I had never seen before, and trust may never see
again. It was only by remembering the atrocious conduct of
the Ajawa, which for the time being had placed them almost
beyond the pale of pity, that I could keep myself from feeling
soul-sick at the scene before me.

Soon after this I fell in with Waller and Johnson at the
head of a band of Manganja. Waller, Scudamore, and
Hardisty had joined the Bishop after I had left him, had
together taken and destroyed the chief's quarters, and then
each had put himself at the head of a number of Manganja
and had done what seemed best to clear the plain.

Shortly afterwards we saw a white man coming towards us
followed by a number of natives; it was Scudamore and his
allies. He reported all in retreat before him. He could give
us no information of the Bishop, but some natives made us
understand they had seen him and the rest of the English but.

a short time before, and that they were taking a road which would lead them back to Chinsunzi's. We waited some time. All signs of the conflict, except the bush burning on the hills, had ceased. The day was advancing. It began to rain heavily, and other natives coming up and confirming the report of the Bishop having been seen going towards Chinsunzi's, we resolved to return also.

It was a wearisome walk, and when we arrived at the village we found to our chagrin we were the first back. Hardisty and Hutchins, however, soon made their appearance, and reported the Bishop close at hand, with a number of people he had rescued from the Ajawa. Adams and Charles were with him, and soon after he came in. A little child that had been thrown into the bush was in his arms, and a crowd of captives, women and children, with him. He had been upon the track of the main body of the retreating Ajawa, and it was thus these people came into his hands.

It was a great comfort to us in the morning, when we were on our way to the camp, to feel that none of our friends at home knew of the danger we were about to incur ; and it was a greater comfort in the evening, when all were reassembled, to find that when they did hear, it would be accompanied with the intelligence that none of us were hurt by it.

It was eight o'clock when we, after prayer and thanksgiving, sat down to dinner, having been without food since four o'clock in the morning, and marched at least thirty-five miles. After dinner, the Bishop, who never tired while anything was to be done, went out to see to the comfort of the people he had brought in. We fed them before we fed ourselves; but he could not rest until he knew they were all properly housed for the night. When he returned he brought a little child in with him, a boy about six years of age. This little fellow was found at the door of a hut, and was so ill that the Manganja shook their heads when the Bishop desired them to bring him along, saying it was no good, for death had laid hold of him. However, the Bishop made a man carry him home ; but he was evidently dying. He was a Manganja child, a captive probably, who when taken ill had been left to starve and die. He was fearfully emaciated. Life was evidently fast ebbing away. We tried to rouse him by forcing a little brandy down his throat, but it failed to produce any but a momentary effect. Seeing this, the Bishop decided upon baptizing him. Scudamore and I acted as witnesses, and this poor child, the first of his race, under the name of Charles Henry, was numbered among the children of God, and in two hours afterwards his spirit fled to that dear Lord who had redeemed it.

This was a blessed conclusion to the work of the day, and when I at last lay down to rest, my heart was so full I could only find relief in tears.

When I awoke in the morning the first thing I heard was the voice of a babe who could just prattle, and who during the night had, by accident or intention, been shut out of, a hut. Waller heard its plaintive cry, fetched it in, and made it happy for the night under his rug. And there it was chatting away to him by the side of the fire, and not at all afraid.

After breakfast all the people that had been taken either by the Bishop or others were assembled in front of our hut. Chinsunzi and a great many Manganja were present.

The Bishop opened the proceedings by saying that all had agreed that the captives found with the Ajawa should be at liberty to go where they pleased, and he was now going to give them that liberty. Some of the Manganja, however, told us that among those who had been brought off the field were many Ajawa people, who instead of being released had been made captive. In making our conditions we had not dreamt of making captives, so we had made no stipulation respecting those whom we now found in that position. But the Bishop soon decided what to do.

First, he inquired if there were any Manganja who had been made captive by the Ajawa, and about a dozen women and as many children stood up. Most of them had friends or relatives then present; and they were told that they might go to their friends. The said friends and relatives had been very impatient, and urged their claims to some of the said women and children, and their interference had been checked by us with a sternness that astonished them not a little. We had resolved that those released should be perfectly free to choose for themselves; and when they made their choice, it was a happy sight to see the reunion of a brother with a sister, a husband with a wife, a father with his children. It repaid us for all we had done for them.

One woman present had been taken with two others. These latter had been killed; her father and her husband had been killed also, but her old chief, a mild looking man, was present, and so she went to him. Before allowing her to do so, we made him promise that he would treat her and her three children kindly, and would not sell them.

Then we divided the remainder into two parties—those who were Ajawa, and those who, though not Manganja, had been made captive by the Ajawa. It then appeared that there were about forty Ajawa women and children, and that the rest, about twenty-five, belonged to the Anguru, a tribe belonging to the neighbourhood of Lake Shirwa, who had been living in Manganja villages, and were thus made captive. To them we gave the same liberty of choice that we had given to the Manganja, and they all found friends among those present. We told them that if those with whom they had elected to live did not treat them kindly, they were to come to us at Magomero, and we would protect them.

Then the Ajawa people had to be disposed of. They were all women and children, and we gave them no choice. They had no home to which they could at that moment return; it was not prudent to leave them with the Manganja, who might have illused them, so we resolved to take them with us to Magomero, keep them for a time, until their fear of us had worn away and they could understand our true feeling towards them, and then send them as ambassadors of friendship back to their own people. We told the Manganja we should do this, and they said, 'Very good.'

After all this was settled I prepared the body of the dead child for burial. The preparations were simple enough. I wrapped it up in some calico, and then tied it up in a sleeping mat. A grave had been dug outside the village. Johnson and Charles carried it to the grave, Scudamore and I followed,

the Bishop said the burial service, and then we left it in the
sure and certain hope of a joyful resurrection.

It was nearly two o'clock before we were ready to return to
Magomero.   Our march home was an anxious and a slow pro-

PORTRAIT OF DAUMA, THE CHILD CARRIED BY THE BISHOP.

ceeding.   We hired men to carry the small children, but some
of the women were lame.   For one little thing (a girl named
Dauma) we could find no carrier, so after she had trudged
along some distance the Bishop shouldered her and carried her
into Magomero.   It was dark before we arrived.

In words written on the spot—for I merely adapt my journal
—I have thus described that event which produced so much
disapprobation from many who are justly ranked among our
wisest and best friends.   I was not greatly surprised when I
heard they had condemned this act.   All things considered, it
would have been strange if they had not condemned it.   They
were perfectly right *in the abstract*, but we had not abstract
circumstances to deal with, and abstract principles were not,

in our estimation, at all sufficient for the emergency of our position; and I feel certain that had those who condemned us been with us, they would have done just as we did. We felt as strongly as they the horror of taking up arms against a fellow creature, but we could no more resist doing what we did than they, if no other aid was at hand, could resist felling to the earth—supposing them to have the power—the wretch they found beating to death a woman or a child. If Africa is to be Christianised, a large, a very large, discretion must be given to those who undertake the work. No greater mistake can be made than to suppose that men who go out there can, at all times, act as though they possessed all the appliances of civilisation and Christianity, or as though the antecedents of the natives were like our own.

VARIOUS KINDS OF ARROWS USED BY MANGANJA AND AJAWA.

I have frequently been asked if we, in this contest with the

Ajawa, killed many. Unhesitatingly I say, No. I should doubt if more than five were killed, and they certainly not by our guns ; the Manganja caught a body of Ajawa in retreat, and some fell under their arrows. When they found our guns carried so far, a superstitious fear came upon them, and they retreated at once. By what we did I have no doubt we saved, for a time, many hundreds from death or slavery, for after these events no slave-trader came within many miles of our station.

CHAPTER VIII.

EARLY DAYS AT MAGOMERO.

AFTER the events recorded in preceding pages, we found ourselves the fathers of a large family ; we had with us nearly two hundred people, mostly women and children. They regarded us as their preservers, their fathers ; we regarded them as our children, as those whom God had given to us, in order that we might first of all convert them to Christ, and then, through their instrumentality, Christianise the people around. We hailed the deliverance we had been able to effect for them as a promise of that higher and spiritual deliverance which we trusted God would vouchsafe to them through our instrumentality.

Next morning the Bishop assembled all the Ajawa we had brought in, and repeated his reasons for not leaving them at Chinsunzi's. They said they would sooner be with us than with the Manganja ; and the Bishop told them that after they had been with us a short time, and knew us better than they then did, they should be allowed to go away or stay, as they pleased.

They were very badly off for raiment—indeed many of the women were not decent, even according to the native notion of decency ; so we gave to each woman a length of cloth, and made all the children presentable. They were quite dumbfounded by this liberality. They without doubt at first regarded us as a very terrible set of men, cannibals, maybe, for we discovered that notion did prevail with regard to us; and they found us feeding them, carrying their babes, speaking words of kindness to them, and clothing them. But their surprise was increased when Waller—who happily knew a little of surgery, and who then acted as our doctor—called to him those who were ill (as many of them were suffering from grievous ulcers), and washed and dressed their poor diseased bodies.

The Bishop appointed me to take care of the stores, to buy food, and to distribute food to all those dependent upon us. My charge was not small, for I had a large family to provide for and satisfy.

Provisions, however, were plentiful, and when the Manganja found we wished to buy, they were very willing to sell. That part of the highlands in which we were was a lean land with regard to animal food. The increase of population had driven away the wild animals, and the only domestic animals the Manganja had were a few—a very few—black-haired fat-tailed sheep, some goats and fowls.

We were much disappointed at the absence of game in the district in which we lived. I am not aware of any definite statement which warranted us in thinking that wild animals abounded on the Shire highlands, yet everyone at home imagined they did because none of the communications from Dr. Livingstone had distinctly said they did not. So much had been said of the abundance of animal life in other parts of Africa, that it was inferred, from the absence of all statement to the contrary, that the Shire highlands were as bountifully supplied; and it was thought that we missionaries would be able to supply ourselves readily and without stint with flesh of buffalo and buck. But the vast plains covered with deer, the herds of eland, buffalo, and gnu, which we dreamed would be always in reach of our rifles, we never found. Near to the coast, water-buck and other kinds of deer are to be met with; in the Lower Shire Valley, they, and buffalo, are also to be found, but the character of the ground makes hunting for most parts of the year impossible; and in the Upper Shire Valley, where hunting is practicable, many animals, I believe, are to be met with—but on the highlands, as far as we were acquainted with them, they were not. One unfortunate eland strayed down to the neighbourhood of Magomero, from the Lake Regions probably, and a whole army of natives turned out after it. This was all the large game that came within our reach while on the hills, so that the missionary who trusted to his gun for food would stand a good chance of starving. Of course, wherever the population is great the wild animals are scarce. The great want of the tribes we met with was cattle, large and small. Without oxen and sheep it is not possible for any number of Europeans to live long in that land in which we were, for a dozen flesh-eaters would soon exhaust the supply of native goats and sheep in a large district. If introduced I have no doubt that cattle of all kinds would thrive.

The natives grew several kinds of corn, the principal of which was the maize, or Indian corn; indeed that was their staff of life: and it was a famous country for yams and sweet potatoes, and, in their season, peas and beans, cassava and pumpkin. Unlike the people on the Shire, those about us did not haggle, they took what we offered without question. I was careful to fix a fair price for everything, and though I gave much less for things generally than had been given on the Shire, the people seemed satisfied, for supplies increased, and it was a pleasant sight to see the continual influx of people during the day to our little peninsula, bearing on their heads baskets of meal, or whatever else in the way of vegetable food they had for sale; or carrying fowls or driving a goat before them. I was kept at this work for hours every day. For a goat or a sheep I gave as much cloth as they had been in the habit of receiving for a man or a woman; a fathom, or two yards; for ten fowls, the same price; and when they found we wanted eggs, they brought them to us literally by the peck; they don't as a rule eat eggs themselves, they seemed to have a superstition about it, and they did not at first understand we wanted our eggs fresh; so, though the poor hen had been sitting nineteen days out of twenty-one on her nest, she was driven away, and the eggs were brought to us, chicks

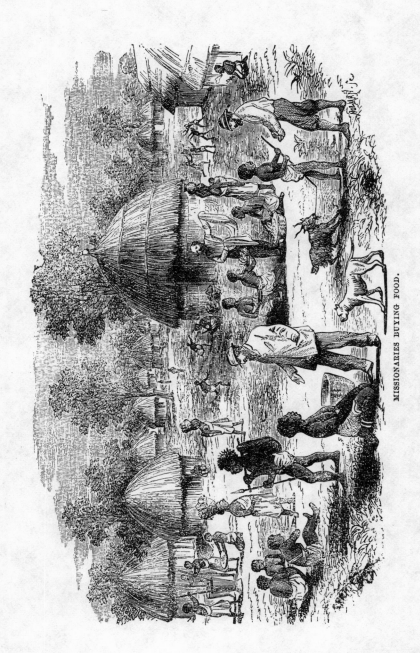

MISSIONARIES BUYING FOOD.

though they contained; and one man, when I pointed that fact out to him, seemed to think, like the Irishman, that I should pay something more for them, because they were already meat.

To all those people who came to us with food we told our object in visiting them. At first they were very suspicious of us; the women were much afraid, would keep outside the stockade, and send some of their. male friends in with their barter; but gradually they acquired confidence, two or three would come in together, leaving their babies outside, and then they brought the babies in also, and at last when they saw that our deeds answered to our words, that our objects were really good, the distrust and suspicion they had of us vanished : they came to us in perfect confidence; even their little children, who were at first horrified when they saw us, lost their fears, and came up to us without hesitation or fear. Indeed we soon found that the land was open to us; go where we would we were cordially welcomed and hospitably entertained.

At sunset—to continue the food question—all the adults under our charge assembled, and I distributed to them a certain measure of meal, or an equivalent in something else. The children had their food cooked for them by an excellent and motherly woman, one released from the slavers, named Jessiwiranga, and twice a day they assembled for food, and I superintended their feeding.

The Bishop soon inaugurated a regular system of work for all. Houses had to be built, ground to be cultivated, our people had to be taught, the language acquired, and the many chiefs who daily came to see us, received. There was occupation for all, and every man's capacity was tried to the uttermost; and with the exception of the man we had brought out with us as a carpenter, and who proved to be no carpenter, nor anything else that was of much use to us, every man's capacity seemed equal to the occasion. We were up at sunrise. At seven we had morning prayer, at eight breakfast. Immediately after this the whole of our people were assembled; the roll of their names called over; and to all who could work was assigned their day's employment. Some went to clear the

ground for cultivation on the north side of us, over the river.
These went under the charge of Charles or William. Others
to cut wood, bamboo, and grass, for building. The boys were
drilled by Scudamore, then broken up into classes for instruction, all the clergy taking a class. I was too busy with my
bartering to be able to take my class at first, so the Bishop
used to take it for me ; it consisted of the smallest children,
and for an hour or more every day he would sit under a tree
with them, trying to make them understand the difference in
form and sound between A and B, &c. Waller was surgeon,
a distressing post, besides superintendent generally of all
secular work, and his hands were quite full. At one we dined;
between two and three we had classes for adults : I generally
managed to be at these, for the principal part of my dealings
with the natives was over by this time. At three we went to
other occupations, getting up the language, visiting the people
about us, or working at our houses, &c. At six, the time for
relaxation, we had tea, and evening prayer at eight. The Holy
Communion was celebrated on every Sunday morning, and on
all Festivals. After evening prayer we generally made a tour
of our little territory to see that all was well, and then we
retired to our respective huts.

At first we were packed closely, for until we built our own
houses two or three slept in one small hut. The freed people
were not so well accommodated ; there were as many as twenty
boys sleeping in one hut, not more than ten feet in diameter.

The evil of crowding so many people together, in so small
a place as the peninsula we were on, was soon apparent in more
ways than one. It became necessary to separate the sexes.
The Bishop assembled all, and told them that henceforth the
men were to live in huts on one side of the village, the women
on the other. This astonished them not a little, and they
asked if it were the English custom for the women to live away
from the men. They were told that it was not the English
custom for men and women to live as they had been living
until they were married. We regarded all as single, and so
they were told that if any man wished to have any one woman
for his wife, and she was willing to take him for her husband,

he (the Bishop) would have no objection, but they must come
to him first and let him know. A day or two after this, a
young man came to us while we were at dinner. He sat at
the door of the hut, and to our enquiry, said he came to talk:
but he did not talk, we could not get him to talk, it was the
last thing he seemed able to do, but at last he informed us
that he wished to have a certain woman for his wife. Upon
our asking him if she wished to have him for a husband, he
held down his head and softly said: 'She says so.' And there
was no doubt about it, for when he fetched her, she did say
so. And then the Bishop, William acting as his mouthpiece,
spoke to them very gravely upon the duty of husbands towards
their wives, and wives towards their husbands; made the man
promise he would have no other wife, made the woman promise
she would have no other husband; and that they would be
kind and faithful to each other. Then he said they were man
and wife, and pointed out a plot of ground outside the stockade
where he intended the village of the married people to be.
We were now in no fear of the Ajawa, and so were no longer
obliged to keep within our barricades.

Next day five men wished for wives, and appeared with *six*
women. There was no difficulty with three of the pairs, all
their arrangements being satisfactory; but in the fourth
instance the woman refused at the last moment to marry the
man, who then went away, and, to prove he was not such an
undesirable fellow, came back shortly afterwards with two
women, both of whom were anxious to be his wives; in the
fifth case the man did not exactly want to marry the woman
he had brought with him, but wanted to have another. Of
course we did not let the man have two wives, and we made
the other business comfortable for all parties. And after this
marriages became popular until all the men were provided for.
Unfortunately we had more women than men: quarrels therefore occasionally took place; the wives began to get jealous of
their prerogative, and would not allow any to share their
husbands' affections with them, though up to this time they
had been accustomed to the arrangements of polygamy. But
in the end, these people lived happily in that condition we had

brought about, and, as a rule, they were kind and affectionate
to one another, and faithful. It was thus we attempted to lay
the foundation of a Christian community. We commenced,
as will be seen, with first principles of morality; and no one
will deny the primitive nature of the materials we had to deal
with.

We had our difficulties of course, and they came quickly
upon us. Our reputation was great, indeed the position we
had acquired in so short a time seemed marvellous. Chiefs
from all parts of the country came to see us and bring presents. On the morning of August 19, a long train of men,
bearing provisions of every description, came to us from
Mongazi—it was his tribute of respect and gratitude for what
we had done. And as he did, so, in their measure, did almost
all the other chiefs. All things seemed hopeful at this time :
and though we had so large a family to feed, we had no difficulty
in feeding them; provisions were abundant, and so cheap that
we were keeping the whole of our people at the rate of 5*l.* per
week.

But we were not long in seeing that our position entailed
in the estimation of the Manganja further responsibilities.
The ease with which we had driven off the Ajawa, made the
Manganja regard us as the possessors of irresistible power ;
as men who had but to will, and what we willed would be.
We soon discovered that they were a very superstitious people,
great believers in witchcraft and medicine (fetish). They
thought that we possessed a medicine that made us invincible,
if not invulnerable. To illustrate this : Some time after we
had been in the land I was sitting by the side of Mankokwe
(the Rundo); Mr. Dickinson, our doctor, was with me. The
chief became all at once very affectionate, he put his arm
round my neck, and I knew then that he was going to ask me
for something. Said he at last :

' Is that your medicine man ?' pointing to Dickinson.

I assented.

' Ask him to give me your war medicine.'

I laughed heartily, and told him we had no such medicine.
He disbelieved me, and said :

'That is not true; you have, you *must* have, and you do not like to give it me. But do ask him for it.'

'I speak the truth,' said I; 'we English have no other war medicine than a brave heart.'

He would not believe, and thus resumed:

'No, that is not true; it cannot be. I have brave heart too; but what is the good of a brave heart; a brave heart alone is no good. Listen. The Manganja have brave hearts; the Ajawa came into their country; they go to fight the Ajawa, but directly they see them they run away. Why? Not because they have not brave hearts; but because the Ajawa have stronger war medicine than they. Now you have stronger war medicine than the Ajawa; so strong, that if only one Englishman went against the whole of the Ajawa, *they* would all run away. Do give me your war medicine.'

Some such feeling as this, I have no doubt, spread at once through the land with regard to us. If men or women met us in the paths, they would kneel while we passed and say: 'Ah, my master!' or 'Ah, my lord!'

Things that we had with us, of whose nature they were ignorant, were looked upon as possessing a supernatural power. To instance what I mean: Waller and I were once halting on a journey in a village, with a number of the men living under our protection, when we heard them telling the chief of the village of all the wonderful things we had, and of all the wonderful things we could do. Said one man at last:

'Do! there is nothing but what they can do! Look here, chief, suppose a man wished to get away from them and they were not willing that he should go—well, he could not get away, do what he would.'

Said the old chief:

'Why, what would they do? Tie him up to a tree?'

Said the man in reply:

'Tie him up to a tree! No, not they, they would not take that trouble. For supposing he had got away, and was gone so far off that, in the distance, he looked no bigger than a fly, they would only have to put *that* thing up to their eye' (meaning a *telescope*, and imitating the action of raising it to the eye), ' and it would bring him back again quite close to their feet. He could never get away from them.'

The fact is, when you go to a purely unsophisticated people, such as these were, the performance of miracles is no longer a necessity, for if you use rightly such things as our science and skill have given us, the effect upon the heathen mind is nearly as great as though you did perform miracles ; and by the time they have acquired a knowledge of the real value of these things, if you have acted fairly towards them, and have lived Christian lives among them, you will have acquired their confidence and esteem, and anything extraordinary will no longer be needed to give you a position among them. If we sanctified to God's service the means we now have, instead of merely using them to increase wealth at home and multiply possessions abroad, miracles, the secondary aids we have lost, would not be needed. With God's grace and God's word the Church would be able to accomplish a divine work among all people. I do not say we saw all this at once; it came upon us by degrees ; but I mention this here, because it will account for the extraordinary position we so readily acquired. But while recording my deliberate conviction that Christian nations now possess in superior power, and in the gifts and refinements of science and civilization, much that is calculated to gain for the Church the attention of the heathen, I cannot but deeply lament the prevalence of that anti-Christian feeling which seeks to promote the welfare of the heathen by the indirect agency of commerce and civilization, instead of the direct agency of the Church, to promote such things as may lead to the social improvement of the world at large, and is careless of the spiritual well-being of the heathen who have been brought under our rule or within the scope of our influence. No policy can be more perilous than this, none so certain to issue in the loss of that political supremacy which it is supposed to foster. ' All these will I give thee and the glory of them, if Thou wilt fall down and worship me ; if Thou will first do homage to me for them,' said the Tempter to Christ ; ' and all these will I give thee and the glory of them, if you will adopt my plans, if you will listen to my suggestions ?' is he now saying to

Christendom, and unless our answer be that which was given
by our blessed Lord, ruin, and worse than ruin will follow.
The secondary aids which the Church ever possesses, like
miracles of old, must accompany, not precede, the ministrations
of the Church. To put them first, to send them forth disas-
sociated from the sanctifying spirit of the Church, is to make
the same use of them that Simon Magus desired to do of the
extraordinary gifts of the Holy Spirit, to use them on behalf of
the Adversary, and not on behalf of Christ.

When we returned from Chirumba, the place where we
encountered the Ajawa, we hoped we had done with them
whom we then looked upon as a mere horde of plunderers,
who, after the repulses they had received from the English,
would be glad to get back to their own country : we did not
for one moment imagine that they were in great force almost
on all sides of us; but so it proved. First a chief named
Katunga sent us a present of three women taken from the
Ajawa, and begged us to come and drive away a horde of that
people, who had long been encamped on his land, and who had
burnt his village. We did not believe Katunga, for we had
already found out that the Manganja, like the ' Cretans, are
always liars.' And we told the women that they were free to
go wherever they liked. They, seeing people with us whom they
knew, and hearing from them of our kindness, asked if they
might stay with us, and we consented.

Then, on August 18, came a great procession of Manganja,
headed by a second-rate chief named Barwi. They came to
solicit our assistance against another body of Ajawa who were
encamped in another direction. Barwi was a young man, a
great dandy, and immensely vain of his personal appearance.
His hair was wonderfully dressed, and he had many brass or
copper rings on each arm, and on each shin. His village was
near at hand, not more than seven miles off, and close to this
village was said to be a large encampment of blood-thirsting
Ajawa. That a large party of Ajawa should be burning and
destroying within sight of us (for in that country the atmosphere is so thin that distance scarcely impairs vision, only
lessens size), and that Chigunda and other chiefs should not

tell of this, seemed incredible, and we did not believe him. He, however, maintained the truthfulness of his story. And so, to make sure, the Bishop sent Hutchins and the four Makololo we had with us, to see if the Ajawa were where they were said to be. These Makololo had been left behind by Dr. Livingstone, and had asked to remain with us until he returned from Lake Nyassa. On their return, they reported that, having arrived at Barwi's village, he would go no farther that night, and wished them to remain with him till morning. This they refused to do, and went to investigate alone. They saw no signs of war, and nothing of the Ajawa. But two days afterwards Barwi sent a deputy, his brother, who declared that the Ajawa were still there. And he seemed so sincere in what he said, that it was thought best to send Scudamore and others to see what the character and strength of the people said to be Ajawa really were. While he was gone, some of the Ajawa women with us said a large body of their people was settled near Barwi's, but that they had been there a long time, and were peaceable, building villages and making gardens. They also told us that the day before we were at Chirumba, some Portuguese slavers left their camp with a large body of slaves bound for Tete. When Scudamore returned he reported that an Ajawa camp did exist within five miles of Barwi's village. He found that chief had assembled his people, and thought Scudamore was going to lead them to war; and they seemed perfectly confident, if he did that, the Ajawa, who were two or three thousand strong, would at once run away. They were wofully disappointed when they learnt that Scudamore had no such warlike intention. He took a guide and went to the camp. He loitered about until sunset, and then he crawled on his hands and knees so close to the Ajawa that he saw women pounding corn, and others, men and women, sitting and talking within thirty yards of him. The encampment was large, larger than that we had destroyed, and he saw that a number of rude huts—things run up in a day—had just been erected. He inferred from this that a number of the fugitives from Chirumba had joined this camp. There were, however, no signs of war; all things around spoke of peace. And subsequently information convinced us that these Ajawa had been living here for some time on friendly terms with the Manganja. Matrimonial alliances had taken place between them; and though they occupied their present position without the consent of Barwi, still they had been peaceable since. No proof could be given of any recent act of war on their part, and we, therefore, did not feel at all inclined to interfere with them.

I believe no set of men could have realized more fully than we that we were ministers of peace, though we felt it our duty, in order to put down cruel oppression and wrong, to use all the advantages we possessed. We drove away the Ajawa at Chirumba because we believed they had been guilty of wanton atrocity, and in order to relieve captives; but we refused to attack the camp near Barwi because we had no enmity against the Ajawa, as a tribe, and had no intention to interfere in a tribal disagreement.

On August 21 we heard that Chinsunzi was sleeping in the village outside the stockade, and we inferred that his presence would entail the presence of a great many more chiefs on the morrow, and that war, and nothing but war, would prove the cause of their gathering. And our inferences were correct. By mid-day not only Chinsunzi, but Kankomba, Kakarara Kabana, Katunga, and a host of other notabilities were assembled in the rear of the Bishop's hut. They came to urge us to drive away the Ajawa near to Barwi; and in order to induce us to give them a favourable hearing, they had brought us a present—a goat and an Ajawa woman. Katunga said he brought the woman, but it turned out afterwards that the man who did bring her lived some way from us, and that the only share Katunga had in the matter was that he walked into Magomero with the man who did bring her. When found out in a deception of this kind, these people seemed in no way abashed, but gave a chuckle as much as to say: ' What clever fellows you are! you have found me out now, but we will see who gets the best of it next time.' The woman was an Ajawa. The Bishop told her she was no slave, but a free woman, and that she might go where she pleased. She had found friends among the Ajawa with us, and she elected to stay at Magomero.

Before the Bishop allowed the real object for which these
chiefs had assembled to be spoken of, he told them that he had
some cause to be angry with them, because they had not kept
the covenant they had made with him, and had taken people
from the Ajawa, and had kept them against their will. This, we
heard, had been done by Chinsunzi and others, and the Bishop
would not listen to anything they had to say unless they
brought these people forth, and gave them liberty to go where
they pleased.

The majority upon this looked very crestfallen, but Kankomba made an eloquent appeal to the Bishop. Said he :

' Forget all that is wrong, and come and help us once more,
and we shall be happy. My village is not in danger now ;
Chinsunzi's home is freed of its enemies ; but Barwi's country
is occupied by the Ajawa ; and Barwi had sent to all the chiefs
and said to them, "The English helped you ; do you, therefore, join together in asking them to come and help me. My
position now is worse than it was before they helped you, for
many who fled from Chirumba have come to me. They have
angry hearts ; they will destroy me." So we come to you,
and we say, help Barwi against his enemies. If you say, "No,
I will not ; I am angry ; I will not listen to what you say,"
then the Ajawa will burn our villages and carry away our
wives and children. You are our master ; you are our father ;
you say you come to do us good ; if you will not help us we
shall all be dead. We cannot stand against the Ajawa ; they
will take first one village, and then another, until all the land
is dead to us, and there is no life anywhere ; you cannot do
us good then, for we shall all be gone. Do not wait, do not
refuse to listen ; drive away our enemies, and then we will
settle our differences afterwards.

This was a good specimen of Manganja special pleading, but
it failed ; for until he felt sure that all who had been taken
from the Ajawa had been set at liberty, the Bishop would not
listen to anything they had to say ; and he refused their present
of a goat.

August 22.—Two women and a boy left us this morning,
not openly but secretly ; the women came from Chirumba ;

the boy a fine lad, was one of the first we released from slavery.

In the evening the Bishop assembled all the people under our protection, and we found that three-fourths were Ajawa, for most of those that had been released from the slavers, to our astonishment, proved to be Ajawa that had been sold by Manganja, instead of Manganja that had been sold by Ajawa. Some had been sold by their own friends, but the majority by the Manganja. When all were gathered together, he told them that any who wished to go away might do so : only he asked them to let him know before they went, not to go away by stealth, for then it seemed as if they had been treated unkindly, and he was sure they all knew that none of them had been so treated. Not one wished to leave ; and one woman, who acted as speaker for the rest, grew quite eloquent in the expression of her desire to remain. ' Where should they go ?' said she ; ' our homes are gone ; our friends are gone ; we have no safe place anywhere. You (the Bishop) are our father, you give us all we need, you treat us kindly and we are not slaves ; we will never go unless you send us away ; we see that it is good to be with you.'

August 24.—St. Bartholomew's day. Holy Communion this morning. The Bishop decided that on all festivals, other than Sundays, we should have a holiday. This gave us an opportunity to visit the neighbourhood. Our hands were so full of work that we gave ourselves but little relaxation.

August 27.—Procter, who had been unwell almost from the time of his arrival at Magomero, was somewhat better.

Walking about all day in the sun with a cap on my head, that had neither peak before nor flap behind, caused me some inconvenience ; for several days I had severest headaches. I only just escaped sunstroke. The heat, however, was not intense, seldom greater than 84° in the shade, and the nights were refreshingly cool.

The Bishop's ' Palace' was progressing towards completion. The roof was thatched, the walls nearly completed, the interior walls being bamboo split and interlaced. It was a famous house, and the astonishment of the natives. The Bishop designed it, and worked the hardest at it. Day by day you saw him with axe, spade, or pickaxe, working as hard as any labouring man in England, and cheering others. He was an excellent leader of men, for he had the power of harmonising diverse dispositions, and keeping men at one who naturally would be opposed. I have never met with another who so quickly disarmed opposition as he; no man obtruded his own opinions less than he, and few men were so likely to carry what they advocated.

On August 28, Barwi came again on the same errand as before. He pleaded his own cause most eloquently, and declared that, since the 14th, the Ajawa had burnt no less than eight villages belonging to him. He told the truth, and if the English found he lied, then let them kill him. Only yesterday Dinde, the chief who sat behind him, had his village destroyed and his people carried away captive. He thought it very hard because Chinsunzi and others had behaved ill that he should be left to be destroyed.

At this point of his oration, Chinsunzi and others came in, bringing with them fifteen women and children that they had taken from the Ajawa. Chinsunzi said they had brought all the people they had, none were now kept back. We knew that this was not true, for a child was not brought that Chinsunzi had taken away from its mother; and upon questioning some of the people present, we discovered that these fifteen women and children had been brought by a fine-looking old chief named Nampeko, and that Chinsunzi still kept those he had taken.

The Bishop was very angry, and told Chinsunzi he was a bad man who loved a lie. It was wrong in any man to tell a lie, but it was worse in a great chief, who ought to set a good example to his people. He must go away at once, and until every captive they had made had been set at liberty, he would not hold up a hand to save the land. He regarded the Manganja as one people, they agreed to make all captives free, and until that was really done he would talk to them no more.

Chinsunzi for the moment was abashed, and said he would go home at once and fetch the child that had been taken from its mother, and all other people that he or any of his subordinates had taken captive.

The assembly then broke up. Barwi went off in a very ill-temper with everybody.

The Manganja in these transactions did not appear to advantage, but we found them upon the whole better than we expected they would be. Before we came to them we talked of them as the most degraded and vilest of men, and we no sooner found ourselves among them than we were annoyed and angry because we did not always find them virtuous. They were heathen, and had the faults of heathen, and, compared with some Christians, I do not think they were so exceedingly faulty. They were a timid people, and had the faults of timid people, and lying was one of them; indeed it seemed as natural for them to lie as to breathe. Their common expression was, 'Ku nama iwe,' you are not speaking the truth; and it seemed to them the drollest thing in life when we said, 'The English never lie.' In the end, however, our truthfulness told upon them; they believed us implicitly, and rarely lied to us.

While we were sitting at dinner on this day, all at once we heard a great uproar behind our hut, and in going out found a young man struggling in the hands of four of our men, and a crowd of our women were ready to tear him to pieces. When we had freed the man from personal danger, and had restored order, we learnt the cause of the disturbance. Sonanagana, one of the most intelligent and well-behaved women we had, and the mother of the prettiest little child on the station, stood forth as the accuser of the man. She said he was an Ajawa, and had married her husband's sister. Her husband was an Ajawa also, but they had all lived among the Manganja. The man before her had persuaded her husband to sell her and her child to the Portuguese slavers a few days before we released her, and the man had then on him a part of the cloth that was paid for them. The man did not deny the charge, but said he had only done as others did before we came into the country. This satisfied us, but it did not satisfy Sonanagana: her blood was up, and had we left him to her and her female friends it would have gone very hard with him. We told them that we could not punish him for what had been done before we had come into the land, and before the Manganja had made buying and selling of men, women, and children a crime ; and so we saw him safely out of the village, but warned him against coming into it again.

What a fearful iniquity human slavery is! what wretches it makes of men! Here, tempted by Christians, a husband had sold his own wife and child for a miserable piece of calico, worth no more, probably, than eighteen pence. One really found it hard to say, ' God have mercy upon those who instigated such a sin!'

September 1.—We discovered this morning that during the night a number of Ajawa women and children had left us. We were grieved that they should go in this way. They were free to go when they pleased, and if they had made known their intention to us, we should have given them an escort back to their own people;. as it was, they could not reach them without much difficulty, hiding during the day, and travelling during the night, for fear of the Manganja. During the next day, however, one woman returned and begged to be received back, and she said others were a short distance off who would like to return also, but were afraid we were angry with them. We sent kind messages to these poor creatures, and they returned to us. Of the rest, about five-and-twenty in number, nothing could then be heard ; we feared they would suffer severely before they reached a place of safety.

On September 5, Chinsunzi, his son Kapanji, Nampeko, Kakarara Kabana, and others again made their appearance, bringing with them the child about which we were angry, and twelve women and children. Chinsunzi made a long speech— these Manganja are the greatest *talkers* on earth—the object of which was to show that now all had done what they promised to do, all were very good fellows, and deserved all the English could do for them. From enquiries we had made among the Ajawa and others living with us, who seemed well informed upon the subject, it did seem likely that all the people that had been made captive had now been produced.

Some of these thus brought in were Manganja; they at

once went to their own friends. They had been made prisoners by the Ajawa some time before, and, had we not interfered, would have been the slaves of their own people. The rest were Ajawa; the Bishop told them they should stay with us for a week, and then they might go where they pleased. One poor girl, about eleven years of age, was dumb and of weak intellect; she and several of the women were literally naked.

Chinsunzi having at last done what he could, and all others having followed his example, the Bishop said he was now willing to hear what they had to say. Of course there was Barwi's grievance, and, over and above that, Nampeko had a tale of woe to tell. The Ajawa had burnt his village and killed his own brother; would the English, therefore, come and 'show themselves' to his enemies? Nampeko lived forty miles away from us, and upon enquiry we came to the conclusion that, if what we heard was true, the Ajawa must be in force all along the southern, western, and eastern faces of Zomba. Having gained this information we dismissed them for the night. Next morning they assembled early, and we told them what we had resolved upon in the interim, viz., to go and see for ourselves. The Bishop tried to 'improve the occasion,' and said:

'I wish I could take all you say as true, but I cannot; you are constantly saying that which is not true, and the English hate a lie. I came here not to take a gun and fight for you, but to teach you to be better men than you are, to teach you God's laws, to teach you to say and do that which is pleasing to God, for you do many things now which displease Him, because you have never been taught His laws. I find you very anxious for us to be kind to you, but you do not seem at all anxious to be kind to others; that is wrong, for we should do to others as we should like to be done unto. If the Ajawa are doing all the harm you say, I will try and stop them; but you must keep to your promises, or I can have nothing more to do with you. I have no hatred of the Ajawa, I love them as much as I love you, but I hate their bad deeds, and if you wish us to love you, you must not act like the Ajawa.'

Nampeko said all the Bishop had spoken was good. He was glad the English were going to see for themselves; they would then know that all he had spoken was truth.

The Bishop wished Nampeko to accompany him, but the chief said the journey was long and he was sorefooted. This was really the case, but he sent some of his best men with the Bishop.

Old Chinsunzi did not like this arrangement; he wished something to be done at once; the country was too hot for delay, the Ajawa were too near, villages were being destroyed, and the Ajawa ought to be driven off at once.

The Bishop sternly rebuked him, and told him, if what he said was true, he was to blame for it, for by his lies he had created delay and distrust; the English could no longer take the word of the Manganja. To this the old man made no reply, though he seemed quite insensible to rebuke. 'My lord Chinsunzi' was too great a man in his own estimation to be affected by any exposure of his faults.

Waller, and the three men belonging to the expedition, with Charles, were not with us at this time. Waller had gone down for additional stores. Hardisty, Gwillim, and Hutchins, had returned to their duty on board the 'Pioneer.'

Waller took with him some of the young men that had been released at Mbame's. It was thought that a sight of the ship would interest them, and it would prove to the rest on their return that they might all safely trust themselves to us wherever we went; and from the time Waller returned with them, our own people, certainly, never distrusted us.

Not long after the notabilities had taken their departure, a great noise 'at the gate proclaimed something extraordinary. Most of the Ajawa women and children who left us on September 1, had returned. Those who had remained with us felt inclined to jeer them.

On asking these people why they left us in the way they did, one woman, to whom we had shown much kindness, spoke up, and said she wished to leave, and she induced the others to go with her. They went in the night, not because they were afraid of us, but because they were afraid of the Manganja about us. We told them they might leave us when they pleased, and if they went away openly they would go safely, for we would send some one to protect them on the road. They seemed to have been short of food while away. I asked Akwinani, a fine bright lad, who had accompanied his mother and sisters, if they had had enough to eat; he shook his head sorrowfully, so we gave them food, and they returned to their old quarters.

Sunday, September 8.—This morning we found a great shelling of peas going on among our people. I had given them none, and the question was, where did they get them? This was not a question for long. William soon found out that they had been stolen from the gardens of the Manganja close to us. All were shelling, and all had participated in the theft. The Bishop went round to every hut, collected all the peas, assembled all the people, and sent also for Chigunda and the owners of the gardens. The thieves had nothing to say for themselves; one or two tried to make us believe that they had permission to gather, but the owners shook their heads, and they broke down miserably. Some tried to laugh it off as a thing of no consequence, but the majority looked subdued and ashamed. The Bishop was much distressed and inclined to punish, but Chigunda and the owners behaved generously. Said they, 'This is the first offence; do not punish anyone. We are sorry the gardens have been plundered, but the thing is done, let the people keep the peas now, but don't let any be taken again.'

The Bishop thanked them for their good feeling, and gave them compensation. That done, he made it a law there and then that, for the future, anyone living under our protection found guilty of thieving should be severely punished, or sent away from us at once. As the owners declined to receive their peas back, they were given to the goats, to the great disgust of the thieves.

We did what we could for those people over whom God had placed us, but for some time we could do little in the way of direct and systematic religious teaching. As circumstances gave us the opportunity we tried to correct their fault, and in doing this we always led them up to God as to One Who was displeased when we did wrong; and that lying, stealing, immorality, and such like sins, were wrong. We fully realised the sacred character of our office and mission, but we felt it would be some time before we could do much more than this for the spiritual welfare of the heathen about us, for though the Bishop and Scudamore made great progress in the language, up to this time, and for some time after, only enough was known to show the necessity of knowing more before we could instruct the people in the truths of our holy religion. We lost no opportunity of preparing them in the way I have indicated for higher teaching; but we were obliged to be content to advance slowly. Very early the Bishop resolved, and I am sure he was right, not to trust to an interpreter in religious matters, for though, up to this time, we had no fault to find with our Cape men, yet we discovered that their religious knowledge was so scant, their spiritual sensibilities so dull, that of the two evils delay would be the least. We kept up our classes, but up to this time we had so much manual labour that nothing like a regular school could be attempted.

September 9.—This morning the Bishop, Scudamore, William, three of the Makololo, Chigunda, and others, left us for the purpose of making a thorough inspection of the Ajawa encampments. The Ajawa difficulty was a very harassing and time-absorbing business—it was our one great cross. But we were not men to sink under our burden; we took things as we found them, and determined, with God's help, to make the best we could of them.

For the time being, the whole care of the home establishment devolved on Procter and myself.

During the day, the chief of a small village near to Magomero brought us a present of four baskets of meal and some pombi, the native beer, which is in appearance like thin gruel, and in taste something like sweet wort. These presents, I should explain, were by no means gifts. Those who brought them expected a present in return. Soon after we were settled at Magomero this system of presents became an actual nuisance. One could understand that it was considered beneath the dignity of a chief to sell, and beneath our dignity to receive from a chief and not give; but in a short time we found almost every one's dignity stood in the way of ordinary barter, all brought presents, and at last things reached such a crisis that one man came to the Bishop and said:

'I intend to make you a present of a pot of beer soon, so will you give me the cloth you mean to give me in return, now, at once?'

This was as acute a trick as that of the individual who sent for change for a sovereign and promised that the sovereign should be forthcoming 'next week.' At last, save in genuine cases, we stopped this giving of presents, by telling those who brought them, that, if they were so generously disposed, they might bring us what they liked, but that we should give nothing in return. So they acted like sensible people and said 'I have brought for sale,' and we bought.

While the Bishop was away I made a calculation of all the barter goods we had, and I found that unless Dr. Livingstone could help us to a bale of cloth we should not have enough to last until December, when we looked for fresh supplies. A liberal calculation of our wants was made for a year, but then we knew not we should have so many mouths to fill. We planned for twelve, and found we had to provide for nearly two hundred. Had not the actual expense in food been insignificant, we could not have done as we did. We saw an end to this expenditure, for when all had gardens our people would provide for their own wants.

The people were behaving well: those who had work did it without giving trouble; those who had no work behaved orderly.

One night, while the Bishop was away, I was aroused by a dismal wailing. I went out and found it proceeded from the dumb idiot girl. She was crouching over the embers of the kitchen fire. For several nights, in consequence of our want of huts, some of the people slept in the open air. The Bishop, however, took this child into his hut, and covered her with his blanket. She had sense enough to appreciate the comfort of this arrangement, and feeling enough to be grateful. She would follow the Bishop, pat his hands, and make extraordinary noises indicative of pleasure. On the day the Bishop left us a large hut was placed at my disposal, so I gave it to some of the women who had hitherto slept out of doors, and placed the dumb girl, Akenena (she cannot speak), under the care of one of the occupants. But she did not like the change; each night I took her to the hut she resisted, and I had some trouble with her. She missed the Bishop, and would sit at the gate watching his return; when he did come back her manifestations of delight were extreme. I made a point of feeding her and three others with the remains of our own food. The three others were girls, mere babes. They were said to be the children of women made captive by the Ajawa, and who had been sold from their offspring. They fell into our hands on August 14; indeed one of them was the child the Bishop carried to Chinsunzi's in his arms. It would be difficult to meet with anything more saddening than the appearance of these children. The elder, Meri, was about three years old, but there was no childish animation about her. She was very emaciated, had a large head, and a wild hungering look was ever on her face. I gave her thrice the quantity of food the others had, but no sooner had she eaten than she was groping among refuse for raw vegetables that might have been dropped, or for bones that might have been thrown away. Of course this morbid appetite was the result of disease, which had been brought upon her by privation. Evidently the little thing had been used to forage for herself for a long time past. But painful as her state was, the state of the other two was still more distressing. At their age, according to Manganja custom, they should have still been nourished from the mother's breast, but they must have been deprived of that sustenance for some time. They, too, were eager foragers for food, though they could scarcely stand. They showed not the slightest pleasure at anything; with the withdrawal of their mother's milk they seemed to have been smitten with an overwhelming sorrow. Their lack-lustre eyes, their hopeless looks were most painful. I tried my hardest to bring a gleam of pleasure into their eyes, but could not succeed. They would watch for me, follow me with their looks; but their looks were always sad, always hopeless. Johnson, who was a kind-hearted fellow, and very fond of the little ones, used to nurse these children and wash them as tenderly as a woman; and 'Please the Lord, we'll make something of these younkers yet,' was his invariable expression of self-satisfaction as he placed them after their bath, side by side, in the sunshine to dry. We did make something of them, but not what he expected. The most hopeful of these two babes while asleep rolled itself into the fire and burnt itself frightfully. The woman in charge of them was sleeping by their side. In the morning when I went to see it, I found it had groped its way to the door, and was holding up its poor disfigured face to the sky. It was quite blind, but knew my voice, and clasped my finger with its uninjured hand; the other was severely burnt. We tried hard to keep life in this little one, but it sank under the injuries it received, and was the second baptised. Its companion seemed in no immediate danger of death, but it was baptised, and died a few hours afterwards.

The death of these children made a Christian burial-ground necessary. We thought of a retired place not far from where we hoped to build our church, but on speaking to Chigunda about it we found he had objections to our using that particular plot of ground because his forefathers were buried near there, but we found a suitable place elsewhere, and both babes were laid in one grave.

The death of these children led me to ask the Bishop what course he was going to pursue with regard to the baptism of the other children: we had nearly seventy boys and girls under twelve years of age. He said if he could be reasonably sure of remaining in the land and keeping these children, that we should not be obliged to leave them, he would baptise them; but, in the uncertain state of the country, we could not be sure of this, and he thought it better, for the present, only to baptise those who were in danger of death. If any are inclined to find fault with this resolution of the Bishop, I would remind them that these were early days at Magomero, and that our position was very uncertain. No one more than the Bishop realised the necessity of baptismal grace, but his previous experience among the Zulus led him to shrink from exposing regenerate children to the danger of being left among the heathen with none to care for their souls.

The Bishop and party returned on the evening of the 14th. Their expedition had not been eventful, but it had been interesting—and they had obtained sufficient information respecting the Ajawa to enable us to come to some decision upon the course to pursue towards them.

Barwi-did not come out of the investigation at all well. When he was at the station on August 28, he solemnly declared that several villages of his had been just destroyed by the Ajawa, and gave the names of them, offered to show the English where they had been, and engaged to forfeit his life if what he said was not true. Notwithstanding all this, the ruins of these villages could not be seen. And when the Bishop pressed the people about him on this matter, they looked at one another, as though they thought he was a very cunning man; and at last said there were no such villages, that the names given were names of men that had huts in a village that was destroyed; but when that village was destroyed they could not say—'many moons ago' it must have been. This made us all feel that we ought to be very careful in assuming the offensive again, merely upon Manganja testimony. The Bishop tried to get an interview with Kempama, the Ajawa chief, living near Barwi, but failed. Barwi, after vainly endeavouring to entrap the Bishop into an affray with the Ajawa, became insolent. The Bishop left him surrounded by his men, sitting on the crest of a hill, looking moodily towards the Ajawa camp. His ebullition of temper, on finding that he could not get the Bishop to do what he wanted done, was like that of a spoiled child disappointed in some pet object it had set its heart upon.

After procuring a guide, the Bishop continued his investigations until he reached Nampeko's; everywhere on the journey he heard terrible reports of Ajawa doings, but nowhere did he find that these reports had much foundation in fact, until he came to the neighbourhood of Nampeko.

Katunga's village, declared to be destroyed, was untouched,.

and the shameless old chief came out with a pot of pombi, and offered hospitality to the Bishop in the very place which he had declared, with moanings and supplications, had been reduced to ashes.

About Nampeko's, however, there were abundant signs of Ajawa depredations, and the smoking of a burning village was seen as the Bishop and party arrived.

The Ajawa encampment was about two hours' march from Nampeko's. It was built on the slope of a hill called Chikala, and approach to it without being observed was impossible. Every village left standing between Nampeko's and Chikala was deserted, and no Manganja dare venture where they once had pleasant dwelling-places. The camp at Chikala had not been formed more than a year, and the slavers from Tete were known to be constantly there. Nampeko said, and probably truly said, that during the year he had lost nearly half his people.

When the Bishop returned to Nampeko's, the chief earnestly entreated him to stay and fight the Ajawa at once; he would soon collect his men, and if the Bishop would only shew himself, and cry out 'The English are here!' the Ajawa would run.

To this the Bishop would not consent, neither would he promise anything, until he returned home and had taken counsel with his friends. Ultimately it was agreed that Nampeko should come or send to us for our answer on the 19th.

On the 15th, about mid-day, Waller returned, followed by a train of eighty Chibisians carrying burdens. He had made 'Queen's messenger speed' on this journey. He reached the ship (seventy miles) in two days and a half, and was only three and a half in doing the journey back, although it was up hill all the way. Dr. Meller, with the steward of the 'Pioneer,' and Rowe, a seaman, left the ship with him, but they knocked up at Mongazi's, and so he left them behind to come on next day.

It was a comfort to have Meller with us, for he was a great favourite with all. He set to work at once and doctored us and our people, and not before we wanted it, for climate, anxiety, and hard work had punished most of us a little, and many of the natives wanted a more skilful treatment than they had been able hitherto to get; though greater kindness and attention than they had from Waller it was impossible for them to receive.

September 17 was an eventful day, and will tend to illustrate the cares and anxieties of our position. First, we heard that Sesaho, one of the Makololo, while strolling about with his gun, had accidentally killed a child. The Makololo went nowhere without their guns, which they invariably carried loaded, and on full cock. Sesaho had been in search of guinea-fowl, the only game in the neighbourhood of Magomero, and while halting in a village he lodged his gun against a tree. The children playing about knocked it down. It went off, and its contents went into the body of one poor child and killed it. Sesaho was the most amiable of all the Makololo, and he was miserable for days. I never saw a man more cast down than he by this mishap: he cried like a child.

It was hard work to soothe the sorrow of Sesaho, as well as of the child's relations; to convince the latter that the death was not the result of malice, but accident; and both that witchcraft had nothing to do with it.

The death of this child made us acquainted with a remarkable fact, viz., that the Manganja distinguished between deaths which they supposed were brought about by Pambi (God), and those brought about by a less benign influence, the Mfiti (evil spirits). They imagined that those who died from old age or from any of the ordinary diseases of the country died of 'God's sickness,' but that those who met with violent deaths, with any but an ordinary death indeed, had their deaths brought about by a malignant power—that they were accursed, in fact. And this idea led them to a different disposal of the bodies. Those whose death came from God were buried in a grave, as we bury our own people, while the accursed were rolled up in their sleeping mats, and hung up in the branches of great trees. We asked why they did this. They said, for fear the ground should be cursed if the accursed were buried in it, and for fear of the consequent famine and distress. This custom brought to one's mind the text, ' cursed is he which hangeth upon a tree ;' and many other of their customs seemed to us to illustrate many other passages of Scripture.

The peculiarity of the superstition I have just mentioned, how-ever, is this, viz. the regarding death in any way as from a good source. With savages generally it is looked upon as an un-mitigated evil. The idea which the Manganja had of God was that of a benevolent deity. They did not profess to know, nor did they know, much about God. Whatever knowledge their forefathers might have had they had lost, but God to them was not a God of wrath—they assigned no wrathful attribute to Him. He was not the author of evil, and they offered, therefore, no terrible sacrifice like the Hindoo, for instance, in order to avert the wrath of God. If they were in trouble or distress they would all meet together, and offer up a prayer to God to deliver them from that trouble or distress, whatever it was. But more of this in its place. To return to the events of the 17th.

Secondly, a complaint was made against three of our men. They met a Manganja man not far from our station, saw he had a handsome copper ring on his arm, seized him, and took it away from him. The man did the right thing, he came to us and complained. The Bishop assembled all our fifteen men, satisfied himself as to the guilty parties, and then gave them their choice, to leave us for ever, or submit to a flogging. Two submitted to the flogging at once, the other went away for two days, but then came back and asked to be whipped—and whipped he was.

This circumstance led Chigunda, who was present, and ad-miring our justice, to say that our boys had been guilty of plundering also. It appeared that they lay in wait on the Sundays for all people who, in ignorance of our custom not to buy on that day, brought things for sale. As these people came in, our boys rushed upon them, expressed their surprise that they should dare to bring anything for sale on Sunday, when order had been given to the contrary, and claimed as forfeit what they had brought. If this was refused, a regular onslaught was made, which usually ended in the flight of the

Manganja. Of course we enquired into this also, found it true, brought the offence home to several boys, punished them, and made arrangements to prevent anything similar taking place again. Out of fifty-seven boys, we found that thirty-five were Ajawa. Their contempt for the Manganja was supreme. The dominant race was manifest in all their actions; and I had begun, by this time, to like the dominant race, notwithstanding their actions.

Thirdly, we heard that small-pox had broken out among our people, and upon enquiry we found it true; and also learnt that it was by no means an unusual disease in that part of the world; it was called Mtondo, and the Ajawa inoculated their children with it, under the idea that it was milder when produced in this way. We had to take precautions to prevent the disease spreading, by removing those who had it from all others; but six children died before we could stop it.

Fourthly, Damanji, the man who wished for two wives, having finished his hut, had taken to it the woman he had chosen; but the woman he had rejected, not having met with another offer, was inconsolable. When she saw her rival established in her new home, she rushed about like a mad woman, talked frantically about killing herself, and seemed utterly wretched because she had not the half of a husband. It was some time before we could reduce her to reason. Indeed, before that was accomplished, she rushed at the wife, and would have been sadly handled, for she was excited, while the wife was cool and also the stronger.

It will be seen, from this specimen of a day's work that we found these poor people very human indeed, with all the faults of our common humanity; and that the work we had to do was a little different from that which the conventional ideas of many good people assign to the missionary to the heathen. On the one hand there are those who imagine that the missionary has but to preach and to pray and to sing, and in an unknown tongue, be it said, and that converts are thereby multiplied; while others, having no faith in such a subjective method of propagating Christianity, would, as some missionaries have done, multiply Christians by Holy Baptism, before it is pos--

sible for those baptized to understand the simplest truths of
Christianity, or to evidence any token of repentance.   The
latter course we did not think it advisable to adopt, the former
was impossible; for though it be an easy matter to acquire a
mere colloquial knowledge of any language, and though the
languages of the natives of Africa are most copious in words
which describe material objects, they are singularly destitute
of words which express abstract ideas, consequently the
preaching of the Gospel, in the ordinary sense of the phrase,
is not at once practicable.   The modern missionary has to do
what the ancient missionary must in most cases have done, lay
hold of words in common use and sanctify them to higher purposes.   This is difficult, doubtless, but not impossible.   Indeed
the Church now has to do just the same kind of work that it
had to do in ages gone by; and if it had but the faith of those
ages, it could do it.

CHAPTER IX.

THE COURSE OF EVENTS AT MAGOMERO.

ON the 19th, we discussed the question of peace or war once
more; not whether peace was preferable to war, but whether
any further warlike demonstration on our part was absolutely
necessary.

We had two applications before us, one from Barwi, the
other from Nampeko, and we had the Ajawa everywhere about
us.   Clearly we had no disposition to go against the Ajawa
because they were Ajawa, but only to put down oppression,
and wrong, and we decided against Barwi's application, because the Ajawa in his neighbourhood, since we came into the
country, and for long before, had been guilty of no oppression
or wrong.   The charges that Barwi had made against them
were not proved.

Then came Nampeko's case.   From the observations of the
Bishop, made on the spot, none doubted that the Ajawa had
ravaged, and were ravaging, Nampeko's country, and that the
life, liberty, and property of the people remaining to him were

in greatest peril. But though none doubted this, some felt
that it was inexpedient for us to go so far out of our way, and
expend so much time and strength as would be necessary to
drive away the Ajawa at Chikala. We had much work still to
be done before the rainy season set in. Houses had still to be
built and finished; gardens were not yet ready for the seed;
there were many sick requiring daily attention; the disorgani-
sation arising from such an expedition would be great, and, for
one, I felt that we were not really called upon to make the
extraordinary effort asked of us.

The gravity of our own position was recognised by all, but
it was decided that the circumstances of the case called upon
us to go to Nampeko's assistance.

The Bishop said that, with the aid of those who had joined
us from the ship, we were strong enough to undertake the
expedition, and to leave so many of our party behind, that our
work at home would not suffer materially. He considered it
of the highest importance to the success of our work, that
peace and order should be re-established in the land. Now all
was terror and confusion; wide districts were ravaged, and the
people not yet molested were fleeing for fear. Half of Nampeko's country had been made desolate during the past year,
and if the Ajawa were not checked, the other half would soon
be reduced to the same position; but if we made an effort
now, we should give peace to the land, and deal another great
blow to the slave trade. The Manganja, who had been driven
away, would return and rebuild their villages, and instead of a
desolated country, we might, when we had an addition to our
strength from home, have a Mission at Nampeko's, the very
presence of which he thought would prevent the slave traders
returning. And so it was decided that we should go to Chikala.

Messengers were sent out to the various chiefs, to assemble
at Magomero on the 21st. On that day, therefore, the various
potentates appeared. They had not much to say; they came
to hear what we had to say. We had to reiterate former conditions, and to make a fresh condition respecting the Ajawa
that might be taken, for we intended to put them on the same
footing as the Manganja captives.

For a time all proceeded satisfactorily to both parties; there seemed nothing to mar the harmony of the deliberations. The Manganja said yea to our yea, and nay to our nay, and all things promised to end as they had begun. But a fault occurred, and there was an end of harmony. One thing which inclined us to aid Nampeko at once, was his distinct statement that the Ajawa had recommenced offensive operations since the Bishop visited his place, and that the very village the Bishop slept in had been destroyed. This, by an inadvertence on the part of one of Nampeko's men, while the deliberations were going on, was found to be untrue. The Ajawa had not, since the Bishop was there, moved from their encampment. On being rebuked for this, Nampeko quietly observed,

'Da nama' (I did lie).

It was necessary to check this untruthfulness, and the Bishop, getting up, told Nampeko he would have nothing more to say to him; he could not trust a lying tongue; he could have no fellowship with liars; and left the astonished assembly.

Nampeko left humiliated. Chinsunzi remained behind, and as he had nothing now to fear, he evidently enjoyed his brother chief's confusion. He knew that he had gone down in our opinion by the lies he had told us, and he was certainly not sorry to see Nampeko in the same degradation. I never saw a man take snuff with more malicious satisfaction.

The greatness of our repugnance to resort to arms again was manifest. When the arrangement was broken off, a cloud was removed from every brow, a weight from every heart. Nothing but a sense of duty, outweighing all other considerations, decided us to take up arms, and nothing but the strong feeling that it was absolutely necessary to punish deliberate untruth, intended to lead us astray in affairs of greatest moment, would have led the Bishop to set aside that sense of duty, in order to mark our disapprobation of the lie of which Nampeko had been guilty.

I was very busy on the 23rd, having much food to purchase, and my storehouse to finish. During the latter part of the week previous, supplies had been scant, and I began to be alarmed for our people, to fear that we had already consumed

the surplus food about us; but on this day I purchased, in two
hours, more than enough to last us for two days.

MISSION STATION AT MAGOMERO.

Our house-building, by this time, was beginning to tell.
Good substantial huts and houses were being built on a regular plan, and Magomero was losing its uncivilised appearance.

Had the Bishop and party gone to Chikala on this day,
those left behind would have had their hands full of work, for
Waller was taken seriously ill with fever, accompanied by a
semi-dysenteric disorder, which more or less had affected most
of us. It was the first time he had been really ill, for he escaped fever better than any of us, but he was quite prostrate

on the 23rd, and did not recover, notwithstanding the care and skill of Dr. Meller, for some weeks. Had not Meller been with us, I think he must have died.

Oct. 1.—This being the anniversary of the Farewell Service at Canterbury was regarded by us as the anniversary of the Mission itself; we made, therefore, what arrangements we could to keep the day suitably and joyfully; and part of the day's proceedings was to erect the first pillar of a church. The site was chosen, the plan made, and the pillar, a good-sized tree, was cut by Scudamore, who was a famous wood-cutter; and after the celebration of the Holy Communion, the Bishop formally erected it, having previously buried a bottle close to it, containing a sheet of paper on which was written—

'This first and corner post of the church of St. Paul was erected by Bishop Mackenzie, and the Revs. H. C. Scudamore and H. Rowley, on this first day of October, in the year of our Lord one thousand eight hundred and sixty-one, being the first anniversary of the departure of the Mission from England.'

Procter could not be present.

We all talked much over this church. The good Bishop was delighted, and spoke sanguinely of having a native congregation, irrespective of our own people, by the time it was finished. Our religious services were exciting great attention among all. At first it was imagined that we assembled together, morn and eve, for the purposes of magic; but when they really understood that we met for prayer and thanksgiving to God, they seemed to have less fear and a more exalted idea of us. We frequently felt the Babel curse to be indeed a curse, for again and again, when we would, we could not seize some favourable moment for the declaration of God's truth; but we felt it better to wait until we could speak freely ourselves, than give instruction through the medium of an illiterate interpreter, who still clung to many of his own old heathen superstitions.

Nothing eventful occurred for some days; we worked steadily. My storehouse was finished; the ground for the boy's dormitory was cleared, and wood was being felled for it. Scudamore, besides his ordinary occupations, cut down more timber for the church. Adams completed a famous night-house for the goats, and was building a large house for our poultry. Johnson was well advanced with his kitchen, and the native men under us had built huts for themselves. The boys' classes had been regularly taken by the Bishop, Procter, and Scudamore, and irregularly by me. We added to our stores considerably, and a few more boxes were brought up from the ship by the men sent down by Meller with botanical specimens, &c.

Our various occupations, and their results, astonished the natives.

The chiefs of various places around were constant visitors. On October 6, however, there was quite an assemblage of the great ones. What they wanted we could only guess at; but Chinsunzi, Katunga, and Nampeko were present, and they never came except on that distressing Ajawa business. We guessed they were on the same errand again.

And so it proved, for, on the 8th, our station was covered with dingy, squatting humanity for some hours, half of whom had food for sale, but the other half formed the suite of the lords and masters of the land, Chinsunzi and Co. They assembled the day before, but we took no notice of them; and for some time this day they were equally unnoticed. The Bishop attended the funeral of a child that had died of small-pox during the night, and then he superintended the getting home of some heavy timber, destined, we fondly hoped, to make us a table, for *we* were tired of squatting; Procter, who had taken Waller's work, was busy with his patients; Scudamore, with the boys; and I with my boys and ‘customers;’ and so the Manganja great ones were left to their own reflections upon the animated scene around them. They were patience itself until three o'clock, when they sent to say they wished to speak to the Bishop. The Bishop went to them. At first it did not seem that they had much to say; they looked at him, and he looked at them, in silence. Then he told them to say what they had to say, and quickly. Nampeko answered:

‘I come to tell you that I am much ashamed of myself for

the lies I told you. I ask you to forget them, and promise
that all I shall say for the future will be the truth.' This was
said with much effort, and the man was certainly ashamed.

The Bishop told him he was glad to hear him speak in this
way, and if he would be truthful for the future he would forget that he had ever told lies, and be good friends again. He
then asked him if he had anything more to tell him.

He replied that the position of the Ajawa was just the same
as when the Bishop was at Chikala. It was not lately that the
Ajawa had burnt villages, but he could not help fearing that
they would destroy him soon, for they had, since they came
down to his country, destroyed many villages near Chikala and
Shirwa, and many of his people had been carried away by the
slavers. The fear was great; the gardens were uncultivated,
and the people were deserting the land or starving. And
this was the real reason he had for asking the English to help
him.

I was too busy to listen to the whole of this conference;
but the end of it was this: the Bishop said he would try and
let the Ajawa at Chikala know that if they refrained from all
further aggression they might remain where they were, but
that we should immediately drive them out of the land, if they
plundered, destroyed, killed, or enslaved again.

He had another plan, and that was to send half our force to
Nampeko's, and establish a Mission at once there, thinking
the presence of any English would be sufficient to secure
peace. This plan did not seem practicable at that time. We
were not sufficiently strong to divide. Our stock of barter
goods was rapidly diminishing; the rainy season was close at
hand, and we had much to do to provide against the inclement
weather coming upon us; we were really not sufficient for the
work we had already undertaken, for the care of all our people was great, and I thought it would have been unwise in
the extreme to have increased our responsibilities at that
moment.

The difficulty was to get messengers to the Ajawa. We
called up our own men and told them the plan. They praised
it in eloquent terms, saying that nothing could promise greater

good; but when we asked them to be the messengers they put their hands instinctively to their throats, and said that could not be, they did not wish to die, and if they went their throats would certainly be cut.

At last it was settled that Scudamore and Dr. Meller, with William and Mobita, the most intelligent of the four Makololo with us, should go to Nampeko's, stay there eight or ten days, and see if they could not, without exposing themselves to danger, open a communication with the Ajawa. This was certainly the best plan, for, if a native messenger had been bold enough to have gone, our message would not have been faithfully delivered, misunderstanding would have followed, and the breach between us and the Ajawa by no means lessened.

We heard many things from our people which led us to conclude that the Ajawa in Manganja territory were not, in the first instance, so blameable as we had been led to believe. They had, it seemed, been forced from their own country by some stronger than they, and were really fugitives, not wilful invaders, had plundered from necessity, and not at first from wantonness; war, therefore, between them and the Manganja was, in the first instance, the result of circumstances which they could not control, and we felt sure that if this were so, and if these people wished for a permanent home, they would gladly accept our proposal to be at peace, and would let bygones be bygones. We were not disposed to let them keep the land in terror, but if they were anxious for peace, we, as ambassadors of the Prince of Peace, would certainly be no terror to them.

Oct. 9.—No rain, but incessant thunder among the hills. The people were everywhere busy putting on additional thatch to their huts, and preparing the land for the seed.

I made a valuable discovery on this day. I found, on looking into the boxes brought up by Waller, two bottles of brandy and a dozen of Pontac (Cape wine), a valuable addition to our very little stock, for we were previously reduced to two bottles of brandy and four bottles of Pontac. Wine and spirits were with us purely medical stores; we did not take any unless illness obliged us to do so, but as one or other of us was constantly invalided, the smallness of our stock was an uneasy subject to think about. A glass of good port, now and then, would have saved us from many a day of prostration, and consequent inactivity.

Sugar we were soon obliged to do without; no great hardship, but a deprivation to those who like it, not so much in tea as with other things, nsima (native porridge), for instance, which is very hard to swallow alone.

Of salt we had abundance. It is a regular article of barter. The natives brought to us three kinds of salt, in bags made of the bark of a tree, and in quantities varying from one pound to thirty. The three kinds of salt are produced from as many sources. The first and best, though a little darker, is equal to good table-salt in England. This is obtained from the shores of Lake Shirwa. It impregnates the soil, which the natives wash, evaporationg the solution twice or thrice. Two yards of calico bought twenty-five pounds of it. The other two kinds are very inferior, and were obtained from certain rushes growing in marsh lands by the lake. The rush is burnt, the ashes washed, and the solution evaporated several times. In the Shire Valley there are several salt marshes.

On October 13, we had news from Scudamore and Meller. Scudamore wrote from Nampeko's thus :—

'We slept at Chinsunzi's on Thursday night, and came by Katunga's to this yesterday. On our way from Katunga's we met people running away from the Ajawa, who had that morning attacked and burnt some villages at the foot of Zomba. We saw the villages burning, but being incredulous, thought it must be grass.

'We found Nampeko's deserted, but the people came in with us. In the evening, we learnt from a man who had been at the fight, that the Ajawa, after burning the villages, retreated before the Manganja as far as the river which we crossed when trying to catch some one to take a message to Kainka (the supposed Ajawa chief,) and that five Ajawa and two Manganja had been killed.

'This morning we went to see the villages; we found them

still smoking, and two others we saw burning higher up the hill. We saw the track of the Ajawa, as if a dense mass of people had passed along from village to village. We discovered two dead bodies of Ajawa killed by Manganja; other bodies were near, but we had seen enough. The gardens were destroyed, and the cassava plucked up by the roots and carried off.

' It appears to Meller and myself to be an unmistakable raid of the Ajawa into the Manganja country. They are said to have been on their way here, but the rain is supposed to have stopped them.

' A great number of chiefs and people have assembled here at Nampeko's, who wanted much to know what we should do. We could only say that we should remain at Nampeko's to protect his village, and should at once write and tell you what we had seen. We anxiously wait for the return of the messenger.

' We can form no idea of the number of the Ajawa, but the Manganja seem very unanimous and eager to drive them away.'

Meller also wrote to Waller. He was more vehement in his expressions, as became him, and expected to see the whole force of the Mission return with the messenger. The Bishop accordingly resolved to proceed on the morrow with all our valuable strength to Nampeko's, and, when there, to act as it seemed good. Our force was not great. Waller was ill; Rowe, the seaman, ill also; Procter was needed at home to attend to the sick: and, though I protested, the Bishop insisted on my remaining also, to take charge of all at home; so that there would be but six Englishmen, viz., the Bishop, Scudamore, Meller, Adams, Gamble, and the steward of the ' Pioneer.'

It is always easy to be wise after the event, and to make sage reflections and judicious excuses when the transaction you speak of is far removed from the excitement attending its performance. I will not do that; but, with respect to this expedition to Nampeko's, transcribe literally what I wrote in my journal immediately after we had decided upon it :—

' We were unanimous in the resolve to go to Nampeko's

help. The occasion seemed to require it. That which was before wanting is supplied, viz., an unmistakable cause for interference.

'The Bishop thought if we divided the Mission force, and had one half at Nampeko's, it would be sufficient to prevent any further aggression on the part of the Ajawa, and so obviate the necessity of actual fighting on our part. I am as much opposed as before to the division of our body at present, nor could I think that our peaceable presence would restrain the Ajawa. I do think that little or no actual fighting will take place, and that the Ajawa will retreat directly they hear that the English have advanced, but I think it necessary for us to advance.

'I own all this appears very inconsistent. Good folks at home will be greatly shocked, I dare say. I advocate to-day what I disapproved of a few days before; and I must confess it is more feeling than reason which inclines me to do so; but it is not possible to be the cold-blooded thing which would sit quietly down unmoved, when you know that you have but to move in order to stop the horror and bloodshed described by Scudamore.

'I feel deeply for the Ajawa, for I am more and more convinced that they have had to endure as much misery as they now inflict; that they have seen their houses desolated, friends killed, children enslaved; but, nevertheless, we must stop their depredations upon the Manganja. Though they may have been forced out of their own land, they are now growing wanton in their success, and are the authors of causeless misery. It is the character of the savage to respect as well as fear those that defeat him, but to pursue to extermination those he defeats; and this, now that the Ajawa here have the upper hand, is what they would do, if not prevented, to the Manganja.

'We had great hopes that Scudamore and Meller would have succeeded in laying the foundation of peaceable relationships between the Ajawa and Manganja at Chikala, but though they have not been able to do that, the Bishop will certainly make another effort for peace, by getting, if possible, an inter-

view with the Ajawa chiefs. I have no doubt in the end all
will come right, and that if we persevere in our good work,
we shall, with God's help, be a blessing to both tribes; but
the present experience is very trying, and " what will they say
at home ?" is often asked by us.

'I cannot see that we could have acted otherwise than we
have done. Our entrance into the land was attended by circumstances which brought about a state of things not dreamt
of by us. Had we Missionaries come into the country alone,
and after the fashion of other Missionaries, under the auspices
of no one, identified with no one, and no one's policy, we
might—I don't say we should—but we might have done as
other Missionaries have done, accepted things as we found
them, and submitted to the circumstances and exigences of the
country, whatever they might be. But as it was with us, we
could not well do this. We were, with Dr. Livingstone, personally engaged in the liberation of the slaves, and we were
heart and soul with him in what he did; and so, in the estimation of the Manganja and all other natives, we were bound
to the policy he inaugurated. The measure taken against the
Ajawa by Dr. Livingstone followed as a natural sequence upon
those against the Portuguese slavers. We were equally identified with this proceeding, and, as my journal must show,
could not well recede. It is not the course we thought to
pursue, but it is the only course open to us—an extraordinary
one certainly; but our position, from first to last, has been
extraordinary, and the position of the people among whom we
live is extraordinary also.'

The Bishop and party returned on October 21. It was not
possible to get an interview with the Ajawa chiefs; and further
provocations from them made it necessary to go against them.
Nearly 2,000 Manganja assembled at Nampeko's, and marched
towards the encampment: but they had no opportunity of
showing their valour, for, as I expected, no sooner did the
Ajawa hear the cry ' the English are here !' than they retreated,
making no resistance whatever. Not a gun was fired. Every
hut was deserted, save here and there by a child that in the
hurry had been left behind. So rapidly did they move off,

that, had it not been for the unmistakable signs that they had been surprised, it might have been thought that they had been warned and gone off the night before.

The camp was filled with plunder. This the Manganja reclaimed, and then the camp was destroyed. During the day the Manganja made many captives—nearly five hundred—all women and children ; and they behaved very well with regard to these people, no brutality was exercised towards them, and all were brought to the Bishop. But, though not ill-treated by the Manganja, they appeared to have suffered horribly, as their emaciated forms testified. They described Nunkajowa, the Ajawa chief, as a selfish tyrant. He used these women, when he went on a raid, to carry home the plunder, but he did not allow them to partake of the spoil. They had to subsist on wild roots, or what little corn they could get by stealth. They might have got away with the main body of the Ajawa had they wished, but they preferred falling into the hands of the English. The next day, October 17, was passed in disposing of these captives ; the majority were Manganja, and returned to their friends. Some of the Ajawa wished to go to the Manganja also, and were permitted. Nearly fifty women and children, however, wished to go with the Bishop, and he could not refuse to take them, though, as chief of the commissariat, I had warned him before he went not to increase the number of our family, as our means were insufficient. But, ' Look at them !' said he, when he returned—and I was looking at them, and wondering how much food they would take before they got into condition—' look at them, you old grumbler, and tell me if you could refuse them !' Refuse them ! certainly not ! It is very well to be prudent, but when you meet with such as these, you act upon the principle, ' God has sent you these people to feed ; trust to Him to supply you with food.'

The accompanying woodcut is the portrait of one of the women who came to us from Chikala, showing the position of the lip ring in old age, when the muscles of the face are too impaired to keep it at right angles to the teeth.

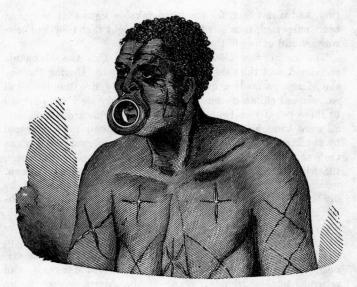

AN ANGURU WOMAN, SHOWING POSITION OF PILELI (LIP-RING) IN OLD AGE.

It was felt by all to be a great thing to have been instrumental, without shedding of blood, in setting at liberty and restoring to their friends so many Manganja captives. Slavery, for the time being, received a severe blow by these proceedings of ours throughout the Manganja highlands. Over all that fair portion of God's earth, before we came, the slaver passed as a conqueror; all submitted to him, and actively or tacitly aided him in his evil traffic. While we were there, he may by stealth have continued his horrible calling, but it was no longer with trumpet-blowing arrogance, but, as the felon he was, slinking from village to village in fear and trepidation. With the destruction of the Ajawa camps his great source of supply was cut off, and the system he had established all but destroyed. It *was* a system : of that there can be little doubt, for at Chikala a large barracoon, capable of holding three hundred slaves, was burnt. In this building, according to the testimony of those we released, the chief Nunkajowa kept those he sold to the Portuguese slavers.

From these people, also, we gained other information respecting the Ajawa at Chikala and elsewhere. They one and all declared that they left their own country on account of war; that the Avisa and other Makoa tribes defeated them, and carried away very many of them as slaves; that those who escaped came down to the Manganja country poor and hungry; that upon their taking food to keep them from dying, the Manganja took many of them and sold them to the slavers; that at last quarrels arose between them, battles were fought, and the Ajawa found themselves able to defeat the Manganja. Then the slavers came to them, gave them guns and gunpowder for men, women, and children, and urged them to continue the war against the Manganja, and take the whole country. Some were tired of war, and wanted to build and to plant, like Kempama; but others, like Nunkajowa, whom they called 'a devil,' were never tired of war: these kept their men always fighting, and would never let them plant, so they had to plunder in order to live. The Machinka, who were neighbours of the Ajawa, and with whom they had often fought, were also defeated by the Avisa; and lately Kainka, their chief, had made friends with Nunkajowa, and it was a mixed horde of Ajawa and Machinka that attacked the villages near Nampeko's. Mutukulu, who at Chirumba was put before us as 'the great war chief,' had fled to Chikala, and, quarrelling with Nunkajowa, had been buried alive by that terrible one.

Bit by bit we got at the history of these Ajawa, and in the end we could not help concluding, that though we found them killing and making captive, yet instead of being pre-eminently the slaving tribe they had been described to be, they had been pre-eminently a slave-producing tribe; for subsequent information enabled us to identify them with the Waiow, mentioned by Dr. Krapf as a tribe that more than any other had suffered from slaving raids. Indeed, for years, thousands of slaves from their tribe alone had been annually brought down to Zanzibar. The Ajawa were in much request as slaves, for, when once tamed, they made the best and most faithful of slaves; many of the petty Arab princes and others above Zanzibar preferring them above all others for their body-guards.

In order to elucidate as much as possible the political history of the country, and especially that of the Ajawa, the Bishop induced some of the most intelligent of our men to tell him their history. The following is the history of Ndoka, a good-tempered little fellow, about twenty years of age. Said he :

'I am Ndoka, not Ajawa but Anguru. The Anguru live on the far side of Lake Shirwa. They are a great people, and once, a long time since, they fought the Ajawa, and conquered them. They killed the old men and women, but they took the young men and women and the children prisoners. They did not sell them; they kept them among them as their own children. As days went on, and moons passed away, these young Ajawa people became men and women. Then the men rose up against the Anguru, defeated them, and killed the son of the Anguru king. Then they came down into Manganja land; they marched right down to the Shire, driving the Manganja before them, and ate of their crops.' When saying this, Ndoka added, with a smile and a bow, 'The English were not in the land in those days.' These people are perfect in the art of paying a compliment. After the body of Ajawa, of whom he was speaking, had done what they willed in Manganja land, they prepared to go back to their old quarters among the Anguru. 'This the Anguru heard, and their hearts failed them, so they left their homes and came to this side of Chikala, and I, Ndoka, with them. There they built villages, and made gardens, and all seemed happy of heart.' Among the Anguru was a maiden who possessed herself of Ndoka's heart, and who said to Ndoka, 'I will be your wife.' He was light of heart then. 'I began to build a hut for my wife; but one day it was said that there was war on the other side of Chikala, and that all the Anguru homes had been destroyed; and the next day it was told that the Chakundas (Portuguese slavers) were buying slaves, and the day after that, the brother of the mother of the maiden I, Ndoka, loved, seized me, and sold me to the Chakundas for two yards of calico and a brass bracelet. I was a moon and a half with them, with the slave-fork on my neck night and day, and then

the English came and said, you are free.' And then Ndoka
all but shed tears at the recollection of his injuries; but he
brightened up quickly, and continued : ' Ah ! the English have
good hearts ; I am of a happy heart while with them. I shall
never want to go away from them.'

CHAPTER X.

THE SHADOW OF COMING EVENTS.

October 30.—From this date the supply of food rapidly dimi-
nished. It did not seem at first that provisions were scarce
in the country, but that everywhere men, women, and children
were too busy in their gardens to be able to come to us. But
in the end we found that food was really scarce, that the people about us had parted with nearly all they could sell until
the first harvest was gathered. We had, however, a good
store of corn, and hoped for the best.

The Ajawa people brought in from Chikala soon recovered
from their emaciated condition. Women who had looked old
and wrinkled, proved comely dames under thirty. Children
who were attenuated to the last degree, filled up, and became
light-hearted, intelligent little fellows. It was at first painful
to witness the eagerness, the wolfish eagerness, with which
they thrust themselves forward when food was given out.
They fixed their eyes on the food I was distributing, and
pushed and jostled violently. Our other people submitted to
be thrust aside without a murmur ; they thought, no doubt,
of the time when they were equally famished, and treated
them with the greatest kindness. With the exception of two
or three old women, who constantly craved for food and
looked none the better for it, these people seemed in fair condition.

For some time we had no more complaints of Ajawa mis-
doing. The Manganja seemed relieved of a great fear, and
went about with an alacrity I had not before witnessed in
them. Peace and confidence appeared restored. But though

the Ajawa were restrained, we had rumours of war from
another quarter. Charles, who went down to the ship to
bring up the remainder of our goods, reported that the Nungwi,
the native population around Tete, excited by the Portuguese
at Tete, had attacked Chibisa because he was friendly to the
English. This did not prove to be true; but we knew afterwards that some of the Tete merchants, when they heard of
Dr Livingstone's and our proceedings against their agents,
the slavers, projected an expedition to consist of a thousand
well-armed men, their slaves and elephant-hunters, to attack
and destroy the 'Pioneer' and Mission Station. The Governor of Tete heard of this and put a stop to it.

On November 8, we moved into the Bishop's 'palace.' It
had been ready for us for some time, but the addition of the
people from Chikala necessitated more hut-building, and, until
that was done, these people occupied the 'palace.' The
change to us was productive of much cheerfulness. Hitherto
we had spread our beds on the ground, now we indulged in a
regular bedstead. We had grown weary of sleeping on the
ground in our clothes. We also sat at a table to meals, a
great comfort. True, the table was a rickety affair, the one
piece of carpentering our carpenter had completed—we had
to lash it to a post to prevent it making awkward movements
at its corners—but it was a table for all that, and in that was
the satisfaction. Wekotani, the lad who waited upon us, no
longer pattered about our plates with naked feet. The Bishop
was highly elated; dear Scudamore was so much Scudamore
that our laughter was incessant, and our liveliness so great
that serious consequences were dreaded for the table. It held
on, however, and having set our merriment at naught, we
agreed to let it shift for itself for the future.

The Bishop was very proud of his house, and proclaimed it
an end to all our discomfort. But alas for his anticipations!
it rained for a few hours during the night, and at once found
out the weak places in the thatch. On waking I found Scudamore placidly sitting up in his bed under an umbrella; puddles were everywhere; and the Bishop looking comically
aghast. This was the first heavy rain we had had. It was

accompanied by much thunder and lightning, such thunder as the tropics alone produce.

We now commenced sending out for food; William, Charles, or Job, who had joined us from the ship, going out with men and women carrying baskets to the villages. I did my utmost to leave our reserve food untouched, but I was obliged to go to it again and again, for, though food was always brought in, the supply thus obtained was not always sufficient for our daily consumption.

On November 12, we were surprised by messengers from Dr. Livingstone, who had returned to the ship from Lake Nyassa. They brought a letter, in which he informed the Bishop that he was going down the river immediately ; that, in consequence of the difficulties attending the navigation of the Shire above the Ruo, he should not be able to bring up our stores to Chibisa's, as he had promised, but only as far as the mouth of the Ruo ; that some of our party must be there on the 1st of January, to receive these stores and any other member of the Mission that might be coming up to join us ; and he strongly urged the necessity there was for the Mission to have a small river steamer for its own use, as it would be impossible for him to aid us again. Altogether, this letter brought us but little comfort. We were, however, too busy at the moment to think much about it. We made up our mail-bag, and the Bishop started for the ship at four o'clock next morning, hardly knowing, from the wording of the Doctor's letter, whether he should find the ' Pioneer' at her moorings at Chibisa's.

About seven o'clock in the morning of Nov. 18, a number of the Chibisians appeared with burdens, and one of them had a letter from the Bishop. It was written at Pingwi, a village half-way between Soche's and Mongazi's. Among other things, it said, to our astonishment and joy :

' Three men from England, to join our Mission, have come up from Quilimane. One, Burrup, a clergyman, is with me now. The other two, a doctor and a shoemaker, are coming. The letters were in time. The " Pioneer" started on Friday, at 10 A.M. We shall rest here to-day, Sunday, and hope to be home to-morrow night, but we are both knocked up. I got down on Thursday, at 10 A.M.' (By this, he did the seventy miles over a mountainous country in *thirty* hours.) 'Burrup has been helping to paddle his own canoe, and has had bad nights. There are letters of date about June in the hands of the doctor. God the Holy Spirit be with you this day. I should like to be among you.'

This was good news, and 'God be praised!' came from our lips. The departure of the 'Pioneer' left us without medical aid, at a time when, if ever, cases urgently requiring it would be likely to arise, and now we heard of a medical brother close at hand. That, and the prospect of letters from England, in a day or two, was a great cause for thankfulness. It was about a year since I left England, and I had not heard from home since then.

The Bishop and the Rev. Henry De Wint Burrup arrived at the station on the 19th; both looked very wearied. No wonder; the Bishop must have gone down to the ship at a killing pace, and Burrup's feat in coming up the river as he did was an unprecedented performance, which must have tried nerve and endurance to the utmost. Dickinson, the doctor, and Clark, the shoemaker, had been left by Burrup in the larger canoe nine days before he arrived at Chibisa's. It was Burrup's intention to have returned to them with the information that he had found the 'Pioneer,' but as the ship was going down immediately, there was no need for him to do so. Charles, who went down with the Bishop, was left at Chibisa's to bring Dickinson and Clark up to Magomero.

Our new coadjutors, it appeared, left England on April 6; the party then consisted of Mr. Burrup, Mrs. Burrup, Dickinson, Clark, Blair, a printer, and Jessie Lennox, a valued domestic of the Bishop.

It was known at the Cape that the Bishop and I had gone up the Rovuma, and that the rest of our party were staying at Johanna, but of our subsequent movements nothing was known.

Burrup, Dickinson, Clark, and Blair, started for Johanna by the first man-of-war leaving Simon's Bay. Mrs. Burrup and Jessie Lennox were left at Cape Town, it being intended that they should come up to us with Miss Mackenzie ; so we expected that they would meet Dr. Livingstone at the mouth of the Zambesi.

At Johanna, great diversity of opinion prevailed among the officers of the navy and others as to the course our friends should pursue in order to join us. Many thought it utterly impossible that they could do it. But neither Burrup nor Dickinson were men to remain idle at Johanna upon the chance of the 'Pioneer' coming over ; and the 'Gorgon' agreeing to take them to Mozambique, they resolved from that place to find their way to us, wherever we might be.

Blair was sent back to Cape Town, he at that time not being sufficiently well to encounter the expected hardships of the journey.

Before leaving Johanna, the old 'Vega' was cleared of the stores we had been obliged to leave behind. Most of them had been spoiled by exposure, and were thrown into the sea, and the remainder—not a tenth part of what we left—was sold to the various ships then at Pomoney. Our boxes of personalities were taken by the 'Brisk,' down to the Cape.

The 'Gorgon' arrived at Mozambique on August 17, and our friends were most cordially received by the Governor, and hospitably entertained by Senhor Soares. Indeed, all the Portuguese at Mozambique seemed to vie with each other in treating our brethren well ; nothing could exceed their personal good feeling. At Mozambique, however, Burrup took the worst type of fever, and for some days his life was in danger. He recovered, but was never after equal to what he had been.

Our friends left Mozambique for Quilimane in Senhor Soares' own vessel, having learned that we had gone up the Shire. Senhor Tito was a fellow passenger ; he made our brethren his guest both on the voyage and at Quilimane, treating them with the same cordial hospitality they had received at Mozambique.

Whatever may be said of the conduct of the Portuguese in East Central Africa, with regard to their treatment of the natives, they deserved and had our gratitude for their great kindness, on all occasions, to us. Indeed, it would have been impossible for any men to have acted more hospitably, more generously, than they did, whenever we met with them.

At Quilimane, Dickinson and Clark had fever, but not so severely as Burrup at Mozambique. It did not seem to be known at Quilimane that we had interfered with the slavers, or, if it were, the Portuguese had the courtesy to say nothing about it to our brethren.

The stay at Quilimane was longer than was expected. Senhor Tito, who made the necessary arrangements for their journey up the rivers, was not able to conclude them so soon as he expected, and as our friends wished. It was six weeks before they could get away.

There was great excitement at Quilimane and elsewhere in consequence of Mariano, a notorious Portuguese rebel, threatening active proceedings again. Soldiers were going hither and thither continually, and it was at one time thought that our friends would have had a military escort up the Shire, it being reported that Mariano had made for Chibisa's. But when they got into the Zambesi, it was found that he had doubled on his pursuers, and was threatening Quilimane. So the military returned and our friends came on alone. They had two canoes, a large one and a small one. The canoe-men were supplied by Senhor Tito, but none of them knew anything of the Shire.

They entered the Shire on October 27, and had a journal been kept of their journey, it would have formed one of the most interesting records of determination and endurance ever written. Of course, the journey was done again and again afterwards by the members of the Mission, but it was the circumstances under which Burrup and Dickinson accomplished their work that made it so remarkable. They were perfect strangers, knew nothing of the natives, did not understand a word of their language, and knew not where they should find us. We felt proud of our brethren.

Both the Bishop and Burrup were very far from well for several days after their arrival. Indeed, the Bishop never really recovered his former elasticity of spirit and active habits. I think he was greatly troubled at the difficulties opening out in consequence of Dr. Livingstone not being able to give us the help we had calculated upon. He did not see his way to a ship for the Mission, and though he was always full of faith, he seemed to lose much of that bright hopefulness which had distinguished him above all other men I ever met.

On the morning of November 29, just as we had finished breakfast, we heard the report of a gun, followed immediately by another report. We knew what it meant: Dickinson, Clark, and Charles had arrived—and with the letters! 'For these and all other mercies, but especially for *this* mercy, God's holy name be praised!' was the Bishop's thanksgiving, and then off we ran to meet the newly-arrived. Dickinson looked worn and weary, but Clark was fresh. We first of all had a thanksgiving service for their safe arrival, and then the day was given up to the news from home.

We had a very happy Communion on St. Andrew's day. With the vivid impressions of home still in our hearts and minds, those at home, from whom we were separated by so many thousands of miles, seemed very near to us. Absence seemed no longer absence—the dreary thing, the uncertain thing, it had been—for with the kindly thoughts and affectionate words still fresh in our memories, it was not possible to think of those who had expressed them as so very far away. We all felt this, and were thankful and happy.

We disposed of our offertory—it was entirely the good Bishop's suggestion—in such a way as to keep up the feeling of communion with ourselves and brethren elsewhere engaged in Church work. Each member of the Mission in turn named the particular work, either in England or the colonies, to which the day's offertory was to be given. From so small a body as ourselves our offerings were but small, but in adopting this plan we did not think of tha , but of catholicity of feeling ; we wished to show that, though o isolated, we were in heart and thought at the most solemn moment of our lives with those who were in other parts of the world striving for God's glory and the good of man.

Dickinson and Clark both had fever severely after Burrup left them, but after several days of much suffering they recovered. They met with the 'Pioneer' four days before reaching Chibisa's; she was then fast on a sand-bank, but Dr. Livingstone was hopeful of getting her off next day.

With the reception of our first mail in England, we felt that with many the interest in the Mission would probably decrease. It is comparatively easy to gain the attention of men to an enterprise when its promoters are struggling for a first success, but when that has been accomplished, and the every-day life commences, then, unless men are vitally affected by the work undertaken, their interest subsides. Some one has said that Missionary effort is the Romance of Religion; certainly there was a good deal that was romantic in our enterprise. So little was really known when we left England of the country to which we were going, so much misconception and undue expectation prevailed as to the immediate possibilities of that country, that many to whom the highest objects of the Mission were not of much real interest, were urged only by secondary motives to support us. We felt, that when our communications reached home, and it became known that it would be many years before the land in which we were could contribute to home wealth, that the abundance of cotton which it was expected would find its way into the European markets had yet to be grown, that there was very little prospect of its being grown, and that we did not find the highland region a better cotton growing country, our Mission would be no longer an object of interest to many.

The cotton supply of the land disappointed us. In the Shire Valley—I speak of it up as far as fifty miles above Chibisa's—the natives grew a little here and there, just enough to make a few cloths for themselves, that was all. That the valley could grow it, there is no doubt; that it might grow more abundantly in parts that none of our party ever visited I can readily believe; but it did not grow largely in that part of the valley with which we became acquainted, and with the exception of a little patch here and there, not at all on that part of the highlands known to us. The people in the high-

lands were rich in iron, those in the valley were poor; so
when a highlandman wanted cotton to make himself a cloth,
he sent down hoes, and such like things, to the valley, and
obtained cotton in exchange. I was told again and again, that
they could not grow it on the hills; that they had tried
and it was useless, it degenerated. The Bishop bought of
Dr. Livingstone, a Manchester cotton-gin for cleaning the
cotton that we were informed would be brought for sale in
abundance; but all the while we were at Magomero, only one
small bundle was brought to us, and that we did not purchase,
for the man wanted more for it than it would have fetched at
Manchester. Evidently he had himself bought it in the valley.
Waller came out with us to inaugurate and superintend the
commerce that was expected to spring up about us at once.
Raw material was supposed to be abundant; but the only raw
material we found was the native. And though Clark, before
coming to us, had learnt the art of tanning in the expectation
that hides were everywhere, the only hides he could find to
tan were those of our little boys. Indeed, Waller could find
no commerce to inaugurate or superintend. Barter for food
there was; but that could be only for a time while we were
simply consumers: as soon as we became producers even that
commerce would cease.

But we were comforted when we thought that there were
those whose holiest sympathies were enlisted in our behalf,
who did not regard us merely as agents in opening out a new
field for commerce, but as the servants of Christ, and messengers of His love to the heathen. These thought little of the
commercial prospects of the Mission, but would rejoice with
joy unspeakable, when news came to them of the conversion
of some poor heathen through our agency; and we could not
help feeling deeply anxious about the judgment they would
form upon what we had done. Doubtful as to the soundness
of our proceedings we were not; but we felt that our experience had been contrary to that which had been hoped for us;
that our proceedings had been unlike the ordinary proceedings
of Missionaries. We did not for a moment doubt of the

loving, hearty support of all, but we were conscious that all would not agree with us.

The Bishop had some conversation with Dr. Livingstone upon the necessity for our procuring a steam launch, and the Doctor urged it strongly. From the first he said we should need one, and as he could no longer help us, he then urged it as the necessity of our existence. No one, at that time, seemed to think that any other mode of communication with the coast was practicable; for notwithstanding Burrup and Dickinson had come up with the aid of the Portuguese from the Mozambique, it did not occur to us that they could give us permanent help, and considering the position of antagonism in which we were placed to them, had we thought they could, we should have doubted their will. Still the Bishop hesitated to write home for a steamer. He had the recollection of the difficulties of the 'Pioneer' in his mind; he thought of the expense, and he could not see what use could be made of either the boat or her crew, supposing other difficulties surmounted, when she was not engaged in going up and down the river. Besides all this, he was full of care as to what could be done until the steamer did come out, for, supposing we wrote at once for one, it would be fully three years before we could get her. We were very anxious, therefore, at this time, about our position, but still hopeful; we felt sure that there was a way out of our difficulty, if we could but see it.

Dr. Livingstone reported that he saw a large body of Ajawa moving along the valley of the Upper Shire, and taking a direction which, if they kept moving, would bring them up towards Magomero. We did not think much of this announcement, as between us and them was a large tract of country thickly peopled, and we felt sure that the nearer they approached us the greater their fear of us would be. Two chiefs, introduced by Barwi, who himself, for a wonder, had no complaint, came to Magomero soon after the Bishop's return; their names were Chinoma and Komba; they came from the neighbourhood where the Doctor had seen the Ajawa, and their object was to complain of an Ajawa chief named Joi, who had established himself in their country, and deprived them of a part of their heritage, and was making their lives miserable with apprehension. We did not give these gentlemen much comfort. These ' wars,' and rumours of wars,' tired us very much. It was a satisfaction, and a cause of thankfulness, to find that for miles about us, ' kondo!' (war) was no longer the invariable exclamation of the Manganja when we met them, but that they were hard at work in their fields, and cultivating more ground than they had ever done before, hoping to get our cloth for their surplus crops.

People, by this time, had ceased to bring food for sale; some of our party were continually out buying at the villages. My principal occupation, to a considerable extent, was gone, so I built a cottage for myself, and forced on the dormitory for the boys, a heavy work, it being sixty feet long by fifteen broad. Clark began a large house in expectation of the ladies; and Dickinson advised the clearing away of the bush around our station, in order that we might get the benefit of increased ventilation. Thus hard work was still the order of the day.

We did all that could be done to prepare for the inconveniences of the rainy season, which we feared would prove a hard time to us, for though Magomero had not then proved to us absolutely unhealthy, we saw, day by day, that we were situated in the most unhealthy place in the whole country.

It was necessary to send some one overland to the mouth of the Ruo, in order to explore the country between us and it, to make friends with the various chiefs, and arrangements for the carriage up to Magomero of those stores, &c., which Dr. Livingstone had promised to bring up to that place; the Bishop decided that Scudamore and Procter, accompanied by Charles, should undertake this work. The Doctor had suggested a route to the Bishop, but Chigunda, with whom we consulted, spoke of another, through a part of the country where all the chiefs were his friends, mentioning their names as Satawa, Saopo, Chipoka, and Tombondira; and, from all he said, we concluded that the distance from Magomero to the mouth of the Ruo was about 130 miles. It was resolved to go on Chigunda's route; and our friends, with eight Manganja as porters, and Nkuto, one of our Ajawa lads, left us on the morning of December 2.

They had not been gone long, before Zomba and Anamisiri, two of the Makololo, were announced. We did not give them a warm welcome, because the Makololo were in disgrace. They had misbehaved themselves in some way when on the Lake Nyassa journey with Dr. Livingstone, and he had left them all at Chibisa's, refusing to have them again in the 'Pioneer.' Zomba, a most intelligent fellow, and his companion, a very inferior man, came to us evidently to enlist our sympathy on their behalf. We could not encourage them after the Doctor had disgraced them, but the Bishop told them that he should see the Doctor soon, and he would speak to him on their behalf. After this, it turned out that they had some captive Ajawa with them. It appeared that, on coming up to us, they had not taken the usual route, but had come up by the other side of Chiradzuro, a mountain about ten miles south-west of Magomero, where they found several villages peopled by Ajawa, into one of which they went with peaceable intentions. At first there were but women in the village, and they behaved kindly, but after a time the men came in, and they were not amiable; they abused with their tongues, and then they took to their bows and arrows. Upon this the Makololo seized their guns, and killed two men. The rest decamped, and the Makololo made some of the women and children prisoners. On being asked what they intended to do with them, Zomba replied, 'We don't want them; do you take them, and do what you like with them.' The Bishop told him that he should send them back to their own homes, otherwise the Ajawa would think that the English sent out the Makololo to kill men and steal women and children. To which Zomba replied, 'I am well pleased. If the Ajawa do not try to kill Zomba, Zomba will not kill the Ajawa.'

When the Bishop informed these women that he would send them back to their own villages, he found they had no wish to go back, but would rather stay, if we would let their husbands come also. They declared further that all the Ajawa about them would be glad to come and live near us, or to have us to live near them.

On seeing Chigunda, the Bishop asked him if he would object to those Ajawa settling near to Magomero. He did object, and very strongly. He had no fear of the Ajawa whom we had released from slavery, for they were our children; but it

MANGANJA PIPES.

would be very different if other Ajawa came; he could not trust them; they would be going backwards and forwards to their tribe. And so the Bishop told these women they must return to their friends, and tell them all he had said. One woman, however, begged so hard to be allowed to return with her husband that the Bishop consented.

We kept the two Makololo with us two or three days in

order to let these women and children have time to get back
unmolested to their homes. And for that time these fellows
smoked the pipe of peace.

CHAPTER XI.

PERSONAL AND OTHER CHARACTERISTICS OF THE MANGANJA AND AJAWA.

THE features of the Manganja and Ajawa, when not wilfully
disfigured, were by no means repulsive. The common idea of
an African is a creature with a retreating forehead, protruding
jaw, and the lineaments of an ape. I do not say our friends
were the handsomest people in the world, but their beauty was
of a higher order than that with which we generally credit the
African. The forehead of the Manganja was high, narrow,
but not retreating; and now and then, among the chiefs and
men in authority, you found a breadth of brain not inferior to
that of the best European heads. The nose, though decidedly
African, was not always unpleasantly flat or expansive; occasionally you saw this feature as well formed as among the
possessors of the most approved nasal organs. The cheek-
bones were not high, indeed they rarely interfered with the
smooth contour of the face. The jaws were small, and not
very prominent ; the chin, however, was insignificant and retreating. But their mouth was their worst feature. Place
your hand over the mouth, and you might think the Manganja
ought to hold their own against all comers; remove it, and
you could not help concluding that, sooner or later, their subjugation, if not extirpation, was certain : it was wanting in all
manly characteristics, and gave to the whole appearance of the
man an expression of weakness.

This was not so apparent among the Manganja in the Shire
Valley ; they almost seemed to be of a different family to those
on the hills. They had less amiability of expression, and they
certainly possessed more determination of character, their river

occupations tending, doubtless, to develop in them more manly
characteristics. In stature, the Manganja were not a tall race,
though you rarely met a little man. Their limbs were well
made and well proportioned to the trunk; the length of the
forearm was as well proportioned to the height of the body as
our own. The large development of heel usually ascribed to
the African races was not common to them. In youth they
were slim in build and loose of limb; in manhood, their muscular formation looked formidable; but the muscle wanted
solidity; touch it, and it was suggestive of nsima—porridge—
the staple food of the land. After middle life, those in easy circumstances had a tendency to corpulency, though the mass of the
aged were lean enough. Before they became decrepit by old
age, they could run like deer and climb like cats; but they had
no predilection for athletic sports—their only amusing excer-
cise being dancing, and in this they were proficients. When
walking they had but little elasticity in their gait; they slunk
along, seemingly ever apprehensive of danger, and ready to
flee. They made their huts with two doors, one before and
one behind, so that if their enemy came in they might at once
run out, instead of trying to turn him out. There were, of
course, exceptions to this description. I have seen instances
among them of a manly and dignified deportment, and of a
headlong dashing impudence, not to be surpassed in the civilized
world; but the mass were as I describe them, an amiable, but
a pitiably weak race, not ugly but contemptible.

Compare an ordinary Manganja with an ordinary Ajawa
man, and the latter was at once seen to be physically the superior: his face was broader; his frontal development more
masculine; the organs of causality fuller; the perceptive
faculties larger; the jaws not more prominent, but more mas-
sive; the chin large, and well to the front; the mouth, though
of full lip, shapely, and expressive of strength of will; while
the eyes, those 'windows of the soul,' had a steadfastness and
an intensity of expression, before which the diminutive souls
of the Manganja fell dismayed. Under favourable circumstances, the Ajawa appeared to be a reckless, jovial, good-
tempered people. Among those with us were three or four

miserable specimens of men, the pariahs of their tribe, I should say, and at first their presence seemed to degrade the whole; but when the others understood what their position with us really was, when the vile thought of slavery was thrown off from their minds, a heartier, or a more manly and trustworthy set of men could not be found in the land.

The Ajawa varied greatly in height. You saw men not more than five feet two or three, and you saw others five feet eight or ten.

The cranial formation of the two tribes was in uniformity with their general appearance. In each the mind had fashioned a 'tabernacle suitable to itself.' Compared with the Manganja, the Ajawa head was large and round. A phrenologist would say in them firmness and self-esteem predominated, while caution, which was developed frequently to a deformity among the Manganja, was barely evidenced: the base of their brain exhibited a breadth and a volume compared with which the shrinking and drooping occiput of the Manganja was really feminine.

The Manganja women were more gentle in appearance and manner than the Ajawa. The latter were large of stature, full-fleshed, and sensual-looking to the last degree. The former were frequently gracefully formed, and seemed of a retiring disposition, though, when they had confidence in you, they were vivacious enough. They exhibited but little of that inanity which characterized their husbands; and had it not been for the odious lip-ring, and for their elaborate tattoo, many of them would have been really good-looking. Chigunda's chief wife, for instance, had really handsome features, and the deportment of a lady. The men tattoo as well as the women, but less elaborately and effectively. With the women the cicatrices were frequently disgustingly prominent, while with the men they were barely visible. The tattoo answers to dress and ornament with the women. Each tribe had its distinct tattoo, by which they could be known as easily as the knights of old by their heraldic devices. The Ajawa women were generally loud-mouthed, but the Manganja women were not blatant. Now and then an old or a young shrew asto-

nished you with the energy of her tongue, but modesty of behaviour and speech was, as a rule, common to them.

In other physiological characteristics there is little or no
difference between the tribes. They attain maturity not much,
if any, earlier than in England, though they are regarded as
men and women immediately afterwards. Child-bearing
seemed unattended with the pain and physical inconvenience
attached to it in civilised life. Immediately after the birth,
the women emerged from the bush, to which they invariably
resort on these occasions, with a yellow-looking 'little
stranger' at their backs, and at once went about their ordinary work, apparently not weakened by their trial. I do not
think the Manganja were a prolific race. Chigunda had
twelve villages, and in every village wives, and by every wife
children, but it was not so with all; you rarely saw, as in
England, half a dozen little ones playing round the door of the
huts of the common people. The Ajawa were lustier, and evidently multiplied faster.

It was difficult to judge of the age of the natives, and they
did not seem able to enlighten you on this subject. There
were plenty of greyheaded people everywhere, though I imagine the appearance of age commenced earlier with them than
with us.

Umbilical hernia was common among children, but besides
this, which they consider no disfigurement, you rarely met
with any distortion of feature or malformation. A born crip-
ple, or a person who squinted, I did not see. If such are
born, they die in their infancy, from wilful neglect probably,
though I could not get any to admit this.

In their social and religious observances, with one important
exception—viz. that the Ajawa circumcised and the Manganja
did not—there seemed very little difference between the two
tribes.

To begin at the beginning. At the birth of a child, unless
the offspring of the free wife of a chief, no rejoicings were
made ; but when such a wife brought forth a babe, the women,
in their gayest attire, went out to the bush to the mother, and
accompanied her and her little one into the village with loud

expressions of joy; and the whole night was made lively with singing and dancing, and copious supplies of pombi. On such occasions, many of the dances, especially those performed by the women alone, were of a very objectionable character. From the moment the child is born, until it can run alone, it rarely leaves its mother's breast or back; with arms out and legs apart, they describe the letter X behind their mothers; they seem made to cling. The mother performs all her domestic duties with this living burden at her back, and when she is engaged in pounding corn, the shaking the poor little creature gets is ludicrous to behold. But as it is born to it, it sleeps in placidity; but should it awake and prove troublesome, the mother leaves off her corn-pounding, puts her hands behind her, and with the tips of her fingers gently taps her darling behind, and you rarely saw the child that could resist this soothing operation.

Should a babe belonging to the common people die, but little demonstration of woe is made beyond the mother's brief wail; but should such loss happen to the wife of a chief, or chief presumptive, the case is very different—all the circumstance of grief is freely exhibited. The mother, with the badge of woe round her head, a band of malusi (bark), walks slowly through the village uttering disconsolate cries; the women flock to her, and soon rend the air with their doleful sympathetic utterances. They go to the hut where the body lies, sit around or throw themselves prostrate on the earth, still continuing their lamentations. Should the father be absent when his child died, a not unlikely circumstance, as great men have wives in all their villages, he enters the village giving utterance to lamentable cries, in response to those of his wife and her female associates, and then the husband and his companions, the wife and her friends, unite their voices, and with redoubled energy mourn for the departed. At night, with strange incongruity, the drums are brought out, and—though the principal mourners are lying prostrate round the hut of the dead child, the pictures of inconsolable woe—dancing commences, varied by pantomimic extravagances of action among the women, who assume all the attitudes of war, pretending to strive with the dreaded messenger that had taken away the life of the child. The cries of the mourners, the shouts and songs of the dancers, the wild screams and excitement of the mock combatants, make altogether a Babel of sounds truly distressing. Some of the dances at the death are as improper as those attending the birth of the child. Like those of the ancient heathen, they represented delights that are of the earth earthy.

The education of children is not an onerous task with these natives : they educate themselves. If a boy, you see the little urchin, as soon as he can totter, drumming away at an imaginary drum, or shooting grass arrows from a toy bow, or digging holes with a hoe large enough to topple him over with its size and weight. As he gets older, the lower lobes of his ears are pierced, his upper incisors are filled so as to resemble sharks' teeth; he takes to other games of play, whip-top, humming-top, ball, and, if he be an Ajawa, wrestling, for all these, and many other games, are common to them as to us. Indeed, it was a question with us, at one time, what it was we could teach these children of ours in the way of amusements. At last Scudamore and Waller thought to surprise them with a kite. The kite was made, the children assembled to see it ascend, but the kite was ill-made, was lop-sided and heavy, would not go up, and the children made merry thereat. Said Waller, ' You have never seen anything like this before, have you ? ' Said a little urchin in reply, ' Oh ! yes, we have, though. We have seen them, but ours were different to yours. Ours went up, yours go down.' A terrible answer. As time progresses, the child accompanies his parents to the garden, and there gets his first notions of agriculture. All knowledge comes to him intuitively, I think, for I never saw a child taught, or chastised for not knowing, or chastised for anything. In the same way he knows how to make baskets from bamboo, &c., twine from buazi, cordage from bark of trees ; to build huts, to smoke bhang and tobacco, to make bows and arrows, hoes, and all the iron things they use; to spin cotton and to weave it; and to do all that a Manganja or Ajawa man is expected to do. The blacksmith's art is not so easy of acquisition as other occupations, and, though all may be blacksmiths, but few excel in ironwork. Chigunda was a famous worker in

MANGANJA BASKETS.

iron, so was Zachuracami, the chief presumptive of Magomero; and these and others that we knew were really skilled workmen, for, despite the rude nature of their tools and appliances, they often made knife-blades, spear-heads, arrowheads, and other things, of such excellent workmanship that they might have come from the hands of some of our workmen. The Manganja were better blacksmiths than the Ajawa; and the Manganja of the hills better than those of the valley, though the valley men excelled in wood-carving, their knife-handles and sheaths, pillows, and snuff-boxes, being generally elaborately and sometimes excellently carved.

The laziness which is said to belong to the African cannot be laid to the Manganja; his work was not always laborious, but he was always doing something; if he had nothing else to do, he would thread beads while talking to you. He had more ndustry than the Ajawa, but I never knew either Manganja or

Ajawa decline work when a fair amount of cloth was offered as an equivalent for their labour.

MANGANJA KNIVES.

A girl's bringing up is as simple as the boy's. She seemed to have fewer childish sports than he. Her pastime consisted principally in imitating the employments of advanced years. As soon as she can walk, she trots along with little burdens on her head, or pounds and grinds imaginary corn. Water-carrying, corn-pounding and grinding, field-work, and household cares soon become realities to her; and capacity for all this, skill in hairdressing, tattooing, making pombi, and the various earthenware pots in use among them, form her principal accomplishments. At an early age her upper lip is pierced in preparation for the hideous pileli, and at the proper time she passes through the Niamwali—of which more presently —and is tattooed. Perfection of tattoo is not obtained by one cutting; it has to be repeated several times before the cicatrices are sufficiently developed. A woman under operation for the tattoo is a disgusting sight. No part of her body is exempted, and she is covered with blood. I once came upon a woman in the condition I have described. She laughed when I told her she was doing a foolish thing, and replied that it

was not foolish but a very wise and very good thing, and that
when her tattooing was finished, she would be the best-looking
woman in the country.   Once get the women to clothe themselves, and they would cease tattooing to a great extent, for
the love of personal ornament, which mainly induces it among
the women, would expend itself in dress.   The assumed necessity for tribal distinctions would prevent for a long time the
practice being done away with entirely, for by its aid the tribe
to which a man belongs is as well known as by diversity of
speech, or difference of uniform.   Various names are given to
the cicatrix on different parts of the body : on the cheek it is
called nkwekwe, on the forehead mpenya, on the breasts kake-
rere, and on the back nteka, &c.

The position of the woman with the Manganja and Ajawa
was in no way inferior to that of the man.   It is imagined
that among the Africans generally the woman is but the drudge,
the slave of the man.   It may be so to a certain extent among
tribes which are pastoral ; there the men are occupied with the
cattle, are a ruder race, and to the woman falls the drudgery
of the field and the house ; but with the people we were with,
who were essentially agricultural, no such disparity existed ;
men and women worked together in the fields, and the special
occupations of the women were thought to be no more degrading that the specialities of our women are to our own women
at home.   The men seemed to have much kindly affection for
the women ; such a thing as ill-usage on the part of a husband
towards his wife I did not once hear of.   Frequently, as I shall
have to illustrate, the position of the woman seemed superior
to that of the man ; in their religious observances, for instance,
the principal officiant was generally a woman.

The Niamwali is a ceremony which boys and girls must pass
through on arriving at maturity.   Among our people were
several girls and lads who had arrived at this state of existence,
and Jessiwiranga was deputed to ask the Bishop for permission
to hold a Niamwali.   The Bishop sent for William, and asked
him if there was any harm in it.   Said he :

'Harm! oh no! no harm.   It is just nothing at all; what
is called in England bringing out, you know.   They dance,

they sing, they make glad, because boys and girls live so long
—long enough to be married—that is all—but no harm any
way.'

Upon this testimony consent was given; and I resolved to
see as much of this Niamwali as I could.

Before the ceremony the girls were light-hearted, merry
creatures, but as soon as they entered upon the Niamwali they
became the pictures of misery. This sudden change was perfectly unnatural, and was, I expect, produced by some narcotic.
First of all they were taken into a hut, and what passed there
I don't know exactly, and if I did, I don't think I could
describe. It was harm, much harm, I fear.

After this they were washed and oiled, and invested with a
profusion of beads; the entire possession, in fact, of our
whole community in the bead line, was hung about the necks
and bodies of the girls, who seemed to be principally operated
upon, and who submitted to everything with depressed heads,
arms hanging listlessly by their sides, and as though for ever
deprived of power of speech. The women then formed themselves into a procession, and with hand-clapping and singing
conducted their charge beyond the village to a place in the
bush where the grass had been cleared away, and boughs of
trees were so arranged as to form a fence and bower. The
girls were seated on the ground in a semicircle, their feet
towards a fire, their hands in their laps, their heads still
depressed, a melancholy spectacle of the superstition that had
transferred them for the time being from laughter-loving,
frolicsome children, to woe-begone looking women. The lads
sat apart, and did not seem to be objects of half the solicitude
the girls were.

Now that things were advanced to this stage, the women
commenced a series of songs, dances, and pantomimic acting,
which lasted, without intermission, for three days and nights,
during which time the only change of posture allowed the
girls was a formal placement of their bodies lengthways on the
earth, or a few minutes' position of upright. As they were
placed, so they remained; and if at any time they inadver-
tently moved either head or limb from the required position,

a woman immediately put it back to its right place. Songs, dances, and pantomimes were mostly to the glorification of sensuality. I saw one or two dances, however, which were quite unobjectionable, the figure not being inferior to some of the best efforts of civilized terpsichorean art, though the execution had something of the savage in it. The most skilful dancer was a young lady decorated with a profusion of wicker-work ornaments. She bounced about with marvellous agility, though you would not have said hers was the 'poetry of motion.' The most singular was a dance on the hands and knees by two women, and a movement in the knees only by one woman. Just before the proceedings terminated, an effort was made to teach the girls the art of oscillating their bodies, which is done in many ways, and is a repulsive custom, but the poor creatures were utterly unable to profit by the lesson, having lost all control over their muscles, and being thoroughly exhausted by the long exercise; they tried to imitate their instructress, a saucy little woman, but they failed. Unmitigated abuse was poured upon them, and their awkward movements imitated; but it was of no use, there they stood, helpless and inefficient. As a finale to the proceedings, the girls were re-washed, re-oiled, and re-conducted into the village, amid the songs and shouts of the assembly.

Notwithstanding William's testimony to the contrary, I felt that this Niamwali had so much of wrong in it, that I represented to the Bishop the advisability of preventing it for the future.

The morals of the young people are not worse than those of certain classes at home. The girl, however, suffers not in reputation for wrong-doing; not that immorality is actually sanctioned, far less encouraged, but it is not regarded with severity; the young people do as they will, and no punishment follows.

When a girl is sought in marriage, the man first offers a present of a fowl to the parents; if they accept it he is regarded as a recognised suitor. Previous to the wedding he builds and furnishes a hut, and hut and furniture are considered the wife's property. The large presents, however, given to the parents of the woman as an endowment for her and her children by the Kaffirs and other tribes in the south, are unknown among the Manganja and Ajawa; indeed, their poverty makes such impossible. Generally, a young man had but little difficulty in getting a wife, though now and then it happened he had to put up with a woman old enough to be his mother.

If those married belong to the common people, but little demonstration is made—a few pots of pombi are consumed, that is all; but if the contracting parties be of the upper classes, then the ceremonies and rejoicings are of several days' continuance.

If a wife be found sinning with another man, the husband in his first anger may kill the adulterer. Should he not do so, he proceeds against him, according to law, for damages. If the offender be a free man, he alone is responsible; but if he be a chief's child—slave—the chief is responsible. If the freeman be not rich enough to pay the damages given against him, his wife and children, if he have any, are taken as equivalents. If the offender's chief pay, the man retains his wife and children, but he and they lose their freedom, and become the property of their chief.

The adulteress may be at once discarded, and her children, which are always considered to belong to the mother alone, become the property of the father, and he may dispose of them as of any other property. As far as I could learn, however, the husband very rarely divorced his wife, but kept her, and took the fine.

By a curious code, in order to preserve freedom, the husband is not responsible for the ill-doing of his free wife. If she offends, and is adjudged to pay a fine, her brother, not her husband, is liable, supposing she has no means herself of paying. She could not become the slave of her brother, but she could of her husband, and she and her children would be slaves, and might be disposed of by him at will, if he paid the fine inflicted for her offence. The slave-wife is, with her offspring, the saleable property of the husband.

The parental feeling is strong in the women. There is an

idea prevalent that the African mother has so little regard for her child, that she will part with it upon the slightest occasion. I can only speak of those tribes with whom we became acquainted, and of them this was certainly not true. They had as much affection for their little ones as the mass of English mothers have, and the affection of the children for the mother is remarkable. It lasts beyond childhood; the common expression of grief is, ' Ah! mai!'—' Oh! mother!' Men will go to their mothers for consolation, will treat them with respect, and will undergo anything, or make any sacrifice for their welfare. The mother is to the man of the first consideration, on the ground, doubtless, that though he may have many wives and children, he can have but one mother.

Of course superstition interferes with the mother's affection at times. If a child fall ill, the mother will nurse it with the utmost tenderness; but should the medicine-man declare death inevitable, she leaves it to die without further effort to save it. I have seen several little ones thus exposed to die outside the villages. I once saw a woman anxiously watching her sick child; greater tenderness no one could have shown. Two men came into the village for the night, one of whom was a medicine-man. His skill was quickly sought by the mother. He looked at the child, gravely threw up his dice, in order to see what hope there was for it. The mother watched the result with painful eagerness, and it was not favourable to her hopes. She entreated the man to try again, promising him a large reward if the prognostication was favourable. The man complied with her wishes, and the poor woman saw nothing but death for her offspring. But she had not then lost hope; she redoubled her entreaties for a favourable cast of the dice, promising additional reward, all her possessions, everything she had, but the result was the same—death. She crouched down in despair; her little one would die; she lost hope; her child was henceforth dead to her; and a low death-wail proceeded from her lips. I tried to give the poor woman encouragement, told her that the medicine-man knew nothing about it, that her child might live if she still cared for it, but my words were as idle tales, her faith in the test was implicit. I was travelling, and left the village immediately after, yet I have no doubt of the result; the child would be taken outside the village; the mother would leave it in agony; and there it would die untended and apparently uncared for. And yet the mother had much affection for her little one, and would feel and mourn its loss as much as mothers would in England: though, like Hagar of old, the African mother cannot bear to see her child die. I am convinced that much injustice is frequently done to these people by travellers, who are not able to trace the effect to its right cause.

I met with no instance of a woman having twins, but should such a circumstance occur, the mother is not disgraced, as in some tribes, neither are the children, or either of them, put to death. The probability is, however, that one of them dies from neglect.

Active cruelty towards the aged is certainly not practised. They may, like deformed and diseased children, be slighted, and so suffer, but I met with nothing like systematic cruelty towards them, and when spoken to about it, both Manganja and Ajawa indignantly disowned it.

They are not a reflective people, certainly, and grief, therefore, is very short-lived. Except in rare instances, they howl for a day or two, and are comforted the next. The only instance I met with, where the semblance of grief was long-continued, was in the case of a woman who had lost her husband. While the man was alive, she was a continual scold; her everyday abuse of the poor man was quite a nuisance to us, for they lived at Magomero. She seemed in a continual state of mental excitement, which could only find relief in constant and violent exercise of the organs of speech. And so when he died her death-wail was more vehement and vociferous than her abuse while he was living; and there was no end to it. The night was made hideous for weeks with her piercing outcries. Poor thing! when she could no longer abuse she lamented, perhaps because she could not abuse.

Neither the Manganja nor Ajawa were a selfish people. On the contrary, they were in many things a very generous people. In matters of food, even when starving—and who would not

NATIVE HOSPITALITY.

be selfish then?—they were most liberal; they never thought
of keeping what food they had to themselves; but shared it
with all about them. Call up a child, as I have done many a
time, in many places; give him a little sugar, and he will put
a little into his mouth, and jump with delight to find it so
nice, but the next impulse will be, not to put the rest into his
mouth, but to call around him all his little companions, and
share with them the precious sweet, leaving but a few grains for
himself.

I recollect seeing Chechoma, Chibisa's man, sitting down
hungry to a fowl and some porridge. It was not often he
could indulge in a fowl, but he had been on a long journey,
had returned faint and wanting food, and the wife in her joy
at his return cooked a fowl. He sat down, as a hungry man
would do, devouring the food with his eyes, and I expected to
see him do, what I certainly should have done under the same
circumstances, eat all; but no, some children and others were
standing about, and off went a leg to one, a wing to another,
and the distribution continued until he had but a small piece
of the carcase left for himself, and with that and his porridge
he seemed perfectly satisfied. I made some remark upon what
he had done, upon which he looked up and said, with much
simplicity:

'It is our custom; we don't eat fowl every day; and when
we do eat it, we share it with others who do not.'

I never found the Manganja, or any native indeed, inhos-
pitable. When travelling, if you are a stranger to the people
of the village where you wish to stay for the night, timidity
or distrust of you may sometimes lead them to avoid you, but
as soon as they have confidence in you, they invariably do
their utmost to make you comfortable. The best hut is swept
out for you, and placed at your disposal, and a fire lighted.
Water is fetched for you, and some present of food is sure to
be made. When once you are known and trusted, every
village you enter you may make your home. This was my experience, and the experience of those with whom I was associated. Where it was otherwise, I should hesitate to say the
cause was with the natives. Of course there are exceptions

to this as to every other rule; you meet with churls and cut-throats everywhere. But from whatever cause arising, I can only say that I travelled in Africa with as strong a feeling of security, and met with as much kindness, as is possible in England. You must live with a people to know what they really are. Travellers merely pass through a land, they are strange to the people, the people are strange to them, both are suspicious, and so both are, more often than not, unamiable. Yet if they knew one another better, they would both see that each had more than one good point belonging to them which they were at first not credited with. Of course the reputation of the people suffers, for travellers return, and more often than not describe as fixed conditions that which is but accidental.

There was, without doubt, something like a judicature among these tribes, and a certain method for the administration of justice. For instance, if a man was certain of having received a wrong from another, he would first of all go to him and say, ' Pay me for the injury you have done. What will you pay ? ' If an unsatisfactory answer be returned, the next step is to send a friend to put the case more strongly than before, and if the offender 'still resists, he may be called to a ' mirandu,' a public assemblage, where crimes charged against any man are investigated and adjudicated upon, and where the chief, if both plaintiff and defendant belong to one chief, acts as judge. Should the parties belong to different chiefs, both chiefs preside. We saw a case where a man, a child of Chigunda, sought redress of another, a child of Sachima, for having stolen away his sister. The accused denied his guilt and refused to pay. A mirandu was called. The place of assembly was about a mile from Magomero, and much pains had been taken to make it suitable to the occasion. The grass was cleared, and boughs of trees so arranged as to protect the principal personages from sun or wind. The assembly consisted of the two chiefs, their officers, the principals in the case, and their respective friends. The chiefs sat together. The principals arranged themselves on opposite sides, leaving the space between them clear. First of all Zachuracami, who acted as clerk of the court, made a long statement in a high-pitched voice respecting the cause of their being called together, and then called upon the accuser to stand forth and make his accusation. Forthwith the accuser stood forward and testified. According to his statement, his sister had worked for the accused, had lived at his place, and no more had been seen of her. The inference was that she had been sold—the idea of murder did not seem to occur to them—and the accused was charged with having sold her. This he denied, declaring that he had paid the woman her wage, and that she had left him at the time appointed.

In support of their respective statements, each party gave evidence by his friends. Their method of doing this was singular. When the accuser testified, he did it in the most dolorous of voices, and broke off in his evidence repeatedly, pausing every three or four minutes. During these pauses, the clerk of the court recapitulated what he had said, and the witnesses rushed into the open space, danced about extravagantly, and clapped their hands. And it was thus they affirmed and confirmed the truth of all that had been advanced. In the same way acted the accused and his witnesses, though their evidence was constantly interrupted by the other party, who repeatedly exclaimed, 'I want my sister; give us back our sister,' &c.

After this was done, each was examined and cross-examined, the chiefs acting in this not as judges, but as counsel for their respective children, and Chigunda showed himself quite an astute practitioner.

When as much was known of the case as could be known, a satisfactory solution seemed as far off as ever. The one side was clamorous for conviction, the other for acquittal—the one saying, pay for the injury you have done, the other calling out for compensation for having been falsely accused, and the judges siding each with his own 'child.'

At last Chigunda consulted with his child—the accused—and, with a view to stop the fruitless clamour, offered that he should drink the muavi (poisoned water), the supposed certain test of innocence or guilt. But this proposal increased responsibility; if the accused by this method was proved innocent,

the accuser would be charged with the serious crime of having
compassed his life, and his position would be full of danger.

So this proposal was declined, and another period of excitement and clamour followed. Chigunda at length lost patience,
and exclaimed angrily, 'Why don't you accept our proposal?
We are ready to take the muavi. Give it. If my child is
guilty he will die, and we will pay. If he is innocent he will
vomit it, and then you must pay; and so there will be an end
of the matter.'

The other side evidently thought the chances were in favour
of the vomiting, and still declined; and at last Sachima interposed, and candidly said he thought his child, the accuser, had
failed to establish his charge, and advised him to withdraw it
altogether. This he did, upon the other side undertaking to
commence no retaliatory proceedings.

Some time afterwards the woman was discovered in a village
some distance off, to which she had gone to get away from her
brother.

This was the most reasonable mode of getting justice in the
land; and, though far from satisfactory in its issues generally,
it was a public acknowledgment that certain acts were wrong,
and that an authority existed for punishing the wrong-doer.
Had this man been found guilty of selling the woman, probably he would have had to pay a goat, or an equivalent, the
worth of the woman in Manganja estimation. But though
condemned, the complainant is left to enforce payment, so he
might, if the stronger man, elude payment, or resist until the
other was wearied out. As here, so there, the law's delay and
uncertainty were truly vexatious.

The Manganja and Ajawa are not idolaters; we met with no
instance where they *worshipped* a visible object under the idea
that supernatural power existed in it. They believed, however,
that, influenced by the great medicine-man, a power was im-
parted for good or for evil to objects either animate or inanimate, and they had an implicit faith in or a dread of such
objects, though they did not worship them. The influence of
these great medicine-men, therefore, was very great. Their
capacity to work evil was thought to be unlimited; nor were

they ever supposed to do a purely beneficial deed, for if they benefited one, it was an understood thing that it was at the expense of another. They employ their magical arts in the detection of offenders, and I once had an opportunity of witnessing some of their proceedings. Some corn had been stolen from the garden of one of Chigunda's people. The owner complained to the chief, who employed the services of a celebrated medicine-man living near. The people assembled round a large fig-tree just outside our station, and the magician, a wild-looking individual, who seemed exceedingly uncomfortable when we appeared, commenced proceedings. First of all he produced two sticks, about four feet long, and about the thickness of an ordinary broom-handle; these, after certain mysterious manipulations and utterings of unintelligle gibberish, he delivered, with much solemnity, to four young men, two being appointed to each stick. Then, from his capacious and greasy goatskin bag, he brought forth a zebra-tail, which he gave to another young man, and after that a calabash filled with peas, which he delivered to a boy. The medicine-man rolled himself about in hideous fashion, and chanted an unearthly incantation; then came the man with the zebra-tail, followed by the boy with the calabash, moving, first of all, slowly round the men with the sticks, but presently quickening their pace, and shaking the tail and the calabash over the heads of the stickholders. For a time nothing came of these proceedings; but ere long the spell worked. The men with the sticks were subject to spasmodic twitchings of the arms and legs. These increased rapidly, until they were nearly in convulsions; they foamed at the mouth; their eyes seemed starting from their heads; they realised to the full the idea of demoniacal possession. According to the Manganja notion, it was the sticks that were possessed primarily, the men through them; it was the devil *in* two sticks; and when I asked the awe-struck spectators, what next? a man in suppressed voice, said:

'Wait, and you will see. The sticks will drag and drag the men, until they drag them to the person who stole the corn.'

And as he said, so, apparently, it came to pass. The men seemed scarcely able to hold the sticks, which took a rotary motion at first, and whirled the holders round and round like mad things. Then headlong they dashed off into the bush, through stubborn grass and thorny shrub, over every obstacle—nothing stopped them; their bodies were torn and bleeding; round to the gaping assembly again they came, went through a few more rotary motions, and then, rushing along the path at a killing pace, halted not until they fell down, panting, and exhausted, in the hut of one of Chigunda's slave wives. The woman happened to be at home, and the sticks were rolled to her very feet, and by so doing denounced her as the thief. She was brought before the now excited assembly, and to their indignation denied that she was the thief. The medicine-man was appealed to. In triumph he was smoking his pipe under the tree, and the only remark he vouchsafed was : ' The spirit has declared her guilty ; the spirit never lies.' But the woman vehemently declared that the spirit did lie, that she was innocent, and to prove her innocence said she would take the muavi. As the spirit could not object, and could not be called upon to pay, save in reputation, the muavi was produced; but, as corn-stealing from a garden was, according to the Manganja code of laws, a petty offence, and she was connected with the chief, she was allowed to take the muavi by deputy. She ran home, came back with a fowl, a cock : this bird's mouth was pulled open, the deadly stuff was poured down its throat, and the expectant congregation looked on, with greedy eyes, to the issue. It was this : the bird, after struggling for a few seconds, threw up the poisoned water, lay quiet for a minute or two, and then, hearing a lusty challenge from a rival bird in the village, stood upon its legs, flapped its wings, and crowed. It was evidently none the worse for the ordeal it had passed through, and all the people pronounced the woman innocent. She carried off her cock in triumph. The medicine-man shrugged his shoulders, and disappeared. Here were two ordeals, both infallible ; but the one contradicts the other, therefore neither is infallible. But that was not the reasoning of the Manganja ; their belief in the muavi was evident. And who could deny the reality of the spiritual possession they had just beheld? The men who held the sticks did not act, they were acted upon; for it was not at all likely men would do as they did, and get themselves torn to pieces, of their own accord. And so their faith, despite their contradictory results, remained unshaken for the time. In the end we shook it a little, and among our own people succeeded in establishing trial by jury instead of these objectionable, and in most cases unjust, proceedings; and our method of proceeding so commended itself to the pockets (for the medicine-men there, like the lawyers here, require a heavy fee before proceeding) as well as to the good sense of the natives about us, that before we left the country one or other of us had to sit in the administration of justice almost every day.

I have no doubt that many of these professors of magic firmly believed in their own power; and cases came under our notice where, when put on their trial for having compassed the death of some one by their supernatural acts, they vauntingly owned they had done so. A man was struck dead by lightning in a village a few miles from Magomero; people came forward and testified that they had seen a certain professor of witchcraft go up into the clouds and bring the lightning down upon the man. It was proved that he had threatened to do so, and, when on his trial, he boasted that he had done it.

There was another class of medicine-men who were not supposed to possess supernatural powers beyond the capacity to produce charms as preservatives from sickness, or to tell fortunes. These men frequently had much skill in the treatment of the simple diseases of the country; they knew much of the properties of various medicinal plants, and were the cuppers and bleeders, though not the drawers of teeth. Of course in their practice there was a great deal of mummery and superstition, and if they had to deal with a complicated disease— one beyond their skill to cure—they would ascribe it to the malevolent influence of some enemy of the patient. I once met with a young woman who was in the greatest distress of mind. She was ill; she had been to the Sinanga—medicine-man—and he told her that her enemy, whoever it was, had

bewitched her, had caused a land tortoise to enter her mouth
while she was asleep, and it was then eating away her heart.
She was evidently suffering from enlargement of the spleen.
Of course, according to the native doctor, the disease could
not be cured until the enemy had been found, and the enemy
could not be found without supernatural aid, such as he and
his fellows could give, and that aid must be paid for. But in
simple cases they seemed skilful enough; they were far more
successful in the treatment of wounds and the ulcerous sores
so prevalent among them than our own doctor. Their *modus
operandi* is not always agreeable; for instance, in cases of
severe fever, they take the sap of a trailing, climbing plant,
called by them Candanarubi, wood-ashes, and castor-oil, mix
them well together, make a few gashes with a knife in the body
of the patient, and rub the compound in through the wounds.
A severe, but generally a successful remedy this. The virtue
is principally in the sap, from which proceeds a very pungent
odour, and which is probably a strong nervine stimulant. The
Portuguese have great faith in the remedies of the native
doctors, and frequently employ them in preference to those
prescribed by their own inefficient medical men. But the
native doctors dislike attending the Portuguese, and in most
cases will not do so unless compelled. ' We can cure our own
people,' say they, ' because we know how they live, what they
eat and drink, and they have only the diseases of our own
country, and they have confidence in us. But you white men
are strangers. We don't know you so well as we know ourselves; your habits are different to ours; you eat and drink
strange things, so your sicknesses are often different to ours;
and though you ask us to save you, you laugh at us even when
you ask this. If we try to save you, we do our best; but we
are only men, and we cannot always cure. This our people
know, but they trust us; and if a man that we are trying
to cure dies, we are not afraid; we did our best, and no harm
comes; our people do not say, ' You have killed him, and we
will kill you.' But if we try to save you white men, we are
afraid. If you get well, all is very good for us; but if you do
not get well, you are angry, call us bad names, and beat us;

and if you die while we are giving you medicine, your friends
say we have killed you, and then they kill us, whip us to death,
or make slaves of us, and take away our wives and children.
So we don't like to give you white people medicine.' And
under such circumstances, it would be a wonder if they did.

A clever medical man, as we found, is a great aid to a Mission ; for one of the best ways of dispelling the belief in witchcraft, is to cure, and explain to them the nature and cure of
those complicated diseases which the native doctors do not
understand, and therefore ascribe to witchcraft.

Among the Manganja and Ajawa very little surgery was
practised. They had a rough method of extracting barbed
arrows from the flesh, thrusting one of their large knives into
the wound, enlarging it, and holding it open, while another
drew forth the arrow. I have known them use the knife to
an ulcer, but beyond this, nothing more. Other tribes, however, practise amputation, and the Maruru, in their method,
had anticipated one of the latest European improvements in
amputation. They take a bowstring, pass it round the limb to
be taken off, tighten it, and daily contract the loop until it has
cut its way to the bone, healing the flesh as they proceed.
Then they lay the limb on a block of wood, and by a dexterous
blow with a heavy knife sever the bone. The result is a clean-
cut amputation. The bone protrudes a little, but they so
manage matters that no sore remains.

The laws relating to land are with the Manganja the same
as among the New Zealanders and other savage people. The
land is the property of the tribe; no individual can possess a
freehold. The separate possession of individuals is secured to
them only so long as they occupy : no one can transfer land to
another. The chief has the power of allowing the alienation
of land, but the common rights of the community restrain
him : without the common consent he could not dispose of any
part of his territory. There is no limit to the extent of land
a man may occupy, but he must cultivate what he holds, for
cultivation alone makes property. If a man gave up a parcel
of ground upon which he had bestowed much labour, he received no compensation ; as the representative of the commu-

nity, the land reverted to the chief, in whom alone the power of disposal rested. But a man going away from the ground he had tilled could sell the crops upon it, and as they ripened the purchaser was allowed to gather them. The petty chiefs derived but little profit from their position. They probably had more slaves, but they worked in the field as much as others. Chigunda used to go to work in his garden daily, and he had but little besides that which he himself produced. He supported himself, his wives, and his families, by the produce of his garden. The agricultural pursuits of the Manganja rendered them less savage than many other tribes, but this was fatal to their independence. They were broken up into small communities, settling wherever ground was most fertile. Each little community had its head man, or chief, and too often its separate interests; and though the subordinate chiefs were nominally under a superior, like Chinsunzi, and those superior individuals nominally subject to the Rundo, to whom tribute was paid from all the chiefs, yet this arrangement produced but little good. Central authority existed but in name, unity of action was not the result of it, and patriotism did not exist. There was a time, it was said, when the Manganja were a very powerful people, and I think it likely, for though the tribes around spoke different languages, the Manganja language was spoken by all. They had been in possession of the land from time immemorial; they knew of no one before themselves; but when we went into the country, they seemed ripe for ruin, a people ready to pass away, unless rescued by a strong and benevolent hand. They needed a new element among them, a new principle of life, and that we hoped to have been instrumental in imparting to them by establishing the Church of Christ in their midst.

There were some very hopeful features in the religious belief of the Manganja. Their form of government was something like a theocracy, for though the Rundo was the supreme chief, he was not the supreme authority; there was a higher than he recognised in the affairs of the country. A certain spirit—whether of some great departed chief or no did not clearly appear—whom they called Bona, was supposed to have an

abode on the top of a mountain called Choro, and to him the
Rundo resorted for counsel in times of difficulty and danger,
so that the Rundo's position was something like that of the
Judges of Israel; if he was applied to by his people, he asked
guidance of Bona. Bona was supposed eminently benevolent:
when his power predominated war did not desolate the land;
drought was unknown; he blessed the seed, and the fruits of
the earth abounded; he was, in fact, a dispenser of peace and
plenty as well as of wise counsel. He had on Choro and elsewhere (for he was thought to be ubiquitous), certain huts consecrated to his service. He was spoken of as having a visible
presence, but no one could say they had really seen him or
heard him. His instructions were made through a woman
consecrated to his service, who acted as the medium between
her people and Bona, and who was vulgarly spoken of as his wife.
It was not necessary that the woman elected for betrothment
to Bona should be a virgin; but after she had become Bona's
bride, she was excluded, on pain of death, from the society of
all others. But though she was so exclusively devoted to Bona,
he appeared to her only in her dreams. If the Rundo wished
for Bona's advice, he, or his deputies, would proceed to the
top of the mountain with horn-blowing and shouting to make
the bride of Bona know of his approach. She then retired to
the seclusion of her hut, heard without seeing those who came
to her, sought and found Bona in sleep, received from him, in
this condition, that which he wished her to make known,
and when she awoke she declared to the expectant people the
message which Bona had given her to deliver.

Bona was often in need of a wife; for, notwithstanding her
eminent position, the condition of the woman must have been
miserable. Under ordinary circumstances, the occupations of
the native women are numerous and constant, and they all
seem born for the fulfilment of wifely and maternal duties; but
the wife of Bona, doomed to inactivity and isolation, separated
from her real husband and family—for choice was generally
made of a married woman—must indeed be a wretched creature, and no wonder Bona needed such a rapid succession of
helpmates. Tingani for a long time supplied wives and food

for Bona, but he, at length, wearied of that honour, and Man-kowe had to do so. Waller once happened to be at the Run-do's village when choice of a fresh bride was made, and found the people in a state of fear and excitement; each woman was apprehensive for herself, and each man for his wife. The Rundo made choice of the woman, and as it was his policy to keep out of the way of his people until the choice was made and the woman carried off, he was not visible. In the dead of the night, however, there was a great cry, and 'Aksai anga!' (my wife) in a man's voice, and 'Amai!' (my mother) in chil-dren's voices were heard above the general turmoil. The choice had been made, and the husband and children were bewailing their loss. In the morning the Rundo appeared, and was very popular, for though the husband and children of her who had been taken were still sorrowing, the rest had escaped and were rejoicing—so painful are the manifestations of false religion.

In this idea of Bona, however, there is good ground work for Missionaries to proceed upon in the promulgation of our holy religion. You would of course ignore the existence of Bona, but Bona would help you to point out a higher than Bona—'Who prepareth rain for the earth, and maketh the grass to grow upon the mountains, and herb for the use of men:' Who 'maketh peace in all thy borders, and filleth thee with the flour of wheat.' We could laugh at the folly of asking counsel of Bona, of seeking to know Bona's will, but, in-asmuch as they did that, we could the readier make them understand that with us they could know God's will at all times, if, with us, they had and knew God's word. And then they would also realize our motive in coming to them to restore to them that knowledge of God which they had lost, to make known to them His will for their guidance, and to impart to them His grace in order to strengthen them to perform that will. I am convinced that such is the spiritual condition of the African heathen, that what they still retain—if we only knew how to make use of it, as St. Paul, for instance, did of the inscription on the heathen altar at Athens—would help us greatly in imparting to them what they have not. And I be-lieve that seeking a groundwork in their common customs, upon which to build the Christian's common faith, is a surer and a better way of making them Christians than by totally ignoring all they know as useless, because superstitious, and everlastingly preaching to them as though they had the same antecedents to help them that we have.

But this idea of Bona was not their idea of God. Both Manganja and Ajawa seemed to have a better idea of the Deity than most savage tribes. The Manganja called God, Pambi, or Mpambi; the Ajawa, Mulungu. Neither, as I have elsewhere said, looked upon Him as a God of wrath; indeed, they did not appear to assign any wrathful attribute to Him, nor did they in any way make Him the author of evil; they supposed evil to proceed from malevolent spirits—the Mfiti. We never, therefore, found them offering up human sacrifices in order to avert God's anger. If great danger, either famine or war, threatened them, they would assemble at an appointed place, and in an appointed way, offer up prayer to God to deliver them from the famine, or to give them the victory in the war. We saw instances of this. At Magomero, soon after the commencement of the first rainy season after we were in the land, there was a solemn assemblage for prayer. The ground had been prepared, the seed sown; the rains came, the corn sprang up—all seemed as we desired it; and then the rains ceased: day by day, week by week, and no rain; the fierce sun seemed withering the young corn, famine appeared imminent. Chigunda assembled his people in the bush outside the village, then marched with them in procession to the appointed place for prayer, a plot of ground cleared and fenced in, and in the middle of which was a hut, called the prayer hut. The women attended as well as the men, and in the procession the women preceded the men. All entered the enclosure, the women sitting on one side of the hut, the men on the other; Chigunda sat some distance apart by himself. Then a woman named Mbudzi, the sister of Chigunda it was said, stood forth, and she acted as priestess. In one hand she had a small basket containing Indian corn meal, in the other a small earthen pot containing the native beer, pombi—the equivalent, doubtless, to the ancient offering of corn and wine.

She went just into the hut, not so far but what she could be seen and heard. She put the basket and the pot down on either side of her. Then she took up a handful of the meal and dropped it in the flour, and in doing this called out in a high-pitched voice, ' Imva Mpambi! Adza mvula!' (Hear thou, O God, and send rain!) and the assembled people responded clapping their hands softly, and intoning—they always intone their prayers—' Imva Mpambi! (Hear thou, O God!) This was done again and again until the meal was expended, and then, after arranging it in the form of a sugarloaf, the beer was poured, as a libation, round about it. The supplications ceased, Mbudzi came out of the hut, fastened up the door, sat on the ground, threw herself on her back; all the people followed her example, and while in this position they clapped their hands and repeated their supplication for several minutes. This over, they stood up, clapped hands again, bowing themselves to the earth repeatedly while doing so; then marched to where Chigunda was sitting, and danced round about him like mad things. When the dance ceased, a large jar of water was brought and placed before the chief; first Mbudzi washed her hands, arms, and face; then water was poured over her by another woman; then all the women rushed forward with calabashes in their hands, and dipping them into the jar threw the water into the air with loud cries and wild gesticulations. And so the ceremonies ended.

Singularly enough, before the ceremony was over a thunder-cloud passed over Magomero, and we had an abundant shower of rain; though the hills about us soon drew it away, and it was some time before it rained again.

Here again was plenty of groundwork upon which to build up in the minds of these people a knowledge of that good God, whom they thus ignorantly worshipped. Enveloped as it was with superstition and folly, this act of theirs might have been made the stepping-stone to a reasonable, spiritual and acceptable sacrifice of prayer and thanksgiving. And I am very sure that there was no impediment in these people, either physical, intellectual or spiritual, to prevent the Gospel spreading among them, as readily as it did among ourselves.

They are suffering as we suffered, before the Church of Christ
was established among us, from all the miseries and ignorances
and wickednesses which arise among men alienated from God ;
but take to them the grace of God, and, sure I am it will correct the spiritual evils of their nature—if we use that method
which God has ordained we should use in imparting it to
them—and produce happiness in their souls.

But though they had this idea of God, of the world to come
their ideas were most vague. They did not think that death
annihilated ; for they had a firm belief in the existence of the
Msimi—the spirits, or more properly ' shadows' of men after
death ; and they even thought that the spirit of some of their
chiefs possessed the power of hearing their prayers and grant-
ing their requests, and it frequently happened that when they
did not immediately get what they had supplicated Mpambi
for, they would pray to the spirits of these chiefs, saying,
' Perhaps God does not care to give us what we want, so it is
no use asking Him any more ; we will ask the spirits of our
chiefs.' Yet though they had this idea of a spiritual world,
of the conditions of that world they knew nothing. They did
not comprehend that this life was a life of probation, and they
therefore had no belief in a future retribution. Though they
did not think death annihilated, they seemed to imagine that
it reduced all to the same level ; the murderer and the thief,
the adulterer and the liar, being no worse off than those un-
stained by such crimes ; they all became Msimi, and as far as
comfort and happiness were concerned, all were circumstanced
alike. Whatever their idea of duty or law was, they did not
believe in any future punishment for the violation of duty, or
the breaking of law ; neither did they expect a reward for a
faithful observance of both. The only rewards and punish-
ments they believed in were of the earth, earthy.

Their religious belief did not influence them as individuals ;
no man, for instance, thought of praying to God alone. If
God were supplicated, it was by all, for the benefit of all ; to
receive common advantages, protection, or favour, or escape
from disaster. Their terror of death was great, and in order
to preserve life they resorted to innumerable follies, but it did

not occur to them to commit themselves individually to the Divine protection; and their astonishment was great when they discovered that we never lay down to rest at night, or awoke in the morning, that we never went on a journey, or undertook any important work, without doing that—asking for God's blessing and thanking Him for His mercies. Our public worship they were not long in understanding, but our private devotions were strange to them for some time. I suppose few heathen at any time ever understood individual holiness. The Greeks and Romans worshipped for their nation, not for themselves; and I expect the essential features of heathenism, like those of human nature, have been one and the same in all ages of the world, and one and the same in all parts of the world.

But I believe that the conversion of the African heathen will be found to be an easier work—humanly speaking—than that of the Hindoo or Chinese. He is dense, dark, barbarous, and degraded; but they have a system of religion, a regular philosophy for which they think no problem in life too hard. Their principle of religious belief, therefore, is a living antagonist not readily overthrown; but with the Africans it is otherwise, for more often than not, they can give you no reason for what they do beyond this, ' It is the custom of our country.' The idea which gave life to their customs has, in most cases, been forgotten. We once met with a remarkable instance of this. Akumtara, the chief of a village a few miles from our station at Chibisa's, died, and we heard that, according to Manganja custom— and this was the most essentially savage custom we met with— one of his slave wives was to have her throat cut and be buried with him. When a great chief died several wives were sacrificed. Upon hearing of this, Procter took William with him and went to the village to see if he could not prevent this sacrifice of the woman in question. He was received favourably by the inhabitants, and when he told them he wished to speak to them about the woman they were going to kill, they said: 'Speak out all that is in your heart.'

' Are you going to kill a woman and bury her with the body of your dead chief?' asked he.

'We are,' was the answer.

'Why do you do it?' was asked again.

'It is the custom of our country,' was the reply, and that was the only reason he could get; not because they did not care to give him their reason, but because they had no other to give. Doubtless this custom originated in some idea of the necessities of the future state, in the same way that the North American Indian conceived that his dead friend had but gone to new hunting-grounds, and would want therefore the means for hunting, and so killed his horse and his dog and put them with bow, arrow, and spear into the grave. But if ever such idea gave birth to this Manganja custom, it had passed away from them; they did what they did because their forefathers had done the same, but of the motive of their forefathers for doing it they were ignorant. This, without doubt, evidenced great degradation; and it is from degradation that the Africans, in common with all other heathen, are suffering. Everywhere among them you behold signs of this degradation, in almost every custom you may detect evidences of a higher state of things than now exists. There are, it is true, those who say that all men, heathen as well as Christian, are progressing from a lower to a higher state of existence; that God, in fact, is actively engaged in educating all mankind, bringing them all to Himself by different ways; but I cannot imagine any one, unless blinded by preconceived ideas, going to Africa, becoming acquainted with the manners and customs of the natives, and yet holding to such an opinion as this. You need not the testimony of Holy Writ to the Fall of Man, the fact is plain before your eyes. Like the heathen of old—not willing to keep God in their knowledge—they are given over to a reprobate mind, and are perishing in their own sinful imaginations. So if we leave these heathen to themselves, we leave them to perish. We have no authority for believing otherwise. Awful as it is, we cannot escape the responsibility of this fact; and awful as is the thought of the future of the heathen who perish in their heathenism, we cannot avoid it. We may indeed hope that God's mercy will surpass our expectations of it; but sure I am, notwithstanding the present shortcomings of the Church with regard to the heathen, that their condition would be far more hopeless than it now is, if we accepted that sentimental idea of the love of God, and of God's moral government of the world, which is now somewhat fashionable, and which regards that love and limits that government to man's capacity to estimate them.

But to return to Akumtara. The degradation which prevented his people knowing why they were going to kill and bury the body of one of his wives with that of this chief, was really no hindrance to an appreciation of a better state of things, for when my brother Procter said to the assembled people, 'Do you know what becomes of people after death— not of their bodies, (that, we know, goes into the grave,) but of their spirits?' and found that they did not know, he told them we knew, because we had God's word, which He had given to us in order that we might know what great love He had for us, how far we had fallen away from Him by wicked works, and what we must do in order to please Him here, and to go to Him when we die. And as he was able—and he was better able than most of us—he declared to them the good news of God and of His Son Jesus Christ. And when they heard that God was angry with those who killed their fellow-creatures, as they were going to kill that poor woman, and that in a future state they would be judged for the deeds they had done here, and that they would then be punished or rewarded according as they had obeyed or disobeyed God's will on earth, they were astounded; it was, indeed, strange news to them, and for a time they made no reply.

At last one, in effect, said it would be a bad thing to make God angry with them; they should be sorry to do that, and if it would make God angry with them if they killed the woman, they would not kill her, they would let her come and live with us if we would permit her. Ready consent was given to this, and they went at once to the place where the woman was, (she was in the stocks, not far from the dead body of her husband) unloosed her, and took her to Procter, who brought her to our station, and she lived with our people.

Such a success as I have just recorded could not always be

looked for; it would be unreasonable to expect any people to give up at once deep-rooted customs, bound up as they are with the most solemn occasions of their life, even though they can give you no reason why they maintain them; but in time you would succeed, for the character of the African is far more hopeful for improvement than many have imagined.

The circumstances of our highly civilised life lead us to expect too much from our own efforts. We not only work for results, but we want to see the results we work for; and we measure spiritual success by temporal, and we do wrong. The perfect sanctification of an individual soul is the work of a lifetime; the conversion of an entire race the work of centuries.

It always has been so from the very beginning, and it always will be so; and if we have not the strength to persevere 'by patient continuance in well-doing' for these poor African heathen, we nineteenth-century Christians are but a degenerate race, and not worthy of the sacred name by which we are called.

CHAPTER XII.

TROUBLES AT MAGOMERO.

I RESUME the narrative of events interfered with by the last chapter.

December commenced badly for us at Magomero. With every fall of rain the unhealthiness of the place was more and more manifested. A stomach sickness, which nothing could cure, afflicted our children, and wasted them to skeletons. The first to fall under it was a little boy to whom life at no time could have been joyful. He was one of those to whom existence in this world means suffering. While here he was a miserable little isolate, his pitiful physical condition unfitting him for the companionship and amusements of those of his own age. It was painful to see him slowly dragging himself along, life a burden to him, but he was baptized, and he died. And then what a change had a few hours wrought. Life no longer a torment, but the possessor of an existence so exalted, so beautiful, so full of loving companionship, so capable of highest sympathies, that we who were left behind could not imagine it! His heathen name was Dzika, his Christian name Charles.

We all suffered from the prevalent complaint. I find the following entry in my journal for December 17 :—

'Since my last entry, December 4, I have been nearer death than ever I was before. This day week I was very ill with dysentery, and it seemed most probable that I should soon follow those little ones of ours who have died of the prevalent sickness. It is only owing to God's mercy, and Dickinson's unremitting care, that I am here to write this. I am still suffering considerably. For the last four days I have been in a hut on some rising ground, a few hundred yards from the Station. By this change I am removed from the foul air of my own hut. The higher ground about us is healthy. Compared with that of our Station, the air where I now sleep is quite pure and refreshing. Since Dickinson has been with us, everything that could be done has been done to make our Station healthy: but, do what we may, we shall never make it so. The place is condemned, and it is only a question of convenience as to when we shall move from it. We cannot move now—there is no place to which we can go; all the villages are occupied, and building at this season of the year is impossible. The good Bishop, who accepted Magomero with reluctance, has grown quite fond of it; but the place must be given up, annoying as it is to have spent so much labour in vain upon it. We cannot enter it now without feeling that we have been robbed of vitality, and without finding our physical powers reduced to lowest ebb. I only hope it will not prove another Linyanti.'

But sickness was not the only trouble that came upon us with December.

On the afternoon of the 7th, Charles, who accompanied Procter and Scudamore on the Ruo expedition, returned alone, haggard and worn, his feet lacerated and swollen, the very picture of a man who had been hunted for his life.

'All are gone—I alone am left—not one besides myself has

escaped!' said he; and then he sank down on the ground and
burst into tears. This was horrible news.

After a time we had further information from him, and it
appeared that at first all went well with our friends; they
found a good road and friendly people, until they arrived at a
village about eight miles off, belonging to a chief named Manasomba. Here they were attacked and plundered, and Procter, Scudamore, and the porters, were said to have been either
killed or made prisoners.

'Twice,' said he, 'was I surrounded. I hardly know how
I broke away from them. And when I was about a hundred
yards off I heard two shots fired. I fear this was all Mr.
Procter and Mr. Scudamore could do before they were overpowered. The natives were all around them firing at them
with their bows and arrows.'

I heard this much, and I could wait for no more, for dysenteric pain was strong upon me. I returned to my own house.
A short time after, the Bishop came in, and said:

'We have just been considering what we had better do. I
did not send for you, because I thought you could not bear it.
But one thing is certain—we must without delay get these
men, if they are alive, out of the hands of Manasomba, and,
in order to do so, I propose to go down to his village, where
we hope they still are, with as large a force as we can muster.
We will at once send down to Chibisa's for the Makololo. It
is not wrong, I think, to make use of their help on such an
occasion as this. We propose to take five or six white men,
and most of the Makololo. The remainder will remain here
to defend this place in case of necessity.'

Brave and good man! His heart was full of feeling, almost
to bursting; but he mastered himself, and was at once master
of the position.

The natives crowded about our doors, sorrowful as though
they had lost their dearest friends.

Johnson came in to me, greatly agitated, for Scudamore had
been a good friend to him. Said he, 'I don't like this at all,
sir. I wish we had all died together. And I would have died

too, that I would!' And so he would, for he was a brave and generous fellow.

But scarcely were these words out of his mouth, when Winapi, one of our women, rushed up to my door, clapping her hands with joy, and exclaiming, 'Johnson! Johnson! Anglesi! Anglesi!' And she pointed to the path leading to our Station.

Johnson rushed out, and I followed, for the effect of this woman's words was electrical; and there, sure enough, were our dear brothers, coming towards us unhurt, though worn and weary to the last degree. We embraced them as those given back to us from the grave.

Our people were as delighted as we. The joy they manifested on the safe return of our friends was very gratifying. They rushed forward to welcome them with a heartiness we had not looked for. A great grief seemed removed from them. They felt with us in our sorrow, and they rejoiced with us in our joy. Men, women, and children—it was the same with all. This sympathy was very encouraging; it showed us that what we had done for them had not been done in vain.

From the narratives of Procter and Scudamore, it seemed at first everything was favourable to their enterprise. They went over new and interesting ground, and derived much information and pleasure from their journey. Their first day's journey lay through a country everywhere well cultivated. Next day, their course lay over a plain. The rains had done wonders for the country, and the ground was clothed with richest verdure, relieved and set off by a host of flowers of every hue. Indeed, the country all around Magomero was a delight, so profuse were the flowers. They crossed the Trojira, a river not unlike an English trout stream. Along the banks of this river, as along the banks of all the rivers on this upper plateau, trees of large size grew, but they were mostly destitute of that peculiar formation and foliage one looks for in tropical countries; but an altitude of nearly 4,000 feet above the sea modifies tropical characteristics into those belonging to temperate regions. A little higher, and as Dr. Meller did

on Chiradzuru, you will find some of the productions of our
own land, viz., the blackberry-bush. The Trojira was found
to flow from the Milanji into the Ruo. The bridge across
this stream evidenced more skill and industry than the natives
usually exercise on their public works. It was not, as usual,
a single trunk felled so that it had fallen across from bank to
bank, but a number of well-chosen logs lashed together, so
that a man might get over without much fear of breaking his
neck, or being drowned by falling off into the stream below.

As they approached the end of their second day's journey,
they had magnificent views of the Milanji, which there faced
due west. They were then above forty miles from Magomero,
and the huge precipices and ravines which we had so often
seen in the distance were there revealed in their majesty and
vastness.

On the second night, our friends slept at the village of
Saopa. Chigunda had spoken of him as a friend, and a friend
he proved. The country about Saopa seemed more fertile than
about Magomero ; it produced a greater variety of the fruits
of the earth, though at that particular time food was scarce
even there.

The next morning, a start was made for Manga, the next
halting-place. In about two hours they came to the pass of
Chore, a flat-topped hill lying just off the Milanji. Then they
crossed a small river, which runs through a large plain called
Manganja, and from which, according to the testimony of the
natives, the whole country is named. The etymology of Manganja, however, is Ma = the people, Nyanja = great water; a
name, probably, given to the lake people generally.

Nothing could be more unlike the 'rolling wastes,' the
'burning plains,' and 'sandy deserts' of Africa, than this plain
—richest verdure, beautiful flowers, and on the banks of the
streams large trees with graceful foliage. The brilliant
plumage of bird and butterfly made this district, as well as
many others about us, at this time of the year almost a paradise in appearance.

An hour before midday our friends halted at a large village,
where was plenty of food, belonging to a man named Na-

komba, who was son-in-law to Chipoka, the chief of Manga.
Here rice, lemons, and pine-apples were produced, good things
to which our brethren had long been strangers. Nakomba,
on being told that the object of the journey was to open a
path from the mouth of the Ruo to Magomero, in order to get
up our stores, and for purposes of honest trade, said that
would be a good thing, for then his people could earn cloth as
porters; and cloth they evidently needed, for scarcely any
were decently covered.

Near Nakomba's village cotton was growing; but neither
on this journey, nor on any other taken by the Mission party,
was anything like a large growth of cotton seen on the highlands.

Nakomba acted as guide to Manga, a village beautifully
situated close under the Milanji. Flowers, fruits, and trees
were around the village, in the village, and around all the huts.
A natural avenue of enormous trees led to a rocky stream—
the Maropa—which came rushing down from a huge cleft in
the mountains.

Chipoka, the chief of Manga, was the great man of those
parts. He received our brethren cordially, and, as the afternoon was advanced, persuaded them to remain with him
till next morning, when he promised to send them on to Tombondira's.

Next morning, in fulfilment of his promise, Chipoka sent
his two sons as guides to Mirode, the village of Tombondira.
The guide from Saopa's also went with them. They had not
proceeded far before a dispute arose between the guides with
regard to the road, the man from Saopa declaring the others
were going astray. As a rule, it is always best to get passed
on from one chief to the next, if you take no guide from your
own place, and so it was resolved to follow the road taken by
Chipoka's sons. The country through which they now passed
became more tropical in its character, palms of various kinds
abounding. In the course of an hour, they crossed the 'Stink,'
a river that had nothing offensive to the olfactory organs about
it. At a short distance from this, they came to another and
much larger stream, the Rikania, which was about thirty yards

broad, but not deep at the ford.   Then, towards midday, they
arrived at a cluster of huts, all of which seemed unoccupied.
One person only, a man, was seen in this place, and he was
lying on the seat in front of one of the huts.   He stared as
our brethren passed, and said a few words, which were not
caught, to the guides, started up, and ran on ahead to a village
a short distance off.   To this village there appeared to be but
one entrance, and that was well guarded.   Impenetrable bush
was on either side, and loose wood and thorns lay close to the
entrance as if for the purpose of blocking it up.   The village
consisted of about forty very large and well-built huts.   This
place had strong natural defences, it being protected in one direction by a thick bush, and by a river, the Ruo, with very
steep banks, on the other.   The Ruo here was about fifty miles,
it was supposed, from its confluence with the Shire.   It was at
this place about thirty yards abroad, with a rapid current
and a rugged bed, not, however, passable, without the aid of
canoes.

   Manasomba, the chief of this village, was declared to be absent.   The men of this place were a tall, insolent-looking set
of fellows, not at all like the Manganja in appearance or bearing.   Their tattoo was like that of the Anguru.   Their conduct
soon gave cause for suspicion.   Charles, while looking about
the village, was accosted by a man, and asked if the white men
did not wish to buy slaves, as they had plenty to sell.   Charles
told him that the white men then present were English, and
did not buy slaves.   This did not seem satisfactory information to
the man.   And finding that the chief did not make his appearance,
and that so much was suspicious about the conduct of the people of this place, our brethren packed up, and resolved to resume
their journey.   But on making their intentions known, Chipoka's guides refused to leave, became insolent, and demanded
twice as much cloth as they had agreed to take for their day's
march.   Our friends left without paying them anything. Their
departure gave great dissatisfaction to the villagers, who abused
them as they left, and declaimed against the meanness of the
English, who bought nothing, and gave no presents ; and a
number of men ran after them, calling out—

'Stop! you must stop! Come back! Where will you go? You cannot cross the river without canoes, and you must cross it to get to Tombondira's, and no one has canoes but us.'

Procter had just then fired at some guinea-fowl; this, the men conceived, was done to frighten them, and they handled their bows and arrows in a threatening manner, and one called out—

'Do you think you can do anything with your guns? You may kill one or two, but after that, what will you do? We are not afraid of them.'

They then divided into two parties, one division preceding our brethren a little to the right, the other on the left, and they shouted to others working in the fields to come and join them. Fearing that if they then persevered in their journey it would provoke bloodshed, Procter and Scudamore drew up, quietly sat down under a tree, and invited the men to come and talk the matter over with them. This they did, and it was explained to them that they were in a hurry to get to the river's mouth, and they asked if Manasomba had come in. The men said he had, and pointed out an old man standing a little distance off. Thinking that they might have infringed African etiquette in leaving without seeing the chief, and that difficulties would vanish upon seeing him, they returned to the village, Manasomba preceding them. He was an old man, once a very powerful man physically, but now feeble-bodied, and in personal appearance much like Chinsunzi. He pretended great friendship, produced food, and would not hear of our friends leaving him until the morning, when he promised to send a guide with them to Tombondira. Finding nothing better could be done, they decided to stay, and settled themselves to dinner. Manasomba brought forward his wives and explained to them that the white men used knives and forks in eating in order that they might not soil their fingers. This was all very well, but the people congregated in an uncomfortable manner, and looked and acted as though they had some sinister intention. Nothing could be done, however, but watch and wait. When it was nearly sundown, Charles heard from one of the men that

accompanied our friends from Magomero, that Manasomba and
his people intended to attack the English, as soon as it was
dark, and kill them. A woman had informed this man that
orders had been given to fire the hut where the English slept,
and to kill them as they tried to escape. In confirmation of
this our brethren saw the women were busy removing their
household utensils, and hurrying out of the village, a thing
they always do when a fight is expected. The men were sitting round the huts with their bows and arrows beside them.
Fearing to excite attention, the bearers were collected quietly,
and while the burdens were being packed up, Scudamore went
to Manasomba to keep him in conversation. But he was not
to be hoodwinked, for Scudamore heard him whisper a man to
tell all to be on the look-out as the English were preparing to
leave. Scudamore then assumed a bold bearing, and told him
that they would not stay any longer with him, but would return at once to Chipoka's. Upon this the old rogue gave a great
shout: all his people were at once on the alert, and although
our friends were ready to leave, the others were ready to prevent them.

It was nearly sunset. As our brethren went towards the
entrance, Manasomba's men crowded before them, but gave
way whenever the muzzle of a gun was brought to bear upon
them. At this juncture a man called out, ' Stop up the gate.'
This was done by men standing inside and outside the entrance,
Here Charles did good service, for, before they could do anything else, he made a dash at the men at the gate, and knocked
away the obstacles they had placed there.

Thus he cleared the way for the rest. Scudamore and
Procter hurried on the bearers, following after, and having
their guns ready, if it became absolutely necessary to use
them. At last one man was bold enough to lay hold of
Procter's gun, but it was readily wrenched from him, and he
drew back in alarm, like all the rest, when it was presented at
him. As soon as the bearers, however, were outside the gate,
they were immediately attacked, their burdens knocked off
their heads, and every effort was made to capture them. Most
off the bearers fell into the hands of their assailants. Scud-

-amore and Procter showed great forbearance in not firing at
this juncture, but they resolved not to do so, unless an actual
attempt was made on the lives of any of the party.

Fortunately, the plunder proved a great attraction, and drew
off the attention of many of their assailants, while others
were pursuing the bearers that had escaped. This enabled our
brethren to get quite clear of the village, though thirty or
forty men, armed with bows and arrows, followed them closely,
shouting, ' Kondo ! kondo !' ('War ! war !')   But whenever
one put himself forward in any way, as though intending to
shoot, a gun was levelled at him, though, had they acted in
concert, one discharge of their arrows must have been fatal to
our brethren.   At last three men sprang forward upon Procter,
and endeavoured to wrest his gun from him.   In the struggle
he fell on his back, still holding his gun, which he tried hard to
get to bear on one of his assailants, and when it seemed he
had done so, he pulled the trigger.   The ball, however, passed
under the man's arm.   Scudamore then fired at the principal
aggressor, but, though he missed the man, they all left Procter
and fled.   Procter again fired, and as he turned round, he
heard a smart pat at his side, and found a poisoned arrow
sticking fast in the stock of his gun.   Had he not been carrying
his gun in a most unusual position, this arrow must have gone
into his thigh.

After this, they were not again molested, though their
assailants tried to get in front of them by making a detour ;
but, as it was now nearly dark, our brethren managed to get
away from them.   After what had happened, they felt they
could not trust any of the people of the country, and so they
resolved to avoid all the villages in returning to Magomero, at
least eighty miles distant.   So, after thanking God for His
mercy in protecting them thus far they again committed
themselves to His protection, and struck out for home.   But a
cross-country walk at night, in Africa, is a rough method of
proceeding, and their falls were numerous, and their bruises
abundant.   They soon came to the Rikania, but not at the
ford.   The banks were steep, the water deep ; Procter could
not trust himself to swim, and three times Scudamore stripped

and plunged in, hoping to find a safe crossing. At last he succeeded. Crossing this river occupied them three hours, but, when over, they felt safe from all further molestation. They continued their journey through the night and the next day, resting a little now and then. Next night they slept in the bush.

As they drew near to Magomero, they entered a village and bought a fowl for a pocket-handkerchief. Here, of course, the people were kindly, and on Procter showing some attention to a sick man, another fowl was produced as a present, and a lad volunteered to accompany them to our station.

When near home a dismal reception awaited them from the wives and children of the bearers that had been made captive. They were wailing most piteously, thinking their relatives dead.

For several days Scudamore and Procter were much fatigued, but no other ill effects seemed to arise from their exposure and excitement.

It was evident to all that Chipoka's sons betrayed our friends into Manasomba's hands. This man was not a Manganja; he was an Anguru that had made himself strong in the land by violence and plunder.

Three days after the return of Procter and Scudamore, two of the bearers made their appearance, one of whom was the man who gave warning of the contemplated treachery. Then two more came in, quickly followed by a third, who was accompanied by some men from Chipoka, one of whom brought an arrow from his chief, and laid it at the Bishop's feet; and this, we were told, was the regular method of declaring that the sender would be the ally of the person to whom it was sent, in all he undertook against his enemies. Two of the bearers had been made captive by Manasomba, but released on the representation of Chipoka's sons, who, when it was done, seemed to be afraid of the consequences of their act, and imagined that the guilt would be visited on them. From these men we learnt what had taken place at Manasomba's after our friends left. The booty was divided, Manasomba taking the lion's share. Chipoka's sons tried to get the other men released, but Manasomba said he would keep them, and if the English wished for them, they must come and fetch them—he was not afraid.

Chigunda expressed great valour, said he would go down and release his children at all hazards, and also declared that Chipoka was a true man, and not to blame, however wrong his sons had acted. There were three men in Manasomba's hands, one of whom belonged to Sachima, a neighbour of Chigunda; he, too, was valiant of tongue.

It was necessary that these men, who had trusted themselves to our protection, should be released, and that Manasomba should be punished for his treachery. And we resolved to do this; humanity and justice demanded that we should. It was from no feeling of revenge, we were too thankful to have our brethren back to have that feeling; it was not with the view of recovering the property that had been taken from us, for the loss of that did not trouble us in the least, but it was that these three men might be delivered from slavery and restored to their wives and families, who daily besought us with tears to restore to them their lost ones, and also that the natives around might know that no act of treachery and violence could be perpetrated with impunity. It was a grief to me that I could not accompany the Bishop. I was too weak to walk a mile. After Manasomba had been dealt with the Bishop and party proposed to go down to the mouth of the Ruo, and there await Dr. Livingstone's arrival.

On December 23, the Bishop, Scudamore, Burrup, and Waller, with William, and the Makololo—who readily responded to our call upon them, and Chigunda and twenty of his men—left Magomero for Manasomba's and the Ruo. As Chigunda complained of extraordinary pains in all parts of his body before starting, we did not expect he would persevere unto the end. But Zachuracami went also, and as he had plenty of courage, and energy and vivacity for twenty, the faithfulness of Chigunda's men was insured.

Fourteen Makololo came up to us, but ten only went with the Bishop. Moloko had a tender foot, Ramakukan would go nowhere without Moloko, and the other two wished to remain behind.

At this time our people were suffering from famine. They
were literally starving. We did all we could to get food from
the surrounding villages, going fifty miles from home to get
it, but we could not procure sufficient for our wants. Our reserve stock was exhausted; and one meal a day, and that a
small one, was all we could give. Though they suffered they
expressed no dissatisfaction; they knew we did what we could
for them, and they tried to be cheerful and content, but it is
hard to do that when you are really hungry. The earliest
crop would not be gathered until the end of January, and a
month's starvation and sickness was a serious thing. It soon
began to tell upon the weak and sickly, and the young.

We lost a child by death on the 22nd. I saw him the night
before, but though he was very ill I did not think him dying,
neither did Dickinson; nevertheless, when Dickinson went to
see him in the morning, he found his 'cold corse lying un-
straightened where the spirit left it.' Two days afterwards, a
lad named Namgwagada died also. He had an incurable ulcer
in his leg, and that gradually drained him of life.

On the 24th I distributed all the corn I had. It was not
half a ration for each, and then I laid hands upon our biscuit,
for it was impossible to see our children die while we had any
food at all.

Dickinson had plenty of patients at this time. Many old
ulcers had been cured, but many were incurable, and new ones
were continually breaking out. The dormitory for the boys
was turned into a hospital, and Dickinson's zeal never flagged,
his charity never failed.

' Christmas-day.—After Holy Communion, Procter, Dickinson, and myself went for a short walk, and the different aspects
of nature about us and in England struck us forcibly. The
contrast was great. At home, in all probability, "the ungenial
day," the rugged cold compelling north wind, or the withering
east: trees leafless, sapless, and repulsive in their nakedness;
the joy of the earth, its flowers, chilled out of existence, or
shrinking beneath the frigid earth; growth everywhere arrested; birds, whose joyous utterances make the heart glad,
chilled and scarcely able to sustain life. Here, around Mago-

mero, Nature is rejoicing, putting forth her greatest strength, triumphing in her power. Look where you will and you behold the earth full of vigorous, beautiful life. Trees have their branches clothed with foliage equalling in hue, excelling in grace of form, anything in England. Myriads of wild flowers rejoice the eye and provoke the hand; birds with bright plumage fly about you, and others fill the air with sweet melody— for no error about Africa is greater than that which declares its birds do not sing. Butterflies, gloriously apparelled, flicker hither and thither, and myriads of other insects, curious in form and beautiful in colour, are on the earth and in the air, and clinging to every tree and shrub. At night the fire-fly scintillates wherever you look; it alights on your person, it enters your house and dispels the gloom with its flickering gleam. It is a joy to see the earth; and if the earth were all we saw there would be no drawback to our joy; but behind all this that is beautiful, there crouches by our side the man for whom this beauty was created, and in him what little cause for joy! What a contrast between him and his brother man in England! There may be many there who are practically as much heathen as he, and far more criminal; but there are others, and, God be thanked, many of them, who are this day joyful, hopeful, exulting; for in their ears rings the angel anthem—

"Glory to God on high, on earth be peace."

Dull and tuneless the ear, purblind and weak the eye, that at this blessed season does not catch something of the heavenly harmony which heralded the Saviour's birth, that does not catch some glimpse of the celestial glory which encompassed the Almighty Babe in His manger cradle at Bethlehem. In England Christmas is a joy, despite all that is sad and sensual in man; a day which causes the bounty of most to overflow its methodical channels, and to the purest and the vilest (for the felon is not excluded) proclaims the gracious news that Christ is born. But here blindness of heart and spiritual darkness are universal. Man is alienated from God, and subject to the spirit of evil; he it is who mars the sweet accord "in all things fair around." In looking upon the earth, beau-

tiful as it is, you seem to detect in it aspirations after a
greater beauty—

> Strong yearnings for a blest new birth
> With sinless glory crowned.

But, looking on man, you have no such fancy, you can find
no such aspiration; he longs for peace that he may indulge in
sensuality undisturbed, but he has no yearning for a better
state of things, and he is ignorant of his degradation.   He is
lively, amiable, will frequently reciprocate your thoughts and
feelings, his social instincts are often tender and enduring; in
casual intercourse with him, so very human are his sympathies,
that you frequently forget that he is without God in the
world; but this day brings him no joy, no hope; he knows
nothing of the mystery of Bethlehem; of the Saviour which is
Christ the Lord; with Cain of old, he has gone out from the
presence of the Lord, and the colour of his skin but faintly
indicates the darkness of his soul.   Yet so it is, and so it has
been for ages; but Lord, how long, how long?'
      So I wrote on this Christmas-day, and so I let it stand.
      On the morning of the 26th all things were calm and fair,
but during the night we had a tremendous storm, accompanied
by a very deluge of rain.
      Death also during the night carried off a poor old woman.
She was one of the last arrivals, and when she came to us there
seemed literally but one step between her and the grave; she
would have died weeks before but for the care and nourishment
she received from us.   It is possible many people may say,
'Why did these men burden themselves with such as she, to
whom they could be of no *spiritual* use?'   They would not say
it, however, if they had seen the good effect our kind treatment
of such had upon all the natives around.   They are quick to
appreciate, and the 'good hearts' of the English Missionaries
will become one of the traditions of the land.
      On December 27 another died; a young girl about twelve
years of age, named Nanuneya.   She also was one of the last
batch of people.   She came to us with a large and incurable
ulcer, which extended from the knee to the instep, and three

parts of the way round her leg, and had eaten into the very bone.

Other deaths quickly followed. Dickinson was not well for some days, and Procter was not up to much. I attended to the sick, but, though the hospital was cleaned out every day, the offensive odour from those who had ulcerous diseases was so great that I was seized with a return of dysenteric symptoms.

A woman named Kuamvala was in the worst condition. She had a babe, which I found beside her in a state of insensibility. I brought it away and baptized it, and it breathed its last on my bed.

Another woman, Usiaga, had a babe several months old. Finding she could not sustain it, the Bishop at first took it in hand. The goats—we had ten—gave some milk, so he rigged up a bottle with calico in such a way that the little one could suck the milk out of it. I came upon him one day while he was thus feeding the child. It was an amusing thing to see the Bishop with the dusky, naked little creature, carefully holding it with one arm, while with the disengaged hand he held the bottle to the tiny lips, anxiously watching the result of his experiment, and brightening with satisfaction when he found it succeed. The little rogue sucked away right heartily, and when he was satisfied he looked about with his large eyes, gaped a little, played a little with the Bishop's big beard, and finally thrust its wizened little face against the Bishop's chest and went to sleep.

Usiaga, however, became so ill that the child was given to another woman to nurse, but with her the babe suffered, and so after the Bishop went to Manasomba's I superintended its feeding. The little fellow suckled hard for life, but it was useless. I baptized him by the name of Thomas, and he died. Usiaga died a day or two after.

On New Year's day I was able to give our people a better dinner than on Christmas-day, for Charles brought in a good supply of corn, and some men from Lake Shirwa brought a large quantity of dried fish for sale. I purchased their entire stock. Dr. Livingstone had kindly supplied us with a bale of cloth, and thus our cloth, though not abundant, was sufficient. Our people seemed to lust for the fish as much as the Israelites did for the flesh. When the fishmen were reported near at hand, they rushed forth like mad things, crying ' Somba! Somba!' (fish, fish). Hitherto we had been unable to get fish-sellers to come to us. They bore a bad character, and came only in times of scarcity, in order that they might get women and children in exchange for their fish. Our presence prevented such exchanges in our neighbourhood, and so they came to us, and were glad to have our cloth.

During the afternoon a man brought in two or three Kakas (cucumbers), the first fruits of the new harvest. These cucumbers were in form like a vegetable marrow, but in taste equal to the best cucumbers our English hothouses can produce. It was perilous food, but we could not resist eating it; though we paid a heavy price for doing so by increased diarrhœa.

January 22 was an eventful day. About eleven o'clock this morning two of the Makololo, Moloko and Maseka, who did not go to Manasomba's with the Bishop, walked quietly into the village, and Moloko said, ' When we left you a few days since we went towards the Shire, not by the way you go, but by another way, which took us up to the waterfalls. When we were near the river we entered a village in which were Portuguese slave-dealers. As soon as we showed ourselves there was a cry, " The English are here!" and the slavers ran away, leaving all they had behind. We took the men, the women, and children, the cloth, the beads, and the brass, and have brought all to you. Do you what you like with them all.'

They then fetched ' all' in. There were five men in slave forks, six women and ten boys; and a considerable quantity of barter goods.

* We set the men free of their cruel yoke, and told all they were as free as ourselves, that they might return to their friends at once, or go where they pleased.

They were Ajawa, and had been sold by their own people. They found plenty of acquaintance among our protégés. They said they did not wish to go back to their own people, for if they did they might be sold again, and they did not care to trust themselves to the Manganja, who were their enemies; they would therefore be very glad if we would let them live with us, for all the Ajawa now knew that the English were friends, not enemies, and that they had good hearts.

We told them that we were in great distress for want of food, that we could not get sufficient for those then with us, so we could not feed them, but the grown people might, if they liked, live under our protection, and we would help them all we could until they could help themselves. The little children it was impossible to refuse, so prudential counsels in their case were thrown aside, and faith gained the day. We believed God had sent them to us, and we trusted to him to enable us to feed them.

We were not inclined to take any of the spoil for ourselves, and told the Makololo to keep it. But when they heard that we were short of cloth they behaved admirably, and Moloko said, 'Take cloth to buy food for the people we have brought you.' And so for the sake of these people we borrowed fifty fathoms for their support.

The men were young and well made, the women, with one exception, were also young, and the boys, varying in age from six to sixteen, were bright-looking and intelligent.

About two o'clock in the afternoon of the same day, the Bishop and party, to our great astonishment, returned. We had imagined them encamped at the mouth of the Ruo awaiting the arrival of the 'Pioneer,' if it had not already arrived. They were all suffering more or less from the effects of their journey. Scudamore was only just alive. When he came in he fell on my bed utterly exhausted with fever and fatigue. Waller was also much exhausted. Burrup was suffering, and had suffered all through the journey, from diarrhœa, and the Bishop also, though he tried to look vigorous, and act vigorously, was evidently suffering from illness and his late exertions.

They had been exposed to almost incessant rain. Every streamlet on the journey had become a torrent, and every path a streamlet. They had been out of wet clothes scarcely an hour since they left us.

They reached Saopa's village on Christmas-day. There they rested and celebrated the Holy Communion. Saopa and his friends said they were sure Chipoka was a true·man and regretted very much what Manasomba had done. A message was sent to him, but as he did not make his appearance by one o'clock next day the whole party started for his place. The rain was frightful, the rivers swollen, and it was with great difficulty they could cross them. Chipoka was away when they arrived at Manga, but he returned next evening. Other chiefs were with him, and a conference was held. Chipoka accounted for his absence by saying the rain had hindered him, a very reasonable excuse, for it must have been enough to hinder any less determined than Englishmen. His explanations respecting his conduct in sending on Procter and Scudamore to Manasomba's were not quite satisfactory, as it was evident he knew the character of that chief, and that he had been before guilty of similar deeds. But he had never injured his (Chipoka's) friends, and so he despatched our brethren by his place because it was the nearest and best road to Tombondira's. He sent his own sons to show to Manasomba that the English were his friends, and he defended his sons by saying they had procured the release of some of the bearers, and had not taken any of the spoil, and to prove his faithfulness he was willing to help the English against Manasomba in any way they pleased, It was thought wise to give him credit for all he said, as the Bishop was not in a position, even if it had been politic, to question its truth.

From further statements it appeared that Manasomba had been in a great fright for some time, expecting the English to come upon him. A few days after Procter and Scudamore were there he sent down to the Ruo for his brother; they had collected all their men and had encamped on the banks of the Rikania, intending to defend themselves there against the English. But the rains brought sickness upon the people, they were obliged to disperse, and the brother returned to his own village. Then he tried to win Chipoka and other chiefs to his side; but finding he could not do that,—for one and all refused to ally themselves with him,—he was living in fear and trembling. Chipoka and the rest urged an immediate attack upon him. Now that they had broken with him they wanted to get rid of him altogether, and Chipoka said, 'Go to him by night, while all are asleep, and then you can kill all easily.' But that was not the intention of the Bishop; his real object was not war but peace, he hoped to bring Manasomba to acknowledge his guilt, and to sue for pardon, and to submit to whatever penalty the English might inflict. So instead of marching at once upon him he resolved to go in search of him in the morning, and bring him to reason without violence if he could.

In the morning they started, the Chipoka contingent being less than was promised. Soon after they crossed the Rikania they saw a large body of men armed with bows and arrows coming towards them, who called out 'Stop, we wish to have a mirandu' (conference). The Bishop and party halted, and answered, 'We wish to speak also; let your chief and four others come and talk with us.' But an incident occurred which effectually prevented this arrangement. Two of the Makololo unwisely made a dash at one of Manasomba's men who was in advance of the main body, thinking to capture him in order that the Bishop might use him as messenger to the rest. They seized him, but he struggled so vehemently that he got out of their hands, and Manasomba and all his followers took to their heels, and ran towards their village. This was vexing, and nothing now remained to be done but to follow them. When they arrived but one man was seen, and he immediately disappeared. The village was deserted. Search was made for the stolen property, but only an empty valise, a pair of boots, and two cooking-pots were found. The huts were full of the usual articles appertaining to the domestic life of the Africans; corn was in the gokwas (bins); sheep, goats, fowls, and ducks in the village; indeed such was the haste with which the village had been left that nothing had been removed. The live-stock was given to the Makololo for food, for they had been badly supplied with provisions on the journey, and then the village

was fired. In a few minutes not a hut remained of all that
had composed Manasomba's village. This was a fitting punishment for his offence. No life had been taken, and the destruction of his village was a degradation that would cling to him
through life; it was equivalent to the brand of the felon in our
land. All men would know of his offence, and all would hear
of his punishment, and evil doers would fear.

Good people at home, judging of our circumstances by those
with which they were surrounded in England, condemned this
act as contrary to the spirit of love which should actuate the
Christian. I will not argue the point with them, for if they
read this simple account of what was done, and of the motives
which influenced us, and are not satisfied that our actions and
motives were the necessity of our position, I fear no argument
I could produce would convince them. As well might they
blame the punishment of criminals in England as vindictive
and contrary to the spirit of Christianity, as censure us for
doing that which our knowledge of the country and people
taught us was most suitable for the suppression of crime
and the punishment of offenders.

The whole party returned to Chipoka's. Had they their
baggage with them they might have gone on to the Ruo at
once, but not having it they were compelled to return to
Manga.

When Chipoka heard that neither Manasomba nor any of
his people had been killed, he looked very grave. It would
have saved him from much disagreeable apprehension if the
old robber chief and his people had been sent out of the world;
being alive, he must conciliate them, or submit to retaliation,
unless sufficiently wary to keep the fear of us before their eyes.

Next day, Sunday 29, was anything but a day of rest; wild
rumours of war floated about, and kept the chicken-hearted
Manganja in a state of excited fear. The Bishop wanted to
resume his journey on the next day, but Chipoka could give no
guides; no one could now venture to go near Manasomba or
his relatives; not a man on that side of the Rikania would
venture to cross it now. And, with the exception of the
Bishop, all thought it inadvisable to go down to the Ruo by

way of Tombondira's. The Bishop thought, and it was afterwards shown that he was right, that the fear of the English
would be upon all, and that he might go on in perfect safety,
but it was impossible to get the natives about him to that
opinion, and it being absolutely necessary to send Scudamore,
who became very ill on this day, back to Magomero as soon as
possible, he gave way to the general feeling and returned.

The Ruo appointment had been most unfortunate. Upon
consultation all thought of the land route was given up: after
all that had happened, the distance and difficulties were too
great, and the Bishop resolved to proceed to Chibisa's, take a
canoe, and go down the river to Malo, the island at the mouth
of the Ruo. It was a gloomy plan at best, but no one could
suggest a better. Burrup accompanied the Bishop, as he expected his wife, and the Bishop expected his sisters. Both
were strong men, but neither took care of themselves ; the
Bishop because he was always caring for others, and Burrup
because he failed to understand that he could possibly need
care.

They started soon after mid-day on the 3rd, the Makololo
carrying their baggage. It rained heavily before they started
and recommenced soon after they left. The Bishop was very
sad when he left us, Scudamore, for whom he had great love,
being in so critical a state that Dickinson feared for his life.
He left us with his blessing.

While giving out food, on January 5—it was but a little I
had to give—I missed Akenena, the dumb girl, and then it
occurred to me I had not seen her for several days. Under
ordinary circumstances her disappearance would have caused
me no concern, for she was of eccentric habits, and liked to
absent herself now and then; but she had, with almost all
others, been ill for some time, and looked as though she meant
to die. After the Bishop left, I was so unwell that Johnson
distributed food for me, and thus she remained unsought.
When I was about again I searched for her, and to my grief
found her dead in an old hut, to which she had gone in order
that she might die out of the sight and way of all. Poor child !
we were very sorry to lose her, for though not full-witted,

she was kindly affectioned, and of a very grateful disposition. The Bishop was very fond of her, and took much pains to teach her habits of order and cleanliness, and whenever she met him she clapped her hands with joy, and gave utterance to the most pleasing sound she could make.

On January 7 a light broke through our gloom. We had not expected the pumpkin crop until the end of the month, but on this day we bought enough pumpkins to last our people for two days. They came from a distance, our own and our neighbours' crops were only just in flower. These pumpkins saved us from absolute starvation.

After fluctuating between life and death for some time, dear Scudamore rallied a little on the 8th, and day by day recovered strength, to our great joy.

Among our people sickness was on the increase, and my Journal at this time is simply an obituary. Dickinson was unremitting in his attentions to the sick, and constantly employed in devising means to better their condition; but a sickly season, a pestilential locality, and semi-starvation, proved too much for him. One after another, the weak and the young died; for, though the pumpkins saved us from death by starvation, they could not save us from the effects of previous privations.

On January 22 I wrote, 'Death and sickness still busy among us.' We lost children by death daily. Our little 'band of hope' was gradually wasting away. And, under God, it was entirely owing to Dickinson that we Missionaries did not die also. I had dysentery again, and all, at one time or the other, became nearly as ill as myself. Anything more truly wretched than our condition at this period cannot be possibly imagined. We were without suitable medicine in many cases, and had no wine, brandy, or flour. Pumpkins, and cucumbers, with a small piece of goat daily, constituted our food. We had a few tins of preserved meat, but these were kept for cases of pressing need in sickness. We strove bravely against the state of things besetting us, and, miserable as our condition was, it was not without its consolations—as the following will show.

On the 27th we were surprised to find a number of strange men, unarmed, sitting in front of our station, desiring to speak with us. They were Ajawa, and they came into Magomero during the night for fear of the Manganja; but they did not fear to put their lives into our hands. Upon our inquiring into the cause of their coming to us, they said—

'Our chiefs have sent us to ask you to let them and their people come and live near you. We know you are not enemies, for we see our people living with you as friends. They tell us, that when the slave-dealer was taking them out of the country you freed them, when they are hungry you feed them, when they are naked you clothe them, when they are sick you give them medicine, and when they die you bury them. An enemy never does that. We wish to live at peace with the Manganja. We are now tired of war, and want to sow and to reap; but the Manganja will not let us live at peace, they will not let us make gardens, they will have war, and so we should like to come and live near you, then we should have peace, for all would know we were your friends.'

I think this is a proof, if any were needed, that our proceedings against the Ajawa were not calculated to make them irreconcilably our enemies, as many supposed.

We had no power to grant the request of these men, for Chigunda would not consent to their coming near him, as his own fears would keep him in a state of perpetual terror, and his friends would regard him as a traitor to the national safety; but we assured them of our friendly feeling, and promised when our chief (the Bishop) returned, we would do all we could to make them and the Manganja friends, as we wished both well, and would try and do both good.

The woman who acted as guide was one of those brought to us by Zomba, and she begged hard that she and her husband, a fine, stalwart, honest-looking fellow, named Chimlolo, and their child, might stay with us, and said the Bishop had promised that if she came back with her husband she might remain. We knew this was the case, and we granted her request, and never regretted it, for Chimlolo proved a most trustworthy and excellent man. She was a handsome woman, despite the lip-ring, and modest and well behaved at all times.

The others went away at night, being afraid to pass through Manganja country during the day. The implicit trust these men had in us was very gratifying. We hoped their interview with us would lead to happiest issues. No other occurrence, since our arrival in the land, had given us so much satisfaction and pleasure.

One other circumstance I will record as a proof, and we had many other proofs daily, that our labour among the Manganja was not in vain.

Ndoka, whose history has been given, consoled himself by marrying a woman some years older than himself. This woman was released from the slavers. She was a widow, her first husband having been killed just before she was sold as a slave, and when she was sold, she was sold away from her little child, a girl about two years old. For some time she could learn nothing of her child, but at last she heard that a Manganja man named Kankadi, who lived about a mile away from our Station, had lately bought it for three baskets of corn. We knew this man. He was a big-boned, knotty-browed, savage-looking fellow, and bore no good character, for he had been guilty of several deeds of violence, it was said, and was generally feared. We sent to Kankadi, and told him to come to us on the next day, and bring the child with him. He came, armed with his bow and poisoned arrows, and his old mother came also, and she brought the child with her. The child was a pretty little thing, in good condition, and had evidently been well supplied with food.

As soon as he fully understood our object in sending for him, Kankadi assumed an insolent attitude, and spoke out boldly and defiantly. The child was his, he said. He had gone down to Soche's village, where he saw a man who said he wished to sell her for food. He had no wife, he had no child, he wanted a girl to grow up in his hut to grind corn for him, and fetch his water; and so he brought the man to his hut, and gave him three large baskets of corn for the child. The child was his, and if the English wanted her, they must buy

her as he had bought her; and he did not care to let the child
go at all.

Kankadi had been with us in all our expeditions; he had
agreed to the conditions proposed by us before we consented
to aid the Manganja against the Ajawa—conditions which
made it a crime for all there, and all whom they represented,
to buy or sell man, woman, or child again—and the chiefs had
promised to punish the criminal. So we desired Kankadi to
follow us down to Chigunda. Chigunda, since his return from
Manasomba's, had been ill, and we found him outside his hut,
surrounded by his wives, and submitting to the operation of
cupping. He had been taking our medicines, but did not give
up his own remedies, and cupping is most popular for many
sicknesses among the Manganja. The Sinanga (medicine man),
made a slight incision with a native razor just above the instep,
and then produced a goat's horn, the root end of which he
dipped into water and placed over the wound. The top of
the horn was cut off; he applied his mouth to the orifice, and
sucked away until he had exhausted the air, and then cleverly
stopped the hole with wax. The horn stuck fast to the foot.
While this was being done, William declared to Chigunda the
particulars of the case between us and Kankadi. Chigunda
was not so fluent of speech as usual. He paused some time
before he made any remark, and when he did speak, his speech
was destitute of the fire and force which generally marked his
pronouncements. What he said amounted to this:

' I have never broken my promise. I have not bought or
sold people; I have been faithful to my word, and will always
be faithful. I knew nothing of what Kankadi had done, and
if I had I could do nothing, for though Kankadi lives near me
I am not his chief—he comes from a long distance and is a
stranger. I have no power, therefore, to make him give the
child to its mother, or to punish him. If I were to do so, my
friends would go away, and I should be left alone. I think he
ought to give up the child. All that the English have said
and done is quite right. All that Kankadi has said and done is
quite wrong. Let the English do as they please; they will
be sure to do right.'

Poor Chigunda! He was a mouse of a man, and a power-less chief, and was afraid of Kankadi, who did not seem in the least afraid of him. We then asked Kankadi if he had any-thing more to say. No, he had nothing more to say. The child was his, and he meant to keep it. We told him that the child was not his, but its mother's, and that he must at once give it up to its mother, and pay a fine for having broken the covenant he had made with us. On hearing this, the expres-sion of Kankadi's face was diabolical; it looked like murder; and he relieved his hot wrath by fiercely plucking up the tufts of grass around him, and at last said:

'It's a lie! I never promised not to buy a slave. All I promised was not to sell to the slavers. I have not done that, and I have done no wrong. I bought the child for myself with my own corn. I will not give her up. The English are strong; let them take her, but——'

What the 'but' meant William could not say; that it meant mischief was certain, for in his wild mood he looked like Cain, and I think he felt like Cain, for he fingered his bowstring spitefully, as though he would like to twang an arrow into the hearts of some of us.

The attempt to influence this man for good seemed hopeless for a time. We might have taken the child from him by force and driven him out of the village, but that we did not wish to do; we wished to develope some better feeling in the man; and though I was hopeless of being then able to do it, Waller was not. He pictured to him the sorrow of the poor mother, her heart yearning for her little one, and trembling with anxiety for fear it would not be returned to her; he told him of the sorrow desolating the hearts of many poor mothers in that land, through their children being sold from them. And while he spoke in this way a better spirit came over the man; his face assumed a milder expression; he ceased to speak or behave insolently; and when Waller said: ' Supposing you had a child, and it was stolen and sold away from you, would you not think it very cruel, very wicked of those who took it from you ? Would not your heart feel as sorry as this poor mother's here ?' an expression of pain passed over the man's features. He did not reply for some moments; he was much agitated; but at last he said, and while he said it he was almost choking with emotion: 'It is true I should feel it. I should feel it here,' laying his hand over his heart, 'and my heart tells me it is a cruel thing to take the children from the mother. Take the child; give it to the mother; I will keep it no longer. I don't want anything for her, I give her up freely.' And the child was given to its mother.

And that man belonged to that race which we, in our insular egotism, are regarding as of an inferior creation to ourselves, or at least branded with such an indelible degradation as to be fit only to be the life-long slaves of the superior families of man. No people have been more misrepresented, because none have been more misused, than the Africans. We made merchandise of them, we treated them as creatures without souls, we kept them in a state of life-long debasing servitude, we did our best to degrade them to the condition of the brutes that perish; and now that we no longer do that, we point to those we have degraded, and say, 'Behold the objects of your mistaken philanthropy—brutes, not men—irreclaimable and vile!' and to support this, propound theories declaring the Word of God a lie, that God has not made of one blood all the nations of the earth.

With the month of February came in the new corn; and though sickness and death still continued active among our people, hunger ceased, and the effects of plenty upon the famishing were pleasant to behold. Applications for permission to dance during the moonlight nights were frequent, and we were too thankful for the change in our affairs to refuse. Indeed the noisy accompaniments of the dance, after our long period of silent sadness, only broken by the suppressed cry of 'Jala' (hunger), and the wail of death, were really music to our ears. These moonlight dances simply for amusement were not in the least degree objectionable; they were less open to censure than many of our own dances; it was only those dances connected with the superstitious observancy of the natives that were of an evil tendency.

CHAPTER XIII.

WE had been for some time very uneasy at the protracted absence of the Bishop and Burrup. They had been away nearly six weeks. We knew that their supplies, unless they had met with Dr. Livingstone, would be exhausted, and a long sojourn at Malo, one of the most pestiferous parts of the whole valley of the Shire, filled us with cruel anxiety. It was little we could take to them from our stores, for we had scarcely anything but green corn and pumpkin, and our stock of barter goods was all but exhausted. But it was impossible to sit still any longer without making an effort to gain information of them, and we resolved, in the event of their not returning within a week, to send some of our party down the river to them. But before the week passed we knew all. We knew that our own large-hearted, single-minded, most charitable Bishop and brother was dead !

We were at dinner on the 14th, talking about the arrangements we had better make for going down the river, when Zomba, one of the Makololo, appeared before us. His manner was constrained, he looked like a bearer of evil tidings. We inquired after the Bishop, and he hid his face in his hands. We were greatly shocked, for the man's expressive action told us better than words could do of our great loss. We were for the moment stunned, unable [to think or feel. At last some one desired Zomba to tell us what he really meant, and he said, ' Wafa ! Wafa !' (He is dead ! He is dead !)

He then told us that Burrup, very ill, and carried on men's shoulders, was close at hand. No men could have been more grief-smitten than we. But we were called upon to act, and Dickinson and I, taking our last drop of wine with us, went forth to meet Burrup. We missed him, he having been brought by another path ; but when we returned we saw how much he had suffered, far more than he knew. He was one of those men who never know what they are suffering until laid low

He was but a wreck of what he was when he joined us, and
Dickinson said he was then but a shadow of himself when
he left England.   Naturally he was one of the strongest of
men.

He was not able to give us any connected account of what
had taken place since he and the Bishop left Magomero; but
from statements made at various times, it appeared that they
experienced great difficulty in getting down to Chibisa's; the
mountain streams were swollen by the heavy rains to such an
extent that they had to wait hours before they could ford
them.   They were in wet clothes night and day from the time
they left Magomero until they reached the Shire.   On the
sixth day after leaving us—that is, on the 8th of January—
having with some difficulty procured a canoe, the Bishop and
Burrup, with Zomba, Charley, and Seseho, three of the Makololo, left Chibisa's for Malo.   Their progress down the river
was rapid.   The first night they slept at Chickwaba.   Next
day the canoe, greatly overladen, was very difficult to manage.
The Makololo, with the exception of Seseho, were not good
canoe men.   They halted as the sun went down at a village in
the Elephant Marsh, belonging to a man named Magala.   At
this place the mosquitos and every other insect abomination
were so numerous, and annoyed them so greatly, that all but
the Bishop wished to go to another village a short distance
lower down the river.   Unwilling to oppose his opinion against
the possible comfort of his companions, the Bishop consented
to the removal, and the baggage was repacked and stowed in
the canoe.   Darkness came on before they could reach the
place they sought.   The Shire in this part is broken into several channels.   They missed the main stream, and the canoe
was drawn into a side current and eventually upset.   The
water was not more than four feet deep, but this accident was
productive of most serious consequences.   Everything in the
canoe went into the water.   Guns were made useless by loss
of ammunition, and the tea and coffee were so damaged as to
be worthless; but, worst of all, the medicines, which had been
carefully selected and plentifully supplied by Dickinson, with
a view to the emergencies of the river, were utterly destroyed.

Burrup lost the valise containing his change of clothing; and
the Makololo lost their little all.   For an hour they were in
the river fishing up their things, and putting the canoe to
rights, and in their wet clothes they slept in the canoe that
night.

Return for fresh supplies they could not, as they were more
than a hundred miles from Magomero, and the return journey
would occupy many days.   It was then the 10th of January;
Dr. Livingstone had made it imperative that we should meet
him at Malo on the 1st: the Bishop expected he would be
impatiently awaiting their arrival; so next morning they
pushed on for Malo, their clothes drying on them as they went,
and arrived there soon after mid-day.   To their great disappointment Dr. Livingstone was not there.   They were told,
indeed, that the 'Pioneer' had passed by only a few days before; and Dr. Livingstone has expressed surprise that the
Bishop, on receiving this intelligence, did not follow the ship.
Possibly he might have done so, had he then known for certain
that it was only five days since the 'Pioneer' had passed, but
with that indistinctness common to the African computation
of time, he could not tell whether the few days spoken of
might not be two or three weeks.   Besides which it was really
useless to follow the 'Pioneer' with the view of overtaking her,
as below Malo the difficulties of the river cease, and she would
steam down to the coast at the rate of fifty miles or more a day.
The Bishop could do no other than he did, seeing Dr. Livingstone
left no letter of instructions for him on the island as he passed
by.   So he waited, daily and hourly expecting the arrival of
the 'Pioneer:' walking to the end of the island several times
a day, to see if he could discern any signs of the little vessel
coming up the river.

Malo is about three-quarters of a mile in length and a quarter of a mile in breadth, and then contained about five hundred
inhabitants.   Chikanza, the chief, was hospitable, and placed a
hut at the Bishop's disposal.   Fowls, eggs, meal, and beans
were to be had on the island in abundance, so food was not
needed.   But when the excitement of the long journeys and
events of the previous month passed off, then it was apparent

that the Bishop and Burrup were very ill. The Bishop's energy
of body failed, and he was occasionally much distressed by the
difficulties in which he was placed through the inability of Dr.
Livingstone to bring stores up to Chibisa's, and the failure
of the land route from the Ruo to Magomero. He several
times spoke as though he thought that these difficulties and
our own incapacity to keep up a regular communication with
the Cape, would prove fatal to the Mission. There seemed
no possibility of getting the ladies and the stores from
Malo when they arrived, unless the 'Pioneer' could give
him help; and of that, knowing as he did the many cares
pressing on Dr. Livingstone, he had but little hope. He
was, however, longing for the arrival of his sisters, and once
said to Burrup he thought it would break his heart if they
did not now come. He was, without doubt, feeling, and deeply
feeling, the need of the support and comfort their presence
and sympathy would be to him. He used to rejoice in the
thought of the pleasure they would experience when they saw
how God had favoured the Mission by giving into our charge
so many children to train up in His fear and love; and I had
many a time pictured to myself his face more than ever radiant
with happy affection as he introduced them to the people
among whom he and they had cast their lot. But, in wishing
for his sisters at that particular moment, he was evidently
hoping against hope that all would be well, and that they
would get up to Magomero without much discomfort. He was
one of the most hopeful of men. This feature in his character often led him to overlook many things in which a less hopeful man would see the germ of much future discomfort: but
it was very pleasant to be associated with him; for if his hopefulness brought upon you a little inconvenience now and then,
it carried you safely over a multitude of difficulties that a
more cautious man would have stumbled at. It was this very
hopefulness, coupled with an entire absence of selfish feeling,
which made him appear negligent of his own personal comfort.
It was not carelessness, but the result of an ever-present
feeling that all would be well, which led him to spare everyone
but himself. This was manifested in every action of his life,

even the most trivial. I used to be apprehensive that this would eventually lead him into trouble and danger from whence there would be no escape, and ventured to tell him so, but his reply silenced me. Could I see how he could act otherwise? I could not; for all that he did was so sanctified by the spirit which prompted the doing, that you could not have him do differently. You could only do as he did—trust that all would be well. But had he been less hopeful and as careful of himself as possible, his position on Malo could not have been avoided. It was the necessity of the circumstances which had beset us ever since we approached the mouth of the Zambesi. From the first, our main difficulty—viz., want of communication with the sea—was present to the minds of all; but the excitement of coming into a strange country, and the extraordinary events which followed, led us not to trouble much about it. For some time at least we had every reason to think the 'Pioneer' would be able to help us, but Dr. Livingstone's letter to the Bishop at Magomero made clear to us the exact nature of our position, and we all saw it to be a grave one. This had, as I said, a very depressing effect upon the Bishop. Still he had not made up his mind to write home for a ship when he left us; but when at Malo, and brought face to face as he was there with the inconveniences arising from want of means of transport, he wrote a letter, since published, to the Boat Clubs of the Universities of Oxford and Cambridge, begging them by prompt and special contributions to supply and keep up a steam launch for the Mission. In doing this, he did all that could have been done; had he written it earlier, it would not have reached home earlier, for it was among the first year's communications from the Shire.

Poor Burrup could give us but scant information respecting the last hours of the Bishop on earth.

It was evident that the longer they were on the island the worse in health they became. Diarrhœa increased, and fever came upon them, upon the Bishop most severely. They had no remedies, nothing to lessen the violence of the disease; the Bishop's physical force was so abated that he could scarcely get out of the hut. On the 24th, he was incapable of collected

conversation; his mind wandered; but even then the one
thing present to it was the Mission; he spoke of that repeatedly. At one time his difficulties appeared overwhelming,
at another he had surmounted them, and sisters and stores
were all at Magomero—to him a haven of safety. From the
25th to the 31st, the day of his death, the fever increased to
such an extent that he was unable to utter a single word; and,
during the last five days of his life, he lay insensible.

The natives have a dread of anyone, especially a stranger,
dying in their huts, and, setting aside the superstitious feeling,
it is a great loss to them, as the hut after a death is closed for
three years; so when Chikanza knew that the Bishop was
dying, he begged he might be removed to another hut, to one
less needful to Chikanza himself. It was from no ill feeling
that Chikanza desired this, it was but the 'custom of his
country,' and, heathen though he was, he had shown 'no little
kindness.'

In all the watchings and requirements of the Bishop's position during the last days of his life, the Makololo behaved
admirably; their attentions were unwearied, and their grief,
when he was no more, great.

It was during the afternoon of the 31st that the Bishop
died. As soon as his death was known, Chikanza was anxious
for the immediate interment of the body. I believe it was a
superstitious fear, not real want of feeling, which produced
this anxiety. The Makololo also wished it, and with them it
was certainly from no lack of affection. Burrup then consented, and he and they went over the river to the north bank
of the Shire, and, clearing away the bush from a secluded
place, dug a grave. It was dark before the body could be
lowered into the ground, too dark for Burrup to read the
Burial Service, but he said all that he could remember. And
there, on the banks of the Shire, away from all but the heathen
to whom he devoted his life, in 'sure and certain hope of a
joyful resurrection,' rests what was the soul's tabernacle of
Charles Frederick Mackenzie, the first Bishop of the Central
African Mission.

A wasted life! say some. A wasted life? No! a thousand

times No! Like Abel, 'he being dead yet speaketh,' and 'the record of his life and death, I verily believe, will inspire hun-

dreds to follow his example, to do and dare, to sacrifice all, all that this world counts most estimable, for the glory of God and the good of man.

In thinking of his great capacity and exalted character, his ardent love and simple faith, it is natural for men to say his proper sphere was home. That such as he are needed at home, and never more so than now, none can doubt, and the need I

fear, will increase until the English Church becomes really a
Missionary Church; until there prevails in the Church to a
greater extent than now that self-sacrificing spirit which dis-
dains to make a sacrifice unto the Lord our God, in foreign
lands, of that which costs us nothing.

Burrup said but little of his own sufferings, and, independent of the distress of mind he must have endured during
the last days of the Bishop's life, he had himself suffered much
he was only not dead when he came back to us.

After the Bishop's death, Burrup resolved to return to Magomero. The river was full of water, the current very strong,
and the Makololo were anxious to return by land. But to this
he was not willing to consent, as he was under an engagement
to restore the canoe to its owners. So, on February 2, they
re-embarked and tried to ascend the river. For three days
they laboured, but made so little progress that the Makololo
declared it was useless trying any longer; the canoe, therefore,
was left in the care of some natives, and they resumed their
journey along the bank of the river. Burrup was so weak that
he fell down repeatedly on the road during the three days they
were in getting to Chibisa's. Nothing but his strong will kept
him going. But when at Chibisa's that will could no longer
sustain him, his breakdown was complete. During his two days'
stay at Chibisa's, the Makololo were incessant in their acts of
kindness; indeed, he had met with unvarying kindness from
the natives all along the road. Mankokwe, the Rundo, through
whose village he passed, conducted him himself to the next
halting-place. Finding he could walk no farther, the Makololo
and Chibisians made a palanquin of wood, and carried him up
to Magomero. This was done without promise of reward, and
without hope of reward. Moloko, when he left, finding he had
no cloth, held out some, and said, with much feeling, ' Here,
Burrup, take this cloth to buy food on the road home.'

The death of the Bishop we felt to be a severe blow, not
only to us, the Missionaries, but to the Mission itself. The
prospects of the Mission, I could not doubt, would be materially altered by that one death: whatever its future might be,

it would henceforth be different in many respects both as to its working and constitution.

After Evening Prayer on the 14th, Procter said that before the Bishop went away he entrusted a paper to him, which he desired him to read to the members of the Mission in the event of his death. It was his Will. That part of the Will which related to the government of the Mission expressed a wish that the members of the Mission would 'act under the temporary headship of the senior priest acting with the advice of the other priests; or if there be no priests the senior deacon; or if there be no deacon the senior layman, acting with the advice of the others of their own degree respectively.' Procter, therefore, became, *pro tem.*, our head. It was a trying and unexpected position for him, and it was a trying and unexpected position for all of us. We did our best to strengthen his hands, and to keep among us 'the unity of the spirit in the bond of peace,' and I believe we succeeded.

In discussing our position, it seemed to us, at that time, advisable to send one of our body to the Cape, if not to England. We did not then know that we could communicate with the coast again for at least a year. The difficulty was to get away. We were ignorant of the temper of the Portuguese towards us, and Dr. Livingstone had strongly advised us to have no commuication whatever with them; but we felt that our position needed extraordinary effort, and we determined that, other means failing us, one of us should go to Sena, and from thence to the coast, where it was hoped a man of war might be met with.

The first thing that claimed our attention after we received the news of the Bishop's death, was the condition of our people. We never intended that they should remain dependent on us. At first, they had not the means to support themselves, and so we fed them, and they worked for us in return; but now most of them had their own gardens, and the first crops were ready to be gathered. We told them therefore that the time was now come when all but the sick and the children must feed themselves. If they worked for us we should pay them for their labour in cloth. None were cast down at this announcement, none wished to leave us. Some of the women who had no husbands had but very indifferent gardens; that, we informed them, was their own fault—if they had not enough food they must work for it, and the Manganja about Magomero would be glad to employ them in their gardens. Damanji and Lonkola made speeches, in which, on behalf of themselves and brethren, they professed eternal friendship for the English, declaring, somewhat in the language of Ruth, that where we went they would go, and that our people should be their people. Further they did not say, but we hoped the time would come when those very men would be able to finish the sentence by saying, 'and your God shall be our God.' They said we were their fathers, for when they were dead we had given them life, by which they meant that when they were captive we had given them liberty, and they desired nothing better than to live and die with those who had been such great friends to them. They spoke in feeling terms of the Bishop, and said when he died there went from them the chief with the sweetest heart on earth.

At this time, nothing could look more hopeful than the condition of the country about us. The crops were yielding more than á hundredfold—with the chimanga (Indian corn) it was a thousandfold. Our English wheat, it is true, did not do well. In ignorance of the seasons, we sowed it too early, and so it had the full force of the tropical rains upon it; but the barley and oats flourished.

Every arrangement that could be made for the health of the place was made. The sick were removed to separate huts outside the village. The dormitory was fitted up and kept exclusively for the healthy children; each child had its own bamboo bedstead, instead of lying on the ground and huddling together like pigs; and Clarke, who proved a most valuable man, fitted himself up a berth in the dormitory, and had the general superintendence.

Day after day passed and there was no improvement in poor Burrup's health. On the 21st his condition excited our gravest fears; we did not think him in immediate danger of death, but he was so ill that we thought his ultimate recovery

very unlikely. He was evidently failing, but he was far from conscious of his danger: only once it became apparent that he knew how very ill he was, and that occurred on the day before he died; finding himself at the moment too weak to get up from his chair to fetch something he needed, as I handed it to him, he said, 'If I don't soon get rid of this diarrhœa, I think it will go hard with me.' But he shortly afterwards expressed his conviction that the vitality of his constitution and strength of body would bring him through; it might have done, could we at first have given him the assistance he so greatly needed—wine and brandy and nourishing food—but he never complained; he had the fortitude of a hero and the faith of a martyr.

PORTRAIT OF THE REV. H. DE WINT BURRUP.

On the morning of his death, February 22, he was up by six o'clock, walked across the village, and called to Johnson to get him some coffee; he drank two cups, and almost immediately afterwards fell back on his bed insensible. His death-struggle continued till a quarter to eleven A.M.: he never recovered consciousness.

We buried him at the bottom of our village, within the enclosure marked out for the Church. It was on Sunday, February 23rd, immediately after the celebration of the Holy Communion; and we were able to give him a more fitting interment than had been possible for the Bishop. Johnson, whose capabilities seemed endless, made a good coffin out of bamboo; Waller, Dickinson, Clarke, and Adams, carried the body to the grave; Procter, Scudamore and the rest of the party followed, and, as I took the service at the grave, I walked in front. The natives stood around preserving a mournful silence; it was a sad duty, and the most difficult I had ever undertaken. It is doubtless an ill expression of affection to be sorry at heart at the death of those who ' die in the Lord,' but nature must and will have its way on such occasions; and our own sorrow was intensified by the thought of the grief that was in store for the young wife, who, with the Bishop's sisters, might be close at hand, ignorant of the bereavement she had sustained.

The probable arrival of the ladies was a great cause of anxiety to us; under happiest circumstances their presence would have been, at so early a period in the history of the Mission, a mistake, a great mistake, involving them and us in much trouble. Only men, capable of doing and enduring much, could hope to stand against the difficulties arising in the pioneer work of such a Mission as ours. That in course of time, when order had been established, security ensured, and comfort obtained, ladies would. be of greatest use, I have not the slightest doubt. The presence of a Christian lady among these poor African women would be a leaven that would spread far and near, and accomplish great good, but at first they would but paralyze the efforts of others. Of course we had to discover all this from the circumstances which beset us. We could not comprehend the difficulties we had to encounter until they came. Bishop Mackenzie did not write for his sisters until he was told that he might safely do so by Dr. Livingstone, who expected his wife to join him, and for whom we purposed building a house at our Station.

Mr. Burrup arrived at Magomero on November 19; and died on February 21. He was with us not more than three months, the greater part of which time he was away from the Station, so he had but little opportunity of joining in our work, neither had we who remained at home much of his society; he was, therefore, to us almost a stranger.

I have not mentioned Barwi lately, but that is not because

we were able to rid ourselves of him; he frequently came with
a complaint against the Ajawa. He had no cause of offence
against them himself, but he constituted himself their accuser-
general, and repeatedly brought men who professed to have
been injured by them. On February 19 he visited us and
claimed our aid against Joi, who, he said, was robbing certain
friends of his, and we told him to go away and to come to us
no more with his complaints, for we had done all we intended
to do for the Manganja against the Ajawa; that the Manganja
had peace now, and it would be their own fault if they did
not keep it. This did not at all satisfy him; he went away,
but said he should come again and bring his friends with him,
perhaps we would listen to them. And on the 28th he came
again, and brought his friends with him—four or five chiefs—
two of them from the Ku Jireka district, which lies towards
the Upper Shire. Of course, upon the testimony of these
worthies, no other Ajawa chief equalled Joi in ferocity and
bad deeds; but we knew something of the cause of dispute
between the Manganja and Joi, and were sure that whatever
they suffered or might suffer from him, they had brought upon
themselves; they had stolen some of his people, his sister
among them, and sold them to the slavers, to the companions
of those very men whom the Makololo had frightened away.
So we told Barwi we knew all that he could tell us about Joi,
that the Manganja had provoked their own troubles, and that
it was wrong in him to come to us so often, and to give his
brother chiefs such useless trouble. Upon this he lost his
temper, and said—

'Ah! Chigunda is not here; you do what he asks you; if
he said go, you would go against Joi.'

Whereupon we looked very fierce; and Barwi looked very
small and slunk away.

Chigunda had been ill for some time. Previous to his illness, and the Bishop's death, he used frequently to visit us,
and, as a matter of course, there was always a place at table
for him. He began to eat like a civilised creature, using knife
and fork dexterously. The Bishop was very fond of him, and,
despite the weakness of his character, there was much to like

in him.   At table he and the Bishop used to laugh and chatter
together like dearest friends.   The Bishop had the power of
drawing him out in a most amusing and edifying way.   On
March 3, Chigunda visited us for the first time since the
Bishop's death, and he appeared to feel keenly the absence of
the Bishop, who had formerly received and welcomed him.
He sat down, and looked all around at us; then he looked at
Procter, who sat where the Bishop used to sit, and then at the
vacant places at table, and sighed.   It is not Manganja etiquette
to speak of the dead, so he said nothing; but he was very
subdued, and we had no disposition to disperse his sadness.

On the morning of March 6, the three men that had been
left in Manasomba's hands returned; he had of his own accord
sent them home.   From their statement it appeared that he
was living in continual fear: his old allies had forsaken him,
he had no friends, his punishment for his treachery was complete.   So without taking life, a bad man had been punished,
law vindicated, and those who had been made captive restored
to their friends.

Our expectation of the arrival of the ladies was not unfounded, for on the morning of the 8th, Masaka, one of the
Makololo, brought us up letters from England, and also a note
from Dr. Kirk, stating that Miss Mackenzie and Mrs. Burrup
were at Chibisa's—to which place they had been brought in a
boat by Captain Wilson, of H.M.S. 'Gorgon,' and that he
(Dr. Kirk) and Captain Wilson had intended to come up to
us, but were lying at Soche's ill of fever, and without medicines.   Upon this information, Scudamore, Waller, and myself
immediately started to their relief.   Scudamore proposed going
on at once to see Miss Mackenzie, who had been apprized of
her brother's death, and to acquaint Mrs. Burrup of her great
loss, Burrup's death not being known at Chibisa's.

We reached Soche's about half-past one o'clock on the 10th,
and to our surprise found Dr. Kirk and Captain Wilson, who
had part of the boat's crew with them, making preparations to
return to the Shire.   We sent off a messenger to Magomero
at once, to bring down to the river all letters and papers for
England.

Captain Wilson had good reason for this speedy return, as will appear when I trace the cause of his presence among us.

His ship, while cruising on the east coast, put into Mozambique for supplies; these he did not find, but he found the 'Hetty Helen,' the brig which had on board a new steamer for Dr. Livingstone (the 'Lady Nyassa'), Mrs. Livingstone, the Rev. J. Stewart, who had been sent out by the Scotch Free Kirk to spy out the land preparatory to sending out a Free Kirk Mission, Mr. Rae the engineer, Miss Mackenzie, Mrs. Burrup, and two female attendants, the Rev. E. Hawkins, son of the Provost of Oriel College, Oxford, who was joining the Mission from the Cape, and Blair, who had been sent back in ill-health from Johanna by Dickinson. The 'Hetty Helen' had taken in the Mission party and stores at Natal, had arrived off the Zambesi safely; but could not get into the river; had waited about for several days, and was finally blown away by a storm, and made for Mozambique. Captain Wilson at once offered to take the ladies on board the 'Gorgon,' and took the brig in tow and brought her back to the Zambesi. When off the Luabo the 'Pioneer' was descried. She went out and towed the brig into the river. But when the 'Pioneer' was laden with sections of the 'Nyassa' she could only take a small portion of our stores. The rest were left at the Kongone with the Rev. E. Hawkins. The 'Pioneer' had greatest difficulty in getting up the river, and when she arrived off Shupanga, Captain Wilson, who had waited to give Dr. Livingstone the assistance of his crew in unlading the 'Nyassa,' &c., came to the conclusion that she would not get up much further, and resolved to bring Miss Mackenzie and Mrs. Burrup up to Chibisa's in his gig. Dr. Kirk, and Dr. Ramsay the surgeon of the 'Gorgon' accompanied him. Besides this, as wild reports were flying about the Portuguese settlements to the effect that we had been severely repulsed in an engagement with the natives, and were even then besieged in our own Station, he kindly thought that if he took two or three boats filled with armed men into the Shire, the news of this would spread among the various chiefs of the land, and be of great service in showing that they were within the reach of other

English if they behaved badly to us. These boats came up the Shire, some distance, but returned before reaching Chibisa's.

Captain Wilson had been informed that ten days would be sufficient for the journey there and back—a grievous miscalculation, for it took him fifteen days to get to Chibisa's; and much discomfort and privation to those in the boat was the consequence. I can conceive nothing more trying than the position of the ladies in an open boat on this long journey up the rivers. Miss Mackenzie must have died had it not been for the untiring attention of Captain Wilson, and Drs. Kirk and Ramsay. Poor Burrup left a letter with Chikanza to be given to any English that came up the river, but it was not delivered, and so while they were at Malo, where Miss Mackenzie was very ill, they heard nothing of the Bishop's decease. The fear of being thought responsible for his death induced the people of this place to withhold information.

Dr. Kirk was told of the Bishop's death by the Makololo at Chibisa's. At this time nothing was known at the river of Mrs. Burrup's loss, and when Captain Wilson and Dr. Kirk started to come up to us, she was thinking that the first person to return would be her husband.

The long hardships endured in coming up the river so told upon Dr. Kirk and Captain Wilson that they found it impossible to get beyond Soche's; and having been away from his ship more than six weeks, Captain Wilson resolved to return to her at once. To our inexpressible comfort, he expressed his intention of taking the ladies back with him.

A slight cessation of fever enabled Captain Wilson to reach Mbame's village, but next morning the fever was again so strong upon him that he could not resume his journey until after mid-day. Waller pushed on to Chibisa's, hoping to be able to secure a canoe to take him down the river, for Captain Wilson and Dr. Kirk thought we might make arrangements with the Portuguese to bring up our stores in their canoes. It seemed to them very clear that the 'Pioneer' would not be able to help us.

Captain Wilson was very ill on the night of the 11th, at a village some twelve miles from the Shire, and next day his men rigged him up a palanquin, in which he was carried down the hills. He rallied, however, before the day was over, and gave orders to start within an hour of his arrival at Chibisa's. Fortunately Charles, after an unexampled journey from Magomero, doing the seventy miles in twenty-eight hours, arrived with the Bishop's papers and our letters for home just before he started.

That the noble and disinterested services of Captain Wilson saved the lives of Miss Mackenzie and Mrs. Burrup I have no doubt.

To say that we were thankful to him would but inadequately describe the feeling with which we watched, from the steep bank at Chibisa's, the boat push off into the river with these two greatly afflicted ladies—would ill describe the gratitude I now feel while I write these lines.

Miss Mackenzie was too feeble to stand, and was carried down to the boat. Mrs. Burrup bore up bravely against her sorrow. It was indeed a painful providence which had taken from them those to whom they came, the only two of our party who had then died. One felt how insufficient mere human sympathy was to comfort, that it was only He who had permitted their affliction who could console and reconcile them to their loss.

Waller went down the river, taking Job with him. And it was most fortunate for us, as I shall presently detail, that he did so.

CHAPTER XIV.

WITHDRAWAL FROM MAGOMERO.

SCUDAMORE and I left Chibisa's on the day after the departure of the boat—March 12—and arrived at Magomero early on the morning of the 15th, not much the worse for our week's marching, though on the average we had walked more than twenty miles a day.

We left Dickinson, Adams, and Gamble ill; the two former

were now, we found, better, but the condition of Gamble seemed hopeless.   Could Captain Wilson have waited, we should have sent him home with the ' Gorgon.'

When at Chibisa's, we found the Makololo revelling in all the good things that part of the world could produce, masters of the village, monarchs of all they surveyed.   They had goats by the score, fowls by the hundred; they ate the finest corn and drank the best of pombi.   They and their numerous wives were clothed and decorated without regard to cost.   They had sprung all at once from poverty to wealth, from a condition little removed from bondage to that of lords of the creation. And how was all this brought about ?   When left by Dr. Livingstone at Chibisa's they had little but their guns and ammunition, and for a time they were in great straits.   But with guns they knew themselves to be formidable ; they hunted the slavers far and near, released the captives and took the plunder.   The women thus released they took for wives, the men and boys they kept as slaves, and with the spoil they clothed themselves and all belonging to them.   They had then no sheep or goats, and no corn.   But the Manganja had, and as in their own country the possession of cattle by a neighbour is in their estimation a good *casus belli*, they were prepared to make war on the Manganja for their flocks and corn if they did not yield them without resistance.   The Manganja yielded, and thus arose the bleating of sheep and goats, the cackling of fowls, and the well-stocked houses of corn in the Makololo habitations.

After having supplied themselves with cloth and beads from the slavers, they might, it is true, have bought from the Manganja, but they preferred to keep their beads and cloth, and to acquire Manganja property in another way.

The English name, therefore, in their neighbourhood, was in bad odour.   And we found it was no comfort to the people of some villages near the river to call out, ' The English are here, don't fear ; ' for they did fear, and until they recognized us individually ran away from us.

It was a great mistake on the part of Dr. Livingstone to leave the Makololo at Chibisa's unprovided with everything

but arms. They were identified with the English, they came
up the river first of all with them, they had been with us on
our journeys, lived with us, and they adopted our name in their
raids, and the consequence was, we were in some places looked
upon as foes instead of friends. We were greatly pained by
the state of things we discovered, and which they scarcely attempted to deny. They had always behaved well when with
us, or when employed by us, and had many good qualities for
which we liked them, but we felt that they must no longer be
identified with us, and that we must at once and entirely re-
pudiate their ill deeds.

Mankokwe talked of driving them out of the country, but
they would have driven like sheep five times the number of
Manganja Mankokwe could have brought against them, and so
he appeared to think at last, for he never interfered to protect
his people from them.

We had not returned to Magomero many days before the old
war-panic broke out among the Manganja as strong as ever.
Chiefs came to us as plentiful as butterflies. They declared
that Joi had united with Kempama, the Ajawa chief in Barwi's neighbourhood, and that they had bound themselves by a
solemn league and covenant not to rest until they had wrested
the land from the Manganja. Even that great Fumo-Mon-
gazi—or rather Bona, Mongazi being the hereditary title—
sent his brothers to crave our assistance against the dreaded
enemy, who were said to be somewhere north-west of Chiradzuru.

Bona had vapoured to such an extent about his prowess, and
the number of men he could bring into the field, that he was
the last man, had we not known the Manganja by this time,
we should have expected to come to us for aid. Soon after the
Chirumba camp was broken up, when Waller and Meller were
in his village, they expressed surprise that he had not been
present on that occasion, or sent men to help, when the object
was the national good. But, said Bona, putting himself into
an attitude—

'What, me? Bona? Look! See Chiradzuru! Well, all
the country between that and this, belongs to me, Bona. Bona.

is a great chief, none greater.   His lands are very great.   Look this way, look that way, look all ways, and still the country belongs to me, Bona.   Bona did not go.   Bona did not send any of his children.   Why ?   Because Bona has nothing to fear from anybody.   You do not hear of anyone making war on Bona.   All know he is a great chief.   Bona does not, like Chinsunzi, like Kankomba, like all the other chiefs, send goats to the English, strangers in the land, to ask them to drive his enemies away.   No ; Bona does not do that, if he did, he would think himself no man.   No ; Bona is able to fight all his own battles, to drive away all his enemies.   Let the Ajawa come.   What would he do ?   He would send his fighting bro- ther with all his fighting men, and where would the Ajawa be then ?   Bona cannot say, but no one would ever hear of them again.'

But there was a rumour among Bona's people that the Ajawa were coming, and Bona, instead of sending his fighting brother against them, sent him to us, and dismal was the report of the fighting brother.   The foe was close at hand, in number so large you could not count them, they had burnt, and they had killed, and Bona and his fighting brother, and all his valiant men of war, were all dead men, if the English did not come to their help.

We reminded the fighting brother of Bona's great speech, and could not help laughing at his confusion of face.   But, said he—

'Bona was very wrong to talk like that, very wrong; but that was a long time ago, forget it now, and do not laugh, listen to what we say, come and help us, aud laugh after- wards.'

But we had no intention to help them, for the dismal tale of the fighting brother was not a true story—we knew that from other sources—and even the fighting brother, upon cross- examination, admitted first of all that only one village, and that a very small one, had been burnt, and only one man killed, and then was forced to own that as yet no village had been de- stroyed and no one killed, but he declared a woman had been carried off.   He stuck to the woman, an d we let him have her, but told him he must expect no help from us, because the Manganja were a set of cowards who made fears to frighten themselves with.

In thinking over the various localities suitable for a station— for we had resolved, as soon as we had the means, to remove from Magomero—we could think of no place more suitable than the neighbourhood of Bona. It was healthy, fertile, well-peopled, and one day's march nearer the Shire. Procter and Dickinson had been talking of making the necessary tour of inspection, and thought they might as well make use of Bona's fighting brother to show them the country. So they went away with him, and determined at the same time to find out the real position and movements of the Ajawa.

They had not been gone an hour before another brother of Bona came into Magomero, and professing to know nothing of the fighting brother's visit, declared that he had seen Ajawa with his own eyes, and in those very districts through which Scudamore and I had passed a few days before and found all security, and the people without fear. And then one Portilla, an ambassador from one Mamvula, chief of a place some thirty miles to the south-west of us, came into the village, and his object also was to secure our services against the Ajawa (oh, how we abominated that word in the mouths of the Manganja!) and, to make sure of our co-operation, had brought us the tempting present of an Ajawa woman and child! He seemed quite unable to comprehend our refusal. What! refuse to help Mamvula? Impossible! So we were very explicit indeed, and still further astonished him by saying that his purposed present was odious to us; and that if his master Mamvula stole Ajawa women and children he would be rightly punished if the Ajawa came against him and destroyed him. So Portilla the ambassador went away very crestfallen.

But Portilla had barely gone before others came, and to our amazement they spoke of peace, and gave us proof of plenty. First came Bango, chief of a place called Misaji, a few miles north of us, and with him came a long train of men laden with corn, which he begged the English would accept as a small token of his friendship and gratitude. Had not the English given him all ? they gave peace to him and his, and they were then able to plant their gardens and reap their corn.

While engaged with Bango, another body of men, also bur-dened with corn, entered Magomero. Their leader was Montongo, the head man of Numyama, chief of Kunumbo, who also said his lord was grateful, and as a proof of his gratitude had sent us of the fruits of his fields. If Bango and Numyama were grateful, so were we, and with thankfulness to the Giver of all Good, accepted these most welcome presents.

But Bango and Numyama were not the only chiefs who brought presents. Chinsunzi, the last man we should have expected to be grateful, came attended by his son Kapanji, and upwards of a hundred men, most of whom were burdened with corn. The old chief was arrayed in his grandest apparel, and his approach was attended with much pomp and ceremony. A vanguard preceded, and announced the arrival of the lord Chinsunzi ; and when he appeared, and had seated himself, his men ranged themselves in order behind him. Kapanji, how-ever, marched backwards and forwards in front of him for some time, making a trumpeting noise with his hands and mouth, greatly to the amusement of our boys, who forthwith began to imitate him. Then Chinsunzi made a very pretty speech, expressive of his great regard and constant affection for the English, who had done such good things for him and his, and his regret that he had not been able to come and see them for so long a time. He had been very busy in the field, and now, having time, he had come, and had brought a little present with him. The little present was a heap of corn.

We were very glad to see a better side to Chinsunzi's cha-racter ; up to this time we had seen but little else than mean-ness and mendacity. He may have been really grateful, for whatever might be the exaggerations about the Ajawa in other parts, it was very certain they made his country a desolation, and his people fugitives. Now his land was a fruitful field, and his people were content and happy in their security and abundance.

Chinsunzi said there were no Ajawa in his neighbourhood, and he was under no apprehension of their returning.

Procter and Dickinson returned on the 22nd. They found Mongazi much inclined to warlike talk, but amiable, and willing to let us live on his land if we could find a place to suit us. A place was found about four miles from his village, appearing to afford all we needed—a slope of a hill removed from all marsh land, and having a fertile soil and plenty of water. But it was not possible to move unless we had cloth; until our stores arrived we could but wait where we were.

It appeared, from the information our brethren acquired about the Ajawa, that Kempama was making war in a mild way, in revenge for an attack which had been made on some of his people by Barwi, when a brother of Kempama had been killed. He had burnt a small village, and in doing that had scared the Manganja out of their wits, all those living near his camp having forsaken their homes and taken to the bush. On the crest of a hill behind Chiradzuru there was a considerable number of fugitives, men, women, and children. The men, great hulking fellows, were crouching in abject terror among the children—their bows and arrows, useless weapons in such hands, lying beside them. Of Joi nothing was known; he seemed to be far away. All that we heard of this fresh Ajawa disturbance confirmed us in the opinion that the Manganja had provoked it, and that Barwi, a persistent and splenetic fellow, who wanted to get rid of Kempama, had been the prime provoker. After living peaceably for three years, Kempama, well knowing all we had done and could do, was not at all likely, unless greatly aggravated, to commence hostilities.

On April the 1st, Mbame, of all people in the world, came to solicit our aid against the Ajawa. He said no place belonging to him had been destroyed as yet—he lived within twenty miles of the river—no place belonging to Soche had been destroyed, nor did he think Mongazi had suffered, but they were all in great fear. The Ajawa had advanced into Ku Jireka, Mamvula's country, and they would certainly in time 'eat them all up' if they were not checked. He admitted that Mongazi and Barwi had sent to him and asked him to come to us—but he maintained as truth that the Ku Jireka district was being occupied and the Manganja flying.

In speaking of this to our own Ajawa people, they said they believed it to be true; and Chimlolo, who came to us from some Ajawa near to Ku Jireka, thought that it was quite true. He had heard before he came to us that a number of his people had been forced out of their own country, and were coming in the direction of Ku Jireka. These would be the people Dr. Livingstone saw when returning from Lake Nyassa, and they might be an annoyance to us, as they could easily get between us and the Shire, and so cut off our communication with it.

This was a serious matter, and we consulted upon the course we should adopt. With respect to Kempama we were quite clear, we would not go against him. When we broke up the camp at Chirumba we did so in the firm belief that the Ajawa were the mere creatures of the Portuguese slavers, and that if they were dispersed a permanent peace would be the result. But now we knew that, though they had been made use of by the Portuguese, the Ajawa were in the first instance no more to blame than the Manganja, and we saw also that if we went to war again it would not be with the pariahs of the tribe, but with the tribe itself, who were, by stress of circumstances, being forced down into Manganja territory, and whose necessities compelled them to take food wherever they found it. From all we could learn there seemed no doubt that the remains of the Ajawa people were being driven into the Manganja Highlands. And our greater knowledge of the Manganja convinced us that even if it were right, it would be perfectly useless to help them again. The more you helped them, the more they would want helping, the less self-reliant they would become. Had the land been ours, had we been merely colonists, we could have held it against all comers, as Christian Missionaries, though we were quite ready to succour the distressed and defend the oppressed, even if we had to resort to arms, we had no inclination to increase our warlike reputation by simply taking the side of the one tribe against the other, when we knew, for certain, that the war was tribal, and that we were not performing a simple act of justice and humanity in ridding the land of a band of robbers and murderers.

These considerations made us resolve that we would not again take up arms against the Ajawa unless they molested us, and that we would give up the Highlands first, and let the two tribes settle the question between themselves. It was perfectly useless to make efforts for peace; give the Manganja peace to-day, and with the characteristics of all cowards when they think they have the upper hand, they would provoke war to-morrow. We told Mbame that he and his friends must expect no help from us.

On April 14, we sent Charles down to Chibisa's to see if he could get any information of the 'Pioneer.' Our entire stock of barter goods was exhausted, and we were tearing up our sheets in order to purchase what we needed.

On the 17th, the dispute between Barwi and Kempama came to an issue, which left no doubt in our minds that war was commenced in earnest; day by day we had been pestered by the Manganja, and every day we heard of doings which turned out to be false, but at last we knew for certain that Barwi had persuaded Mongazi and some other chiefs to join him with their forces, and they had gone against Kempama, and endeavoured to surprise and defeat him; but he was not to be surprised, and before the fight took place there was a parley. He asked why the Manganja had come to destroy him? He did not wish for war, and he had not made war, he had only burnt the village of the man who killed his brother. But since they wished for war they should have it, and it should be a war as long as he lived, for he would never make peace with them again. Whereupon a fight took place, and the Manganja according to custom were beaten; the whole country was quickly covered with fugitives, who fled either from good cause or unreasonable fear. Kempama, joined by some more of his countrymen, then advanced his position, and threatened Barwi's villages.

Of course if we intended to have fought Kempama, it would have been our policy to have gone against him at once; but it would have been decidedly wrong to have helped the Manganja in this instance, and much as we pitied the poor trembling creatures who came to us and implored us to drive their enemy away only this once, and they would never make war again, we were obliged to be deaf to all their appeals. The Manganja themselves did not attempt to deny that Kempama's brother had been killed by Barwi, and that that circumstance provoked him to retaliate, and there was every reason to believe that during the previous five months the Manganja had killed and made captive many of the Ajawa who were living in villages away from the large camps.

The question was, what should we do? Remain at Magomero and see the country desolated about us? That was more than we could do. It would have been impossible to have remained, and see the Manganja reduced to extremity, and not have helped them. And so we resolved to leave Magomero at once, and go down to Chibisa's, if we could not find a good position near Soche's or Mbame's.

We sent down to Charles, and bade him bring up as many men as he could get to carry down our baggage. We came to that resolution with much pain. It did in this case certainly require more courage to give up than to hold, for it would have been easy work to have shouldered our rifles and driven Kempama and his people, simply from the neighbourhood of Barwi. But we all clearly saw that if we took up arms again we should be obliged to enter upon a regular campaign; that a single effort would have been worse than useless. Sooner or later, it was evident the Ajawa must occupy the country; our presence, unless we fought, would only complicate matters, and indeed, unless we fought we could not live, for the crops and all the live stock would be destroyed, and we should be left without food.

We resolved to take our children with us, and such of the elders as cared to accompany us; our numbers were greatly reduced, for by death alone since the beginning of December we had lost more than fifty women and children. The Bishop's class, the class he took for me, consisting of our youngest boys, were all dead save one little fellow named Katolatola (literally, Drop me down and pick me up); and fever was still very active among us through March and April. We managed, however, to keep up our classes, despite all troubles;

and many of the children were improving greatly in habits and manners.

On March 20, being Easter Day, for the first time since the Bishop's death we sang the Psalms and a hymn. The previous Easter Day the Mission party on sea and land were so prostrated by fever that it was not possible to celebrate the Holy Communion; but now our condition was better; and, despite the anxious cares upon us, we were far from unhappy—who could be so on such a hopeful, life-giving Festival?

On the 21st, a man whom we sent down with Charles, returned, bringing with him a bundle of cloth, a bag of newspapers, and a letter from Waller. Blair had come up the river with Job, and had brought us supplies in two Portuguese canoes. Waller remained at Shupanga. His letter was dated 17th of March, and stated that the 'Pioneer,' unable to ascend the river, had landed the sections of the 'Lady Nyassa' at Shupanga, and, with Captain Wilson and the ladies, had returned to Kongone. And then, to our consternation, he added, '*out of the very large stock of stores brought out for us to the Kongone, scarce any of the essentials are left.*' This really proved to be the case, for out of fifty boxes of flour we received no more than eight; our biscuits were gone, so was our salt meat. Out of four casks of wine we had less than one cask. Our cloth had been freely used; our brandy was tapped to a cruel extent, and other things in proportion were, in a like manner, lost to us. And how was this? Our stores were landed intact, they were put under a tent on shore, and when the 'Pioneer' and Captain Wilson with his boats ascended the river, Mr. Hawkins remained in charge. But he was taken ill with fever, and was ordered on board the 'Gorgon.' The 'Gorgon' was blown away from the coast in a storm, and was absent some weeks. Thus our stores were without protection. The natives at the Kongone may have stolen, and others may have helped themselves. It is certain that, when the boats of the 'Gorgon' returned from their river trip, there were ninety sick and hungry sailors for nearly three weeks without sufficient food or medical comforts. An idea seemed to prevail among those at the Kongone that we

Missionaries were revelling in abundance at Magomero, be-
·cause Bishop Mackenzie, thinking the supply of goats would
not fail, had asked Dr. Meller to sell to the ships' crews any
preserved meats and also the biscuit that might come out to
us. A little considerate thought, however, must have convinced all, that in consequence of leaving so large a quantity
of our first year's stores at Johanna, there could not but arise
a deficiency of food in a land which as yet produced scarcely
anything suitable for Europeans. This, of course, could not
have been surmised in England; but the painful result was
that five-sixths of what was really necessary to our existence
had been taken from the second year's supply which the Cape
Town Committee with so much care and feeling had sent to
us. It is true we did not really want food, but we suffered
much from the character of the food we were compelled to eat.
Pumpkins, cucumber, and new corn, are delicious things when
you do not have too much of them, but they do not form the
best of food for men worn by hard work, exposure, fever, and
dysenteric complaints. Our breaking-in to native diet was
too severe. It annoyed one to be continually obliged to think
of what we could eat, what we could not eat, or whether we
could eat at all. I suffered less than most; but it was very
painful to see some of my brethren enduring, and sinking
under illnesses which would have been avoided altogether, or
from which they would readily have recovered had they had
proper food. I blame no individual in saying what I do on
this subject; and had it not been necessary for me in writing
this narrative to trace effects to their true causes, I should
have been silent upon this point: but as the loss of these
stores entailed much privation, and extraordinary exertions,
which aggravated the natural difficulties of our position, and
helped to fatal issues, I cannot avoid the responsibility of de-
tailing what we justly regarded as one of our most serious
misfortunes.

But we were not men to grow morbid in thinking over a
trouble that could not be remedied. We received with thankfulness the bundle of cloth Charles sent up to us, and went on
with preparations for our departure, growling now and then,

or we should not have been Englishmen, but, upon the whole, grateful that things were no worse.

April the 24th was a day of excitement for us, and of some suffering and much terror to the Manganja. We were hard at work, packing up our personalities, when the cry of ' Ajawa! Ajawa!' was raised, in such a manner as led us to believe a horde of these folks were upon us, so we snatched up our guns and sallied forth, but there was nothing but smoke visible— the smoke from a fire six or seven miles from us. We went on to the top of a hill, and saw that it was Barwi's villages which were being destroyed. One after the other, in rapid succession, they were fired, and many people were rushing from the burning villages towards Magomero. Adams and Johnson looked at us in a beseeching way, for though both in calmer moments thought it impossible for us to take part in this conflict which Barwi had without doubt provoked, both were warm-hearted, impulsive men, ready at any moment to defend the weakest, and we required all the power we had to resist their appeal.

Having burnt these villages, killed two or three people and made some captives, the Ajawa retreated to their camp. The Manganja made no resistance, nor did they attempt to harass the Ajawa as they retired.

As the fugitives flocked into Magomero, one could not help deepest pity for them, they looked so helpless and hopeless. We could do no other than follow the course we had decided upon, it would have been both weak and useless not to have done so. Leave Magomero under any circumstances we must ; it was death to remain. To go after the Ajawa and rout them from their camp would have done the Manganja no good unless we followed up what we did by driving them and all their fellows out of the land altogether. If we were away, in order to save their homes, the Manganja would accept the Ajawa as their masters. It was their fate as the weaker, unless we stayed with them, became their champions on all occasions, and destroyed all stronger than they. That we would not do ; and we clearly saw that the land must then pass into the hands of the Ajawa, and that it was manifestly our best policy to

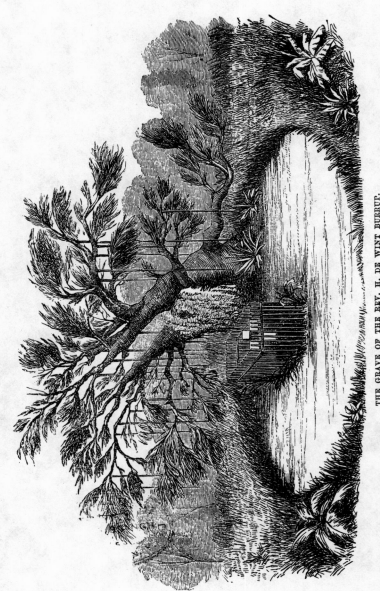

THE GRAVE OF THE REV. H. DE WINT BURRUP.

retire from the hills for a time, and when the Ajawa had the land, go and complete among them the work we had begun with the Manganja.

We sent for Chigunda and told him that we should leave Magomero in a day or two. He expressed no surprise, for he knew of our intentions to leave some time before this fresh outbreak of war. At first he expressed a wish to go with us, but after consulting with a brother chief, he said he would stay until driven away, and then he would come to us.

The Manganja have all the domestic faculties largely developed, inhabitiveness especially ; but, though they do not like to leave their homes when they are in danger, as is here shown, they make no effort to defend them.

During the day Barwi was reported to be outside our station unhurt. He simply went out as the Ajawa came in, and left his wives, with the exception of one, in their hands.

The Ajawa tactics were simple enough. They left their camp before daylight, marched direct to the principal village, assailed and destroyed that, and fired the others which lay in their line of march home. They made prisoners of all they could pounce upon, but they did not pursue any.

Charles returned towards evening with about seventy Chibisians, and so we resolved to leave Magomero next day.

Early in the morning, the 25th, we had finished all our preparations, and after paying a visit to poor Burrup's grave which we had surrounded by bamboo rails, we distributed food to all, and gave to each man his burden. Our departure caused greatest excitement among the Manganja, crowds of whom assembled to see us off. Those of our people who were going with us were all ready. The wives of our men prepared meal for the journey. One poor girl named Chesika, who was unable to stand from an apparently incurable ulcer, was immoderate in her grief until we found a man to carry her, and then she was as immoderate in her joy. We had saved and kept her from death, and had we left her she would have died of sorrow.

CHESIKA, AN AJAWA GIRL.

We resolved to go by Chiradzuru instead of by way of Mongazi's village, that route being nearer, and affording two halting-places before we got to Soche's. Scudamore took the lead, I the rear. Taking the route we did, we had to wade through the river. Just as I was about to cross, I heard a child screaming piteously, and immediately afterwards a little girl, about five years of age, rushed down to the river after us, and would have thrown herself in if I had not caught her. She was a poor wizened little thing that I had especially cared for, but whom in the hurry of the morning's work I had forgotten. She begged hard not to be left behind, and we had no intention to leave her, so I took her across the water, and finding she could not keep up with the main body, I had to carry her for the first three or four miles. She was not heavy, but I was weak, and had my gun and knapsack to carry. So when I reached the place where Scudamore had halted in order that all might come up, I was glad to turn her over to the care of an unencumbered woman.

The distance from Magomero to the village of Bobo (where we halted for the night) was not more than ten miles, but the day was hot, and it was a wearisome march for the women and children. A panic existed among the inhabitants of the villages along our road; they were ready to take to the bush at any minute. Bobo was in hiding, but as soon as he saw us, all fear was at an end, he and his men came forward, and preceded us to the village. The presence of the English ensured safety for that night. All the huts, with the exception of two, were placed at our disposal, but as the village was small, there was but accommodation for the women and children. We, and the native men of our party, slept out in the open air. It was a strange experience. The huge mountains hanging as it were over us, and here and there reflecting the many fires our people had kindled, the wild appearance of the men as they ate their evening meal, the discordant din of many voices, and the circumstances of our march, made an altogether only to be realised in a country like this.

Next day we moved on to Pingwi.

The incidents along the road were numerous, some were pleasing. For instance, it was pleasant to notice the great concern most of our men felt for the safety and well-being of their wives. They would go a-head some distance with their burdens—and the natives on level ground always walk faster with a burden on their heads than without one—but at every halt would run back to look after the Akasi (woman). It is not usual for natives to manifest so much affection, but our men were somewhat humanised, and happily coupled, and each, having but one wife, bestowed upon her all the care and feeling he would have dispensed to a dozen.

Katolatola, the only survivor of our very small boys, marched along famously for five miles, and then his strength failed him,

and I found him yelling with apprehension. I discovered a
big fellow skulking in the bush, and promised him cloth if
he would carry the child to Pingwi; he promised to do so, but
three or four miles farther on I found Katolatola deserted and
disconsolate. Clarke coming up, gave his gun to a boy, and
shouldered the little urchin, and so he arrived at Pingwi.

It was nearly dark before the last of our party came in.
Our own men behaved admirably. The man Chimlolo proved
himself a noble fellow, helping those who were weak, and encouraging all by his hearty word and laugh. Our own men
bore the heaviest burdens, and must have been very tired; but
finding that Akumsama, and another lad who had ulcered legs,
were some distance behind, two of them, Akumtonda and
Ntula, returned for them, and brought them in on their
backs.

Poor Adams was the last to arrive; he had developed fever
on the way, from which he and Dickinson were seldom free.
Constitutionally, however, they were most unlike, Adams
being robust, and Dickinson the reverse.

We found Pingwi deserted.

The next day, Sunday, we wished to make a day of rest;
but the Chibisians were anxious to get on to Soche's, so we
sent them on with Charles and Gamble.

Having seen Dickinson and all others off on Monday,
Procter, Scudamore and myself, accompanied by William and
six of our men, went back towards Magomero, in order to
bring on some luggage that had been left behind; so we did
not get to Soche's until the next day.

A thunderstorm met us on the way, and we were never
more wet than when we entered the village. Soche's, with its
groves of banana, might have been a charming place, but it
was dirty. Rotting vegetable refuse lay about in all directions.
The puddles were expansive and knee deep. There were a
great many people in the village, and we were with difficulty
accommodated.

The Socheians seemed in a thriving condition, the children
were fat beyond all precedent, and the country was certainly
the most fertile in the whole land. This was the district Dr.

Kirk recommended, and the Bishop wished to occupy. It was no good to attempt to halt here now, for Mongazi was close at hand, and his fate we knew to be sealed; and Soche had Joi and his horde coming up behind him. By staying here we should not have been free of any of the Magomero difficulties.

Next day, Job came from Chibisa's with thirty additional men; and as it was raining hard when he arrived, a more miserable set of fellows than those Chibisians no one ever saw. The native loves not rain or wind; under their influence he seems half dead: give him sunshine and he expands to the full extent of his capacity. We were all very moist, and all more or less unwell, but Job had brought us a bottle of brandy, and so for the first time for six months we were able to comfort ourselves with a little spirit and water; we had been so long without anything of the kind, that the brandy, though good, did not taste at all pleasant to our simple palates; nevertheless, its effects were beneficial. It threw off the fever coming upon me, and the rest suffered far less than they would have done. Johnson had no more than a table-spoonful, but it made him so joyous that he produced his fiddle and drove the Socheians nearly mad with admiration.

Next morning we moved on to Mbame's. Master Katola-tola marched before me the whole distance, and talked about the affairs of the country more like an old man than a babe of five.

I did not stay long at Mbame's, but went on to Chipindu's, the first halting-place from the river, intending to start for Chibisa's early in the morning, in order to make preparations for the arrival of the rest.

We had some consultation upon the advisability of halting altogether at Mbame's. But we found that at his elevation the country was suffering from drought. The first terrace had had none of the rain that had been so plentiful higher up; crops were failing, and our people declared we should want food if we stayed; we talked to Mbame, and though he would have given his best to have had us settle beside him, he could not say that food was likely to be plentiful; on the contrary, he was fearful that he and all others at his altitude would suffer from hunger, so little rain had there been. We resolved to go down to the Shire, and rest for a time on the south bank below Chibisa's.

Circumstances were not happy at Chipindu's; the chief was out, and the people were sad at the prospect of failing crops. It was with difficulty I could get a dinner. A breakfast next morning I could not get, so I started for the river without one, and arrived at the banks of the Shire a few minutes after nine.

I found Blair seated at the door of his hut eating ground-rice porridge, swimming in milk, and sweetened with sugar; I never coveted food before, but I did covet this—it looked delicious. I had walked twelve miles without a breakfast, I was faint from hunger, and so I said to Blair:

'Are you hungry?'

'No.'

'Then turn your breakfast over to me, for I am.'

He did so, and till then I had not known what was meant by the word delicious, as applied to food. It was almost worth while going through the privation to have such an enjoyment.

Blair was not well—he had had fever on the river, and was not recovered from its effects.

As soon as I was rested I went in search of a site. The place where I first began building was too circumscribed. I went lower down, and there found an excellent position. When Scudamore saw it on his arrival he said:

'This is a glorious place—all we want—high enough above the river, and water easy of access.'

The bank here was eighty feet high, and there seemed no limit to the view from it: mountain peaks on a clear day were seen a hundred miles distant; and the valley scenery up and down the river, backed as it was by the Manganja hills, was beautiful.

The soil was good, a light supersoil upon stratified sand. We did not deceive ourselves, and think that this place would probably prove as healthy as the better parts of the Highlands.

We knew that no position by a river in Africa could be so healthy as the higher regions, but it was the best position along the river, and we felt sure that it would prove healthier than Magomero. We moved to this place with our eyes open to the full consequences of our act. It was the only place to which we could retire, until peace was given to the Highland districts, and we could return to them. It was not our choice, it was our necessity, which led us to come down to the valley.

As soon as I had fixed upon the site, I summoned the great men of Chibisa's, and fortunately the great man's greatest man was over from Doa, where Chibisa resided. I told him of our intentions, and he expressed his delight to hear that the English were going to live near them. Chibisa would be honoured, all would be honoured; the country was before the English, they might take what they liked, they might build where they liked, and he hoped they would remain for ever.

Nothing could be more amiable, nothing could exceed the profound bowing, and foot stamping and scraping, the latter trick they had learnt from the Portuguese, with which these worthies received the present I gave them on concluding our proceedings. Chechoma, the talkative, was there; and as he was second head man, and medicine man to boot, I had to propitiate him by a present. That done, he sent a herd of men and boys to clear away the bush from the ground upon which we intended to build. I would mention that presents with us were not the formidable things they appear among tribes north of where we were. There they require whole pieces of cloth, while with us two yards were considered a liberal present unless to a very great man indeed.

All our party were down by the 6th of May. It seemed incredible, so thickly had events pressed one upon another, that it was but a year since we entered the Zambesi. Yet so it was. If time were measured by experience, we were ten years older than we were twelvemonths before.

After we had paid the porters, and the Makololo, for we owed then not only the fifty fathoms Moloko advanced, but for going down to Manasomba's and to Malo, we found that we had all but exhausted the stock of cloth Blair had brought

up, and as Job was fond of the river, we decided to send him
down to Shupanga again for additional supplies.

The giving up of the Highlands depressed us greatly; but
though cast down by our difficulties, we were by no means in
despair. We each felt inclined to echo the sentiment of a
verse of a simple poem, of which the Bishop was fond:

> Father, I know that all my life
> Is portioned out for me,
> And the changes that are sure to come,
> I do not fear to see;
> ˙But I ask Thee for a present mind
> Intent on pleasing Thee.

CHAPTER XV.

SETTLEMENT NEAR CHIBISA'S.

FOR a few days, until we could get up huts, we remained at
Chibisa's village, and then made ourselves fully acquainted
with the proceedings of the Mokololo. They had plundered
the country on all sides, and so great was the terror of them
that the Manganja were afraid to come to us with food. It
was necessary, therefore, to take vigorous measures, and catching one of them in the act of taking from a man the cloth I
had just given him for a goat, I laid hold of a stick and gave
the fellow a good thrashing.

We then called them together, and told them that if they
continued to act as they had done, we would hold no intercourse with them, and not allow any of our people to come
near them. Moloko and Ramakukan denied that they individually had been guilty of plundering or ill-usage, but admitted that others had done both. I do not suppose that
Moloko and Ramakukan had been personally engaged in
robbing the Manganja, but they had a number of men whom
they had released from the slavers, and these they employed
in the bad work. We found that that was the policy pursued

by most of them, and it was thus they were maintaining themselves.

When we forced this fact upon him, Moloko replied;

' Well, it is true we have taken food when we wanted it, and what else could we do ? We were left without food, without gardens, without sheep or goats, without anything but our guns. We cannot go to the Portuguese. We cannot go to Linyanti. We must stay here. What shall we do then ? die of hunger ? no, not while we can take food. All men would take food rather than die.'

They promised us they would make gardens, and go elephant hunting if we would sell their ivory for them, and this we engaged to do. They did not leave off pillaging altogether, but our presence kept them in check, and in the end the natives around brought us corn in abundance, and for a time there was no want of goats' flesh.

The change from the hills to the valley did our native people good; the sickly recovered health, and all were much improved. Up to our leaving Magomero, death clung to them; a boy named Kasarima died the day before our departure. But death seemed to have taken farewell of them at last. We did not bring all down, as some preferred to remain on the hills and return to their own brethren; but all our married people, a few women, and the children came, in all about seventy souls.]

There was plenty of work for the men and women, and as we paid them for their labour in cloth, they found their own food. The children we fed.

But the change of locality, though beneficial to our native friends, distressed some of my English brethren. The heat of the valley was greater than that of the hills; long exposure in the sun while house-building was at first necessary, and considerable fever was the consequence. My health, however, was greatly improved by the change, and I soon lost all symptoms of dysentery. Procter did not suffer more than usual; but Scudamore, who had not recovered from the effects of that last journey to Manasomba, was greatly tried by the increased heat. Dickinson, Adams, and Clarke, suffered most severely;

fever with them seemed all but incessant. Gamble brightened wonderfully, and Blair, after he had shaken off the attack I found upon him, was no more open to fever than a native.

Altogether, though the change could not be regarded as satisfactory, we had then no reason to regret that it had been made. It was a comfort, which we gratefully appreciated, to be living free from the distractions of the hills, the everlasting cries of 'Kondo!' and 'Ajawa!'

Waller, to our great delight, returned on the 27th of May. He brought with him the remnant of our stores, and some necessaries he had purchased from the Portuguese. We had less than we needed, but the question of ways and means no longer harassed us. He informed us of the death of Mrs. Livingstone, and the return of Mr. Hawkins, broken in health, to the Cape, whence he came to England, only to die. We met him at the Cape, when *en route* for the Zambesi, and hoped for much satisfaction from his companionship.

Mariano, the Portuguese rebel, was reported wickedly active above Shamo and Morumbala, not fighting the Portuguese, but slaughtering and capturing the natives. He was said to have 2,000 armed men, and was depopulating the country, sending those he made prisoners to the slave agents on the coast. The Government had ceased to interfere with him.

The position we assumed towards the Makololo troubled them greatly. We had quite dispelled the idea among the Chibisians and others that they were English, and they were very uncomfortable. We expected they would make some move, for they became careless in their domestic economy, killing goats extravagantly, and doing other things quite contrary to their ordinary habits, and so we were not surprised to learn, on June 1st, that they had all gone away. When we went to the village we found it empty. With the exception of Chechoma, Tambala, and a few others, they had driven the original inhabitants away, and now that they had flitted, the place looked desolate enough. It was said that they had gone to Doa, to Chibisa.

The day after their departure, eight Ajawa men and their wives, who had been released from the slavers by the Makololo, but who refused to accompany them to Doa, begged that they might be on the same footing with us as our other native friends. We were not anxious to have these people near us, as they had been the agents of the Makololo, and we advised them to go back to their own people. That, they said, was impossible. War had passed over their country and their friends were killed or dispersed. If they returned, they would be enslaved, and most likely sold again. They promised to keep all laws we might make, and do nothing contrary to our will. They acknowledged that while with the Makololo they had robbed the Manganja, but urged as an excuse that in doing that they only did their master's bidding. We took time to consider, and in the interim, Damanji, Akumtonda, Chimlolo, and others of our old stock, begged very hard for their countrymen, promising to be surety for their good behaviour. We did not put them on the same footing as the others, but we gave them permission to build near us, and promised we would protect them so long as they were honest, industrious, and sober. There was a great deal of clanship among the Ajawa, and that one thing made them stronger than the Manganja.

Our people, adults as well as children, were daily becoming a better and a purer people under our teaching and example. Their confidence in us was unbounded, and their opinion of our superior wisdom and goodness as extensive as their confidence. Of course, what they did different to what they had been in the habit of doing, and what they left undone, was probably the result of no higher motive than the wish to please us; but as we always directed them to a higher than ourselves, they were, I think, beginning to recognise God's will as their rule of life. Whether a more demonstrative promulgation of our holy religion would have accomplished greater and more immediate results, is a question open to discussion. I should, I confess, like to see the experiment made among the African heathen.

As soon as we were able, we recommenced, and more systematically than before, the study of the language. The mantle of the Bishop had fallen on Scudamore. He knew more of the language than any of us, acted as our preceptor, and was looking forward to having a religious service for the natives in their own tongue. Our best plan was clearly this : While we were compelled to wait in the valley, to do all we could for our people, confine our attention as much as possible to them, so that when we did return to the hills they might in a certain sense act as missionaries to their own tribe. Every week made it more and more evident that the Ajawa would possess the Highlands, and that quickly.

I know my narrative is not like the generality of missionary records—the religious element and effort are not always apparent, *but they were always there.* Our object was to make Christians of these poor heathens, and we did not for one moment lose sight of that object. All we did, was done with that one great end in view. What we did, and the way it was done, may certainly be open to objection—it would be strange if it were not so ;—but we, clergy and laity, did our best, and it was done heartily as unto God. We were pioneers, and had to clear away an immense amount of lumber and rottenness, and all things unwholesome, before we could even lay the foundations. And we had to do that, it must not be forgotten, with very imperfect tools—with our tongues, not absolutely tied, but with only an infant's power. I never felt so forcibly as on Whit-Sunday, June 8th, how great a punishment was the Babel curse, how great a blessing was the removal of that curse with the outpouring of the Holy Spirit on the Day of Pentecost.

We were not to be long in the valley, however, without hearing that hideous word, Kondo! again. For some time rumours of war between Chibisa and a Portuguese half-caste had reached us, though we placed but little reliance on what we heard. But on the 11th of June, Chechoma came to us attended by a long train of dismal-looking Chibisians, and informed us that the fortune of war had gone against Chibisa, and he had been compelled to retreat from Doa, and was even then close at hand with all his people.

'All his people' proved to be about six hundred souls. They arrived a few hours after Chechoma came to us, and encamped in the bush outside the village. The Makololo returned with them—indeed, they met Chibisa on the road.

On the 13th, Chibisa visited us in state. Having heard so much of this man, and not having had his person described, we imagined him to be of large stature and imposing mien, and were surprised to find him a little man, about forty years of age. When introduced, he shook hands after the fashion of Europeans, and following us into a hut, seated himself on a chair, as though he had never known what it was to squat. Then he surveyed us individually, not rudely, but as one well versed in physiognomy, nor did he lose his self-possession for a moment. He had a very large and long head and a very peculiar cast of features, and he had stamped this physical peculiarity on his children; having seen their father, you could single them out from among a crowd of others, for they had the same length of skull and the same form of feature; but they had not the father's powerful spirit that shone out of the eye now and thén, even when the features were passive.

We opened the conversation by expressing our sorrow that he had found it necessary to leave Doa, and our hope that now when he was here he would stay, as we should like to have so distinguished a man for our neighbour as well as our friend. He replied quietly:

'I know the English are my friends, and that they feel sorry for my trouble, but I am not going to stay here. I shall go back to Doa soon. This is a poor land. There are no elephants and no buffalo here. I have brought the women and children for safety, but I shall return soon, and if Makururu (the man with whom he was at variance) comes against me again, I shall go out and meet him. And if I die, I die.'

He said this without any attempt at Manganja eloquence, scarcely raising his voice to the ordinary conversational pitch, and while filling his pipe with tobacco.

We then explained to him our object in coming into the country. He listened attentively to William's translation of our words, and seemed to realise all we said, for he replied:

'My people told me that you came to speak about God, not to fight, and that you left the hills because you wished to be quiet. I know that some white men teach, and some fight.'

He made no appeal to us to help him, but acted like a man who knew what work he had to do, and meant to do it.

We then spoke of the state of the hills, and told him of the want of courage and union among the Manganja. He smiled and said, 'Oh! they will not fight alone or together, and they want me to be their leader! I have enough of my own troubles. I must take care of myself, and they must take care of themselves.'

He did not allude to the cause of the quarrel between him and Makururu, but said that he was taken by surprise, and having but little ammunition—while his opponent, who had received the assistance of a man named Belchior, a man in a state of semi-rebellion against the Portuguese, had plenty—he was obliged to retreat. We expected to hear more about the ammunition, but did not then.

We saw that Chibisa's determination and pugnacity had not been over-rated. He spoke and acted like a man who was only stooping to conquer, and we felt sure that it would go hard with Makururu yet, whatever the merits of the question in dispute. Chibisa had that peculiar appearance and manner which all have who are not easily overcome. He said that he was on good terms with the Portuguese generally; the quarrel was a personal affair between him and Makururu, and his ally Belchior, or Matichoro, as the natives called him.

Before he left us, as he had always behaved well to us, we gave him a considerable present, and also a fathom of cloth to each of his head men.

Chibisa's people were more curious than he, and our various properties greatly interested them; they were especially as-tonished at a small pendulum-clock in my hut. The continual movement of the pendulum confounded them at first; they looked at one another, each trying to see what the other thought of it; listened, laughed nervously, then listened again. At last one merry fellow wagged his head from side to side keeping time with the pendulum and ejaculated, 'Da-da— Da-da' in imitation of the tick, and a shout of laughter from all was the result. A burning-glass was also great fun; I tried it on their hands and legs, and when they experienced its effects, they leaped about like wild things. But when they saw the fun of it, they brought others ignorant of its power, and enjoyed their consternation when the new comers felt the heat. They ejaculated no end of surprise, when, after seeing the glass set fire to a piece of calico and light a pipe, they discovered it to be quite cool. Next to the clock and burning-glass, photographs interested them most. The portraits of the 'Mamuna Anglesi,' the English *men*, did not surprise them much, but that of the 'Akasi Anglesi' (the English woman) was a real wonder. The dress, the hair, the absence of lip-ring, great or small, were all noticed and commented upon. The women fetched their friends to see their English sister, and contrasting their own semi-nude condition with the well clothed figure before them, and their own shaven crowns with the well-covered English head, they looked at their naked legs, put their hands to their bald pates, and laughed in greatest glee.

In the afternoon we visited their camp. It was a scene of sadness. Long exposure and hardship had brought illness upon many. The majority of the women and children looked weary and dispirited. The men seemed more fatigued than dispirited—they did not look like men who had been thoroughly beaten. The retreat from Doa was evidently no rout, for the goats and sheep had been brought off, a considerable quantity of corn and all household furniture. Their inanimate properties were piled up against the trees, and formed a strange medley. Here and there you saw tokens of intercourse with civilisation, for the simplicity of the household chattels of the unsophisticated native was broken in upon by various articles of European manufacture. Among Chibisa's effects were a cane-seated couch, a chair, a child's cot, and some of his people had similar articles. As Chibisa did not deal in slaves, these things probably came from the Portuguese in exchange for ivory.

It was a happy thing for the women and children that their flight was not in the rainy season. Had it been, many of them must have died; as it was, a few days' rest revived them.

Next day Chibisa paid us another visit. He was less formal in his approach, but was splendid in his attire. He had on his head a scarlet cloth cap ornamented with gold lace, and around his body a richly coloured wrapper of European manufacture.

Dickinson showed him some micro-photographs, one of which was a portrait of Dr. Livingstone, which he instantly recognised. He was a little less official in his manner than on the previous day, but he was always self-possessed. He said little about his own affairs, and seemed too much interested with the many things we showed him to talk about himself.

Checoma, no longer the talkative, and shorn of all gay apparel, for he wore a goat skin, and had not a single ring on wrist or legs, attended him. I made some remark about his altered appearance and manner. Upon which Chibisa gave a little chuckle and said very quietly:

'Yes, Checoma has been acting the great man; but I looked at him last night, and now you see what he is.'

Poor Checoma! That look must have been highly significant.

In the afternoon Waller and I again visited his camp. We found Chibisa lying prone on the earth, with his head a little raised, and surrounded by his principal men. They were evidently holding a council of war, but ceased their conference significantly as we approached. Chibisa rose and led the way to his own habitation, a secluded spot fenced in by trees and shrubs, and where we found all his wives and children. Their name was legion, and upon our remarking this, he said he had wives 'Kumi! kumi! kumi!' which means ten thrice told, and as many more as you please.

The children were of all ages, from the young man of twenty to the babe just born. I counted eight infants at the breast, and Chibisa was the father of all of them.

One of the wives was ill with diarrhœa, and Dickinson attended her.

During the day we had a host of Chibisians about our huts

—men, women, and children—all anxious to see the manners and customs, and the possessions of the Missionaries. They manifested neither timidity nor presumption. The women and children kept at a little distance off until invited to come nearer, but when invited they came without hesitation. Now and then a little fellow too old for infantine unconsciousness and too young for the bravery of boyhood, would cling to his mother and roar lustily for a time. These big babes, for children are frequently kept to the breast until three or four years of age, are uniformly great cowards, but they harden as soon as the mother turns them off. The African child appears to require the maternal nutriment longer than the European, for if they are deprived of it before the time I have mentioned, they become wizened and prematurely grave, such miserable little specimens of humanity as are not seen elsewhere.

Chibisa's next visit related to ammunition. He made a formal request for gunpowder! Said he:—'Without gunpowder I cannot go back to Doa, for if I have no gunpowder I cannot defend myself, and I cannot live. You are my friends, friends always help one another; you have gunpowder, give it to me in exchange for ivory; I have plenty of ivory with me.'

He had several large tusks.

That we had gunpowder was quite true, and that Chibisa should ask for it was natural enough, considering our relations with him. But upon principle we had always refused to give gunpowder to any native, and we could not consistently let Chibisa have it. So we made him understand that it was our rule not to give or sell gunpowder to any one. He looked angry and disappointed for a few seconds, but at last said:

'If the other man (Dr. Livingstone) was here, he would let me have gunpowder, I am sure. He is down the river; will you send a letter to him and tell him I will give him ivory in exchange for gunpowder?'

This we said we would do if he could find messengers to take the letter. He then went away not at all satisfied, but accepting the arrangement we proposed as his only chance of getting what he wanted.

Chibisa was soon in trouble with the people on the Shire.

The day after the gunpowder conference he came to us and told us that some of his people had been killed in the village belonging to one Akuchapa, who lived about three miles above us. He did not attempt to blame Akuchapa, for said he, ' My people were hungry, he found them stealing his corn, and so he killed them.'

He did not ask us to mix up ourselves in this matter, but said he was going to fetch home the bodies, and though he should not go to war with Akuchapa for this act, yet when his people were hungry they must have food, and if he had to stay where he was much longer they would all be hungry, and he must fight for them, he could not see them starve.

We saw clearly enough that Chibisa was in a critical position. None of the river-chiefs liked him. Mankokwe was at variance with him. He was regarded as an interloper on the Shire, and his personal characteristics were so much superior to the Rundo's, that under any circumstances it would have been uncomfortable for the latter to have the litttle man near him. We felt sure that if the Chibisians took to plundering, the chiefs would find out they had no gunpowder, and would unite against him.

For a time after the Makololo returned our relations with them were not pleasant. We discovered that there was a feud between them and our Cape men, and it seemed to us that our men, Charles especially, were to blame. Moloko accused Charles of having enticed away his wife, and I fear there was some truth in the accusation. In the dispute that arose Moloko appeared to greatest advantage; our men were in the wrong, and the consciousness of that made them act worse than they would otherwise have done.

In consequence of this, and of other circumstances which had come to our knowledge from time to time, beginning before the Bishop died, we resolved to send these men back to the Cape upon the first opportunity. They had worked for us faithfully and well; they had in many ways been of the greatest assistance to us, but we could no longer trust them; the temptations of their position with us were too powerful for them, and for their sakes—for we had excellent characters with them as good Christian men—as well as our own, we determined to dispense with their services as soon as possible.

Chibisa was determined if possible to get gunpowder from us, and the messengers to Dr. Livingstone were not forthcoming. Our relations with him for some days were not amicable. He found himself in an uncomfortable position with the other chiefs, and tried to conciliate them by suggesting a combination against ourselves on account of the ill-doings of the Makololo, though he had sought them as allies against Matichoro. He was the most crafty man we had to deal with in Africa. He did not blame us face to face, because he knew that would provoke an open rupture with us, and he could not afford to do that. So he sent an invitation to Johnson and William. When they arrived at his camp they found Kapanji, Chinsunzi's son, and several other chiefs, or representatives of chiefs, assembled. Chimbeli, Mankokwe's head man, was there also. Then Chibisa made a speech, the object of which was to prove that he was a greatly injured individual, and that the ill-will against him from those present arose from what we had done. Said he :

'I am here, and I cannot go back to Doa, because the English, who say they are my friends, will not help me. I received them as my brothers. They build on my land. I do not ask them to fight for me ; I can fight for myself. I only ask them to sell me gunpowder, but, though they have plenty, they will not let me have any. Whose fault is it, then, that I am here ? Mine ? no, not mine, but that of the English. You say the English are good people ?'

And the assembly replied, ' Yes, the English have good hearts. They take nothing from us ; they pay us well for all they have ; they give us cloth for our corn, and goats, and fowls, and if we go a journey for them they give us cloth for that too. Yes, the English are good people.'

Nothing discomposed, Chibisa resumed his speech.

' Yes, the English do all that, but what else have they done ? You come to me and say—Go away, we do not want you here ; your life is not safe here. And I know my life is not safe here, I am in danger of dying. But why ? why is all this? Because the Makololo have been robbing and beating the Manganja. But did I bring the Makololo into the country? No! Who brought them here? Why the English! Then why blame me? Blame the English, for they are the people to blame, not me.'

This speech had the desired effect upon the assembly. 'Ah,' cried some, 'it is quite true the English did bring the Makololo here, and if they were to give you gunpowder you could go away. They would be our friends then as well as yours,' and they all smoked in moody silence for some time.

Johnson then replied:

'We have heard what you say, Chibisa, but what is the use of your talking that way to us? We are only servants; go and talk like that to our masters.'

'They will not listen to me,' said he.

'No, not if you talk as foolishly as you now do. But if you talk like a sensible man they will listen to all you have to say. You know very well that though the Makololo came up the river in the same ship with us, that they are not our children. You know that if they were left behind we missionaries did not leave them behind.'

'You English are all one,' broke in Chibisa.

'That is not true,' shouted Johnson, 'and you know we are no more one than you and Mankokwe are one, suppose you go over the river in the same canoe. You say you have nothing to do with the Makololo. That is not true. You gave them permission to live in your village, you took their presents, and you asked them to fight for you. We have gunpowder, but we will not give it to you or to any other chief. We wish to be your friends, but if you talk and act foolishly, as sure as your name is Chibisa, you will be sorry for it. You go on as you are now doing, and you, Chibisa, will soon be a dead man. I tell you that.'

'Kodi!' (an exclamation of incredulous surprise, meaning, 'is it so?') said Chibisa.

'Ah! kodi!' (It is so) continued Johnson, imitating his manner. 'For what I tell you is truth, so don't you act foolishly, but go and talk to our masters like a sensible man.

What they say they mean. They will give you no gunpowder, but if they can help you in any other way I know they will do it.'

It was Greek and Greek, or rather African and African, and Johnson had the advantage. Chibisa no longer talked grandly, but explained that he could not send his people down the river to the ship alone, for it would be sending them to death, as all the river chiefs were his enemies. What was he to do therefore ?

We felt for the man, and asked him to come and eat with us next day. He came to dinner. When he had eaten, we told him that Johnson and William had informed us of what had passed, and though we should not alter our determination upon the gunpowder question, we were ready to do what we could to show that we desired his friendship. And, it seeming very clear to us that if he sent his men down the river alone they would surely be killed or made captive, we told him that one of us would go to the ship with his messages.

' Jekoma!' (That is good!) was the gratified exclamation of himself and followers, and all his troubles seemed at an end. He then talked and laughed, and acted altogether like a man from whose mind a heavy load was removed, for he made sure he should get the gunpowder through Dr. Livingstone.

As I was the author of this proposal, I was, of course, anxious to carry it out, but Scudamore thought he ought to go, and, the others thinking with him, he went. He was also to come to some understanding with Dr. Livingstone about the Makololo. Job went with him, and Chibisa sent three men with three tusks of ivory.

Chibisa did not stay long by the river after the canoe was gone. Information was brought in by his scouts that his enemy had left the neighbourhood of Doa, and that some of his crops were still standing, so he and his men packed up and went. Most of the women remained; others went to Mika-ronko, Kapichi's place.

Our intercourse with him before he departed was as friendly as could be desired. He was frequently at our table and comported himself like a civilized man. Indeed, intercourse with the Portuguese had civilized him a little, and vitiated him a great deal. He was fond of ardent spirits, but, of course, we gave him none, for we kept our brandy from the natives as carefully as we did our gunpowder. Once he asked for it, and I told him we used it only as a medicine, whereupon he laughed heartily, and turning to his men said:

'What do you think? Kasisi (literally, without hair, a name given by the natives to the Portuguese priests) says brandy is physic. Did you ever hear that before?' And they all laughed.

The same afternoon he became eloquent to Johnson, for whom he professed great friendship, upon his love of brandy.

'Your English Kasisi,' said he, 'is a strange man. He says brandy is medicine; but I know it is English pombi, and I like it very much. Why don't they give me some? When I go to see the Portuguese they give me plenty, as much as I can drink. I sit in their houses and drink, and drink, until I get drunk, and then I go to sleep, and when I wake I drink, and get drunk again. It is good to get drunk on brandy.'

But this was said to Johnson only; to us his conversation was more sober.

Before he went we told him that we had not chosen the valley as a permanent residence, and hoped soon to go back to the hills, they being more healthy for us. He said he hoped we should live on his land.

'I know,' continued he, 'that you came to teach us about God, and to make us a better people than we are. That is very good. And when I am over all my troubles, I shall come back again, if you stay here, and listen to what you have to say, for I want to know about God.'

Chibisa certainly was the most remarkable man we met with in Africa.

Pending the return of Scudamore, we resumed friendly intercourse with the Makololo, and to remove from them all possible necessity to plunder we gave them cloth now and then to buy corn. Moloko, Ramakukan, and others went hunting, a drove of elephants having been reported about twenty-five miles below us.

About this time, the beginning of July, we were much troubled with fever. I subjoin Dickinson's report for the previous month :—

	Date of attack. June	Disease.	Duration.	Remarks.
Procter	. 6th	Fever .	Three days	
,,	. 26th	Fever .	Two days	
Scudamore	. 11th	Fever .	Six days	
Rowley	. 20th	Neuralgia	Two days	{ Produced in face by decayed teeth
Waller	. 1st	Fever .	One day	
Dickinson	. 26th	Fever .	Five days	
Clarke .	. 26th	Fever .	Four days	Ill from last month
,, .	. 15th	Fever .	Four days	
,, .	. 27th	Fever .	Two days	
Blair .	. 9th	Fever .	Eight days	
Gamble	. 6th	Fever .	Three days	
,, .	. 22nd	Diarrhœa	Four days	
,, .	. 26th	{ Laceration of Cornea }	Four days	
Adams .	. 7th	Fever] .	Three days	
,, .	. 18th	{ Diarrhœa Dysenteric }	Four days	
Charles .	. nil			
Johnson	. 16th	Fever .	Four days	
William	. nil			
Job .	. 26th	{ Dysenteric Diarrhœa }	Four days	

Dickinson attributed what increase of fever there was—and it was really but a very small increase upon what we had at Magomero—'*chiefly* to our leaving the Highlands for the Shire, though other circumstances considerably influenced the result,' and to the ' depression resulting from our exertions in coming from Magomero—daily exposure to the full effects of the sun while house building, and—oh! what a blessed cause! ' to the full and excellent supply of stimulating food we have received since our arrival here.'

It must not be supposed from the mention of a ' full and excellent supply of stimulating food,' that we fared sumptuously every day, or ate and drank to excess. We had two meals a day; but those meals consisted of good food,—as bread, rice, oatmeal, sugar, eggs, milk, fowls, or goat,—and that diet, compared with what we had at Magomero, was ' full

and stimulating.'   The little brandy we had allowed ourselves
weekly was, however, discontinued.

I don't think Blair had fever more than once after this, and
the removal *from* the Highlands could not have affected him,
as he had not been on them.

By putting on a higher roof, and a thicker thatch, I lowered
the temperature of my hut during the greatest heat of the day
from 95° to less than 90°.   To me, however, the heat was
rarely distressing, though some of my brethren suffered considerably from it.

CHAPEL AND HOUSES AT CHIBISA'S STATION.

We heard from time to time of the state of the Highlands,
and it seemed certain that Joi had possessed himself of the Ku
Jireka district.   Mamvula had taken refuge with the Maravi,

and large numbers of fugitives were encamped on our side of the river above Matiti, the first of the Murchison cataracts.

July 8. Having been for some time closely occupied with work at the station, Dickinson and I—accompanied by Charles and four of our men, Chimlolo, Chimwami, Ndoka, and Sesamanja, and with Dadwa, an old Chibisian acquaintance, as guide—started on an excursion to the cataracts. This was the first journey that had been undertaken by any of the mission which had not graver objects in view than mere relaxation and satisfaction of curiosity.

The morning was favourable for walking, the fierce heat of the sun being modified by cloud. The characteristics of the valley up to Matiti differed in nothing from those of our immediate neighbourhood. Here and there was a large baobab, the grotesque feature of every landscape about us; the sterculia was more abundant—it is a tree with a stem as smooth and as bright as that of the silver ash, and which, without knob or branch, rises from the ground to the height of sixty or seventy feet, and then developes a parachute-shaped crown of graceful foliage. But the many varieties of the never failing Acacia—which is, next to the Palmyra, the most graceful tree in Africa—were the most abundant. Everywhere there was a profuse undergrowth, consisting of prickly shrub and stunted wood, scorched-up grass and flowerless creepers, with an occasional mass of odoriferous jessamine, gladdening the eye with its pure white and delicate petals, and gratifying the senses with its sweetness. If we add to this, fields of corn that would never come to maturity, the stems sunburnt and withered, the ears blasted and fruitless, with a few patches of cotton here and there, the precious wool bursting from the pod and looking like frosted silver, we have the main features of the vegetable productions of the Shire valley, situated between Chibisa's and Matiti.

These fields of withered corn filled us with apprehension; for though the supply of food at the station had been good, yet we knew that the principal crops of the valley had failed from want of the latter rain. The Indian corn was not largely grown in the valley, nor along the first range of hills, the soil suiting the Mapira (Holcus Sorghum) best. Everywhere, nevertheless, we heard that the Mapira had failed; but we did not, at this time, see much indication of the terrible state of things which ensued in consequence.

After passing through the country, nominally Chibisa's, we entered upon the land of one Somo, and then we were unpleasantly reminded of the Makololo. The paths were blocked up, and when any of the inhabitants met us they ran away. We next came to a ruined village. The huts had been pulled down, and this also was said to be the work of the Makololo. It might have been, but when once in Africa a people have a bad name, every bad deed committed in the land is laid to their account. We were glad, however, to get beyond Somo's land, for from some unknown cause, it was certain we were no favourites with the people.

After this we came to Chuari, a very large village, the chief of which was named Amarinda Chinbandu, who turned out to be the Rundo of the country above, as Mankokwe and Tingani were of the country below.

The village was surrounded by a dense growth of euphorbia. The huts were old and badly built. The inhabitants looked well fed and contented. When we entered the village we were met by several men, who conducted us to the travellers'-tree, and invited us to be seated. When we told them that we were English, journeying for our pleasure, but wishing to pay our respects to the chief as we passed, we were told that we were the brothers of Amarinda Chinbandu, and that our visit had made the hearts of the people of Chuari glad. A man went to inform his chief of our arrival, and quickly returned with the intelligence that his lord and master was ready to embrace his English brethren. We found the chief seated on a leopard skin at the door of his hut. He was a very old man, with hair and beard perfectly white. Around his shrivelled body was one of the gay-coloured scarfs we had brought into the country, and on his right leg he had several large ivory rings. The old man smiled and smiled, and did his best to show that he was not a villain. A mat was spread for us quite close to him; and again he claimed us as brothers, and declared Chuari was ours. We then told him where we were going, and he said we should find many of his children up above, and many people who had fled from Joi. We asked him if he were afraid of Joi, upon which he spoke up most valiantly, 'Afraid of Joi! What me! Oh, no! He will never come near me!' And the old man chuckled as though the notion of Joi coming near to such an old lion as he, was the best joke he had ever heard.

After this expression of confidence in himself, he got up and went into his hut, a work of some difficulty, for his attenuated legs would scarcely sustain his withered body, and he lurched about like a ship in distress. When he reappeared, he was accompanied by a youth bearing a basket of pombi. He apologised for not having anything better to offer us, but said that if we would call as we returned he would give us superior cheer.

We were very pleased with this old man; a more genial welcome we could not have had.

As we were leaving the village, a man in authority—he ought to have been Lord Chamberlain, for in figure, manner, and voice, he was an African Polonius—stepped forward, and begged to be our guide. He was complaisance itself. We thought he was going with us to Matiti, and intended to devote himself to our service; but when we were in the thick of the euphorbia surrounding the village, he wheeled round, and, with a voice and manner indicating the disclosure of a state secret, said :

'I, too, have pombi.'

'Fowls and meal?' interrogated we.

'Fowls and meal I have. You shall have them. Wait but a little,' said he.

And off he went, full of the importance of his mission.

He quickly returned with pombi, and immediately afterwards there was such a cackling of hens that it seemed as if all the people of the village were chasing fowl.

'Do you hear?' said he, smiling; 'you shall have fowls;' and then, recollecting that we had asked for meal, added, with an assuring smile, 'and meal; I had not forgotten.'

And we had both.

The noise of turbulent water told us when we were near
Matiti.   Machikalonga, the village we proposed staying at for
the night, was on the bank of the river, just below the Falls.

Here we found fugitives, and very woe-begone they looked.
Some of them were engaged in putting up rude huts outside
the village.

Ngua, the chief, was a common-place, timid man, but took
pains to show that he was friendly.

The waterfall was a disappointment.   There were huge
masses of rock in the bed of the river, and the water dashed
about here and there in a wild, extravagant way, and that was
all.   The fall of water was insignificant.   A huge crocodile lay
stretched at full length upon a rock in the middle of the stream,
quite regardless of our presence.   We both fired at the creature at the same instant.   'Wafa!' (He is dead) shouted the
natives, and the animal did seem to be in a death struggle ;
but with the characteristics of his cold-blooded race, he would
not die easily.   He writhed and wriggled until he wriggled
himself off the rock, and then sank into the water like a
stone.

The next day was again favourable for walking, and in a
short time we came to Sengaro, the second fall.   Here the
Shire assumed the features of a mountain torrent ; dashing for
three hundred feet from rock to rock, in a furious manner.   A
wilder scene than this could not well be ;· but it was not grand,
it fell much short of that.

Our road from this place for the next two miles lay over and
beside huge masses of basaltic rock, which looked as though
some mountain had exploded, and flung its fragments here.

From this place for several miles the force of the stream was
considerable, and as it everywhere met with obstructions, a
perpetual roar and foam was the result.

Along the bank of the river there was recent spoor of buffalo and deer.   The hippopotamuses were numerous ; in many
places the ground was covered with their dung.   Crocodiles
were frequently visible on the rocks, and birds were plentiful,
but we saw none with which we were not familiar.

On the north side of the river the hills sloped down to the

water; here and there they rose abruptly, to the height of a
thousand or more feet.   And behind these hills lay the great
plain of Ku Jireka.

For ten miles after leaving Matiti, the country was but
thinly peopled.   But then we came to a large village, and near
it lay an encampment of fugitives from the Ajawa.   There
must have been a thousand men, women, and children, congregated there.   When they saw us, they were at first greatly
alarmed.   The men seized their bows and arrows, and, according to custom, ran into the bush; the women ran into their
huts for anything they could seize, and the children were fast
making off.   We called to them not to fear, and one of the
men recognised us.   He had been to Magomero while we were
there, and the revulsion of feeling from extreme fear to perfect
confidence made the poor fellow almost mad.   He seized our
hands, he danced about us, and actually screamed with plea-
surable excitement.   When a little cooled down, he insisted on
going with us.

From this place until we halted for the night the line of fugitives was unbroken.   They were encamped along the south
bank of the river for miles.   We wished to go to Patamanga
Fall; but the sun set before we could reach it, and so we slept
at one of the encampments.   The chief here was one Gomi.
Gomi was said to be buffalo hunting when we arrived, in
reality he was in hiding, but his wives received us hospitably.

These people were not badly off for corn; they had large
quantities stacked up about the camp, and I had not seen such
large ears of Mapira since we came up the Shire.   The crops
in the Ku Jireka district had been abandoned, but the fugitives daily stole across the river, and brought corn over from
their gardens.   The Ajawa, however, being masters of their
country, they did this at the risk of their lives.

It was a beautiful night, the air was soft, the moon resplen-
dent.   Fires were lighted outside, and we sat around, with the
people about us.   Dickinson, in the enjoyment of the hour,
forgot the sciatica which had troubled him during the day, and
astonished me by his proficiency in the Manganja tongue.   He
astounded and delighted Gomi (who had come out of hiding),

his wives and people, with details of English customs, manners and appliances. And they, while listening to him, forgot their troubles, and light-hearted merriment rewarded his efforts. The confidence and honest purposes of the men, the gentle ways of the women, their generosity in giving us a perfect Benjamin's mess from their evening meal, and the affection they manifested for their little ones, formed as pleasing an experience of unregenerated humanity as I ever met with. We did not leave them in ignorance of our motive in coming to Africa; we did our best also to make them understand something of God, and His love to man.

The men we took with us from our station were capital fellows to travel with. They cared for us as though we were their own children, and yet they never presumed. Chimlolo was a most valuable man; his ready wit led him to anticipate our wants, and his good feeling inclined him to provide for them. We knew by experience what he was, and so we were not surprised when daylight came to find him in our hut with hot coffee, fowl, and porridge; though to accomplish such a breakfast at that time, he must have been awake and at work nearly half the night.

In dealing with the Manganja, the single sentiment of pity is ordinarily evoked; but a good Ajawa one really likes.

Patamanga was said to be 'Pu fupi' (very near): it proved to be seven miles off, seven miles of as wild a country as you could well meet with; the road was rugged and rough, a continual scramble up and down the rocks.

When we had been walking about an hour, Gomi halted, and called out 'Oni!' (Look!), and when we looked, we saw a troop of large baboons; and when they saw us, the old males showed their teeth, set up their manes, and barked savagely. The natives called them Nyani, and declared they were so fierce and powerful that when angry they would attack a man. They were of a light brown colour, and the largest of them looked quite four feet long.

Again, Gomi halted and said :

'Here is the water you wished to see.'

'Where?' said Dickinson, looking about.

'There!' said Gomi, pointing downwards, for we were on a
rock nearly a hundred feet above the river.

'That! what an imposition!'

And the Patamanga Falls did not impress me otherwise.
There was a ledge of broken rock extending across the stream,
by and over which the water dashed furiously enough. The
whole, however, was something like a large tumbling bay.

We retraced our steps, halting at Gomi's to rest for a short
time, and then proceeded to Machikalongwi, which place we
reached about half an hour before sunset. In coming back
we took a road more inland; the road over which Dr. Livingstone purposed to carry his steamships. We were but ordinary men, and were amazed at the boldness of the idea.

Next morning we borrowed a canoe of Ngua, and returned
home by water.

We passed many canoes on our way down, some quite new.
The launching of a canoe is attended with much festivity.
The owners accompany its progress to the water with dancing
and singing, and all other things that tend to lighten labour
and make the native heart glad. When the canoe is in the
water, a trial trip is made, and if it does not sink or capsize
under the mass of excited men who crowd into it, it may be
safely trusted.

We enjoyed our excursion, but were glad nevertheless to see
our own home again. Poor Chesika was hobbling about on
her crutches on the cliff, and shouted a welcome down to us
as the canoe passed by ; and when we arrived at the landing-
place, a troop of our merry little fellows with affection in their
eyes, and ' Jekomas' on their tongues, clustered about us,
shouldered our guns and baggage, and preceded us up the hill
to our houses in joyful excitement. Our hearts were drawn
very closely towards these children.

CHAPTER XVI.

I HAVE said little about the natural history of the country we were in. And I have really but little to say, for I am no naturalist.

Our associations in the wild beast line were far more numerous in the valley than on the hills. The hills were singularly destitute of wild animals; but when in the valley, we had no difficulty in believing that we were in a country which contributes largely to the Zoological Gardens and the British Museum.

The cat tribe was numerous in the valley, though the roar of a lion was rarely heard, and not one of our party ever saw the creature.

A schoolboy knows, or should know, that tigers are not found in Africa, although Du Chaillu and others will talk of tigers when they mean leopards. Leopards were seldom met with on the hills, but when we came to Chibisa's, Chechoma warned us not to leave our goats out at night, as the nialugwi (leopard) was close at hand. We took great care of our flock, but with all our care the leopards managed to get at them. One night we heard the death cry of a goat, and rushing out just caught a glimpse of a leopard bounding away. The carcase of the slain animal was left behind; we carried it away, and blocked up the gap in the fold which the leopard had made by scratching away the earth and forcing the stakes on one side. But in the course of an hour a doleful shriek warned us that another goat was slain. The leopard had returned, had again forced himself into the fold, and was making off with this fresh victim; but on our turning out was compelled to drop it, and take to the bush. Thinking hunger might induce the brute to return yet once more, Waller poisoned the carcase of the goat which was first killed with strychnine, intending to exchange it with that which the leopard had just dropped, and which for the moment we left in the bush. But the cunning beast had watched us, and during the few minutes we were in the hut doctoring the body of the goat, he returned, and finding the coast clear made off with his prey. But cunning met cunning with fatal effect. In the morning our boys discovered the partially devoured goat; this also was seasoned with strychnine and left to work its mission, which it did so effectually that *two* leopards were afterwards found dead near to it.

The ocelot was even more numerous than the leopard; its skin was frequently brought to us as an article of barter. But beyond a wild-cat, whose skin the natives wear as an ornament, and the native domestic cat, than which a more miserable-looking creature does not exist, we met with no other of the felinæ.

The quadrumana were not numerous. Among the mangroves a pretty little monkey existed, and was plentiful, and there were monkeys that used to watch us from the trees at Magomero while we were bathing; and there were long-tailed and tail-less baboons on the hills and in the valley; and some of the baboons, as I have said, were large, but we saw no monkeys, I expect, which could not be found in any ordinary menagerie in England.

Squirrels, not unlike our own, and a pretty little creature answering to the description Du Chaillu gives of his ivory-eater; and rats and mice, and several kinds of shrew, comprised the rodentia that came under our notice. There are several species of rat, and the bewa, or field rat, a harmless-looking creature, small in size, slender of form, and of the colour of the lavender, is regarded by the natives as the best of all meat. At certain seasons of the year there is a regular rat harvest, the boys being the reapers. You see them coming home with dead rats on a reed like larks on a skewer. They dry them, smoke them, and hang them up in bundles, like sprats, at Billingsgate, and eat one now and then as a dainty.

One evening my boy Juma (one of the boys now with Dr. Livingstone) came into my hut with his supper, a lump of nsima, and something which looked like a burnt sausage.

'What is that, Juma?' said I.

'Bewa,' said he.

'Is it good?'

'It is good. Better than sheep, better than goat, better than bird or fish, better than all other meat. Shall I roast one for you?'

And he pulled out a fine rat from his bag, and held it up for admiration. I nodded assent, and off he ran delighted. He returned with the rat frizzled and black, cooked to a turn. Its odour was savoury—but it was a rat, and I hesitated.

'Did you skin it, Juma?'

'No!'

'Did you take the entrails out, Juma?'

'No! They are the best of it—the fattest!' said he, in surprise at my want of power to appreciate what a rat was.

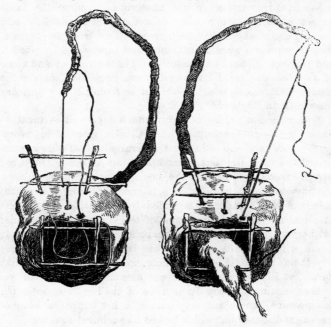

TRAP SET.   RAT CAUGHT.

NATIVE RAT-TRAP.

I did'not taste it, though I afterwards thought myself weak
to allow prejudice to interfere with my taste, for I have no
doubt the boy was right, and that rat was pleasant food, and
the method of cooking it was no worse than our method of
dressing snipe.

The elephant was found along the entire length of the Shire
valley, and in some parts, as I have said, hundreds of these
noble animals might be seen together grazing like cattle in
our meadows.   But the character of the country made hunting very difficult.   The Manganja rarely attempted to molest
them.   I once asked a man why they did not hunt them, and
his answer was, ' We have no guns, and it is useless to hunt
the elephant with bows and arrows.   Suppose you shoot at an
elephant with an arrow, he feels, it is true, but no more than
we feel the bite of a fly, and he turns his head round and
says, " What fly bit me ?" and then he knocks off the arrow
with his trunk, and goes away not caring at all.'

The knowledge of the power of the gun had put these people
quite out of conceit with their own weapons.

The Makololo had guns, and were good hunters, but upon
the whole they were very unsuccessful : they said the valley
was not a good hunting-ground.   We did really nothing in the
way of hunting, not having a Nimrod among us.   Dickinson
and Clarke tried for an elephant in coming up the Shire.   The
beasts were feeding close to their halt, a small village on the
banks of the river.   The villagers took no notice of them, and
the children played about as unconcerned as though they were
donkeys ; but in the breasts of our friends the ardour of the
chase was kindled, they shouldered their rifles, double-barrelled
Enfields, and started in pursuit.   The elephants saw them
coming, and moved quietly away, whisking their trunks from
side to side, and feeding as they went along.   They followed a
fine bull with good tusks, who gave them a long walk before
he permitted them to come up with him, and at last led them
into a swamp, where he turned round and quietly looked on.
Dickinson levelled his rifle right at the creature's forehead,
made sure he would bring his game down, but the caps snapped
and that was all.   Clarke did the same, and with the same

result. Fortunately for them, their rifles had been lying all day at the bottom of their canoe, and water had come upon them. At best, with the weapons they had, they would but have wounded the beast, roused him to fury, and he would have been upon them before they could have turned round, and trampled them to death in the swamp. As it was, he went his way, and left them to do the same.

It has been said that the male and female elephants are not seen in herds together. Whatever their habits in this respect may be in other parts of Africa, in the Shire valley they certainly consorted; large herds of males and females, with their little ones, were frequently to be seen.

Elephant meat is considered food, but unless he be a native, a man must be very hungry before he could eat it. The carcase I have never tasted, but the choice parts, the trunk and the foot, have several times fallen to my lot as a dainty; the first was like India-rubber, with a slight flavour of meat to it, the second like glue softened in water without any flavour of meat whatever.

But though elephants may have been more numerous, hippopotamuses were more frequently seen; they were continually trumpeting up and down the river. I could not look upon the hippopotamus as a savage beast; as a rule there seemed nothing savage about him. His deep bass utterances were the very expression of jollity, and I frequently felt inclined to sing :—'He's a jolly good fellow,' when listening to his vociferous Ha! Ha! But they can get furious. Sometimes the males, like all other males, will quarrel about the females, and then they fight; and a fight between these animals is a sight that, once seen, you are not likely to forget. When a male hippopotamus gets old, the ladies frequently forsake him, the young bulls unite against him, and drive him from their society. He is compelled to live alone, and then, like an old rogue elephant, he is dangerous, and will attack everything that comes in his way. I met with one such as I was going down the Shire on my way home. The canoe men were paddling and singing, when a tremendous blow at the bottom of the boat stopped their song, and scattered them on either side.

Zalwakuti, a little boy, who was sitting in front of me, was
sent spinning into the river. Fortunately, the boat righted
itself, and I was not thrown out. After rescuing the child, I
seized my rifle, and looked out for the aggressor; he rose
about ten yards from the boat, his eyes flashing fury, and
evidently intending to come on again, but before he could do
that, he had a bullet into his head, and down he went with a
yell, and away we paddled, glad to get from the neighbourhood
of so desperate a brute.

SHOOTING THE HIPPOPOTAMUS.

The rhinoceros did not come near us; once and once only,
when on a journey, I saw its recent spoor, and once only did I
see a horn that had been recently taken from the animal.

The wild boar was plentiful in the delta of the Zambesi, but
very few were seen in the neighbourhood of our stations. A
man came to us one day and said he had one for sale, but
upon being questioned, it turned out that the brute was still

in the bush, and that we must first catch our boar before we could cook him.

The zebra was found on the Zambesi delta, and according to native testimony it was at one time common on the High-lands, but like all other animals, had been driven out of that district in which we lived. The tail of the zebra was the sym-bol of chieftainship—the Manganja sceptre, in fact—though it frequently played an important part in the medicine man's arrangements.

Near to the coast, water-buck, bush-buck, and several other kinds of deer, as I have previously mentioned, are constantly to be met with; they exist also in the lower Shire valley; but on the Highlands we found them not, and but one miserable little bush-buck was ever seen near Chibisa's while we were there. The Missionary must go to thickly inhabited districts, where people are plentiful, and there of course wild animals are scarce.

The buffalo of the Shire valley may be numerous, but in the swamps he is almost unassailable. Wherever you went, the Highlands excepted, you saw signs of this creature, but you rarely saw the animal itself.

The native domesticated dog, like the cat, is a very inferior animal; a low-looking, long-nosed, yelping, contemptible little brute—what its breed is it would be hard to say. I like a dog as well as most men, but it was impossible to have one of those ugly natured creatures near you.

Hyænas galloped past our doors every night in the valley, but we rarely heard their lamentable whine on the hills.

Jackals were on the hills, but much more numerous in the valley.

But neither of these animals, beyond contributing at night to the causes which frequently made sleep impossible, was an annoyance.

The most notable of the Insectivora was a long-snouted creature like in some respects to the Cape elephant-shrew. A man brought one for sale one day, not as a curiosity, but as a delicate morsel for the palate; I had eaten elephant, hippopo-tamus, crocodile and monkey, but I had no fancy for a shrew.

But of animated nature, birds formed the largest as well as the most beautiful portion.

Of the raptores, the hawk was by far the most numerous; it abounded in many varieties, and formed a graceful feature in every landscape. The larger kinds attacked our poultry frequently, and our boys were ever on the watch to protect our fowls, and to shout ' chikwatu!' (hawk) as an invitation to those skilful with the gun to show their skill.

The owl was next to the hawk in interest and numbers. Some were as small as pigeons, others equal to the great horned owl; many were beautifully feathered. In the stillness of the night you not only heard their hoot, but frequently the sweep of their wings as they passed close to your hut.

Of the perchers, the nightjar with its charming metallic note, and the hornbill, were the most interesting. The hornbills were numerous about Chibisa's, and were not bad eating.

At Magomero there was a large and handsome kingfisher, whose derisive, laugh-like, ' ya-ya-ya,' was constantly heard along the streams; his body was refulgent with crimson and green. On the Shire there were several kinds of kingfishers, the most conspicuous being the belted, but there was not one so glorious in apparel as our own magnificent little fellow.

The starling in the valley and on the hills had a glistening bronze-coloured plumage, but he was not so handsome as our English chatterbox.

Of crows there were three varieties, viz., two black and one (the hooded crow) with a magpie plumage. Of the black, one was not much larger than a sparrow, the other was nearly twice the size of our own crow.

Bee-eaters were numerous. Rollers scarce. Parrots were of two kinds, one with brown, the other with green and yellow plumage. They astonished me, a stranger to their habits, with the rapidity of their flight. There was a great variety of pigeons, though they were not sufficiently numerous to form a regular article of food. The golden oriol attracted your attention wherever you went, and sun-birds and honey-birds scintillated before you in all their glory. And, more numerous than our own sparrow at home, were the pretty little amadavats, who, in a suit of pink or sky blue, were seen on every twig. On the hills the whidda was common, and so were many other birds of the same class with pleasant plumage and sweet voices.

Of the Rasores, besides the domestic fowl, a breed capable of great improvement, for they were not much larger than a pigeon, there were the African pheasant—a mean flavourless bird, not abundant—and the Guinea-fowl, a fine handsome creature, more abundant, and so good for food, that our regret was that it was not more numerous.

Crane, heron, and birds of like kind, were past computation in the neighbourhood of the swamps. In going up or down the river we were never without plenty of fowl for food, for besides the birds I mention, we met with ducks, geese and plovers, hammerheads, spoon-bills, bittern and ibis, pelicans, cormorants, darters and flamingo, the last of all being the most delicate eating.

Among reptiles, the crocodile of course holds the first place. For some time it was doubted whether the merc iless-looking beast in the Shire was crocodile or alligator, but the authorities on this point decided at last that it was crocodile.

The heat of the valley made bathing a necessity of existence, and when we first came down from the hills, we had not that fear of the crocodile we should have had, and used to bathe in a shallow but unprotected part of the river. One morning, however, an unfortunate goat came down to drink at our bathing place, but a few minutes after we had left it, and before he could finish his ' ba-a!' of terror, a crocodile seized him and he was no more seen. We bathed no more in the river until we had protected ourselves with a stockade which ensured our safety, even though the ferocious brutes were nosing about on the outside.

Three women were carried away by crocodiles while we were in the valley. Two while bathing, the other while stooping to get water.

But though this creature is the most cruel and loathsome looking animal you meet with, I think his flesh, as food, is as much underrated as that of the elephant is over-estimated.

I once had a steak cut out of the tail of a crocodile which we killed. It was broiled, and brought in with other things for dinner; I liked it, though I am bound to confess no one else did. Dickinson complained that it was 'fishy,' Waller pronounced it ' beastly,' Proctor tried it, but made for the door looking very pale, and though Scudamore thought we might have been glad of it during the pumpkin time at Magomero, he declined the offer of another slice. Altogether the result was not satisfactory, and, upon the whole, though I still believe in the correctness of my taste, I think few would care to use this creature as food.

A crocodile's nest will contain sixty or seventy eggs; I have seen crocodiles twenty feet long, but the egg is not larger than that of a goose, and in flavour not unlike it.

At Magomero chameleons abounded. They were larger and more beautifully coloured than any I have elsewhere seen. Some were fully eighteen inches long, and had flapping ears like those of the elephant, and a fleshy protuberance on the nose, in shape and position like the horn of a rhinoceros.

The lizard was not wanting either on the hills or in the valley; it was constantly about our houses.

When we came into the country we expected much discomfort from the snakes; and snakes were everywhere, on the hills and in the valley, in your hut, and sometimes in your bed. But though some had deadly natures, very few accidents occurred from their presence. Once only did we know of a person being bitten; it was one of our women; the snake, a cobra, was rolled up in her sleeping mat, and on being disturbed bit the woman in the arm. She came to Dickinson at once, who, without hesitation, cut away the bitten part, and dosed her with ammonia. She was very ill, but did not die, and Dickinson's fame as a curer of snake-bites was great. I one day had an interview with a cobra. I was in pursuit of butterflies, for butterfly catching gave zest to a walk, and often induced exercise. I was watching a beautiful creature flitting about a tree, and was intent upon securing it, when I heard a

slight noise behind me, and looking, saw ' a snake in the grass.'
It was a cobra of the worst kind, and as I turned my head it
reared itself. I was within its striking distance. My first
impulse was to strike it, but I had but a butterfly-net, and
that was a bad weapon to kill a snake with. So I looked
at it, it looked at me, and we looked at one another without
moving for a few seconds, and then it turned round and went
away.

It is strange how soon you get used to the conditions of
the country you are in. I should feel inclined to run from a
common hedge snake in England, but one soon ceases to be
nervous about such things in Africa. At the time it did not
strike me that I had any special cause for thankfulness, for I
was less surprised at seeing the snake than I should have been
at seeing an earthworm, for that I did not see in Africa; the
latter may be there, but if so they are very scarce.

We were in a land of frogs, but they were modest animals
and kept to their own proper localities. Many of them were
very pretty, both in form and colour, much prettier than I
had imagined a frog could be. Among them were those who
had a hideous croak, but others, and they were the most
numerous, had a liquid utterance which was by no means dis-
pleasing. As evening closed in they mingled their voices with
those of the cicadæ, and together they made a tolerable concert. When once used to their evening hymn you liked it
rather, it was soothing.

A frog that inhabited the rivers on the hills and looked all
body and no limbs, was roasted and eaten by the natives.

There should have been plenty of fish in the Shire, but if so
we were bad fishermen, and so were the natives, for it was not
often that we could get fish. A native would sit by the river
all day long angling, and think himself well repaid if he caught
a fish weighing four ounces. Had we had a suitable net we
might have taken more, but our cast net, the only useful net
we had out, was stolen at the Kongone.

Many of the fish were strange looking creatures: one, for
instance, carried its teeth outside its mouth, there was nothing
like a lip to cover them.

Molluscs were very scarce both on the hills and in the valley, though some were very large.

A land crab used to haunt us at Magomero, especially in the rainy season. It was not large, and it looked unwholesome, but our people when hard pressed ate it. Spiders were everywhere plentiful. Some were really beautiful, others were very ugly. One, a creature about the size of the palm of a man's hand, and called the gudji gudji, by the natives, was the most hideous and repulsive thing I ever saw. But it rarely molested us.

There were several kinds of hornets, but they were the most amiably disposed hornets imaginable—leave them alone and they left you alone. They flickered about your head sometimes and looked angry, but that was all.

The African flea was not the pest with us that it is in Egypt and elsewhere. There were two kinds, one as large as that in England, the other so small that you only felt it; but the smaller flea was the most annoying.

Bugs were in the house and in the field: those in the house were a torment to some people, but those in the fields troubled no one; many of them were of large size and beautiful colour.

The mosquito was not on the hills, but it was a trouble in the valley. Biting flies, though not numerous, were frequently a nuisance. Once we had a swarm of flies whose advent was so mysterious, and whose numbers were so great, that they might have convinced the doubting of the truth of the plagues of Egypt; it was a large, dark blue fly. One morning we awoke and found it on every blade of grass, on every leaf, on every twig; in the air, and in your house, there and everywhere, flies, nothing but flies. Their perpetual buzz would have driven a nervous man mad, and their presence was irritating to those who were not nervous. But they left us as suddenly as they came, not, however, without leaving a memorial of themselves behind: they deposited their larvæ on all things woollen, and in a very short time our rugs and blankets were instinct with things that crawled. But this was an exceptional experience.

Ants of course predominated. The most formidable was the litumbo, a creature answering to Du Chaillu's lesser bashi-kouay ; and, the most abominable, a big black fellow fully an inch long, which, though it rarely bit you, emitted so horrible an odour that one of them in your hut made it loathsome.

At Magomero the litumbo was a real annoyance ; they love humid localities, and, therefore, seldom left us. The ground was tunneled by them in all directions. When they came to the surface they would disperse themselves over a large space of ground and hold it against all comers. For three days they occupied our store-house and all the approaches to it, and we were helpless. Though it deposits no venom, the bite of this creature is enough to madden you, and it lays hold of you with so resolute a gripe that it will suffer itself to be dismembered before it will leave go. They vary greatly in size ; in the swarm you will see some not more than a quarter of an inch long, while others are nearly four times that size. They travel in armies, and the larger appear to act as guards to the rest. When crossing an exposed path the giant ants range themselves on either side of the main body, and with heads erect and jaws distended threaten all intruders. When on a journey few things turn them aside ; they surmount all obstacles, and will even cross a stream of water. I saw a swarm on the hills crossing a stream which was about two yards wide. Some of the lesser ants rolled a straw into the water, floated on it until it touched a stone, to this stone they clung, and then managed to shift the straw until it formed a communication with the bank. This process was repeated until a bridge was formed from bank to bank. On either side of this straw bridge was a living parapet of small ants, many of whom were in the water and clung to the others to prevent their being washed away. At intervals of about an inch a larger ant mounted the parapet on either side, held on below with its legs, and leaned forward and clung to the ant opposite with its mandibles : by so doing they formed a girder, and left the straw-bridge unob-structed upon which the main body passed over ; and no army of men could have moved more orderly. Myriads passed over while I watched, and the work was still going on when I left.

But when I returned a few hours afterwards no trace of ant or bridge was left.

The white ant of the lower Shire valley erected huge mounds, but that of the upper part of the valley and on the Highlands made no mound, though it was very destructive to your boxes and furniture.

There was a semi-transparent brown ant, about half an inch long, on the Highlands, which did raise a mound. I took some of the soil from what I thought was a forsaken hill, in order to make a floor for my house; but the creatures were in the soil, and in a short time they began to build. They seemed to increase mysteriously, and they ran galleries of mud up the walls, and in a very short time I was living in an ant-hill, and the thing became so unbearable, I was obliged to turn out of my house.

A very small black ant, a thing so small that it might almost creep through the eye of a needle, did the work of a scavenger in the valley. Their scent was most acute, for though you could see them nowhere near you, if you dropped a bone or a piece of meat, or left an unwashed plate on the table, in a few minutes they were swarming upon it. They rarely molest you, but when they do bite you feel it. If you are a collector of insects, they will ruin your collection, unless you make it very secure. These little creatures avoid damp, and choose a light dry soil.

Among the masses of rock scattered about the hills you frequently saw a gray ant, one of the busiest little fellows in existence; but his motions seemed objectless, hither and thither without any apparent plan.

There were several other kinds of ants, but none were so annoying as they are said to be in some other parts of Africa. All things else favourable, the discomfort caused by insects, especially on the hills, would be as nothing.

Of the beetle and butterfly much might be said, for both were numerous, some were rare, others unique, and many were very beautiful.

Cockroaches, mantis, crickets, grasshoppers and locusts, were all but endless in variety and numbers.

Of the vegetable kingdom I wish I were competent to speak. I can only say that I know a large tree from a small one, a timber tree from a creeper, and a bulbous flower from a mere seedling. And as I write this merely to give a general idea of the country and its productions, so that they who read may form some estimate of the suitability of the country for missionary enterprise, perhaps such knowledge may suffice.

On the highlands good timber trees were scarce. On the upper plateau the trees generally were stunted, wizened things, seldom so large that you could not span them with your hands, though by the side of the streams, and in the deeper depressions, trees of large size and beautiful foliage were frequently met with.

Fruit-bearing trees were very scarce. At Soche's you found the banana, above Soche's we rarely saw it. The kombi, the native name for the fruit of a giant creeper, which twined itself about the tallest trees reaching to their topmast branches, whose blossom was white and sweet scented, was when ripe in outward appearance like a lemon; the rind was thick, and yielded abundantly a milky-looking juice, which thickened on being exposed to the air. Each kombi contained at least ten stones, in size and appearance like tamarind beans, around which a yellow pulp adhered. The pulp was juicy, and the juice was an exquisite acid. Boiled down with sugar, this fruit makes a delicious preserve.

The maposa, the produce of a small tree, is another fruit indigenous to the highlands. It is about the size of an orleans plum, and when quite ripe is in flavour something like the custard apple, but it must be quite ripe before it bears this similitude, otherwise it tastes strongly of turpentine.

Besides these there are—the fig, which is rarely eatable; a fruit in appearance and taste like a medlar; another like an indifferent cherry; a few more indescribable things; and the tamarind.

It is thought, and I have no doubt rightly thought, that Africa abounds with what we greatly require, and the general feeling and expectation when we left England was that the particular part of Africa to which we were going was of all others abundantly favoured. That we did not find it so I need scarcely say.

Of cotton I have spoken—it will grow, but to any considerable extent it was not cultivated.

Oils of no kind were to be had as an article of barter. A little oil was made from the castor oil bean, and a still smaller quantity from the ground-nut, for neither bean nor nut was grown to any extent. Palm oil we did not meet with. Shea butter and other vegetable greases were not known.

Gums were not plentiful. Now and then you saw a little gum exuding from a tree, but a hundred people would be a long time before they could collect a hundredweight of it.

Ivory was of course abundant, but the Portuguese had the trade entirely in their hands, and as they wished to keep it, and held the ports on the coast, a profitable competition with them was not possible.

Dyeing woods were not plentiful. Ebony and a certain kind of lignum vitæ were found in certain parts of the Shire valley between us and the Zambesi, but neither for quality nor quantity could they be valuable as articles of export. I say this advisedly, for though splendid specimens of lignum vitæ may have been met with in the valley of the Zambesi, there were none such in the Shire valley below the ¡ cataracts. Of the productiveness of the Upper Shire valley in this respect I cannot speak from personal observation.

The only thing I saw that I think might have been made profitable was tobacco. On the hills it was grown [abundantly, and it was excellent and cheap.

No doubt the country could be made more productive; in some parts of the highlands and in most parts of the valley, limes, lemons, oranges and pines would grow. And I think that there are few things which are produced in England which would not flourish on the hills, but its present produce is insignificant. The raw produce, in a commercial point of view, was, as far as we are able to see, simply nothing.

The highlands, however destitute of the larger vegetation, were rich in some kinds of flowers, and the liliaceæ were beautiful and abundant. It would be an easy thing for a Mission-

ary in a favourable locality to have a garden of flowers such as
could not be found for glorious colouring in England. 'God
might have made the world and not have made the flowers,' or
have limited them to localities where alone they would be appreciated. Had he done so, however, the Manganja Highlands
would have lost their greatest charm. Yet the inhabitants
have but little appreciation of this charm, for they were not
able to express the various colours of the flowers about them.
Of black, white, red, green, blue, and yellow they could speak,
but for any combination of these colours they had no word.

But though flowers were there, honey was not. In two
years, though we offered large prices for it, we only succeeded
in getting two pounds weight of it.

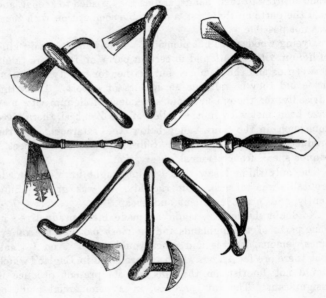

BATTLE AXES, &c.

Of the mineral kingdom I have also but little to say. I
certainly know granite from metamorphosed sandstone, and

basalt from quartz, but of mineralogy, properly so called, I
know nothing.   Limestone or lime in any form we did not
find.   Ironstone was most abundant; and the natives used an
apparatus in smelting it which Tubal Cain might have invented
—perhaps did; and their iron work was good, witness their
axe heads.   Plumbago was there, but in limited quantity—the
natives used it to ornament their pottery.   And good clay
for earthenware and bricks was to be met with in most
places.

The conclusion of this matter is this: setting aside other
difficulties, with a little outlay and much care you might make
the country produce enough for the wants of moderate men,
sufficient therefore for the wants of the Christian missionary.
More than this my experience will not let me say.

CHAPTER XVII.

BEGINNING OF TROUBLE AT CHIBISA'S.

DICKINSON suffered from a severe attack of fever soon after
we returned from our trip to Patamanga, and he suffered so
constantly, and so severely, that it was evident to all that to
save his life, he ought to return home by the first opportunity.
In constitution he was most unfitted to the climate.   His
system seemed readily to sympathise with the diseases of the
country.   He suffered considerably on the hills, but in the
valley his life was a continual suffering.

Thinking it possible we might be able to return to the
Highlands before the rainy season, Waller and I went in
search of information, and of a healthy locality, within easy
reach of the river, and free from the distractions of war.

We found that the Ajawa were everywhere prevailing, that
Mongazi was destroyed, his villages burnt, his people scattered;
and we could not find the position we sought.   The only place
we could occupy was near to Mbame's, but this spot was most
ineligible, as there had been no rain there since January; the
crops had failed, and famine was setting in.

Our expedition lasted several days. We visited every position likely to be of use to us, and were forced to conclude that a move to any of them was at that particular time impossible.

We found Soche trying to make friends with the Ajawa, and in order to do so was proving a traitor to his own tribe, making prisoners of fugitives, and sending them as presents to Joi.

We found Dickinson on our return more ill than ever. He was suffering from a complication of diseases, which we dreaded would prove fatal. It was a good thing for us that Waller knew something of the method of treating the sickness to which we were most subject, and had the courage to use his knowledge; had it not been so, we should have suffered much more than we did. In this fresh attack he was instrumental to a great extent in pulling Dickinson back from the jaws of death.

This increased illness of Dickinson determined us not to leave any effort to return to the highlands untried; so ,Procter and Clarke explored among the hills lower down than we had been. They returned on the 1st of August, and reported that on Mount Choro, they had found a site which they thought would be suitable for a station. The summit of Choro was a small plateau, three thousand feet above the sea, with a good soil, plenty of water, and but seven or eight hours' march from the river. The people on this mountain, though a timid race, were in no fear of the Ajawa, for a very hilly and thinly peopled country, offering no temptation to the invaders, lay between them. Mankokwe was the Rundo of this place, and Mjowa the chief. But though Mankokwe was professedly willing, and showed every wish to be friendly with us, the people on the mountain would not hear of our residing there. When Waller went to make arrangements with them, he found them in a state of consternation at the very thought of it. Superstition was the cause of this dislike of our presence, for Mount Choro was the supposed residence of the spirit Bona, of whom I have spoken; it was consecrated to him, and the favoured few who lived on the mountain; and the superstition of the people was so strong that they seemed resolved to submit to anything, to do or dare anything, rather than permit us to come on to the mountain. Nothing that could be said or promised was sufficient to do away with their prejudice against our presence. They did not care or dread Mankokwe's displeasure—what was that to the displeasure of Bona! And finding their prejudice was unconquerable, Waller was forced to admit that any attempt to occupy Choro would be hopeless, unless we drove away its inhabitants, and so possessed ourselves of it by force; a thing clearly impossible. The people were almost mad with superstitious apprehension; they seemed as though they believed they were living in the actual but invisible presence of a mighty spirit, to whom we were antagonistic, and whose wrath would be visited on them. We might have killed them before they would have consented to our coming.

Bona's sanctum was among the pleasant verdure on the mountain top, and of their belief in his presence there could be no doubt. Had they not had proof of it? People had fled from war in the valley, to the summit of the mountain : they had but little food with them, only a few pumpkins; these they hanged on the trees, and immediately every branch put forth pumpkins, and the tree continued to bear fruit until no more was needed. Could any but Bona have done that?

We were never before so openly opposed by the superstitions of the Manganja. Their religious belief, whatever that belief was, had not before been so thoroughly manifested as the enemy of the truth. Their belief in dæmons and devils was certain; that they believed in fetish was also certain, for their consecrated trifles were everywhere met with; and that they had something like an adoration of a Supreme Being I have shown, but I was never able to harmonise these various phases of their belief. They did not as a rule like talking about their religion, and invariably tried to shirk definite inquiries. Had they a legendary lore which they loved to recite, we might have been able to have arrived at more definite conclusions than we did; but we did not find that they had anything of the kind. They talked about food and women, but they seemed to be without heroes, and without traditions to illustrate their creed.

But though Choro was not open to us, we were determined to avoid, if we could, the danger of staying in the valley during the rainy season, and we made other efforts to find a home among the hills, but all failed, and at last it was simply this— remain, or leave the country. Of course we remained, and committed ourselves to the keeping of Him who was able to defend us from 'the pestilence that walketh in darkness,' and from 'the sickness that destroyeth in the noonday.'

Had there been no prospect of our being able to return to the hills at any time we should not have remained, we should have left that part of the country altogether; but we could see clearly that it was only a question of a few months more or less, and we should be able to go back to the highlands— not to the Manganja, it is true, but to the Ajawa, and we were sent to them as much as to the Manganja. Bishop Mackenzie was consecrated Bishop to the 'tribes dwelling in the neighbourhood of Lake Nyassa and the River Shire,' and the Ajawa were one of these tribes.

The Makololo after the departure of Chibisa again occupied his village. We had constant complaints of them, and upon investigation found more often than not that the complainants had really suffered from the lawless violence of the people living with them, if not from the Makololo themselves. Of course their ill-deeds were exaggerated and multiplied, but making all allowances for misrepresentation, they were the authors of much misery to the Manganja about them, and of much trouble to us.

Scudamore returned on August 4th apparently in good health, having successfully accomplished the objects of his journey. The Chibisians had gunpowder, not from Dr. Livingstone, but from a Portuguese who took their ivory in exchange; and the Doctor sent a letter to the Makololo which had the effect for a time of putting them on their good behaviour.

With Scudamore came Mr. Stewart, the gentleman sent out by the Free Kirk of Scotland. He was our guest for several weeks.

It did not seem probable that the ships would be able to ascend the rivers for some months to come, as the Shire, owing to the long drought, had much less water in it than when we came up. This drought was beginning to make itself felt. Less food was brought to us; indeed the supply of corn had well nigh ceased. There had been no rain in the valley sufficient to moisten the surface of the earth for nearly eight months. On the line of river itself the consequent dearth was not apparent; for on the islands and along the banks, just those places which received moisture from the stream, you found chimanga continually growing; but looking beyond this thin belt of bank, you saw a hard, arid soil, fields of withered corn that had never come to maturity, and every prospect of the woe that too surely came upon the land, but of the extent of which we at that time could form no conception. How could we imagine so dreadful a visitation as that which ensued when we found the people bringing us corn as though they had sufficient for themselves and to spare? They might have known what was coming upon them; but they are not a reflective race; the present gain of cloth blinded them to the certainty of future starvation.

One effect of Dr. Livingstone's letter was to send most of the Makololo elephant-hunting again. The bush-burning was now general, and they had a better chance of success than before.

A few days after their departure, however, tidings came that Moloko had been gored by an elephant. Mr. Stewart, who knew something of surgery, and Scudamore, went down the river to where the poor lad was lying, and returned with him more dead than alive.

It appeared that they had come up with a herd of elephants, all of whom, with the exception of a male and a female and their young one, made off. On being fired at, the male decamped, but the mother remained with her young. Moloko fired at her and wounded her, but could not get out of her way; she bore down upon him, caught him up and threw him, gored him with her tusks several times, and then dropped down dead by his side.

He had a wound in his chest, another in his back, a rib was broken close to the spine, and pressed upon his lungs, and his thigh was pierced in four different places.

His fortitude and endurance were remarkable. He uttered no groan as Dickinson examined him; and his spirit seemed in no way subdued. He did not die, but he was a long time before he was able to get about again. The wound in his chest spoilt his hunting for ever. Ramakukan, one of the roughest and burliest of men, attended to him night and day for months, and with a woman's tenderness. It was really beautiful to see the devotion of this man for his friend. He was the blood brother (not the brother by blood) of Moloko, and blood brotherhoods are the strongest ties of friendship it is possible to imagine. When the alliance is first formed, each man partakes of the blood of the other, and for good or for ill they are friends till death.

Mr. Stewart naturally wished to see as much of the country as he could before he returned to England, and we wished to know the exact state of the Highlands, so we planned a journey, and he and I executed it.

We left the station on the 19th of August, and our first day's walk to Chipindu's was unmarked by event.

The country was not looking its best, for a great bush-burning had destroyed all the verdure in the valley and on the hills and covered the surface with black ash. For several days before our departure this fire had been burning. At first it appeared like a long line of light on the crest of the hills; then in zigzag, angry-looking streams, it descended to their base, where it set fire to the luxuriant but sun-dried grasses and shrubs of the valley, and a mighty conflagration was the result. Up to that time I had seen nothing equal to the descriptions I had read of bush-burnings, but this surpassed everything I had imagined, and put to flight my incipient incredulity. The fire extended at one time more than ten miles, and in many places rose above the tallest trees, and reduced them to ashes by its irresistible energy. It was a magnificent sight, and as we felt sure no village was being destroyed, we could look on without apprehension.

Chipindu and his people were as friendly as ever, but he, poor fellow, was very ill, sickening for death.

We did not find Mbame at home, but his wife gave us such information about the Ajawa as decided us to proceed. Since destroying Mongazi they had been less active, though bands of them were prowling about the country. Magomero was said to be untouched. We had Chimlolo with us, and as he said we might go on to Magomero, we went on.

Soche at first gave us a very unsatisfactory reception. He did not want us to stay the night in his village, but that we were resolved to do and did. We found out afterwards that he expected some of his men to return that night from the Ajawa camp, and he did not wish us to be present. Chimlolo said it was quite true that Soche was employing men to steal women and children from his neighbours in distress, and was sending them to the Ajawa as a propitiatory offering. Want of food was beginning to make itself felt even at Soche's.

When at Pingwi we halted for rest and food. While there a lad came out of hiding and sat by us. In answer to our enquiry if there was war, he answered, in a feeble voice, 'No, not to-day, but there will be to-morrow.' The appearance of this youth, his dejected bearing, and hopeless condition, coupled with the melancholy condition of the country, gave rise to a long talk about God's moral government of the world, and the issue was that to which all Christian men must come, 'Shall not the Judge of all the earth do right?'

Within a mile or two of Bobo's we saw several Manganja women, who having, with many others, been made prisoners by the Ajawa, had escaped from them. They told us nothing but what we knew, but their testimony was valuable as it confirmed what we had heard, viz.—that the Ajawa were concentrating their forces in the Ku Jireka. That was a bad fact for Soche.

We found Bobo's village in a dismal condition. It is surprising in what a short time neglect and desertion reduce a decent Manganja village to a dungheap in appearance. In one of the ruined huts were men and boys crouching round a little fire. As soon as they heard our footsteps they ran. Fortunately, I recognised one of Bobo's children and called to him; he recollected me and reassured the rest. Bobo came to us soon after and did his best to provide for us for the night. He said no one thought of making gardens; it was useless, now Mongazi was gone, Soche would go, and all would go. They were dead.

It was with very sad feelings I approached Magomero next morning. When about to cross the river we were recognised by some women, and the shrillest of lurley looing was the result. At first I thought it fear, but Chimlolo said—' Fear ? it is not fear. Do you not hear? They say, Atate (father).' And it was for joy, not for fear, the women cried out when they recognised me. Zachuracami came rushing down the bank to meet us, and seemed overjoyed to see me again.

The stockade was re-erected, and the boys' dormitory and my house had been pulled down to supply the timber. Storehouse and kitchen were also gone for the same purpose.

On entering the gate my heart sank like lead within me. Nor did the joyful salutations of the women and children, who actually danced round me with delight, raise my spirits. They looked famine-stricken, aud the whole place was suggestive of misery and desolation. The Bishop's house, though standing, was somewhat dismantled. The cotton gin, most useless of all the things taken up to Magomero, and the only thing we left behind, was still in it.

Burrup's grave was as we left it.

Chigunda's outward appearance was much changed; he had on a cloth frock coat, which had been Gamble's, and he had turned the skirt of my Inverness cape, which had been spoiled for my use by rats, into an under wrapper, which he wore like a petticoat; and on his head he had a cloth cap, which he wore inside out. His appearance was not at all improved by this costume.

He confirmed all that Bobo had said, but did not think himself in much danger, for said he :

' This is the home of the English, and the Ajawa will not touch it; they will burn all others, but they will leave this standing.

My men were anxious to remain the night at Magomero, but the place was so suggestive of sorrow I could not stay. When we left we took the road to Mongazi's.

We had some difficulty in getting along, as many of the old paths were blocked up on account of the war.   The defensive operations of the Manganja were like most other things they did, insufficient.   They hedge up the way with thorns, but so carelessly that no native would be impeded, much less stopped on his way.

We slept that night at Nsamba's.

Next morning we saw no real signs of the war until within five miles of what had been Mongazi's, the great Bona's village. There the evidences were plentiful; village after village had been burnt.

The crows were busy about the ashes of the great village, and we found on the path the remains of a man, which were horribly suggestive of the food upon which the carrion birds had fattened.

Mongazi had evidently been taken by surprise.   The ruins were strewed with half-charred furniture, and pottery in all conditions, shapes and sizes.   At the other villages we saw nothing of this; the Ajawa had apparently employed their old tactics, made a sudden dash at the head-quarters, and destroyed the lesser villages on their return; thus giving the inhabitants of these places time to get away, and take most of their things with them.

We were glad to be at Soche's again, having walked nearly thirty miles fasting, for no food was forthcoming at Nsamba's; we had none with us, and were not able to get any on the road.

We slept at Soche's, and made a Sabbath day's journey to Mbame's next morning.

We left Mbame's soon after sunrise, and reached the station about 2 P.M., having been away just a week.

The result of the journey convinced us that the Ajawa were practically masters of the highlands, though they were not as yet in occupation; and that the poverty and misery of the Manganja made it impossible for us to go back to them at that time.

On Sept. 3, Procter and Mr. Stewart left the station, on a tour of observation, for the Upper Shire.

They returned on the 11th; having a sad tale to tell of war and famine. The fugitives above us had greatly increased, while their food had decreased, and deaths from starvation were already numerous among them. All seemed in a state of utter dejection, lying about on the ground helpless and hopeless. A little time and these too had passed away, and the ground was strewn with their glistening skeletons.

On Sept. 12, poor old Mbame came down to us, looking very haggard; he was on his old errand. The Ajawa were close to him, and he wished us to go and drive them away. Soche, he said, had Ajawa living with him, and allied himself with them in their attacks upon the Manganja. We comforted Mbame as well as we were able, but we could not fight for him.

Food became more and more difficult to get; and we saw that unless we could get supplies from the Portuguese, we must leave the country, and our people must starve. So it was arranged that I should go down to Shupanga with Mr. Stewart, who was leaving us, and thence to Quillimane, if needful, for stores.

But on the 14th, the day before we had arranged to start, a canoe arrived from Shupanga, with letters from England and the Cape. The 'Ariel' (Capt. Oldfield) brought them to the Kongone, and Dr. Livingstone, who had gone to the Rovuma, sent them up before he left the Zambesi. From the Cape we learnt that the Bishop of Cape Town had gone to England, to get a successor to Bishop Mackenzie, and that fresh stores were about to be sent to Mozambique for us.

It was therefore necessary that arrangements should be made with the Portuguese at Quillimane, for a regular transit of stores from Mozambique; and Waller thinking that the committee expected him to undertake this duty, resolved to go down the river instead of me.

Dickinson would not go home at once, but wrote to resign his office, and resolved to await the arrival of his successor. ' I cannot leave you men without medical assistance. If God spare me I shall be thankful; if it be His will to take me to

Himself, let me die in the performance of my duty,' was his noble reply to my earnest desire that he would go home.

Mr. Stewart saw the country at its worst, and his impressions were, we imagined, far from favourable. His visit gave us great pleasure; our sorrow was that we were not able to give him a more bountiful reception.

He and Waller left on the 19th. As the canoe pushed off from the bank, we, and our people who had assembled to wish them farewell, gave them three cheers, as a supplementary blessing to the good wishes already uttered; and in a few seconds the canoe had rounded the bend of the river and was out of sight, on its journey of peril.

Food was now so scarce that it was seldom I could give more than half rations to the children. We struggled on, however, and did our best, not relaxing in our daily duties, keeping up the classes, doing what we could to get a little of the light of truth into the grown people, and working hard at the language.

It having been reported that chimanga was to be bought down the river, Dickinson and I went to Mankokwe's. As we left, some of our women called out, very sorrowfully, ' Don't leave us; if our English fathers go from us, there is no life in us, we are all dead—don't leave us—do come back.'

They were comforted when we told them we were going in search of corn.

Everywhere down the river we found hunger prevailing. Corn was growing on some of the islands, and in some few places on the banks, but it was not sufficient to supply the wants of more than five per cent. of the population. Where the corn was ripening argus-eyes were watching it; every ear was carefully secured against the ravages of birds, and the potent koño was there also to protect it from the cupidity of man.

The koño is an invention of the medicine man, to punish those who pilfer from their neighbours' gardens. An ear of corn is here and there smeared with a fatty substance—fat of what, I cannot say;—these ears are artfully connected with a band of bark, which is thus made to pass all round the garden.

If any thief stumbles against, or in any way touches this bark band, he is a dead man to a certainty, according to Manganja belief; he may not die directly, but he will waste away of an incurable disease.

Nevertheless this koño did not prevent the owner from watching his crop day and night, and woe to the thief when taken; a knife was drawn across his throat, and his body was thrown into the river.

Mankokwe professed himself glad to see us, but he could help us to no corn—he, the Rundo of the whole land, was barely able to supply us with enough meal for our dinner and breakfast. Had we not shot birds in coming down we should have fared badly.

Just before we left, Mankokwe sent for me to his hut; and I learnt from the speech he made, that he was now very sure that the English were friends, and not enemies; when they first came into the country he thought they wished to take his land from him, but now he knew they had good hearts, and only came to do good. He, therefore, and all his people were at our service, and the land was before us to go where we liked. Seeing the Ajawa were daily despoiling him of his territory, that generosity did not amount to much.

Chimbeli, his ambassador, accompanied us to the canoe, and on his way said that all the trouble that came on the Manganja was owing to the Rundo not doing as Rundos did in days gone by. They went from village to village all over the land, every year, and at each place they prayed to Pambi to send rain, and to keep away enemies. Then they were a happy people; there was no war, no starvation, but now all things were against them, for the Rundo cared for nothing but his pombi and his wives, shut himself up with them, and got drunk every day, and would go nowhere.

Chimbeli and the Rundo were evidently not on good terms, and we found that there was a feud between them. Chimbeli had been playing the chief at some villages to which he had been sent, and the Rundo to mark his displeasure at this assumption of power, had not long before selected his principal wife as bride for Bona. Still what Chimbeli told us was very

interesting, as illustrating another phase in the religious belief
of the Manganja.   According to that, it would seem that the
Rundo was a sort of high-priest, whose duty was to make a
yearly circuit of his land, and offer sacrifice.

As we returned we landed at the various islands and villages
where corn was growing, but only at one place could we induce
the natives to sell.

Not long before we came to our halt for the night, we saw a
very pretty woman on an island smoking a pipe; corn was
growing about her home.   I had some glittering brass chain in
my bag, and so I took the chain, held it before her, showed
her what a nice necklace it would make, and expressed a desire
for corn; she said, 'There is no corn, there is no giving in
exchange.'   But she looked very hard at the necklace of brass,
and at last her desire for the ornament became so great that
she went away to ask her husband if she might give corn
in exchange for it.   And the result was the same as it would
have been at home—beauty is omnipotent all over the world—
the woman had the necklace and I had the corn.   I felt rather
ashamed of having ministered to the vanity of this poor Manganja woman, but the little ones at home were hungry, and
though the corn I received was not a meal for half of them, yet
it was a something.

It was a tedious journey homewards, wearying in the extreme.   The fatigue of a land journey is far preferable to the
weariness and inaction of canoe travelling.   I pitied Waller
from my heart, he was doing the rivers to Quillimane and
back.   Day after day for weeks, without the excitement of
novel scenery, the canoe sticking close into the muddy banks,
inconvenienced by the spike-leaved reeds, a hot sun inflaming
your brain, cooped up into the smallest space; truly unless
you can reduce yourself in thought and feeling to the condition
of a mollusc, or elevate yourself to that of a saint, existence,
under such circumstances, is very trying.

Job, who went with us to Mankokwe's, and whom we had
left to come home through the villages by land, hoping he might
pick up some corn on his way, returned soon after we arrived.
He brought five goats with him, but no corn.   He was faint

and irritated, for though he had passed through many villages,
during his walk of twenty-five miles through one of the most
fertile parts of the Shire valley, he had been unable to get a
meal of porridge for himself, and he was not to be soothed.
He went to his hut, exclaiming, ' Oh, dis Manganja country
no good! Neber no good! No breaffast! No dinner! No
nuffin! No food nowheres! Oh, dis Manganja country, too
much humbug!'

The children looked very woe-begone when they found that
we had brought so little corn back; all that we could give
them was one ear each.

Next day Charles was more successful in another direction.
And so day by day we went on struggling for the life of those
committed to our care. We tried to hunt for them, but the
heat had become intense: it was frequently 110° in our huts,
and 25° hotter than that in the sun; we could not stand the
exertion of hunting. We shot birds, and looked out for crocodile and hippopotamuses, but all the people of the land were
doing the same thing, and the beasts were so cunning we could
rarely get a sight of them.

It was a good thing the heat could not have it all its own
way. When it was most fierce its very fury defeated itself. In the
morning as the sun mounted towards the zenith, it seemed as
though the intense glare would scorch up all things, but its
power was limited by its own evokements. The rarefaction of
air was so great that wild gusts of wind came rushing over the
earth from cooler regions, and greatly modified the heat of
the atmosphere. When we had been some time without these
refreshing breezes the hot air almost choked us; coming out
of your hut about 2 P.M. was like facing a furnace fire. The
natives felt this extreme heat, those I mean that came from the
hills, almost as much as we did. And when you wished them
to continue work as the day advanced, they complained that
the heat of the sun was so great it made their heads ache.

The nights were no longer cool; between midday and midnight there was rarely more than a difference of 10°; between
the water in the river and the atmosphere in the morning there
seemed to be the same difference of temperature as between

midday and midnight. I have taken the temperature while bathing and found-the air 95°, the water 85°. During the extreme heat of the day the difference of course was greater, for while that of the atmosphere rose, that of the water remained all but stationary. But despite this great heat, the health of our party at the station was during the month of October better than it had before been. Dickinson improved in appearance, and though others had fever now and then, the attacks were feeble in character and of brief duration. Prickly heat, however, was very annoying to most.

Early on the morning of the 14th of October two of Chibisa's sons, accompanied by a number of people, came to us and solicited an audience. From their statement it seemed that when Chibisa returned to Doa he formed an alliance with a half-caste Portuguese rebel called Tireri (rebels are common in the Portuguese African colonies), and with his help attacked and defeated Belchoir and Makururu, who therefore retired and no more attempted to molest him. But Tireri had established himself at Doa, and having more guns and ammunition than Chibisa, had made himself master, was ill-using the Chibisians, was appropriating their property, and threatening the life of Chibisa. Chibisa, therefore, wished us to go to Doa with the Makololo and drive Tireri away. Finding we would not do that, we were asked to write a letter to Tireri, and a letter to Senhor Feroa of Sena, of whom Tireri was said to be afraid. This we could do, and did, for Scudamore knew a little Portuguese.

Chibisa had evidently caught a Tartar in Tireri, and we had little hope that our letters would be of any service to him.

Next day I and William, with twelve of our men, started for Mikaronko, the capital of the Nungwi, of which tribe Kapichi, Chibisa's old ally, was chief. Corn was, we were told, to be had at this place; and to it people went in times of scarcity like the Canaanites of old to Egypt. It lay fully fifty miles to the N.W. of us, and was on the high road to Tete.

We had some difficulty in getting a guide. Tambala, who was the man to tell us ot corn being at Mikaronko, refused to act as guide; he made some domestic excuse to us, but to

Chimlolo he said he did not go because there were a good many
Chakundas in that part of the country, and the people therefore did not wish to see us.   It is a mistake to suppose that
the natives generally were hostile to the slavers, they were
generally friendly, and under ordinary circumstances would
rather have seen them than us, as we had to teach them to
appreciate us.   The slavers came to the village and bargained
for the human commodity as we did for corn or a goat.   They
themselves, rarely took slaves by force, though they incited
others to violence in order to get the market supplied.   They
entered a place quietly, offered their cloth, brass rings, or
beads for people, like any less objectionable trader.   And the
chiefs and principal men thus acquired the property they
coveted without parting with their own personalities ; they sold
those they had made captive, or who had become objectionable
to them.

But if corn was to be had we were not to be deterred from
going to get it because of the Chakundas, and having procured
one Kongo for a guide, we commenced our journey.   We were
late in getting off, the sun was well up, and the heat already
very great.   The earth was so thoroughly burnt by the sun
that it seemed as though you might dig to its heart before you
found moisture; but many of the trees were already anticipating the fertilising rains, and in their innate vigour were
putting forth fresh foliage, the beautiful colour of which was
more grateful to the eye, than the bare branches we had
for so long a time been looking at.   During the winter in
England a leafless tree appears natural enough, it is in harmony with the general aspect of nature, but in the bright
glare of a tropical sun it is not a pleasant sight, it looks
ghastly and unnatural.   It is not all the trees that shed their
leaves, many retain them throughout the year, but though the
eye may generally find a patch of verdure somewhere in every
landscape, yet for many weeks before the rainy season these
regions presented but few cheerful features.

When about twelve miles from home we found the ground
everywhere strewn with masses of dark basaltic and other
rock.   Now and then they were heaped up in huge barrows.

It seemed as if a planet had shivered in its course and had here deposited its fragments. The path was rugged in the extreme, and the heat was very great, far greater than I had ever before experienced. A less hardened hand than mine on touching the rocks would have been blistered. The atmosphere near the ground was heated to a temperature of 140°. The sole of the native foot is as hard as horn, and as thick as cowhide tanned; but my men complained dismally of the way, their feet suffered severely and 'Jira Chæipa' (very bad road) was their frequent cry. We had some miles of this distressing country, and then we entered upon a more fertile district and an easier road, and at last came to a halt in a large, dirty, and ill-constructed village, whose chief was called Chasita. Here we rested, and here I first really under-stood what a grateful thing water is to a thirsty man in a hot country. The gratification of drinking was intense, and my capacity to imbibe seemed unbounded.

The next village to which we came was called Chiposonga, and the chief, an old man, decrepit with age, was a miserable picture of the physical infirmities attendant on longevity. The sight of this old heathen was very saddening. A young vigorous heathen, one can regard with somewhat hopeful feelings, for the sight of youth always inspires hope, but the miserable condition of this old man was painful in the extreme. So near to eternity, yet without a thought, or the possibility of a thought, beyond the present, and the gratification of his enfeebled appetite. Poor old man; so wretched in life, so doubly wretched in death. I was glad to get away from him.

Beyond this place the road was again rugged and rocky, and then we commenced the ascent of a low range of hills on the other side of which was the plain of Mikaronko. These hills were not high, but they were extensive, and barren, and only once between Chiposonga and our halting-place for the night did we find the means of assuaging thirst. The water had collected in a hole dug in the sand of a dried up water-course. With greedy lips and parched throats we drank until our thirsty longings were satisfied. I did not know of the scarcity of water on this road, or we should have carried it with us.

We halted for the night at Michirinji, half-way from Chibisa's to Mikaronko ; the chief, one Mpaka (Manganja for cat), was a big-bodied, but small-souled man, who looked afraid of his own shadow. Food was not plentiful, but Mpaka sold us a goat for our immediate use, in the enjoyment of which my men forgot the fatigues of the day.

We left Michirinji soon after sunrise next morning. For more than three hours our way lay over the hills which were here thickly studded with small trees, and occasionally dotted with immense blocks of basaltic rock. Just before descending, we had a very fine view of the plain, which was about fifteen miles in breadth, and which, compared with the arid country through which we had passed, like Jordan of old, looked ' well watered everywhere.' To the Mwanza and another river is owing its superior fertility. A range of thickly-wooded hills bounded the plain on the other side, and beyond these, many miles away, were the crests of mountains that must have been at least 10,000 feet high. Altogether, this was as fair a scene as any I had beheld in Africa.

Michirombo was the first village to which we came. We made no stay there, but saw two young men who formerly lived at Chibisa's, which place, according to their own testimony, they had left in consequence of the violence of the Makololo.

The further we went into the plain the more fertile it seemed. The soil was a rich black loam, evidently of some depth, for we saw no trace of rock, and trees of largest growth abounded. One, a magnificent fig-tree, called by the natives Mtondo, was of admirable symmetry, had a rich green foliage, and was larger than our largest oaks.

Between Michirombo and Mpondi, a large village about four miles distant, were several lesser villages ; the ground was everywhere cultivated, there seemed little or no waste ; and—sight long looked for, but not seen till now—there were several acres of cotton growing !

We stayed at Mpondi for a short time in order to make

acquaintance with the chief, but he would not see us, and the people were by no means friendly; they evidently distrusted, but did not fear us; and corn they had none to sell, though it was certain they had plenty in the village.

After leaving Mpondi we soon came to the Mwanza, which is about sixty feet wide. Its banks were steep, but not rocky. In the rainy season its volume of water is no doubt large, but then it was not more than eighteen inches deep, but beautifully clear, and flowed quietly but quickly over a bed of sand. We all bathed, and my foot-sore and scorched companions rolled about with the greatest glee.

About a mile beyond the river we came to a village, of which Chinkoka was chief. There, to my surprise, I found many old acquaintances who had disappeared from the neighbourhood of our Station, but who had frequently been employed by us as porters. I rejoiced at this, thinking my journey ended, and my corn bags filled, for of corn these people had plenty. But my rejoicing was shortlived. These people were even more unamiable than those of Mpondi. Chinkoka was a very stolid individual; he seemed incapable of manifesting any feeling but that of indifference. He was a blacksmith, I am sure, for you may tell a blacksmith, as well as a tailor, all the world over. I was annoyed at their behaviour, but did my best not to show it, hoping to bring about a better state of things. But it was all in vain; I was not wanted there; nor would they take my cloth for their corn. I appealed to Chinkoka again and again to tell me the reason of this ill-feeling; but he only looked more obtuse, and took snuff more frequently. I was angry at last, and was instructing William to give these men a good scolding, when Kongo, my guide, came up to me in a state of great excitement; he could scarcely speak from emotion, but at last he said—

'I can go no further with you. I am sick here,' laying his hand on his stomach. 'I have no more heart. I am dead. They tell me I have done wrong in bringing you here, and they say they will cut my———,' and he drew his hand significantly across his throat. 'If you go to Mikaronko you will not be allowed to enter the village; and as soon as they see you the drum will beat, and it will be war?

And the poor fellow in his fear shed tears.

'But why is this? What have we done to be treated in this way?'

'Oh, you have done nothing, but the Makololo have. The people you see here were driven from their homes on the Shire by the Makololo, who took away their corn and their goats, and threatened to shoot them ; and they think that now you have come here the Makololo will come also, and they are angry with me for bringing you, and that is why they will not sell you anything.'

'Save us from our friends!' we missionaries had good reason to say. I could no longer feel angry with these people, for I felt, according to their method of reasoning, they had good reason for being angry with me. So I endeavoured to make them understand the true position of ourselves with regard to the Makololo, and showed them that we were in no way responsible for what they had done. They admitted that the greater part of the ill-usage they had suffered took place while we were up in the hills, and so might have been without our knowledge. And having got so far with them, I asked if the Makololo had behaved as badly since we had been in the valley.

'No,' was the reply.

'Why is that?'

'We don't know.'

'Then I will tell you. It is because we, as soon as we found what they were doing, were angry with them. And, when they came to us and said they had no food, we gave them cloth to buy corn rather than let them steal it from the Manganja. Was that good or bad?'

'That was good.'

'You say that was good. Can you tell me of any one act of the English which has not been good towards the Manganja? If Chibisa is in trouble, to whom does he come? To the English. At this very moment his sons are at our place asking us to help him against Tireri. And yet, when our children are hungry, and we come to you to buy a little corn, you treat us like enemies. That is very bad. It is you who are to blame.'

Chinkoka grunted something, moved about as though on an uncomfortable seat, took snuff quietly, and was as impassive as before. The rest were visibly excited; this news about Chibisa was fresh to them. At this juncture the old man who was in authority at Chibisa's village when we first arrived made his appearance. I knew him well, and had showed him kindness before I went up to Magomero, and the old man had not forgotten it. In his hut he had heard all that had been said, and he now made a speech in my favour. Then turning to me, and laying his hand on my shoulder, he said, 'The Makololo have done us much harm, do not let them come here. It is a bad thing to be driven from our homes, and to have all we possess taken from us.'

Of course I promised that the Makololo should not molest them again. And then he said to Kongo, 'Don't you fear; go to Mikaronko with the English; no harm will come to you.'

After this he took my hand and invited me to his hut to drink pombi, and added—'I want my wife to see my good brother, the Kasisi.'

Good old heathen! I felt very grateful to him.

As I was leaving, a man brought two small baskets of corn as a present from Chinkoka. I felt half inclined to refuse them, as they still declined to sell me anything; but Nchuru Bango, divining my thoughts, said—

'Take it, take it; we can talk of buying when you come back.'

So I took it; but sent back a present exceeding its value.

Kongo recovered confidence, and we resumed our journey, halting occasionally to make friends with the people of the villages through which we passed. At one of these villages we bought a bundle of very fine sugar-canes. Those that were ripe yielded a good supply of excellent juice. In this locality I have no doubt the growth of cotton and sugar need only be limited by the boundaries of the plain.

We arrived at Mikaronko at about five p.m. This village occupied a larger space of ground than any other village I saw

in Africa, and was surrounded by large trees, and impenetrable
bush.   It seemed a residence for magnates, more than for
common people. It consited of circles of huts, family residences,
situated at some distance from each other.   Each circle was
surrounded by a high wall of grass.   Everything looked well
built, and in good repair.   The village was free of vegetable
and other filth.   Kapichi's circle was in the centre of the
village, and his hut towered in height above the rest; it must
have been twenty-five feet high.

As we entered, the inhabitants came out of their enclosures
to look at us, and 'Anglesi! Anglesi!' passed from mouth to
mouth, not exactly in welcome, but certainly not in anger.
All looked well fed, all were well clothed, all were profusely
ornamented with beads, ivory, and brass rings.

I enquired of a man, who looked like one having authority,
if the chief was in the village.   He looked at me deliberately,
first up and down, and then down and up, and in a loud but not
unpleasant voice answered, 'Kœa,' (I do not know).   I felt
sure there was no real mischief in the man, so I placed myself
right before him, and very deliberately looked at him as he
had looked at me, and mimicking his voice, said, 'Ku nama!'
(that is not true), whereupon he laughed heartily, and followed us to the traveller's halt, a magnificent acacia, whose
branches had an outspread, according to my pacing, of one
hundred-and-fifty feet.

Men and boys crowded before us, and looked all curiosity
and expectation.   Seeing a knot of elderly men I sent William, who was skilled in African diplomacy, to let them know
my wants, and to give them information respecting Chibisa;
for Chibisa, as I have said, had a great reputation at Mikaronko.   William's communications had the desired effect.
The chief was not to be seen until the morning, but a hut was
at once placed at our disposal.   Our hut was one of six in an
enclosure close to Kapichi's.   As soon as it was known that
Kapichi had thus welcomed us, everyone became friendly.

These people were Nungwi, a tribe nearly allied to the
Manganja in appearance, language, and customs, but without
the timid bearing of the Manganja.   They made no secret of

their connection with the Portuguese, or of their dealings with the slavers; and one man, the brother of Kapichi's principal wife, entered fully into the causes of Chibisa leaving Mika-ronko, and gave his opinion of his present position at Doa, which he seemed to think all but hopeless.

Early in the morning Kapichi sent for me to his hut. He was a tall, burly, low-natured man, belonging to a class of men met with all over the world, who will give you good reason to fear them unless you can first make them afraid of you. When he came out of his hut he seated himself on a chair, evidently of American make, and in a very rude way kicked a mat towards me for my accommodation. I saw at once that unless I could subdue him all my hopes of corn were gone, and trouble was close upon me. So I set my teeth together, and looked him hard in the eyes, and then gave the mat another kick, which sent it spinning away from me. He lowered his eyes in confusion, for though physically brave, he was men-tally and morally a coward; and then I sent Chimlolo for my railway-rug, upon which I seated myself with much affectation of dignity. And so we sat facing one another in silence for some time. He became restless and uncomfortable, and at last said, in a voice which he meant to be defiant, but which in reality betrayed fear—

'What brings you here? Speak, and tell me what you want of me?'

I replied, 'You have corn. We need corn, for until our boats return from Quillimane our children are hungry. Chibisa is your brother. Chibisa is our friend. I come to you for corn, for which I will give you cloth.'

'Who told you we had corn? We have none to sell. You want something else,' said he in a dogged tone, and he looked so unamiable, that William said to me—

'I no like that man. He look as though he got something black in his heart.'

I did not doubt that, but I knew also that he had corn in his gokwas, and so replied, 'I want corn, nothing more. You need not sell it unless you like, but if you do not we shall know what to think of you; we shall know what message to send to your brother Chibisa when he sends again to ask our help.'

'Did you come for nothing else ? '

'We English say what we mean, and mean what we say. We do not lie.'

He looked hard at me for a second or two, and became less aggressive in his bearing. I daresay he thought my motives were not simple in coming to Mikaronko, that I was going to charge him with the guilt of slave-dealing, and I was glad to hear him say :

' Well, how much corn do you want ? '

' My bags filled.'

Upon which he jumped up, and shouted out in a boisterous voice—

'Ah ! I want to see what you have in those bags ; something to show me, something to give me ; come along ! '

And he ran off towards my hut with boy-like eagerness. He had evidently received an exaggerated account of our possessions at the Station, for some of Chibisa's people who had been to us were at Mikaronko, and expected I had brought something wonderful with me. When I reached the hut he called out—

' Bring out your bags ; bring out your bags ; quick—let me see what you have. I want a bottle. I want a cup like Chibisa's. I told Tambala to tell you to send me a knife and a spoon like you gave Chibisa. Give to me ! Give to me ! ' And he looked inclined to bluster again. I replied—

' We give to whom we like, and to no one else. You want to see something. Well, here is something,' and I showed him my revolver.

' Mfuti pa nona ' (a little gun), said he contemptuously.

I put him aside and fired—once, twice, thrice ; and his eyes were opened to widest extent. Three balls from one barrel ! it was astonishing. Again I fired, and he collapsed entirely. He put his hand on my arm in downright fear, and said in awe-struck voice—

' Wina ? ' (again ?)

' Yes,' said I, ' again ! ' and he evidently thought I could go on firing to any extent without re-loading ; and, with such guns as that, he looked upon himself and his as dead, if we were not his friends. So he sat down and became quite docile, and told me that corn was not plentiful with him, for his crops had been bad, and all people were coming to him for food; but, if I would send my men to the villages where the corn was kept, he would send his head man with them to tell the people to sell. And so, for the time, my contest with Kapichi ended.

Then I gave him a piece of red calico, and a brass chain necklace for his wife, and a clasp-knife for himself; and he stayed and had breakfast with me, drinking coffee, cup after cup, until we were obliged to have another brewing, and we looked like the best of friends.

William went, and so did Kapichi. But his place was supplied by others, from whom I bought several large baskets of corn.

About midday Kapichi rushed into my hut, and in a boisterous voice said—

'Here, Kasisi, my wife has made you some meal, and I have brought corn for sale. Give me the cloth, give me the cloth.'

As he was in a genial humour I made him sit down, and did my best to make him understand our object in coming into the land. He listened patiently, but made no remarks. In the course of the day he sent me a small leopard's skin as a present. And towards sunset I heard him describing his interviews with me to a number of his people who were collected about him; his descriptions frequently provoked roars of laughter.

William returned with a considerable quantity of corn. Our men also bought for themselves, and altogether we had as much as we could carry home.

We found, on our return, Chinkoka as stolid as ever, with no more animation in his face than if it had been carved out of a block of ebony. The people of his village were now more cordial. The heat was very great, and my men wished me to remain here till the day was well advanced; but, as I wished to be home on the morrow, I had made up my mind to halt for the night at Michirinji, so we pushed on at once. When

we reached the village at the foot of the hills the men begged
hard to be allowed to rest there for the night.   I pitied them,
for it was exhausting work, but the thought of the children at
the station closed my ears to their request, and my ' come on !'
was decisive.   Climbing the hills was hard work, and the stars
were out before the last of my men arrived at Michirinji. They
were too tired to talk ; ate their supper in silence, and immediately went to sleep.   I was too exhausted to do other than
throw myself on a bundle of straw, and drink coffee, into which
Chimlolo had beaten eggs.   But long before daylight my men
roused me, and proposed that we should at once resume our
journey, in order to avoid the greater heat of the day. To this
I gladly assented ; for though foot-sore, my sleep in the open
air on my straw couch—and a bundle of straw is a comfort
when you are really tired—had greatly refreshed me.

There was moonlight until the sun arose, and we walked,
without stopping, to Mitondo—a village ten miles from our
Station.   Here we halted, breakfasted, and bought some goats,
and then started on our final stage.   This was a most punishing walk.   The sun was overhead.   The air was as though it
had been heated in an oven.   I felt all but desiccated, and it
was with joy unfeigned I beheld our Station.   It was home ;
for ' wherever your heart is, there is your home ; ' and my
heart had been with our little ones for many hours.

It was a great relief to find that, since I had been away,
they had fared better than I thought they would.   Scudamore
had killed and secured a crocodile ; and as, upon investigation,
no beads or bracelets, or anything else indicating that the beast
had fattened on man, was found in it, they feasted upon it, and
things therefore were looking cheery.

Upon taking off my boots, I found my socks blood-stained,
and discovered that I had lost several toe-nails.   All who took
that walk to Mikaronko were foot-sore, and hobbled about for
days.

On the afternoon of October 25, we heard the well-known
Shupanga boat-song, and presently there appeared a large
canoe laden with corn and rice; which Waller had sent up under the charge of Maseka, the Makololo who went with him

to sell the ivory which he and his companions had gained by hunting.

This timely supply relieved us at the Station from all immediate apprehension of want.

Waller had gone on to Quillimane.

Of course all these distractions arising from scarcity of food interfered greatly with our Mission work, properly so called. We could do little more than keep things together. Our classes were not given up, though regularity was not always possible. But though all was not as we wished it to be, yet there was great hope of more satisfactory results in time. We were getting more and more influence in the land. Our people, the longer they lived with us the less they followed their own superstition and follies. We were seed-sowing, and longed for the arrival of the new Bishop, when, with increased strength, we might return to the hills and reap the harvest.

CHAPTER XVIII.

THE FAMINE.

FOR many weeks we were anxious for the November moon; rain, said the weather-wise, must come then, it always did; but the November moon came, and the drought still continued in the valley. It did seem at first that it would be as predicted, for on S.S. Simon and Jude (October 28), the clouds, dense and black, gathered round about, the lightning flashed, the thunder reverberated among the hills; we momentarily expected a deluge of rain, but we had but the spray of the storm, which spent itself far away among the mountains. The earth about us was not moistened. Several times after this we had similar manifestations, which were followed by similar results. The clouds collected towards the afternoon, the wind became furious, a storm right overhead seemed imminent; but the seductions of the highlands proved irresistible, and away sailed the clouds, leaving us a clear sky,

from which descended an 'unclouded blaze of living light.'
And so November passed away, and we had no rain.

On November 5 Waller returned, having been away seven
weeks. His exertions had been great, incessant, and successful. He brought up three canoes laden with corn and rice,
two bales of cloth, some few other things necessary to our
well-being physically, and a considerable quantity of clothing,
which had been made up and sent out to us by good friends at
home for distribution among our people, but had been left at
Shupanga. He had also purchased a large canoe, the want of
which we had often felt, and which would be of great use
whether we stayed in the valley or went on to the hills.

We went into our chapel to return thanks for the safe
return of our brother, and for God's mercy towards us as
manifested in the bountiful supply of food he had brought
us.

We were now compelled to feed our people : it was useless
to give them cloth : they would go many miles to buy a little
food for themselves and wives, but it was rarely they could
get it; and before Waller arrived they had endured the greatest privation with much fortitude, and upon the whole with
patient honesty. Only once did they fail. One day they returned in a state of great excitement after having been away
a few hours, bringing with them one of their number, Akumsama, wounded with an arrow. We sent for them to know
what they had been doing. Through Matuira, a man who
came to us from the Makololo, a wild, impulsive fellow, the
personification of brute force, but who had hitherto been
docile and obedient, they told their story, from which it appeared they had been used very badly by some people on the
hills. They had, he said, gone to buy food at a village where
a little food was, and the inhabitants, without receiving any
provocation, attacked them, and wounded Akumsama. For
which cause, as they had been guilty of no offence, they wished
us to give them permission to go and avenge themselves upon
these people.

The selection of Matuira was a mistake on their part, for
though he could act with vigour, he could not speak with dis-

cretion ; and we felt sure from what he had said that they, not the people on the hills, had been the aggressors. So we forbade them, one and all, to cross the river again until we gave them permission, and declared our intention of going up to the highlands to inquire for ourselves, threatening at the same time to send all from us who disobeyed our order.

A threat to Matuira was like fire to gunpowder. His eyes flashed defiance, and he exclaimed, ' If you send one away, all will go. We don't want to wait four or five days before we revenge ourselves, we wish to do it at once, or we shall stink in the noses of the Manganja.'

Prompt was our action upon this : we dismissed them in anger. Matuira's impulsiveness had carried him beyond his companions' intentions, and gave us an opportunity for an assertion of power which, for their own sakes, it was necessary to keep constantly before them. They went away from us subdued and crestfallen.

Next day they all came to us—Matuira was no longer in the ascendant ; a better feeling prevailed among them. They owned, and they did it with shame—I never saw shame so forcibly depicted on any men's faces—that they had been the aggressors ; that when the people to whom they came refused to sell, saying they could not eat cloth, they became angry, for they were hungry, and tried to take by force what they could not get by barter ; and, without seeking to justify themselves, they pleaded their hunger as an excuse for what they had done. We felt for them deeply, and could not retain anger. Nothing demoralises, either the civilized or savage, so much as want of food. We were forced to blame but we could not punish. They promised that they would not offend again, and they kept their promise.

It was a hard thing for men who felt themselves the stronger to go about the country like famished hounds in search of a meal, and not be guilty of violence in order to secure it.

When the canoes returned to Shupanga, Gamble went with them ; he was in better health, but other circumstances made it necessary for him to leave us.

About the middle of November hunger prevailed everywhere

about us. It made our hearts ache to see strong and healthy
men and women reduced to feeble helplessness for want of
food. When we went into the villages we saw the people
lying about dejected and hopeless, in appearance mere skeletons, with a dusky skin stretched over them. The weakly and
the little ones died off quickly. We did what we could to relieve any case of extreme necessity when it was brought directly
under our notice, but we could do nothing to stem the tide of
starvation that, like a flood, swept over the land and destroyed
multitudes. It was the same on the hills as in the valley.
Damanji and other of our men went up to Mbame's, and on
their return gave a lamentable description of the condition of
the people. Mbame's village was a mere abode of death. In
several of the huts they found the putrefying remains of those
who had died of starvation. Mbame was not at home, but
they met him and brought him down to us. Poor old man!
he was looking very gaunt and hungry. He was naturally a
fleshy man, but now it seemed that, like the bear in time of
scarcity, he had been subsisting on himself for many days past.
His muscles were shrunken, his skin hung loosely upon him.
He stayed with us two or three days; and when he returned
he went away with a lighter heart, but a heavier person, for
we fed him well, and gave him a bag of corn. He had had no
rain, and just before he started he saw hanging over his home
heavy masses of densest vapour; he thought rain was falling
on his fields, and the old man danced and sung, whirling and
twirling and shouting with the agility of a younger and less
heavy man. It was a ridiculous manifestation of joy, but we
sympathised with it nevertheless. His joy, alas! was prema-
ture. It did not rain: his fields remained unblessed for some
time after this.

   The famine became sore in the land; there was not a village
where people were not dead or dying of starvation. At first
those who died were buried in graves, then the survivors being
too weak for the exertion of grave-digging, carried the bodies
outside the village, and laid them decently under a tree: if a
man, his bow with the string cut, would be placed beside him;
if a woman, the fragments of a broken water-jar. But as time

went on even this attention to the dead seemed impossible—
where they died there they remained. You met with the
putrefying remains of human beings on the paths, in the villages, everywhere; there was no place where they were not.
The river Shire was literally the river of death. Poor hungry
wretches would come from the hills, or from the destitute parts
of the valley, and attempt to steal what little corn there was
growing on the islands and along the banks; no matter that it
was not ripe, they took it unripe: but the owners with wolf-
like vigilance caught them, and with wolf-like ferocity killed
them, and threw their bodies into the river. Mothers also,
having no food to give their children, threw them into the
river, and jumped in after them. Men did the same with regard to their wives. The crocodiles were gorged with human
food.

One morning I saw from the top of our bank what seemed
to be the dead body of a child floating down the river. As I
turned aside, sickened at the sight, a little arm was thrown up,
and I heard a child's voice beseeching help. The child was
alive. We ran down to the river, launched a canoe, and saved
the little one. When he recovered from his fright, he told us
that his father, who lived at a village about seven miles above
us, had thrown him and his mother into the river, and that he
had been a long time in the water. Poor child! he could not
sink; his stomach was so inflated and distended by scarce and
unwholesome feeding, that it kept him up like a bladder. We
did our best to keep him alive, but dysentery carried him off;
but before he died we baptized him by the name of Moses.

The distress was so terrible to bear, that we resolved to get
up more corn from Shupanga, and distribute a portion of that
we had to the people in some of the villages near to us. Two
men were found willing to take a letter down to Senhor Vi-
anna, with whom we dealt, and we despatched them on their
errand.

Relying on this supply we began at once to distribute small
rations of corn amongst the survivors in some of the most ne-
cessitous villages. It was a painful duty; the hopeless, half-
idiotic condition to which most were reduced made us realize

to the full that 'they that be slain by the sword are better
than they that be slain with hunger, for these pine away
stricken through want of the fruits of the field.'   So extreme
was their necessity that we almost wondered that that most
hideous of all hideous expedients, cannibalism, was not resorted
to in order to prolong existence.   For if in olden times the 'tender and delicate woman,' who 'would not adventure to set her
foot upon the ground for delicateness and tenderness,' if this
woman who knew of the God of Heaven and Earth, had an
evil eye 'turned towards the husband of her bosom, and towards her son, and towards her daughter,' and did in the extremity of her hunger 'devour the fruit of her womb for the
sustenance of her body,' it would not have been surprising if
the poor famishing heathen about us had followed her example.
But among the Manganja no thought of cannibalism existed ;
the whole race might have perished without such a thought
occurring to an individual, so foreign was it to their nature.

The Ajawa were not altogether guiltless of man-eating, but
it was superstition, not hunger, which led them to it.   Under
certain circumstances they ate man, as other tribes will eat
lion, in order to make them brave.   They told us of a certain
chief named Niria, against whom the Ajawa fought for a long
time without success, and who sustained his cause almost sin-
gle-handed.   When at last he was overpowered and killed, his
body was cut up into minute portions, the flesh being eaten by
the Ajawa warriors in order that they might become as valiant
in war as he.

It would not have been difficult to make these people realize
the truth that our souls are strengthened by the Body and
Blood of Christ, as our bodies are by the bread and wine.

And so things went on for days and weeks, the sun for most
part of the time a blaze of unmitigated heat, the earth hot
even to burning, panting for the rain, and man dying for want
of the fruits of the field.   There is nothing which so awfully
convinces man of his own impotence, of his absolute depend-
ence upon God, as the suspension of rain in its season.

On the 3rd of December, however, there was a great accu-
mulation of clouds on all sides of us ; they seemed heavy with

rain. The lightning flashed far away incessantly. The distant
thunder kept the air in continual agitation. The clouds were
bearing a torrent of rain upon the surrounding heights for
hours, before the hopes we had of a similar blessing were realized. Then the tempest came upon us. In an instant we
were in the strife of the elements. It was astounding. The
lightning blinded us, and the thunder made every nerve in our
bodies vibrate. The rain came down in such torrents as we
thought could never have been known since the days of Noah.
A hurricane of wind lashed the river into wave and foam, tore
up the trees by their roots, and dismantled whole villages. Yet
above all the turmoil were heard the shrill and joyful exclamations of the women, who rushed out into the storm, and ran
about like maniacs for very delight; but their cries of joy mingled with the wail of the dying : at the very moment the storm
came down upon us, four of our lads were crossing the river in
a canoe; the canoe was upset, and Akumsama,—he who was
wounded in the affray on the hills,—was drowned; the others
managed to reach the shore.

The storm passed away almost as suddenly as it came; the
clouds rolled away in gloomy grandeur, and again the sun was
paramount.

But the rain had done a good work; it had fitted the earth
for the seed, and those who who had seed rushed off at once to
their gardens and commenced sowing. But many had no seed;
in the extremity of their hunger they had eaten their seed-
corn, and before the day was over, and during the days following, poor famished men and women dragged themselves to our
doors, and their piteous cry was, ' Give us seed, fathers.' Some
—marvellous instances of self-denial and hope—sowed what we
gave; all meant to do so; but hunger prevailed with many,
and we knew that the cravings of appetite had overpowered
them; they ate, they did not sow. But those who sowed and
those who ate, died; while the corn was growing the people
starved. Had the rains prevailed at the ordinary period, the
pumpkin crop would have been harvested early in November;
but the seed was not sown till December, and then it came to
nothing; for though on the 5th we had rain again for several

hours, and occasionally all through December and January, yet it was not sufficient to bring the early crops to perfection—the people still died.

On December 6, to our great vexation, the men whom we sent to Shupanga with an order for more corn, returned, without having gone farther than the Ruo. As they went down the river they heard such dismal reports of Mariano's doings, that their hearts failed them ; they left the canoe at Malo and returned by land. Mariano was destroying just below Malo ; plundering and making captive, and sending the captives to the slave-agents on the coast.

The return of these men made it necessary for one of us to go down the river, for we saw we should need more corn before we could gather in a harvest. Johnson offered to go, but Dickinson would not let him, as he had been suffering from slight congestion of the brain. I volunteered to go, but Procter would not let me ; he decided to go himself. We expected our stores for 1863 would be at Quillimane ; if so he would bring them up, as it was necessary in consequence of the disturbed state of the valley through Mariano's proceedings, that a white man should be in charge of them. He left on the 9th, taking Chimlolo, and his own little attendant, Sambani, one of our most intelligent children, with him.

These canoe journeys were a great trouble. Going down the river was easy and pleasant enough ; but coming back, especially during the rainy season, was as great a trial as a man could be called upon to submit to. But they were then unavoidable. By our experiences we were making the work easier for others, but our experience, like that of all pioneers, was very punishing.

A great change came over the face of nature after the rains of the 3rd and 5th. No longer bare and burnt, the earth was covered with verdure. No longer the ghastly skeleton-looking things they were, the trees became beautiful in their prolific foliage. Vegetation of all kinds sprang forth with a power unknown to more temperate climes. The fertility of the earth after its long season of barrenness seemed marvellous. You all but saw the growth of grass. Hidden stumps put forth young shoots so vehemently, that a large shrub appeared where but a few days before no sign of vegetation was apparent. Seed germinated, and the blade was a few inches above the ground in the course of a fortnight.

Our people went to work with a right good will; they gave themselves no rest. We did our best to incite them to good husbandry; and the industry they displayed, and the fruits of their industry, were most pleasing. They brought a large extent of bush under cultivation for the mapira crop, and we managed to purchase for them gardens by the river for the pumpkin and chimanga. Misery and death continued to prevail, but not without hope, for we saw the fruits of the earth coming forth in their order, and were cheered. We looked upon every patch of growing corn with far greater delight than we should upon the most beautiful flowers, for in these we saw a limit to the suffering around us.

The Makololo worked hard in their gardens; but the misery of their position was this: to get good gardens by the river they had to dispossess the original owners. It is useless entering into particulars, but they did without doubt greatly aggravate the misery of the surviving Manganja about us. I do not say this in a fault-finding spirit, for I liked these Makololo, notwithstanding the trouble they gave us. They were a brave set of men, and had we needed assistance at any time when on the Shire, they would have given it unhesitatingly. Among natives such as the Manganja, they would never be less than paramount; and they elevated themselves into the position of chiefs. They were strong enough to hold what they had acquired, and they will, I have no doubt, inaugurate a more masculine state of things in the valley above and below Chibisa's than that which existed under Manganja rule.

Another element of fear came upon the poor Manganja who still survived, in the people of Chibisa, who had left Doa in consequence of Tireri's proceedings. They wanted food and garden ground; and they managed to get it, for they lived and cultivated while others perished.

To us the sufferers appealed in their trouble; and we did our best for them, frequently, when a case of wrong could be clearly brought home, compelling restitution, and by our constant vigilance preventing much oppression. But we need have been twenty times stronger than we were to have done half the work that needed doing at this time of trouble and strife. Hunger and the prospect of death had made men reckless; right was nowhere regarded; the strong hand and the strong will prevailed. Those who had, kept if they could; those who had not, took if they had the power.

Our own people were our great consolation. They were far from perfect, poor things, but they afforded a marked contrast to those around us. It is true they were not subject to the same temptation as many others, for day by day we gave them just sufficient corn to keep them in health; but in times of excitement and lawlessness, it showed that our labour among them had not been in vain, for they steadily pursued the path of honest industry we had marked out for them.

Once, however, we had to proceed with severity against one, who was a lad when released from the slavers at Mbame's, but who grew burly, married, and became mischievous, as a man. We always had to keep a tight hand upon him. His name at first was Kombi (a spoon), which at his marriage he changed to Kandalira (I cannot cry); and he was an Ajawa. He had garden ground as good as the rest, but he coveted another piece by the river side; and in order to get it we were told he had thrown its owner, a boy, the sole survivor of his family, into the river.

We put him on his trial before a jury of his own country-men, and he was convicted by them, upon evidence which there was no gainsaying; for though it is natural to them to judge and act upon impulse, the 'logic of facts' was as irresistible to them as to more imperial minds.

We were the judges, but they convicted. We explained to them what was the punishment for murder in our own country, and told them we should not punish Kandalira as our own countrymen were punished, because he was ignorant of our laws; but we burnt down his hut, and sent him with his wife and child across the river. We took away his gardens, and we threatened to flog him severely if he dared to come near our station again.

His companions looked upon this as an awful punishment; they fully acquiesced in its justice, but they came to us and begged for mercy. He was wrong, they pleaded, but he would not do the like again; therefore, think of the wife and child, and forgive him. We were pleased with the feeling they thus showed, and the Ajawa had no idea of turning against a friend in distress; but the sentence was put into force, and the report of it spread through the land, and created a good impression in our favour.

The wife, Winapi, was a pretty little creature, and when we found out that they had settled on the other side of the river some distance down, we took care that she had sufficient food to keep her and her babe alive, until the first crops growing were ready to gather.

The thunderstorm phenomena during the months of December and January were very grand. We had an extensive view from our station, and we almost daily witnessed scenes which are among the most sublime as well as the most beautiful in nature. We rarely experienced the full force of a storm, but on and over the hills, far and near, the tempests raged with awful grandeur; at times it seemed as though they would rend the mountains. Occasionally the clouds were exquisitely coloured; the rays of the setting sun gave them a glory and a beauty impossible to describe.

As Christmas-time approached, animal as well as vegetable life became profuse, and all things living appeared to awake to renewed activity.

> There was life in the air,
>   There was life in the clod,
> On the earth, everywhere,
>   There was life and to spare.

But there was death also; death not only among the poor heathen around, but nearer home. The great change in the condition of the atmosphere brought increased sickness. I escaped with little inconvenience, for my system happily accommodated itself to change of circumstance; but it was not so with others. Clarke had fever severely, and Scudamore became very ill. For some time he had been suffering from diarrhœa, disordered liver, and a general weakness. He strove vigorously against this—too vigorously we feared—and tried to shake off by increased exertion that of which only a long rest would have rid him. Much has been said about the danger attendant upon a sedentary life in Africa, but we led so active a life that our danger arose from over exertion.

Fever attacked our dear brother, and this upon his previous indisposition quite prostrated him. His condition alarmed us greatly, for his stomach was so sensitive that it rejected the medicines which alone could give him relief.

On the 23rd the fever was at its height, and there was danger that the slight consciousness he then retained might be lost, so Dickinson advised me to acquaint him with the danger of his position. It was a sorrowful duty, but he was fully alive to the critical nature of his illness, and with a serene mind dictated his last wishes.

It was a hard matter to be happy on Christmas Day. One had a lively sense of the cause for spiritual happiness existing in the all important event commemorated; but wearied with watching and anxiety, we were not able to rise above sadness. Dear Scudamore was no better. The fever seemed a little less violent, but its effects were most distressing. His tongue and throat were much ulcerated, and an abscess was forming dangerously near the larynx. Dickinson had fever also which made him totter, but nothing could exceed his loving and incessant attention to Scudamore, for whom, in common with all of us, he had the greatest affection. He showed much skill in meeting the difficulties of the case; and we thanked God that we were provided with abundant remedies, for though the greater part of our store of food was lost at the beginning of the year, the medicines came safely to us.

Procter being away, and I being at that time in deacon's orders only, we could have no celebration of the Holy Communion on Christmas Day. This was for some hours a great distress to Scudamore.

On St. Stephen's Day he seemed to improve a little: his

pulse was down considerably, but he suffered much pain. We had hope, nevertheless, for Dickinson had at last succeeded in getting medicine to stay on his stomach. And this hope continued to grow up to the night of the 28th; then Dickinson, who at that time was watching him, became alarmed. A great change for the worse took place. The inflammation from the abscess extended rapidly externally and internally, and the immediate result was so serious, that Dickinson at once apprised us of the danger, and our dear brother expressed his conviction that he should die. He suffered greatly, but he was quite resigned.

Soon after this, delirium, but in a milder form than at the commencement of his illness, came upon him, and continued, with brief intervals, until the moment of his death. These brief intervals were precious moments; they evidenced how well prepared our dear brother was for the great change that was coming upon him, and gave us—what from the heavenly mindedness of his life we did not really need—a joyful assurance that he who was passing from us would die in peace, rest in hope, and rise in glory.

During the whole of the 29th he continued to breathe with greatest difficulty, and his speech was so much impeded that he could scarcely articulate intelligibly. Every means that could be adopted to give him relief were tried, but in vain. His strength was exhausted; he gradually sank. His mind occasionally failed him, but his spirit remained faithful, and did not cease to commune with heavenly things. Once, after being greatly tried, the cloud cleared away for a brief instant, a gleam of Divine satisfaction shone from his eyes, and he murmured several times:

'There remaineth a rest!'

This was on the afternoon of the 31st.

Having been up during the previous night, and Dickinson and Waller being both much worn, it was arranged that Clarke should be with him from nine till midnight, that Waller should succeed Clarke, and that Dickinson or myself should take the early morning watch. When Waller entered, he soon saw that a change had come over him, and called up Dickinson,

who did all that could be done, as a last effort, to stimulate
his failing powers. But there was no rallying. He was in
the last struggle ; and Waller seeing this to be the case, called
me from my sleepless rest, and I went to behold the last
moments on earth of one who had been to me more than a
brother ; an example of what is desirable in a man, and lovely
and of good report in a Christian.

The Southern Cross was shining brightly over the hut in
which he lay, and though my heart was full of sorrow, when I
looked at that cross, I thought of the Cross of Calvary, and if
my sorrow could not at that time be turned into joy, it was
mitigated.

REV. H. C. SCUDAMORE.

When it was evident that he had but a few minutes to live,
we called up the rest of our brethren, in order that they might
behold, for the last time in life, him who had won all their

hearts by his gentleness and goodness, by his readiness in season and out of season to spend and be spent in the service of his Divine Master.

He died at ten minutes past four, on the morning of January 1, 1863.

Thus, in less than a year, we had lost three by death : the Bishop on January 31, 1862, Burrup on February 22, and Scudamore on the morning of the New Year, 1863.

Dickinson chose the burial-place, and perhaps in doing so had some presentiment that he was also choosing for himself. It was a lovely spot, quite close to our station, commanding a beautiful view of the river, the valley, and the ascent to the Highlands—just such a place as he whom we had just lost would have chosen for himself.

We buried the mortal remains of our dear brother about four o'clock in the afternoon, just twelve hours after he died.

Our people showed considerable feeling. No one went to work, and the men, from an early hour, sat around the hut where the body lay, in a posture of grief.

Moloko, Ramakukan, and several other of the more respectable of the Makololo, attended also. Their words were few, but their countenances and actions expressed unfeigned sorrow. They were fond of Scudamore, and in him they lost a charitable friend.

The Manganja still living about us were not backward in the expression of their sorrow, and Chibisa's two sons came with a number of people to express their regrets, and wished to fire off their guns during the day—that being their method of expressing grief on the death of a chief.

The immediate cause of death was erysipelatous inflammation of the throat and neck; but this was really one of the after-effects of fever.

It was a melancholy satisfaction to us, when we considered the many privations we had been compelled to endure, to know that in his illness our dear Scudamore had wanted for nothing. Great as the loss was felt by us to be, it would have been more grievously felt had human means been wanting to aid his recovery. Had we, before his fatal illness set in, while he was but weak, been able to give him nourishing food in abundance, it is probable that this last fatal illness might have been avoided.

We were all much depressed in spirits, and our physical condition was far from vigorous. We wanted wine and even bread; for those really ill we had just sufficient, for daily use none.

Scudamore was a man of considerable ability—next to the Bishop the most able man we had. This was not at first apparent, for his extreme modesty was such, that it was rarely a stranger was aware of the manly dignity, the depth of purpose, the energy and mental power he possessed. His amiability of disposition was apparent to all. As a companion he was charming; his quiet, genial wit, illuminated everything it touched. We lost much when we lost him; how much we did not know until we missed his influence for good on every subject we had to discuss, and in all the work we had to do. We lost much strength in losing him, and strength of the highest kind. He knew more of the language than any of us. What we knew of its construction was owing almost entirely to him, for he had the gift of unravelling what appeared to most of us a tangled web at best. Had he been spared, he would soon have commenced a regular religious service for the natives; and had he been a less diffident man, he might have done so three months before he died; I say diffident—I ought to have said reverent—for it was more the fear of doing harm by his incapacity, when speaking of Divine things in the native language, than aught else, which made him defer what he so fully purposed to do.

The rains were bountiful in January, but the heat, when the sun did get play, was singularly distressing, really more so than in the fierce days of the dry season. And death still stalked through the land, and gathered an abundant harvest. Wild-looking, famished men, with cords tied tightly round their waists to lessen the pains of hunger, roamed about grubbing up roots, until, unable to go on any longer, they sank down and died. Most of the banana trees were destroyed, the roots, after a certain preparation, being eatable; and before January had passed more than half of the inhabitants of the valley and the first range of hills were dead.

We had the testimony of all, that such a famine as that from which we were suffering was most rare. No one could recollect such a visitation, though most had heard of a 'Magumanya,' the name they gave to a famine when 'heap upon heap' perished for want of food. There is rarely a season in savage Africa when people do not die of hunger. But such deaths are the result of their own imprudence, or are the inevitable consequences of heathenism—deaths which might be avoided; and if Christianity prevailed, such a calamity as the famine of 1862-1863 would have been impossible. With Christianity would come law and order, security for person and property, and stores of food to fall back upon when the crops failed. I do not think that part of Africa could ever be a wealthy land, but under a happier state of things it would supply abundantly the wants of its people. There is a wide field for the missionary, though but small scope for the merchant. In the course of years a commerce of some kind, other than in ivory, might be developed, but I do not think it would be extensive. There can be no doubt that its capacities, at the time we left England, were greatly over-estimated, and its difficulties underrated. When the natives lost their corn crop they lost all; for the land produced them nothing else in sufficient abundance to sustain life.

On the evening of January 21, Chimlolo, with three canoes laden with corn, was reported between the station and Mankokwe's, and in due time the good fellow made his appearance, having performed his duty faithfully and well.

He brought a letter from Procter, which, among other things, informed us that our stores for 1863 were at Quillimane, that the 'Pioneer,' after another trip to the Rovuma, had returned to Shupanga, and that Mariano had ravaged the lower part of the valley of the Shire up as far as Kalubve, and it was his intention to force his way right up the river, so as to get an entrance into the ivory-producing districts of the interior, away from the Portuguese settlements. From him, however, we had no cause to fear. A party of his men stopped

Chimlolo in coming up the river, but as soon as he learnt that the canoes belonged to the English, he let them pass without molestation, and with a promise that his people should not interfere with us.

Procter was going on to Quillimane to secure our stores.

Chimlolo said there was nothing but hunger all the way down the river.

This man, Chimlolo, was an excellent specimen of the Ajawa. His capacity was considerable, his aspirations good, and now that we had won his confidence, his integrity was unassailable. His great ambition was to be like the English in all things. In the matter of dress he very quickly eschewed native costume; and knowing his predilection, I, in return for his attention to my comfort on a journey, gave him a shirt and pair of trowsers. On the Saturday evening after I had made him this present, it fell to my lot to pay the men the wages they had earned during the week. I saw Chimlolo coming across the village to where I was standing, arrayed in shirt and trowsers, and evidently in that state of blissful self-consciousness which our volunteers know something of when they pass up the streets for the first time in uniform. In due course I called out:

'Chimlolo!'

He looked at me with a droll expression, and said:

'Chimlolo? Chimlolo paribe.' (Chimlolo? Chimlolo, he is not here.)

I looked at him for an explanation of that statement, as he was standing before me; when he laughed heartily, and replied:

'Chimlolo, he is dead! He is no longer Chimlolo, he is an Englishman!' giving his trowsers a hearty slap, to show that he had English clothing on.

The new supply of corn enabled us to recommence giving rations thrice a week to some of the surviving but starving Manganja living close to us. There was one village, Maduga, about a mile from our station, and where lived many of those men we used to employ to carry up our baggage to the hills. Many had died, but some were living; so Waller and I went

THE FAMINE. — MISSIONARIES DISTRIBUTING CORN.

to them as soon as we received the corn. We had not gone three hundred yards before we came upon the corpse of a boy who had fallen down and died of hunger. A little removed from this was the body of a man nearly reduced to a skeleton by the ants; and when we arrived at the village, we found the body of another man, who that morning had perished of starvation. As soon as our object in coming to Maduga was known, the unhappy inhabitants came out of their huts to welcome us. Men who had carried heavy burdens with ease up the hills tottered towards us attenuated beyond recognition; others too weak to stand dragged themselves along on their hands and knees; women in the prime of life crawled to the doors of their huts, and could get no farther; and the little children were in such a horrible condition from long famishing, that the sight of them was more than one could bear. Much misery hardens the heart, and, heaven help me! by long contemplation of suffering, I had become somewhat inured to the sight of it. I had seen men and women die almost with indifference, but the sight of these little ones went like a sword to my heart. I could not refrain, I was forced to turn aside.

We were not able to save more than five or six of the people of Maduga; the long privation they had endured, and the disgusting things they had devoured in order to allay the pains of hunger, brought on dysentery, and the village was literally depopulated.

After such a fearful experience as this, a little corn thrice a week was not sufficient; they wanted incessant care, and the most delicate as well as the most nutritious food.

With so much starvation, one might have supposed we should have been exposed to constant depredations from those starving; but it was not so. Now and then a poor, famishing creature would try and steal from us, but the cases were of rare occurrence, considering the general necessity. With one or two, however, the propensity to steal became a monomania. The most remarkable instance was that of a boy of about eleven years of age: he kept us for days on the lookout; there was not a hut from which he did not manage to steal something. If you took him out of the village, he was back before you, and was again trying to steal. He seemed more like an automaton, that could not resist the impelling power, than a human being; and what he did, he did with a gravity and unconcern that was astonishing, manifesting no shame, showing no fear. He belonged to Maduga, and at last, as the least trouble and expense to ourselves, we decided upon keeping him tied up in our village, and hoped by plentiful feeding and physic to cure him. But he managed to undo his fastenings, and though he had eaten until he could eat no more, he forced his way into our store-hut. We made him at last secure, but after two or three days' confinement his health seemed to be suffering, so we gave him his liberty, and no sooner were our eyes off him, than he was found in a hut stealing, or seeking food, though he had food by him uneaten. Of course this was disease, and the poor child died. And there were others similarly diseased, but only such as these attempted to rob us.

Again, it might be supposed that these people, seeing they were the slaves of superstition, might have attributed the famine to our presence in the land. They did not do that. They had received nothing but good at our hands, and they had too much confidence in our good intentions towards them to connect us in any way with the evil from which they were suffering. I look upon this as one of the most satisfactory proofs we had that our influence for good was great.

Unfortunately, the promise of continued and abundant rain at the commencement of January was not fulfilled. Towards the end of the month but little rain fell. The sun resumed its wonted sway, and it seemed as though the rains were ended. The pumpkins and beans withered, the mapira dried up, and only the chimanga in the gardens by the side of the river looked hopeful. The people, by the 10th of February, were eating the corn grown in these gardens, and sowing for fresh crops. As a matter of course, these gardens were productive of much contention. The Manganja who owned them could scarcely hold them against the Chibisians and others, and at last, to ensure them from depredation, we took all the Manganja gardens about us under our protection; who touched them touched us, and so they remained uninjured.

On February 15, we had definite intelligence of Procter. Chimlolo, who was watching his garden by the river, came running up to us, and told us that an English boat, a boat like that in which the ladies came up, was but a little way from us. Off we ran, Waller ahead, I close behind, and the rest nowhere. After running a mile, we caught sight of the white sails of the little craft. For a few seconds we were uncertain, for no one returned our salutations. At last a strange voice replied. It was not Procter, but Mr. Richard Thornton, the geologist, who had lately returned to the Zambesi from a successful expedition, in conjunction with Baron von der Decken, to Kilimanjaro, the snow-clad mountains lying inland from Zanzibar. His 'All well!' gave us much relief, for we had been in considerable anxiety about Procter's welfare. When he landed, we learnt that the 'Pioneer' and 'Lady Nyassa' were hard aground in the neighbourhood of the Ruo, and likely to be so, and that Procter, when the ships left Shupanga, had not returned from Quillimane.

Mr. Thornton was a great acquisition to our party. He seemed, and indeed was, but a youth; but his frank, manly, genial, and generous character soon engaged our warmest affections in his behalf. He proposed making our station his headquarters for some time, while he made theodolite observations of the country about us.

On February 24, Procter, to our great relief, returned, having been away eleven weeks. He brought with him stores and medical comforts of all kinds. The 'Rapid' brought them to Quillimane, and Dr. Livingstone happening to be there at the same time, most probably saved them from destruction, for the launch which our agent, Senhor José Nunez, sent out for them, would have been swamped, had not the Doctor taken the greater part of our stores out of her into the 'Pioneer,' and towed her in.

The news from home informed us of the condemnation of our proceedings against the Ajawa by some of our friends at Oxford. This did not come to us officially, for the Committee simply expressed confidence in us individually and collectively. I do not think any of us were surprised that our Ajawa policy had been condemned, seeing the men who condemned it did not understand the causes leading us to adopt it, and the motives actuating us. We were not angry, but we were thankful that the Bishop and Scudamore were removed from the pain which the manner of some in condemning would have given them.

By the end of February, war and famine had done their work, and ninety per cent. of the Manganja were dead; save in our immediate neighbourhood, the land was a desolation.

We sent Charles, William, and Job down to the coast with the canoes that came up with Procter, and in due time they found their way to the Cape.

CHAPTER XIX.

JOURNEY TO TETE.—DEATH OF DR. DICKINSON.

PROCTER brought no meat with him, preserved or salt: our stock of goats was exhausted; and there were no more to be had nearer than Tete. The depredations of a leopard reduced us to extremity in a night; he scratched away the soil, loosened the stakes of the goat-house, entered and slew three goats and two sheep.

As the people perished the wild-beasts increased upon us; they were not more numerous than before, but they wandered about more, because there were no inhabitants in the villages to check them. Through the depredations of this leopard we were thus left with one old he-goat, and the flesh of those slain, which we tried to preserve by salting—not a promising process.

Dr. Livingstone was as badly off for fresh meat as we, and Thornton said as he had some influence with the Portuguese, and wished to complete at Tete certain triangulations neces-sary to his survey of the country; he would go to that place with either of us, and use such interest as he had to put us and the Expedition in possession of fresh meat. We felt sure that it was his generosity more than the necessity of his work which led him to make this offer, but we thankfully accepted it, and I volunteered to go with him.

We had some difficulty in getting off; we wanted a guide and men to carry food and baggage. When we first came into the country, had we needed a hundred porters, we could have collected them in an hour or two, but now there was, with the exception of our own men, scarcely a man in a physical condition fit for the journey; for those the famine had not killed were barely able to stand without support. At last we found a guide among Chibisa's people, a gentleman in reduced circumstances, who would carry no burden himself, but had no objection to see his own son, a lad of fourteen, half starved and spiritless, laden like a donkey.

Of our own men seven were sick, and as the rest were anxiously watching their fast-ripening corn, I had no wish to take them, seeing that, with two exceptions, they had been released from Tete slavers. But there was no alternative, so I called them together and informed them that I was going to Tete for sheep and goats, and wanted men to go with me. When the terrible word, Tete, was mentioned, for a moment a suspicion of my object crossed their minds; were we, after all, going to sell them for slaves? But it was only for a moment; Chimlolo was the first to volunteer, Damanji followed, and then others, until I had, not as many as I needed, but as many as my conscience would let me take, for some were really wanted at home to look after the gardens of those away. Thornton took his own two men and a boy.

According to latitude, Tete was a hundred miles distant from our station; according to actual mileage, very little less than a hundred and fifty. We therefore calculated upon being a month away.

We left those at the station far from well. Clarke had been suffering for a long time from so severe a form of fever that I feared I should not see him alive on my return. Dickinson was very feeble. As we were leaving he ran after us with a small bottle of spirits of wine, into which he wished me to put anything curious I might meet with in entomology; he especially wanted the Tsetse, and it was thought we should pass through a Tsetse district. He followed us some distance, giving us kindly and useful hints about caring for our health, and uttering affectionate last words, and then he left us.

We left the station on the 27th of February. To get to Tete we had to pass through Mikaronko, the route to which place I have described. The road was not less rugged, but in consequence of a decreased temperature it was less distressing. It was hot enough, for the sun was sufficiently powerful to force up the mercury in Thornton's thermometer, when exposed to its rays, to 120°. But that is a heat which, if not comfortable, can be endured with equanimity. When it is 20° hotter than that, it makes a considerable difference in your personal feelings and temper—you don't like to be contradicted.

But though the road was not altered, the appearance of the country was; the growth of grass and the thick foliage of the trees had so changed its aspect that it was only from two or three prominent features which no vegetation could change, that I was able to recognise it as the same through which I had passed in October.

There was also a change in another respect. The famine had done its work; the land was without inhabitants, until we arrived near the Mwanza. The villages were left standing, but not a single human being was found alive in them; skeletons were everywhere—in the path and in the villages. It was horrible.

Thornton was not in good marching condition; he had been suffering from an inflamed eye, and some old sores above his ankles troubled him at first, so we were three days in getting to Mikaronko. The first night we slept in the bush, the second at Mponda's, from whom we had a cordial welcome. We found Chinkoka's people harvesting their chimanga, and so careful of it that they were not willing to part with an ear.

The Mwanza is the boundary between the Manganja and the Nungwi; and while on the one side we found nothing but death and desolation, on the other there was life and hope.

The Manganja everywhere seemed marked for destruction. Seeing some women and children turn out of the path as we approached on the Nungwi side of the Mwanza, I thought they were going to run away, so I called to them not to fear. At these words the guide, himself a Nungwi man, said:

'Fear! they have no fear! They are not Manganja!' with a contemptuous emphasis on the name of the all but extirpated race. Nor did they fear, for they laughed heartily when they heard the guide's assertion.

Thornton and his men, who were more used to water than land, were so distressed by the hardships of the way that we resolved to rest a day at Mikaronko. We brought Blair with us thus far, hoping to be able to buy a few goats for him to take back; but our hopes were not realised. He went back as he came.

At Mikaronko I was received as an old acquaintance. Provisions were scarce, a few ears of corn and a skinny fowl were all the food I could buy. The chimanga crop was not good, and the other crops were not fit for gathering. Kapichi and those in the village did not look as though they had suffered hunger; but want was said to be in the villages around, and Kapichi told me that hunger was so bad among some of his people that he had been losing by death as many as ten a day. Chimlolo explained that those who died were destitute Ajawa and Manganja, who came to Mikaronko hoping to find food.

The country between Mikaronko and Karambo, the next halt, was very thinly peopled. There was but little ground under cultivation, and hunger had been severely felt.

The scenery between Mikaronko and Karambo was not interesting—a grass-covered plain, thinly wooded, and without streams.

The chief of Karambo was called Yaminyaantu (an eater of men), but despite his ominous name, he had nothing of the canibal about him—porridge and nothing but porridge was visibly stamped on every feature. His village was a miserable collection of badly built huts, his people a miserable collection of half-starved men and women; the children, diseased and famine-stricken, were crawling about stark naked. A poor woman was sitting in front of her hut, watching us at dinner and vainly endeavouring to shield her new-born babe with her own ragged cloth. The wind just then was blowing freshly, and caused the babe to suffer, so I wrapped it up in a bit of blue calico, and I shall not readily forget the mother's look of gratitude.

Mengenichuri was the next halt, and the country between it and Karambo was as uninteresting as unlimited grass and stunted trees could make it. But it was a country well stocked with game. Bucks of various kinds were here; we saw some, but were not disposed for the chase. A huge wild boar, tail erect, plunged across our path in a state of great nervous excitement; and just before we arrived at the village, a leopard sprang up almost at my very feet, and bounded away in great affright.

The Jobfa, an excellent stream of water, flowed by Mengenichuri. It had no great volume of water, but close to the village it formed itself into a deep pool more than 200 yards long and 30 broad. The banks were covered with trees large and small, the tropical element in them being unmistakable, and a pleasanter stream for a bathe I met not with in Africa.

The village was foul; vegetable refuse, fish bones, the bones of buffalo and the larger kinds of deer were festering in heaps. The huts were tumbling to pieces; grass and weeds choked up the approaches; and the stench from human ordure was intolerable. Yet the inhabitants, of whom there seemed no lack, were fat and healthy. As we entered, some people were bringing in the remains of a buffalo, which a lion had killed the night before just outside the village.

A party of Tete elephant-hunters were there, the chief of whom were fine athletic men, with a cast of countenance expressive of great courage and determination. These men were slaves belonging to Tete merchants. The hunters are chosen from the general herd of slaves by their masters for their bravery and fidelity; and as it is to the interest of the owners to treat them well, they very rarely betray their confidence.

The life they lead accords well with their predilections. Servile labour is not imposed upon them. They may be away months in pursuit of their huge game; during which time they are always the welcome guests of the villages around their hunting-grounds. They are supplied with corn and shelter when they need it, and in exchange they supply their hosts with flesh, when they happen to kill either elephant or buffalo.

A successful hunter when he returns to his master meets with many favours; he struts about in gay attire, a slave still, but a very Hector in his bearing.

Ordinarily, a hunter will bring his master in £100 worth of ivory in the course of a year.

Besides this, these hunters form the best defence of Tete. Regular troops are there, but these men—active, hardened, daring, and good shots—form a more efficient guard in time of danger from hostile tribes than the European soldiers.

We left Mengenichuri soon after five in the morning, and though the distance to Machedwa, our next halt, was not less than thirty miles, we did it without much fatigue, for we had a good path through a level country.

The appearance of the country did not alter materially. We passed two or three conical hills, thickly wooded, but every-where else it was a plain, covered with grass—unlimited grass, and the usual complement of trees, which, though of larger growth than those passed on the previous day, were not more than 12 or 15 inches in diameter in the trunk.

At noon we rested by and bathed in the Moladzi, a very African-looking stream—shallow, rocky, and bordered with a tropical vegetation, among which the fan-palm was pleasantly conspicuous.

There was no lack of water in this march; we crossed streams every hour, though the country had certainly been without rain for some time.

We entered Machedwa about 4 P.M.; and Machedwa, though owning larger, better-kept, and more fertile gardens than any we had passed on the road, was more filthy in itself than Mengenichuri. We could not sleep in the huts—the odour made you vomit. In the morning a blue mouldiness was upon all our baggage, and a fierce cold had settled on myself. A walk of five hours through a well-cultivated country brought us to Inya Mitarari, a well-built, well-kept, clean, and comfortable village.

We were now on Portuguese territory. With the exception of two or three miles, the road to Tete from this place lay through the valley of the Rivuba, a considerable river, and where we crossed, about 100 yards broad. It is in this neighbourhood that coal was found, and we passed over a considerable tract of coal shale.

The valley of the Rivuba is the most fertile district in the neighbourhood of Tete ; it was thickly peopled, and the crops were looking better here than elsewhere. At one time the Portuguese had many residences in this valley ; now there was not one, for Chisaka, of whom I have spoken, ravaged it, and destroyed the houses—and the owners had not rebuilt.

When you leave the valley of the Rivuba, you are but a few miles from the Zambesi. You do not, however, see the river until close to it—a ridge of rocky ground which runs down to the water's edge, shutting it out from view.

The Zambesi by Tete is fully a mile broad. The appearance of Tete from the north bank of the river, from want of white-wash and verdure, was far from effective. The town rises gradually from the water's edge. The houses are large, well built, and of stone. The streets run parallel to each other and to the river. Behind the town, running parallel with it, but extending far beyond it on either side, is Mount Caroera, a hill of sandstone, destitute of vegetation, between 2,000 and 3,000 feet high. As is the mountain, so is the soil upon which the town is built, brown and bare ; and as are the soil and the mountain, so are the houses, brown and bare ; so that brown, brown, nothing but brown prevails everywhere. In consequence of this uniformity of colour, at a short distance you can scarcely distinguish the houses from the soil they stand upon.

Many cattle were feeding upon the stunted herbage by the brink of the river. Some of these beasts were fine animals, and would have brought no discredit upon an English farm. These lusty brutes were a pleasant sight to the eyes of a man fresh from a land of leanness and famine ; and their bellowing was equally pleasant to the ears.

When we entered, two European soldiers came up and saluted us, but recognising Thornton, they asked no questions. The Governor, who was sitting in the porch of his house, saluted us as we passed.

Thornton's chief friend was Senhor Clementina, who received us as hospitably as the most hospitable of his race.

The Tete merchants, generally, are men of no standing among their countrymen elsewhere than in Africa. They come principally from Goa with a small capital, which they hope in a short time to increase a thousand-fold, and then to return as great men to their Indian home. Sometimes their hopes are realized, for the profits of the Tete trade are enormous ; but more frequently their hopes are long deferred, and sometimes never realized. Great risks have to be run from hostile tribes, for the Portuguese traders have not, as a rule, a favourable reputation among the natives in the interior ; for some among them have not scrupled to plunder as well as to trade. Ivory is the thing they professedly seek.

Senhor Clementina had no acccommodation for us in the house he was occupying, so he assigned to us the half of one of the several large houses he owned in Tete ; but invited us to his table at all times.

We had but just entered upon our domicile when the Governor sent a soldier to enquire after our welfare, and in reply we said we would do ourselves the honour of waiting upon his Excellency.

The Governor was a gentlemanly and well-informed man ; and nothing could be kinder than his reception of us. He was married, and the father of several children ; his house was well cared for and furnished, and looked as though the owner was a man who loved his family, and studied to make home comfortable. He was not popular with the Tete merchants : he was said by them to be too much of a gentleman. The merchants, as a rule, do not think of making Tete a home ; they simply regard it as a place where they halt for a time, and care not to improve it in any way, or to cultivate the

comforts of home. But the Governor had a care for these
things, and commenced certain sanitary works which touched
the pockets of the merchants, and made certain regulations,
which tended to an improved public morality ; and so he was
not popular.

Of the Mission he had nothing to say but what was agreeable. He had heard of our difficulties, hopes, and privations,
and offered us all the assistance in his power. His wife, a
most agreeable lady, was vehement in her expressions of sympathy. Their padre, she said, was well cared for, had but
little to do, and was provided with all the comforts of
life ; so he must take his chance with the rest of them here-
after. But the English Missionaries, who had left their
country, their friends, and all that was dear to them, to come
out to such an 'abominable country,' in order to teach the
heathens, were in a very different position. They would suffer
a great deal, that was certain ; they would all die, that was
certain too ; but what then ?—they would all go to heaven.
And so, notwithstanding hardships and trials, they were greatly
to be envied.

Having made the Governor aware of the immediate occasion of our visit, he said that Senhor Manoel, who had a farm
about twenty miles below Tete, was the most likely person to
supply our wants ; but he added,—

'Should you fail in getting what you require, let me know,
and though I have but few cattle, large or small, and have no
intention of parting with them for an ordinary purpose, yet
they shall be heartily at your service.'

This was a practical proof of kindly feeling, for Tete was
suffering greatly from famine—indeed, so much so, that all trade
was suspended : and the masters, not having food to give their
slaves, had allowed them to go where they pleased ; and more
than three-fourths had gone away.

We went down the Zambesi to Senhor Manoel's on the 10th
of March, but started too late to arrive at our destination
before dark, or that night at all, had not Thornton been perfectly acquainted with the river.

Senhor Manoel (a Goa man) did his best to please us, and

make us comfortable for the night, and upon hearing of the object of our visit, at once said we could have as many sheep and goats as we pleased; and that to him a promise to pay from us was as good as payment itself. So Thornton, as the simplest way of transacting this business, made himself the Senhor's debtor, and our creditor, and this done, promised to pay £60 for sixty goats and forty sheep; and we then went to rest with minds relieved of a great anxiety. Thornton slept on the table; I, in consideration of advanced years and fever-aching joints, on a less obdurate couch.

As he left us for the night, Senhor Manoel, with a grim smile said:

'Don't leave any of your things on the floor, for the dogs will come in; they are purposely kept hungry, and are apt to eat anything they find loose, no matter what.'

I took my revolver from my knapsack, and put it at hand ready for use, and was careful of my boots; but Thornton was not so careful of his worsted stockings, and in the morning we found the dogs—big, ferocious brutes—had torn them to pieces.

Next morning I saw what Senhor Manoel's establishment was. There were two small houses for himself and family, a few sheds for the slaves, a large store-house, houses for goats and sheep, and a large rectangular cattle-yard, admirably fenced in. Cleanliness was the marked characteristic of the whole place; and slaves swept everywhere with a care and caution which showed that this was a duty they dare not perform negligently. Six men came from one of the sheds, chained together by the necks. Two of them looked fiercely sullen; three looked careless; but the other, as though he would escape his fetters shortly—emaciated in body and thoroughly broken in spirit; the stamp of death was upon him—he could scarcely stand. Our host explained that these men had robbed him, and that the chain was their punishment. How long their punishment was to last he did not say —till death probably. A girl and a boy were also chained together; each at the extremity of a long chain, which could not have weighed less than fifty pounds. When they moved from place to place, while at work—for their ordinary occupations were not dispensed with—each took up in a bundle the half of the chain, and carried it on the shoulder. What their offence was I did not learn, but from their sickly appearance it did not seem that they could endure their punishment much longer. The slaves, however, not in punishment, looked well fed and contented. Their education was completed; they had lost all sense of freedom; they were evidently reconciled to their life of bondage.

Chimlolo, Damanji, and others of my men, who had not been subject to this system of education, were chilled with horror; they were almost afraid to breathe or speak while we stayed at this place.

Our hostess—the Senhor's wife—was the daughter of a native chief who once sacked Tete. This man was dead, and his son, a very mild edition of the father, in order to get the assistance of the Portuguese against another chief with whom he quarrelled, had acknowledged himself a Portuguese subject.

Senhora Manoel seemed a help meet for her husband, or for his circumstances rather. Her civilization had not advanced very far, but she had a good head, was good-looking, eschewed the lip-ring—as indeed do all the Nungwi and Tete women—and was not much darker than her lord and master. In her communications with the slaves, she was the cold, self-possessed, and imperious woman, whose word was law to be obeyed by the sturdiest; but with her husband and children she was submissive and amiable.

There were three children—two girls and a boy, of the respective ages of four, five, and six. These little people gave themselves great airs, and spoke to the attendant slaves in haughtiest tones. Their manners would have excited laughter, had you not seen at the same time, men with strong and lusty thews, crouching down and trembling like beaten hounds before them.

Thornton climbed a mountain—Pingwas—to take observations during the day; and I, after an ineffectual attempt to get to the Ruenia, a river where gold dust was found, stayed in the house shaking with fever.

During the day a messenger informed Senhor Manoel first, that Chibisa had been shot by Tireri; secondly, that Tireri had been made prisoner by Belchior, put into chains, and sent down to the Governor of Sena.

Chibisa committed a fatal error in disregarding our advice to go back quietly to Doa, and in seeking revenge upon Makururu by allying himself with Tireri. The bone of contention which was the immediate cause of his death was a tusk of ivory. An elephant was killed close to Doa; a tusk was brought to Chibisa, as chief; Tireri claimed it—Chibisa resisted —and Tireri shot him with his own hands. And this was the end of Chibisa; a man who had raised himself to eminence among his countrymen by an unusual display of daring and ability, and who naturally had capacity for great things.

We walked back to Tete on the 12th. The goats and sheep were sent on the night before.

There were three classes of soldiers at Tete. Those who came out as colonists as well as soldiers, who were men of good character; the degradado, Europeans also, but convicts for life; and the native corps. These last were the most useful, despite their shambling gait, for they can live like the natives, and the climate is all their own.

Such of the officers as I saw were gentlemen.

There were not many European women in Tete—most of those there were the wives of the soldier colonists. The better class of European women are here very short-lived. They may have themselves to blame to a great extent for this. They live idle lives, rarely exerting themselves to walk; if they visit a neighbour, or go to church, they are carried in a masheela (palanquin); and most of them die in child-birth. The Governor's lady was said to be most active; she looked after her family herself, and when she visited or went to church, frequently walked. But she also died before I left the country.

The half-caste women in Tete held a very equivocal position —few were married.

Before we left, the Governor made us a handsome present of goats, and offered to be responsible for sending to us any number of cattle we might need at any future time, if we would

send him a letter. And he also offered in the name of his
Government, any amount of territory to the Mission, should
our necessities compel us to leave the Shire, and our inclinations lead us to settle near Tete. A thing we were not at all
likely to do, for slavery demoralizes all, and paralyzes all effort
for good, and Tete was the stronghold for slavery; where the
town cross should have been, they had erected a whipping-post
for slaves.

WHIPPING-POST FOR SLAVES, AT TETE.

Our return home was wearisome and tedious in the extreme.
Our animals were a never-ending cause of anxiety, for we had
to keep them from straying during the day, and from being
carried off by wild beasts during the night.

It was my first experience as a shepherd, literally, and it did

not lead me to regard the occupation with favour. Had our
flock been all sheep, it might have been less harassing, for the
sheep keep together and go along without much trouble ; but
the goats are incorrigible vagrants. Was there a bye-path
they should not take, they were sure to take it; did they pass
anything they had no right to eat, they made frantic attempts
to devour it. I do not wonder at the Scriptural distinction
between the sheep and the goats. We had to carry the creatures over the rivers, and sometimes to make folds for them at
night, to doctor them by the way, and to nurse the young
ones.

I had not heard the roar of a lion in Africa until this journey. The first night we heard it we were safely sheltered in a
village, and though the beast made the night hideous with his
roaring, and our creatures were in a state of great fright, we
were not much concerned—they and we were both safely
housed. The next night we had to camp in the bush, and
then two lions visited us; they went round and round our
little encampment, and made sleep impossible. We kept them
off by fires and gun-firing. We found next morning that they
had been very close to us, for we saw their foot-prints within
thirty yards of where we had been lying. The scent of our
flock was strong on the ground, and the lions did not leave us
for several days; we saw their foot-prints in the path by day,
and we had them about us several times after by night. I
think they must have followed us to the Shire, for soon after
our return we heard lions for the first time in the neighbourhood of our station.

In returning we all had fever—Thornton so severely that
we were obliged to halt at Mengenichuri for three days ; Damanji was quite knocked up, and we were obliged to bring him
on in a litter. At one time I had five of my men in furious
fever. They laid it to the karapat, an insect met with at
Tete, in appearance something like a woodlouse, whose bite
produces fever of a very severe character. Two or three
times, fever was so strong upon me that, though I did not lie
up, I was in greatest pain, and staggered along the road like a
drunken man. It was a most painful journey, but by God's

help, and dint of dogged endurance and perseverance, we reached Mikaronko on the 27th of March.

I sent our guide on to the Mission station two days before, apprising our brethren of our intention to wait at Mikaronko until they sent us medical comforts and more men, as we were very short-handed. And I also sent forward an instalment of our flock, twelve of our sturdiest sheep and goats, for I was most anxious on Dickinson's account, feeling that in his delicate state of health, deprivation of fresh meat for any length of time would probably be death to him.

Kapichi acted like a thorough good fellow, and swore a never-ending friendship for the English.

About midday on the 28th, Blair arrived at Mikaronko with the requisite assistance. He brought a letter from Procter, which wrung from me an expression of grief that I could not repress on reading the first sentence :—

'Your letter, which I received last night, gave us the greatest possible pleasure, and I would I could offer in return as good news as that which it brought us; but alas! I

DR. DICKINSON.

have to tell you, in the deepest grief, that our dear Dickinson, after a severe illness of eight days, has left us for the better home, where his will be the rest, we believe, which is granted to the faithful and devoted like himself.'

Dickinson was dead! Dear, good, gentle-minded, loving-hearted, truly Christian man! He died on the evening of March 17. The news of his death was a great blow to me, for though I knew he ran great risk by continuing with us, I was not expecting to hear of his decease. Physically he was most unfitted for our life of privation and hardship, but spiritually and mentally no man could have been better qualified than he. He was a true Christian missionary.

The remainder of Procter's letter, and another letter from Dr. Kirk, with the information which Blair could give, put us in possession of the state of affairs at the Mission since we had been away.

A few days after we left Clarke became worse, and Dickinson so bad that Procter and Waller sent down the river to the 'Pioneer' for help. Drs. Livingstone and Kirk at once came off to their assistance, but Dickinson had died half an hour before they arrived. Their arrival, however, saved Clarke's life, for though Dr. Livingstone was compelled to return to the ship, Dr. Kirk stayed in attendance upon him for several days, and he now reported hopefully of him. Poor fellow, his head had been distressingly affected.

Waller was all but knocked up—exhausted by fever, and sorely tried by constant watching and anxiety. Change seemed essential for him.

This state of things made me resolve to get home as quickly as possible, for now that Blair with additional help had arrived, my presence would be of more use at the station than with the flock. Thornton thought so too; so next day, after walking to Chinkoko's, where the flock halted for the night, I took a man and a lad with me, and went ahead. I slept that night at a village at the foot of the hills, and would have gone farther, and slept in the bush, but a storm was brewing —indeed it had been stormy during the whole of the journey back, and I dreaded another drenching.

We were off, however, long before daylight, and walked till midday, without resting. After our rest, the men's speed did not keep pace with my inclinations, so I left them, and went on by myself, trusting to my own sagacity for finding the right path. But the grass had grown considerably, and in many places quite blocked up the paths, and I lost my way several times, and so walked much farther than I should have done had I remained with the men; nevertheless, I was home two hours before them, and though during the day I could not have walked less than forty miles, the excitement of my brain was such that I was not at that moment conscious of fatigue.

I found our usually quiet station in a state of astonishment. The 'Pioneer' and the 'Lady Nyassa' had just arrived. Nearly seventeen months had elapsed since the 'Pioneer' had gone down the river. I mention this because many have thought that Dr. Livingstone was more or less with us during the whole of the time we were in that part of Africa.

The first-fruits of the flock had also arrived, and had been equally divided between the Mission and the Expedition.

Poor Clarke was looking very shattered in body, but he was bright in mind and spirit. Dr. Kirk and Mr. C. Livingstone had dysentery. Dr. Livingstone looked careworn and aged. All were cordial and rejoicing at our success, for all had been reduced to a great strait for want of fresh meat.

I was very thankful to be back again, but the sight of Dickinson's empty hut, the loss of his affectionate welcome, sent me to my own hut with a sad heart.

I visited his grave ; it was close to that of Scudamore. Side by side, until the great awakening, lie the two friends. They were indeed 'lovely and pleasant in their lives, and in their deaths they were not divided.' I know there are those who look upon the loss of those who thus died in Africa as a great calamity, as one of the greatest misfortunes that could have befallen the Church. Anguish of heart at their deaths I certainly felt—I should have been something less or more than human if I had not—but as a calamity I could never regard their loss. Death is not the worst thing that can befal the Christian. The Church flourishes most when it can point to

THE GRAVES OF THE REV. H. C. SCUDAMORE AND JOHN DICKINSON, ESQ.

its martyrs. There is no conquest without suffering. We have no right to expect to be able to accomplish a Christ-like work without, in some measure, enduring a Christ-like suffering.

I cannot sympathise with that state of feeling, now so prevalent, which willingly sacrifices thousands of lives in the pursuit of commerce or political aggrandisement, but reprobates as an uncalled-for sacrifice, the lives that are given up for Christ's sake.

We were away just over the month. We left on February 27, and returned on March 30. Thornton arrived two days later, leaving the flock at Michirinji under the care of Blair, who came in with it on April 3.

The ships went on to Matiti on April 1—Waller, who greatly needed change, going up with them.

CHAPTER XX.

DEATH OF MR. THORNTON.—LAST DAYS AT CHIBISA'S.

BEFORE the ships left, we consulted upon future plans, and decided, when Waller returned, to make preparations at once for a move back to the hills. Mbame was dead; we could occupy his place, and this we resolved to do. It had not been possible to get back to the hills before this; we had not the means, and the whole country was in a state of distraction. Now our means were abundant, the country was quiet, for the Manganja were not, and the Ajawa, though they had not yet entered upon a thorough occupation of the Highlands, would soon do so, for events proceed with such rapidity in that land, that we felt certain that in the course of a year the old villages would be rebuilt, as they occupied the best positions, and that the only difference we should find in the Highlands would be peace, and the Ajawa and the inhabitants instead of the Manganja. Of the Ajawa feeling towards us we had no reason to fear; our people declared they would be glad to have us among them as friends, and they were joyful when they heard that it was our intention to live with them.

Thornton, after staying a day or two with us to rest, went up to the ships. He seemed to have recovered from fatigue and fever, and was cheerful and very happy, for [he made ;his first Communion with us on the Sunday, and I expected to see him back in a few days, as he did not intend to stay with the ships. But when Waller returned to us on April 14, he said that dysentery and fever still prevailed on board the ' Pioneer,' and that Thornton was suffering severely. I did not think that his illness was more serious than any other we were constantly witnessing or suffering from, and so did not go up to see him; but on the evening of the 21st, messengers came down to us from Dr. Livingstone with such a sad account of Thornton's state of health, that I resolved to go up to Matiti next morning.

But death was beforehand with me; indeed before the messengers sent by Dr. Livingstone arrived at our station, my dear young friend—I had learnt to love him as though he were my younger brother—had breathed his last.

I found all hands assembled around his grave. The funeral service had just been said by Dr. Livingstone—earth was being cast on earth—and there, under a large baobab tree, about two hundred yards from the river, rested all that was mortal of Richard Thornton. He was but twenty-five years of age, having come out to Africa when only nineteen.

Thornton was an able and energetic young man, and had it pleased God to have spared him, he would have been distinguished among the most distinguished of our adventurous men of science.

The journey to Tete, without doubt, greatly contributed to the fatal termination of his last illness. It was not simply the journey with him, for he was up every hill on the road, hewing his way with axe in hand to the summit, when there was no path, in order to make theodolite observations of the country. He was an enthusiast in that walk of life which he had chosen for himself, and his never-tiring energy was an astonishment to many of the Portuguese debilitated by sinful excess, and incapable of understanding exertion save for filthy lucre. During the time he was travelling with Baron von der Decken he rarely had fever, and on his return to the Zambesi he had also, I believe, escaped it, until the journey back from Tete. Being constantly with him on that journey I did not perceive any change in his personal appearance, but others said he looked worn out and exhausted, and that the constant exposure and fatigue to which we had been subject had greatly changed him.

Our move to the hills was again and again deferred. Dysentery attacked Procter; he had not been really well since his return from Quillimane. Those river journeys were grievous things. Burrup and Dickinson had their strength undermined by their exertions in coming up the rivers, and Dickinson was of opinion that Scudamore's journey to Shupanga greatly contributed to weaken him, and Waller came back in November in a very painful condition. He was greatly distressed by boils, and I doubt if he recovered from the effects of that journey for months afterwards.

Thinking change would do Procter good, we sent him up to Matiti, but he returned on May 13 rather worse than better. Then I fell ill. The reaction was a long time coming, but when it did come, I felt how much that Tete journey had punished me. It was not so much fever, as an entire prostration of strength, accompanied by violent pains in the head, which were almost overpowering when I attempted to move. I was ignorant of it at the time, but for some days I was in momentary danger of a paralytic seizure. So the preparations for the move to the hills were of necessity deferred.

The news that we received from the expedition, from time to time, was not encouraging. The attempt to get the 'Nyassa' on to the Upper Shire seemed hopeless, and after a little time that attempt was given up. Men and other means were wanting.

Dr. Livingstone suffered from dysentery severely: the condition of the majority of the members of the expedition was physically wretched, and Dr. Kirk, Mr. C. Livingstone, and four of the European sailors left for home on the 19th. Clarke went away with them, for Dr. Kirk said that it was impossible for him to stay longer with us without utmost risk to life or reason.

On the 27th, Procter, fancying himself better, went with Waller and Adams, and a party of our men, to find a site on the hills for our future station; bnt he overrated his powers; he broke down exhausted at Chipindu's, and the whole party returned next day.

I was still quite unable to make the least exertion.

I think we must both have died had it not been for the constant care of Dr. Meller, who came down to us repeatedly from the ships, aided by suitable medicines, good food and wine.

Before the people on the hills died out, they sowed their corn seed; that seed was bearing good fruit, with no one to reap it, so our people asked if they might go and gather from the deserted gardens. We gave them permission, and they, with others, reaped a good harvest.

Owing to the abundant latter rain, there were successive crops of chimanga on all the islands, and in all the gardens on the banks of the river, and plenty abounded in the huts of our village. Our people were better off than they had been since they had been with us; they had corn in the house, and corn in the field, and another crop, if not two, in prospect—altogether enough to carry them on until the first fruits of the next year's harvest. It had been a hard fight to get them into that position, but they were at last independent of us, wealthy, free men. And they were proud of their position, and thankful to us for having, by God's help, made them what they were. A happier set of people you could not find. To see them at this time working heartily, eating heartily, getting broad with good living, no one would have dreamt of the starvation period through which they had passed. Now and then a poor creature, a mere animated skeleton, the last existing, may be, of some Manganja village, appeared, and reminded you of what had been, and what still was, with the remnant of that people. We felt it to be our duty to take charge of several of these destitutes for a time, and our people took to others, treating them kindly, and paying them well for any help they were able to give them.

I know it has been thought by friends at home, that taking the people released from the slavers under our protection was a mistake, and that the keeping of them until they could keep themselves entailed a very great expense upon the Mission. I care not to discuss the first objection, but with regard to the question of expense, it is simply a mistake to imagine that our poor friends were a great expense to the Mission. At Magomero it cost but little to feed them, for while food was to be had it was cheap enough. Their keep during the famine, in consequence of our having to purchase corn of the Portuguese, was much more expensive; but from the time we released them, until we ceased to provide for them, they did not entail a greater expenditure than £500. But if we deduct from this the price of their labour for us, certainly worth £200, we have nearly 200 souls saved for the time being from slavery, starvation, or death, for £300.

But all this, without doubt, if nothing more had been contemplated or attempted, would have been, considering the highest object of our mission, unsatisfactory. I believe, however, that with them, as with many of our own people at home, the way to improve their spiritual condition, is to show that you are not indifferent to their bodily wants, always keeping before them, that what you do for them is from highest motives. It is true these people had made but little advance in spiritual matters; but their lives were purer; they were giving up old superstitions; and God, as a Being to be adored, loved and obeyed, whose will was to be their rule of life, was now common to their minds, and to a certain extent influencing their actions. But we could not say of any of them that they had been 'fully instructed in the truths of Christianity,' or that they had manifested 'a desire to conform their lives to the Gospel standard,' or had given any 'unmistakable evidence of a change of heart.' None therefore but those who died were baptized, because, as yet, none had exhibited that standard of repentance which our Church requires of adults before receiving baptism. But it seems inconsistent to expect the heathen to be experimentally conversant with the Christian religion before baptism.   Personally I should not have hesitated to baptize Chimlolo and several others under our care, and had we remained with them doubtless they would soon have been baptized.

On June 16, Mbame's sons, and two men who belonged to Soche, came for permission to live near us.   From them we gained information of the Highlands.

Chinsunzi, Kankomba, and every other chief of importance about Zomba, were dead, or fugitives among the Anguru.   Magomero was destroyed, but Chigunda was said to be living with the Ajawa.   All other villages about Magomero were also destroyed, and the inhabitants fugitives, or in the hands of the Ajawa.   Mongazi was dead, and Soche had sought sanctuary on Mount Choro.

Mbame's sons had been made prisoners by the Ajawa, but had managed to escape.   The Ajawa were still living in their camps, but it was evident that want of food, divisions among themselves, and the incapacity of the land to support any great number of people in one place, would compel them to separate, and settle in various parts of the country.

Every day it was more and more certain, that if we were to continue the Mission in that part of Africa, it must be among the Ajawa.   Speaking to Chimlolo upon this subject, he said :

'Those Ajawa who fear you do so because they think you are their enemies.   When they know you are their friends, they will fear no more ; they will like their English fathers as much as we do.'

Procter still continued ill.   There was no abatement of dysenteric symptoms, and his liver was manifestly affected, not incurably, it was hoped, but fast hastening to that condition, do what Meller could to better it.   His only chance of life, or future usefulness, was to get home as soon as he could, and it was agreed that he should quit the country with Dr. Meller, who was leaving the expedition, on August 1.

There was no help for it ; he could not stay ; though when he was gone, I alone of the original staff of clergy would remain.

Towards the end of June we were daily expecting reinforcements from home.   And we had not to expect long, for on the
morning of June 26, our boys raised the cry of ' Galawi Anglesi!' (an English boat), and that boat contained Bishop
Tozer and the Rev. Charles Alington.

Having heard from the Portuguese of the deaths of Scudamore and Dickinson, and knowing also that the expedition was
recalled, Bishop Tozer thought it inadvisable to bring all those
he had brought out with him up to the station, and had left
Dr. Steere, Mr. Drayton, who had been engaged to the Mission by Bishop Mackenzie, and three artisans, at Mazara,
while he and Mr. Alington made themselves acquainted with
our position and circumstances, and consulted with us.

The older members of the Mission were unanimous in thinking that the Shire Highlands offered the best, and, under all
circumstances, the only position we could occupy in that part
of Africa.   And we did not think the attempt to hold it hopeless at all.   Our influence among the surviving Manganja was
great, the Ajawa were inclined to be friendly, we had stores
and medical comforts for eighteen months, war had ceased,
and peace was not likely to be quickly disturbed, as there was
no one to oppose the Ajawa, and with the people we had about
us we judged we might make a successful return to the hills.
At all events, we could not help thinking, considering how
much had been paid for the experience and position which we
had gained, and that we had made arrangements with the Portuguese for a regular transit of stores from Mozambique,
that the attempt to hold that country longer was warranted.

The difficulties in the way were doubtless great.   The river
journey was long and dangerous; the land had been desolated
by war and famine; the original inhabitants were all but ex-
terminated; the Ajawa were predominant, and they (some
thought) might regard us as enemies; animal food—an absolute necessity—was not to be had nearer than Tete; Dr.
Livingstone was going out of the country, and the original
staff was now reduced by death, or departures for home to save
life, to one clergyman (myself), Waller, Adams, Blair, and
Johnson.   Added to this, my health was so impaired that Dr.

Meller stated that longer continuance in Africa would be attended with the most serious consequences, and that a return home was absolutely necessary to stop the effects which the climate was daily producing on my constitution.

These were, without doubt, grave obstacles in the way of a return to the hills; and Bishop Tozer informed us that he had given Dr. Steere instructions to go to Quillimane, while he came up to us, to ask permission of the Governor to occupy Morumbala, if it were found suited for the purposes of the Mission, and it was deemed advisable not to return to the Shire Highlands.

Nothing definitely was settled when Bishop Tozer left us, on July 6, taking with him Procter and Blair, the former to go home at once, the latter to return to us with final instructions. Mr. Alington was left behind to supply Procter's place.

The immediate necessity for leaving the land was not so urgent for me as it was for Procter: indeed I thought that if we removed to a healthy locality, I should, with renewed hopes, recover former strength.

Before the Bishop left, he saw Dr. Livingstone at Matiti; and heard what he had to say upon the practicability of re-occupying the Shire Highlands. I need scarcely say that Dr. Livingstone urged an immediate return to them.

Dr. Meller left the expedition on July 17. He had been a good friend to the Mission. We were greatly indebted to him; and though for our own sakes we deeply regretted his departure, for his sake we could not be sorry that he was leaving a land where life had been to him almost perpetual misery, for he suffered constantly from fever.

On August 6, a boat arrived from Mazara with a letter from Bishop Tozer to myself and Waller, informing us that he had decided to make the experiment of reorganising the Mission on Morumbala, and giving instructions for the removal from Chibisa's. There was also another letter addressed to myself, privately, in which the Bishop informed me that, considering the strongly expressed opinion of Dr. Meller, it was clearly my duty to go home: he would not admit of any other alternative short of an immediate return to England.

Johnson was, at his own request, to leave with me.

The removal to Morumbala involved the giving up of all our people, with the exception of the orphan boys. Had it been possible, however, to take them, the people themselves would have refused to go; with the exception of a few poor women and girls who were destitute, they had all decided upon remaining where they were. At Morumbala, they felt, they would have been an isolated body in the midst of strangers and possible enemies, far away from their own tribe.

They were very sad for the moment when we told them that we were really going away. But long depression of spirit is not natural to the African: he rarely doubles his misfortunes by anticipating them; not from design, but from constitution, he acts literally upon the injunction 'let us eat, drink, and be merry, for to-morrow we die.' And as they had both to eat and to drink in abundance with a few exceptions, they put off thought of the morrow.

After I had said farewell words to them, and had gone back to my hut, poor Jessiwiranga, 'the excellent Jessiwiranga,' as Bishop Mackenzie styled her, came to me with her babe, for she was married to Sesimanja, and sitting down on the floor began to cry; not loudly and boisterously, after the usual fashion of the natives, but quietly and sadly. Said she:

'I do not like our English fathers going from us; they said they would never forsake us. It is bad, very bad, to lose them. When they are gone, what will happen? The Chakundas will come and make slaves of us again, and then what will become of my babe?' And she hugged her little one as though to shield it.

I comforted her as well as I could, but my heart was as sad as her own. Good, motherly woman! I shall never forget the unwearied kindness she showed to our suffering little ones at Magomero.

It was about 3.30 P.M., on August 7, when I took my leave of Waller, Alington, and Adams. The people assembled to wish me farewell—sorrowful enough for the moment. I watched them, as they stood on the bank waving their hands, until the bend in the river hid them from sight. And then— Oh! to me this was a very bitter parting.

During the first hour, the people that were left in the valley, hearing the songs of the boatmen, came to the bank of the river, and shouted and waved their farewells. I knew most of them personally, for all, more or less, had in some way or another been brought under our influence, and it was owing to our protecting presence that they had been able to cultivate in security, and to reap their harvests.

We were at Malo on Sunday morning, the 9th. After we passed Mankokwe's, until we reached this place, we did not see a single human being in the valley. All seemed to have perished.

THE HUT IN WHICH BISHOP MACKENZIE DIED.

I visited the hut in which Bishop Mackenzie died. It had not been occupied since his death.

I visited his grave. The place was so overgrown with giant rushes, grass and bindweed, that it was with greatest difficulty I could find the precise spot where he lay. All traces of the grave were obliterated by the heavy rains, and had it not been for the bamboo cross, which Captain Wilson and Dr. Kirk put up when taking the ladies down the river, no one would have been able to say with certainty, ' Here lies Bishop Mackenzie.' The cross which Dr. Livingstone erected was some distance from the grave itself.

I approached this holy ground with a very full heart—with saddest feelings. But as I stood by the resting-place of this first Apostle to Central Africa, his spirit seemed to be about me, and a glow of hope, the first I had felt for many days, relieved my sorrow. I was cast down, but I no longer despaired; I felt, and I still feel, notwithstanding the mysterious movements of Almighty God with respect to this mission, that the going forth of Bishop Mackenzie was not only not fruitless, but that it was the first step in the wisdom of God towards the conversion of the tribes to whom he went,— the first right movement towards the extermination of that iniquitous traffic, the slave trade, which keeps these tribes in a state of constant terror and strife, and degrades them nearly to the condition of the brutes that perish.

The wisdom of God has ever been foolishness with men, because they see but an abstract act, the present result of which is the very opposite of their wishes or intentions. What did Adam and the Old Testament worthies understand of the infinite meaning of the ' Seed of the woman,' who had been promised as the Curer of human woe, until that promise had quickened into meaning by subsequent events—until in the fulness of time the Eternal God flashed upon the prophetic vision, and the Messiah stood forth as he who was to come ?

What did the sorrowing Apostles know of Him for whom they mourned when they said, ' And we trusted that it should have been He who should redeem Israel ? ' And what can we now understand of the wisdom and intentions of the Providence which raised up in Bishop Mackenzie a chosen vessel, and allowing him just to breathe the holy Name of Jesus to the Heathen, then removed him from his work, reserves his labour for another, and withdraws the mission to another part of the wilderness ? We can say nothing but ' Thy will be done.' It is not as we hoped; it is not as we in our blindness expected it would be. But to say that the life and death of Bishop Mackenzie were in vain ; that the life and death of those his fellow-workers, who so soon followed him to the grave, were in vain, is to question the purpose of Almighty God, to murmur at His method of fulfilling His own intention. No, they did

not live in vain; they did not die in vain.   That land of darkness and death is consecrated to Christ as the resting-place of
those good men.   Their dust, and the dust also of that little
band of native infant Christians, who, as they died of the
pestilence and the famine, received holy baptism, and in the
full purity of their regenerated nature entered Paradise, will
cry aloud to God, ' Lord, how long wilt Thou hide Thyself, for
ever ? '   And it will not cry in vain—it cannot cry in vain;
but it will be, I doubt not, the first fruits of a glorious resurrection of multitudes from that very land, when our Blessed
Lord shall come in glory to gather His people to Himself.

     We halted on the night of the 10th inst. in the Morumbala
Marsh, and arrived at Morumbala on the afternoon of the 11th,
where we found a good house had been built at the base, and
another about a third of the way up the mountain.   I found

NIGHT HALT IN MORUMBALA MARSH.

Blair and Kalloway, the carpenter, at the lower house; from
them I learnt that the Bishop and Harrison were still at

Mazara; that Dr. Steere, Mr. Drayton, and Sivill, the brick-layer, were at the upper house. I slept below.

Next morning I went up the mountain. As far as the house, the road, though rough and steep, was less difficult than that up to the Shire Highlands. The difficulty was higher up, and I did not attempt it. Dr. Steere looked very well; Mr. Drayton like a man who had made acquaintance with African fever. Sivill I did not see, he was shivering under the blankets.

We left Morumbala, and went on till midnight; and then moored ourselves to a sand island in the middle of the Zambesi.

Next day, the 13th, we fell in with Bishop Tozer; he, with Harrison, was going up to Morumbala in a canoe with the last of the Mission stores. We sat talking together for more than an hour, and then parted; he went up, and I down the river.

It was past sundown when we reached Mazara.

On the 16th I joined Procter and Meller, who were at the Kongone awaiting a ship, which, according to arrangements made known to Bishop Tozer by Captain Gardiner of the 'Orestes,' was daily expected.

But these arrangements were not carried out. We waited at the Kongone until October 23. Procter then made his way across country to Quillimane, while I and Meller, who was too ill to undertake the land journey at all, or the river journey by himself, went up the Zambesi in a canoe to Mazara: from thence we descended the Naquaqua river to Quillimane, and then sailed to Mozambique in a trading yacht. Two days after our arrival at Mozambique, H.M.S. 'Ariel' came in, and her commander, Captain Chapman, at once most kindly agreed to receive us on board, and take us down to the Cape, at which place, after leaving Procter at Natal, we arrived on December 15.

I cannot conclude these my personal experiences with the Mission in Africa, without expressing my gratitude for the kindness we received while waiting at the coast from the Por-tuguese generally, and especially from Senhor Mesquita, the officer in command of the military stationed at the Kongone, and Senhor José Nuges, of Quillimane; to the generous hospitality of these two gentlemen it is owing that we were saved from much inconvenience and privation.

ADDENDA.

AFTER I left the Station, my dear friend Waller made final preparations for the removal to Morumbala. But it seemed to him, as to me, a terrible thing to leave our people for whom we had struggled so long, and who had proved, themselves worthy of all that we had done for them, to the mercy of the first gang of men-stealers that might come to Chibisa's. An alliance with the Makololo could not be depended upon for them, and they were cut off from the main body of their tribe. If Kepane, the Ajawa chief, who held most of the Highland districts with which we were acquainted, would regard them as his friends and give them his protection, their position would be more secure, as in case of molestation from any quarter they could then go safely to the hills. So, after consultation with Chimlolo, Damanji, and some others, Waller resolved to send them up to Kepane to invite him to the Mission Station. They were gone several days, but when they returned they were accompanied by Kepane and about fifty of his principal men, most of whom were armed with guns. The conduct of Kepane proved that, had other circumstances been favourable, we might have returned to the hills with perfect safety—that the Ajawa were quite willing to receive us as friends.

Waller, who had become skilful in the native tongue, told him of our object in coming into the land, explained the motives which led us to interfere with the slavers, and the people of his own tribe at Chirumba and Chikala, and dwelt upon all the horror and misery which came upon Ajawa as well as Manganja through their dealings with the slave traders.

Kepane listened to all that Waller said, and replied that he

well knew that the English were not his enemies or the enemies of his people, and assented to all that had been said
about the evil results of the slave trade, and expressed his
willingness to engage in other and less injurious trade if we
could show him how to do so.

Then Waller made him acquainted with the principal object he had in view in sending for him, and he at once cordially responded. He would look upon our people as the
children of the English; he would treat them as he would
treat his own offspring; he would defend them as long as he
could defend himself; he was master of the hill country, and
they might come and go whenever they liked, and no harm
should come to them; and when we came back, as he hoped
we should do, we should see that he had not abused the trust
we had placed in him.

Kepane stayed several days at the station, and he visited
the 'Pioneer' at Matiti before he returned to the hills.

Waller managed to bring about a reconciliation between him
and the Makololo; for before this they had been at variance,
he having received some injury at their hands.

One would be glad to know whether this man has kept
faith with our people? I think he has. They were left with
him in trust, and the African has a strong sense of the responsibility of such a position. They will be living in the
constant expectation of seeing some of us again; they will
keep alive that expectation in his mind, and he will fear to
deal treacherously with us. I have no doubt that they are in
some sort acting as missionaries among the Ajawa—not, of
course, in the highest sense, they were not prepared for that
—but in every assembly they will speak of what we did, they
will tell of our love and kindness as well as of our power, and
they will be able to say that love for God, the desire to do
God's will, and to make them acquainted with the knowledge
of the Lord, were the mainspring and motive of all our
actions. For years to come the English missionaries will be
talked about in the villages of the Ajawa. Around their fires
at night, by the blacksmith's forge, under the khotla tree,
wherever men congregate in that land, our words will be re-

corded, our deeds recounted, and the simple lessons of right and wrong, of truth and goodwill, which we were able to instil into their minds, will not be lost—they will be disseminated. For years to come these people will live in the expectation of seeing us again. They will visit the graves of our brethren, and they will say ' Surely the English will return;' for the African, unless carried away by force, never forsakes the graves of his brethren. And shall their expectations be in vain? God forbid! I live in the hope that a way back to these people will ere long be reopened, that the Church will again send forth to them a Bishop and a goodly staff of clergy and laity. Temporary causes, it is true, made it necessary that we should leave them when we did; but they did nothing to warrant us in deserting them.

There was another subject which gave my friend Waller much anxiety. Among our people were some ten or twelve girls and women who were entirely dependent on us—most of the women being old or infirm, and the girls orphans. The Mission was now no longer able to protect these poor creatures, but Waller could not find it in his heart to forsake them, and so he resigned the position he held under the Bishop and took them with him, on his own responsibility, to Morumbala, where he supported them until he was able, five months afterwards, to carry them with him to the Cape of Good Hope, and there distribute them among various Christian families for protection.

My connection with the Mission having now ceased, I give the remainder of its story in the words of the Report for 1865 :

' A residence of a few months at the new station (Morumbala) showed that it would be quite impossible, for many reasons, to make it the permanent head-quarters of the Mission. Early in 1864, therefore, it was determined to leave that part of Africa altogether, and to attempt to reach the interior from some other point. With this view the whole party left the Zambesi for the Cape. After staying there some weeks and fully discussing the different plans of future operations which suggested themselves, the Bishop determined to make

Zanzibar his starting-point for the interior; and a favourable opportunity occurring of obtaining a passage in a man-of-war, he at once started for that place, accompanied by Dr. Steere. Of the rest of the party, Mr. Waller,* Mr. Drayton, and Mr. Alington eventually returned to England; of the mechanics, Blair and Adams have since joined missions in Zulu-land; the others returned to England, the Bishop thinking that a considerable time might probably elapse before they could be actively employed again, and that to keep them in idleness would be bad for them, and also a useless expense.

'We must not omit to mention an important addition made by Mr. Waller to his long catalogue of good services to the Mission. About twenty native boys were brought down to the Cape, for all of whom Mr. Waller succeeded in finding suitable homes.'

These boys, I must explain, were our own children—those whom we released from the slavers—and who for so long a time had been under our care. They were with Bishop Tozer as long as he occupied Morumbala; but after he left that mountain, Dr. Livingstone, according to arrangements made with Mr. Waller, took them, and the women and girls for whom Mr. Waller had made himself responsible, on board the 'Pioneer,' and thus brought them out of the rivers.† Mr. Waller left in the 'Pioneer' also, so he took charge of all these people, and with the aid of the 'Orestes,' and another of H.M. ships, succeeded in getting them all safely to Cape Town, where they are now, with the exception of Wekotani and Juma, who accompanied Dr. Livingstone in his last expedition.

* I have given this sentence as it appears in the Report, by which it would seem that Mr. Waller up to this time formed part of Bishop Tozer's staff. I have, however, been reminded by my friend that he was not of Bishop Tozer's party in any way.

† In the First Edition this sentence reads thus :—' They were under the care of Bishop Tozer at Morumbala; but when he left that mountain he had no means of taking these children with him, so he wrote to Dr. Livingstone, and begged him to convey them to sea in the "Pioneer."'

Mr. Waller informed me that this statement did not quite represent the facts of the case; I have, therefore, upon his information, made such alteration as seemed to be necessary.

MR. WALLER AND A GROUP OF AJAWA.

It is not too much to hope that these people and children thus
provided for may at some future time return to their own country
and declare to their own friends the great things the Lord hath
done for them.   I do not say this lightly.   They are Christians,
and from what I have heard from Clarke, who is now a
catechist at Cape Town, and from others, there seems good
reason to hope that at least some of them may be qualified to
act as missionaries to their own countrymen.   The younger
of them, especially, are very susceptible of religious impressions ; they readily manifest the graces of the Holy Spirit ;
they are gentle in disposition, and are very intelligent ; indeed
in most things relating to character, moral and intellectual,
they are as unlike the vulgar idea of the African as can well
be conceived.   The fact is, the various African tribes differ in
character and capacity as widely as the different races in Asia
and Europe.   All are, it is true, distinctly African ; but compare the Bosjesman with the Zulu, the Massai and other kindred tribes whom you may extirpate but cannot enslave, with
the readily-degraded West Coast Negro, or the people of
Dahomey with the amiable Mozambique tribes with whom we
became acquainted, and in physical attributes and social characteristics they are most unlike.   It is absurd as well as
most unjust to include all Africans in the condemnation which

the least elevated among them may provoke. I am perfectly certain that the ideas commonly entertained of the mental and spiritual capacity of the Africans generally are to the last degree erroneous. It is not true that they are all ' brutal in instincts,' ' bestial in capacity,' ' mean and ferocious, cruel and treacherous ; creatures grovelling in the lowest pit of moral defilement and intellectual abasement ; wretched materialists, without any idea of a Supreme Being, and so spiritually obtuse as to be incapable of receiving the Christian religion.' They are heathen, it is true, they are suffering from all the ignorance and superstition which have accrued to them from long ages of heathenism, but though degraded they are not wholly corrupted,—they can appreciate justice, and are grateful for kindness ; and when their confidence is once gained, they are faithful, affectionate, and trustworthy. And, God be thanked ! wherever the Church has zealously worked among the Africans, has faithfully used those mighty powers, the powers of the world to come, with which she has been entrusted by her Divine Head, converts to Christianity have been made ; these converts have manifested the fruits of the Spirit equally with the European, have thereby shown themselves to be members of Christ, true descendants, spiritually, of the Second Adam, the quickening Spirit, and have thus proved themselves to be the descendants, naturally, of the first man Adam, the living soul.

I have lately seen letters from Dauma, now Anne Mackenzie Dauma, for Bishop Mackenzie's sister is her godmother, which show much intelligence and aptitude for acquiring knowledge, and the lady at Cape Town who has taken charge of her speaks most highly of her religious disposition and sweet temper. Among the boys, the most hopeful, perhaps, is Chimwala, a bright, energetic lad, represented as standing at the left of Mr. Waller in the last] woodcut, who is now learning the art of printing, with Mr. Blair, at Dr. Callaway's Mission Station, in Zululand; but I hear from Blair that his heart is with his brethren in the Shire Highlands, and that he would readily respond to an invitation to return to his own country ; though not to his old heathenism, for

the lad is growing in grace.   Then there is Chinsoro, who·
stands up to the right of Mr. Waller, and who is now
married to Chasika, and Sambani, the boy leaning forward
on his hands and knees, and others of those we were able
to rescue from temporal and spiritual bondage, who would
be able to give most valuable assistance supposing it were
determined by the church to send another Mission to the
Ajawa.

When, in company with Mr. Procter and Dr. Meller, I left
Quillimane, we brought away with us an Ajawa boy named
Chirumba.   In the first instance he was given to Mr. Procter
by Colonel Nunes, his master.   When Procter left us at Natal,
Chirumba was consigned to the care of Dr. Meller.   On his
arrival in England he lived with me and my friends for some
time, and after suitable preparation he was baptised at S.
Thomas, Oxford, by the name of Mark Augustine Mackenzie
Meller.   I could fill many pages with details of this boy's
gentle deeds and words.   He evidenced the graces of Christianity to an extraordinary degree, considering the horrible
nature of his antecedents.   It was no fancy, it was a reality.
Bishop Crowther came to Oxford while he was with me, and
Mark had an interview with him.   From that time his heart
seemed set upon becoming a missionary to his brethren in
Africa ; and had he continued under my care I have no doubt
this might have come to pass. He went, however, with Dr. Meller
to the Mauritius, and I hope his thoughts and feelings have not
been directed into another channel.

I have entered into these details in order to show first, that
though we were not permitted to accomplish what we went forth
to do, yet we have in the highest sense had some fruit of our
labour ; secondly, to prove that the Africans are capable of par-
ticipating in the spiritual blessings which we, by God's mercy,
possess : and thirdly, to point out the necessity of raising up a
native ministry.   It is not possible that a great land like Africa
can be Christianised by foreigners only, but we, as Christians,
foreigners to Africa though we be, have a duty to perform towards that land.   The providence of God, by the recent discoveries of our countrymen, and by the position we have for a

long time past occupied in Africa, seems to point out that land
to our church as a field of labour. Of course there are limi-
tations to all duties, and if we take for example the labours
of the first missionaries of the church, we see what those limi-
tations are with respect to our duty to Africa. S. Paul, for
instance, made Ephesus at one time a base of operations; he
succeeded in converting many of the Ephesians; he raised up a
ministry from among the newly-made converts, and having established the church in the completeness of its organization
at Ephesus, he removed from thence and worked more immediately elsewhere. This is what we must do. We must first
of all establish stations among those African tribes that occupy
the best positions and are most easily reached; use these van-
tage places as garrisons of faith from whence conquests for
Christ can be made in the country around; raise up a native
ministry from among the converts; and repeat this work in
other places, making our stations centres of religion and
civilization: and having thus established the church among the
Africans, we have done our duty—we must then leave it to
them to subjugate the less accessible parts, and to perpetuate
what we begin. Great sacrifices may be required of us before we succeed in doing this, but what of that! It has ever
been so with the followers of the Crucified.

I know the temptation to Christianity now-a-days is to take
the world on the devil's terms rather than on God's—to hold
for commerce and not for Christ—to seek the welfare of the
heathen by the indirect agencies of commerce and civilization,
instead of by the direct agency of the church. Wait, cry the
men of commerce; wait are now saying the men of science
and adventure, wait until we have prepared the way, the
church can come in by and bye; it has not the power to convert unless we are its harbingers. And thus it is that the
tempter is still at hand, tempting Christ in His members.
'All these will I give Thee and the glory of them,' said he to
our Divine Head. 'if thou wilt fall down and worship me.'
'All these will I give thee and the glory of them,' is he now
saying to Christendom, if you will but listen to my suggestions,
if you will but adopt my plans. But we must not listen,

we must have none of his fine and glittering schemes. As the first missionaries fought so must we if we could conquer like them.

That Christians now-a-days possess in superior knowledge and skill, in the gifts and refinements of civilization, much that may win the attention of the heathen to the higher gift of eternal life, I have shown; but these things, like miracles of old, are but secondary aids, and must accompany not precede Christianity. To employ them without the sanctifying influence of the church, is to make the same use of them that Simon Magus would have done with the extraordinary gifts of the Spirit, employ them on behalf of the adversary and not for Christ. Attempt to civilize and not to ristianise, and in most cases you make Christianity almost impossible. Make commerce, and commerce alone, your pioneer, let it have full sway before the church commences to work, and there will spring up obstacles to the spread of our Holy Religion such as prevail in many parts of Africa, India, and China, and which those who are now most strenuously advocating the commercial and civilization policy, declare to be beyond the power of the Church to remove.

The Church, however, is the channel of all grace. It is indwelt by the Holy Spirit, who, by Christ's duly authorised ministers, acts upon the souls of men as He acts by none other. But it is only by following the example of the Apostles, and establishing the Church among the heathen upon that model, which the Holy Ghost inspired his own first missionaries to set forth, that we have any right to expect success. It is because we have in these latter days not sufficiently realised this, that our success against the adversary has been so small. Human nature has been one and the same in all essential features in all ages of the world. Human error also has ever been essentially the same, flowing from the same perverted sources, however varied its manifestations in different ages and localities, and the Church now possesses the same spiritual powers to combat and overcome error which it possessed in the days of the Apostles and their successors, which it possessed in the days of S. Patrick, S. Columba, S. Augustine, and S. Boniface; it has all that is necessary for making the present heathen world a Christian world. Oh! that the Church of England would awake to the full sense of her position as a Missionary Church! Let her do this, and the blessing that would accrue to her work at home, would be incalculable. In the words of an eloquent writer on missions, ' The spirit that undertakes the duty and makes the sacrifice, will not be borne abroad and then given to the winds, but will be wafted back again, and distil as the dew to refresh and revive the Church. The sight of tribes converted, civilized, disciplined, united, will bear witness to the graces still dwelling within it. Its power will be seen. This token of life will silence many a taunt, awaken many a tender regard; turn the hearts of the fathers unto the children, and convince gainsayers, "that God is with us of a truth." The faith of many will wax strong, and piety will burn brighter in the individual breast that has learned to sympathise in the salvation of the heathen. And examples of men who have hazarded their lives for the name of our Lord Jesus Christ, "will call forth a kindred spirit of sacrifice at home. They will chide the slumberer and self indulgent. They will plead the cause of Christ with us. As we follow them, as it were, into the very dominion of Satan, and stand in the face of the great enemy of Christ—surely our animosities will be laid aside—our spirits, now estranged by jealousies, will be drawn together—our work at home will be consolidated and sanctified, and our Church will shine forth as it did in darker and less prosperous days, a light to the heathen, a mother of Churches, and a glory of all Christendom.'

But to return to Bishop Tozer. As a base of operations the choice of Zanzibar was wise. There is, perhaps, no better standing ground from whence we can better make an aggression upon the benighted tribes of the interior of East Central Africa. Mr. Richard Thornton travelled for some time among the tribes inland from Zanzibar, and from all he told me, and from what I have since read in his journals—and he had no missionary enthusiasm inclining him to take a too favourable opinion of the country and natives—I feel sure that there are people living in healthy highland fertile districts, not far from the coast, who possess all the favourable characteristics of the people to whom we went, and who are less likely to be distracted by war.

What object Bishop Tozer had in view in going to Zanzibar, he tells us in a letter written soon after his arrival at that place. 'I wish,' he says, 'it always to be remembered, that I did not select Zanzibar as absolutely a very good field for Mission labour, but as the *best for ultimately reaching Central Africa.*' And still later he has declared that he shall not rest satisfied until he finds himself in some sense the *Bishop of the Tribes in the neighbourhood of the Lake Nyassa.*

THE END.